I WILL GREET THE SUN AGAIN

I will greet the sun again,
greet the stream that once flowed in me,
the clouds that were my unfurling thoughts,
the aching growth of the grove's poplars
who passed with me through seasons of drought.
I will greet the flock of crows
who gifted me the grove's night perfume
and my mother who lived in the mirror
and was my old age's reflection.
Once more I will greet the earth
who, in her lust to re-create me, swells
her flaming belly with green seeds.

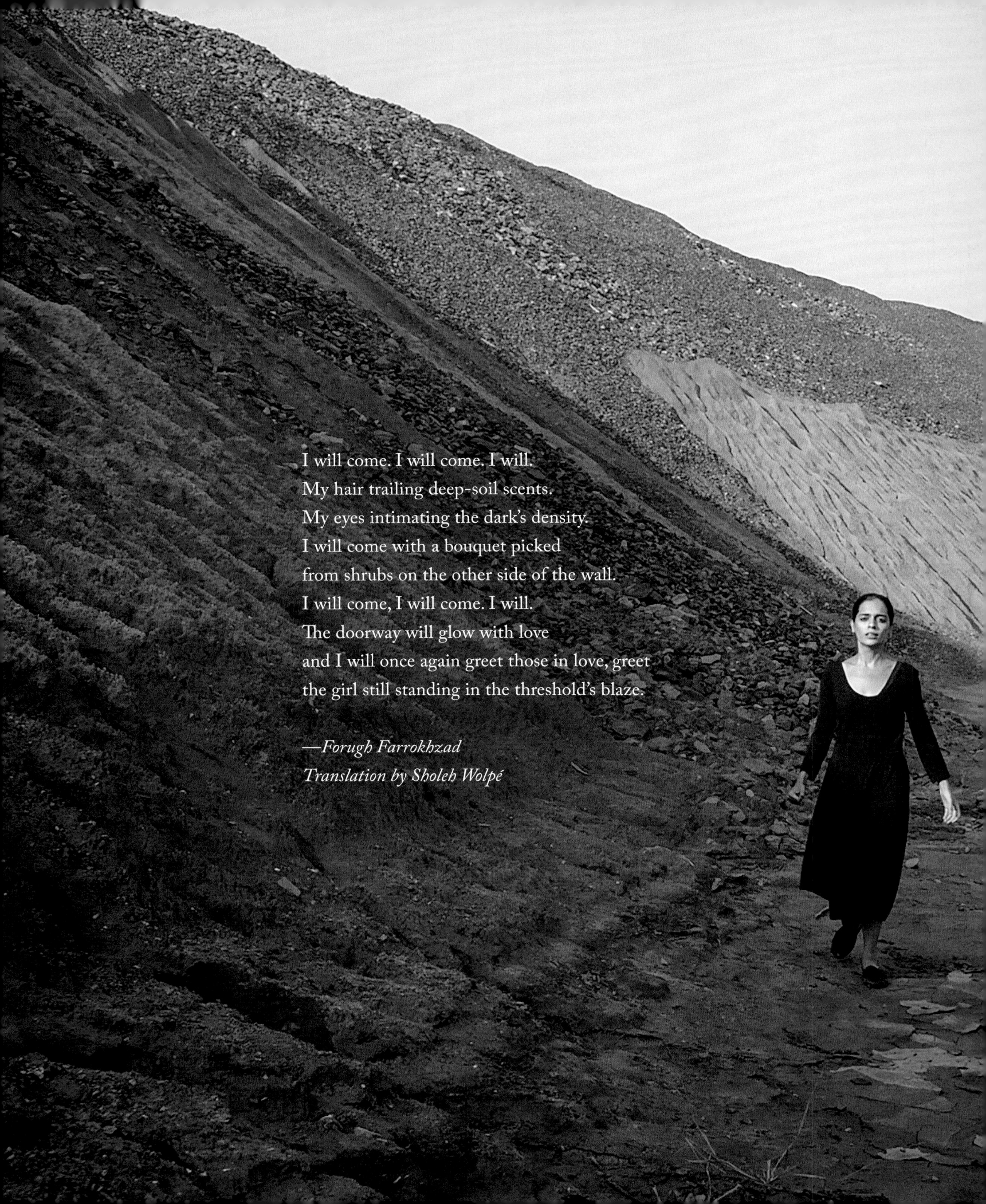

I will come. I will come. I will.
My hair trailing deep-soil scents.
My eyes intimating the dark's density.
I will come with a bouquet picked
from shrubs on the other side of the wall.
I will come, I will come. I will.
The doorway will glow with love
and I will once again greet those in love, greet
the girl still standing in the threshold's blaze.

—Forugh Farrokhzad
Translation by Sholeh Wolpé

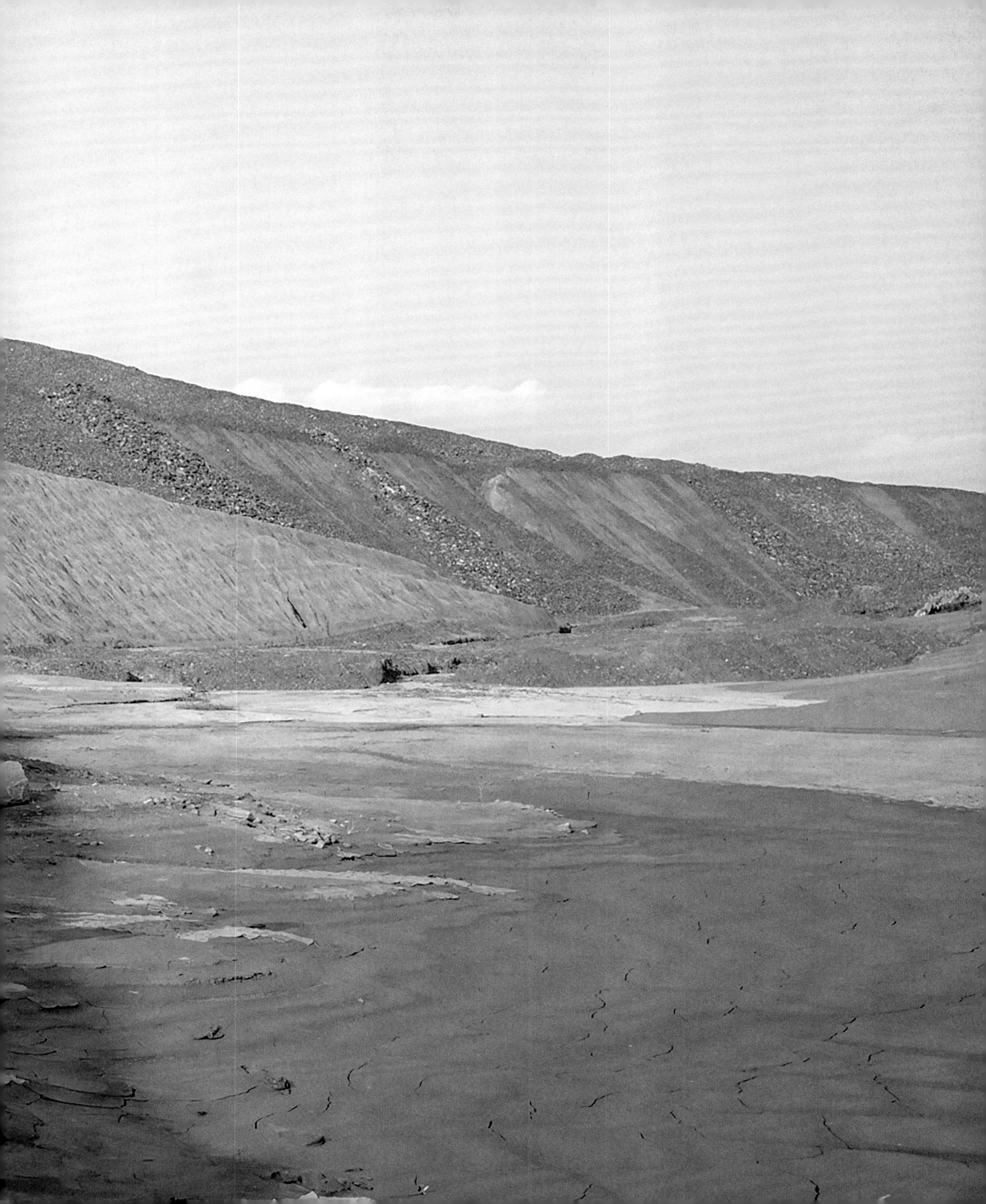

I WILL GREET THE SUN AGAIN

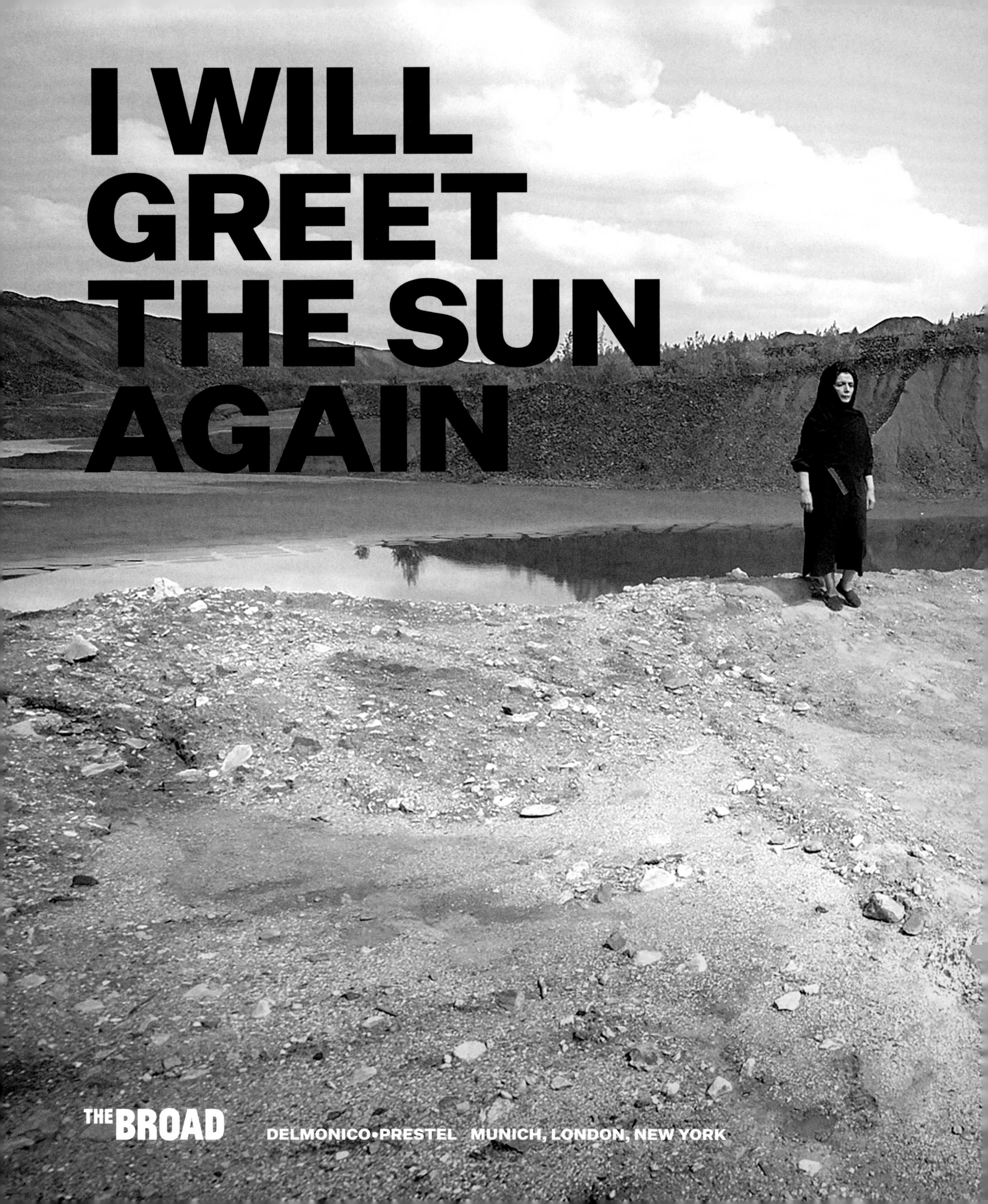

THE BROAD

DELMONICO•PRESTEL MUNICH, LONDON, NEW YORK

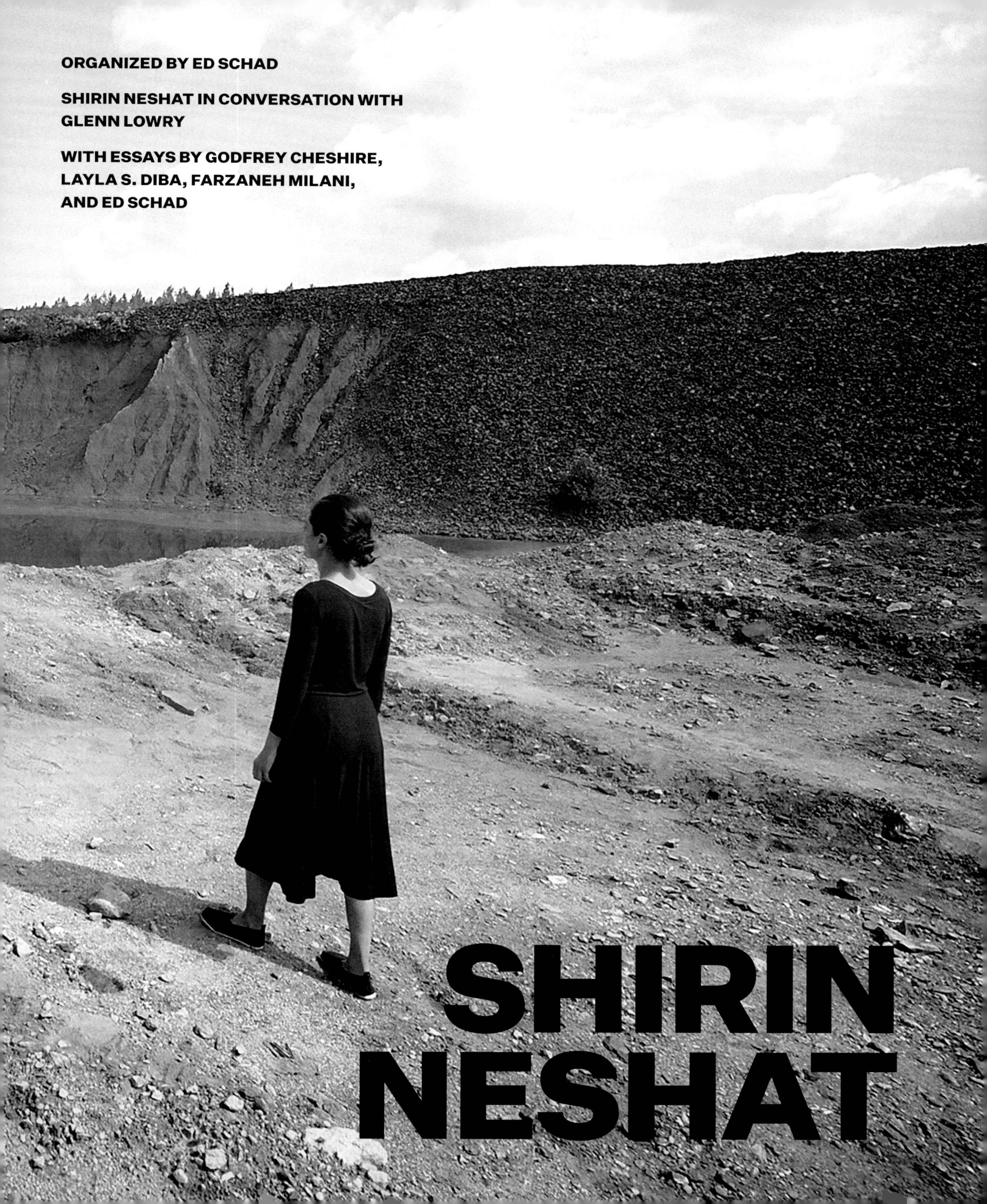

ORGANIZED BY ED SCHAD

SHIRIN NESHAT IN CONVERSATION WITH GLENN LOWRY

WITH ESSAYS BY GODFREY CHESHIRE, LAYLA S. DIBA, FARZANEH MILANI, AND ED SCHAD

SHIRIN NESHAT

CONTENTS

FOREWORD

Shirin Neshat's long exile from her home country of Iran started in California. At her family's request, and as the tensions that would erupt into the Islamic Revolution continued to build, Neshat came to Los Angeles in 1975 when she was seventeen years old. She attended University High School, residing in the Westwood neighborhood with her sister Mahdokht and later with a Jewish French family on Manning Avenue. She spoke no English on arrival. She lived in the city until 1979, when she moved north to attend the University of California at Berkeley. Neshat's story as an artist begins in California, but surprisingly, she has never had a major museum exhibition on the West Coast. *Shirin Neshat: I Will Greet the Sun Again* marks a return of sorts to the place that was her first home in the United States.

Over the last thirty years, Neshat's photographs, videos, performances, and films have pictured exile and displacement with beauty, dynamic formal invention, and poetic grace. Her story and art resonate with many who have left their country in the wake of political conflict, a legacy deeply interwoven with the history of the United States. This exhibition, organized by The Broad's curator and publications manager Ed Schad, is the largest show of her work to date. Arranged chronologically in the museum's twelve first-floor galleries, it takes visitors from her early photographs, *Women of Allah*, through iconic video works such as *Rapture*, *Turbulent*, and *Passage*, monumental photography installations such as *The Book of Kings* and *Our House Is on Fire*, and ambitious video/photography projects never before seen in a U.S. museum. We are especially excited about *Land of Dreams*, a new body of photographs and two immersive videos that will make its global debut here.

Neshat entered The Broad collection in 1999 with the acquisition of *Rapture*. Notably, it was among the first video works—and the first multiscreen video installation—to come into the collection. Neshat's work was a key addition to a collection that, from the early 1980s to the present, has been committed to politically engaged artists whose work witnesses the world's rapidly changing historical landscape, artists like Jenny Holzer, Cady Noland, Barbara Kruger, and Glenn Ligon. *Rapture* is on view in this exhibition, joining three other works from The Broad's Neshat holdings: photographs from her series *Soliloquy* and the film *Possessed*.

Neshat's story and artwork also speak locally to our community here in Southern California, home to an estimated half-million Iranians and Iranian Americans, the largest concentration of people of Iranian heritage outside of Iran. They have congregated in Westwood—nicknamed "Tehrangeles"—and are heavily represented in Glendale, Irvine, Long Beach, Burbank, and beyond. We welcome this audience to The Broad, where, through the eyes and experiences of Shirin Neshat, visitors may gain an understanding of not only recent events in Iran, but also the deep history of Persia. We are thrilled that this exhibition and related programming will bring the films, poetry, music, and other rich traditions of Persia to our extended audience. The majority of works included are on view in Los Angeles for the first time.

It is the core of The Broad's mission to cultivate exchanges among visitors by making contemporary art accessible to the widest possible audience. Our visitors' deep engagement with art has transformed the museum into the vibrant cultural destination that our founders Eli and Edye Broad envisioned. The average visitor is young and often characterizes his/her knowledge of contemporary art as beginning or intermediate. The Broad's audience reflects the diverse demographics of its home city, and we view this exhibition as an opportunity to offer extraordinary work to fresh eyes.

Every staff member of The Broad has had vital responsibilities in the presentation of this exhibition, from visitor service associates, to the preparator crew, to security. In particular, I extend profound thanks to Ed Schad, who curated the exhibition and edited this catalogue; Alice Chung, Director, Marketing & Communications; Stacy Lieberman, Deputy Director; Vicki Gambill, Director of Collections Management; Anne Mersmann, Registrar, Collections and Technology; Nate Rusch, Director of Information Technology; Jeannine Guido, Associate Director of Museum Operations; Rob Hudson, Director of Retail Operations; Christine Steiner, General Counsel; Curtis Weaver, Head Preparator; Stacey Swanby, Associate Director of Visitor Services; Sarah Loyer, Associate Curator and Exhibitions Manager; and Ed Patuto, Director of Audience Engagement.

As always, without the ongoing support and patronage of Eli and Edythe Broad and the board members of The Eli and Edythe Broad Foundation, The Broad Art Foundation, and The Broad, this exhibition would not have been possible. I am deeply appreciative of their profound commitment to collecting and their tireless philanthropy in the arts.

We are grateful to our individual and institutional lenders, especially Barbara Gladstone and Gladstone Gallery, as well as the Whitney Museum of American Art, Shulamit Nazarian, Goodman Gallery, BNY Mellon, and Art Berliner and Marian Lever. We thank Glenn Lowry, Farzaneh Milani, Layla S. Diba, and Godfrey Cheshire for their wonderful contributions to this publication. We also thank our Cultural Partner, the Farhang Foundation.

Finally, and most importantly, we thank Shirin Neshat for her penetrating and beautiful work, her guidance, and her generous support. Her warm and open spirit, her endless energy, and her heroic witnessing and courage in the face of great political and personal hardship are the pulse of this exhibition.

JOANNE HEYLER
Founding Director, The Broad

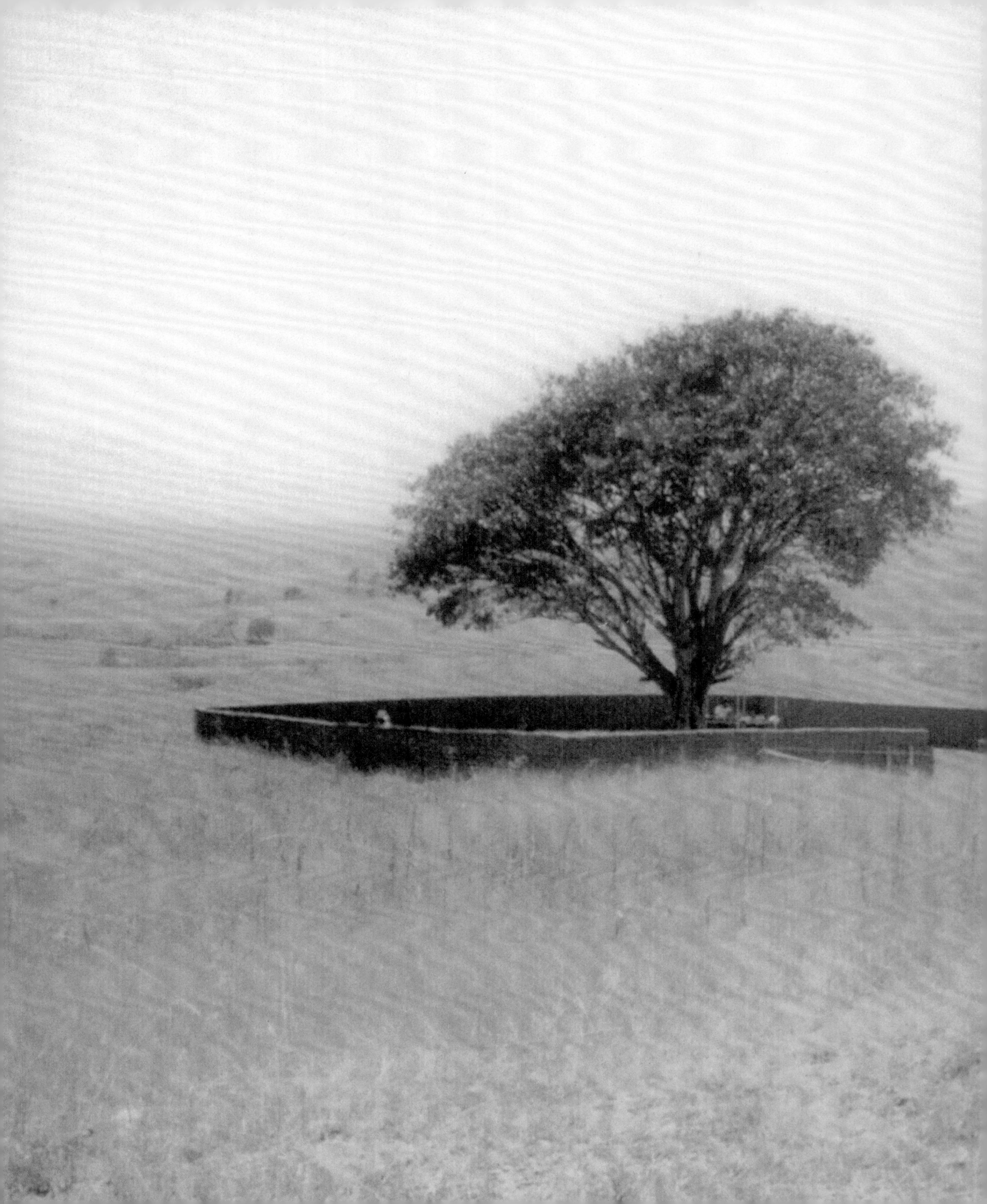

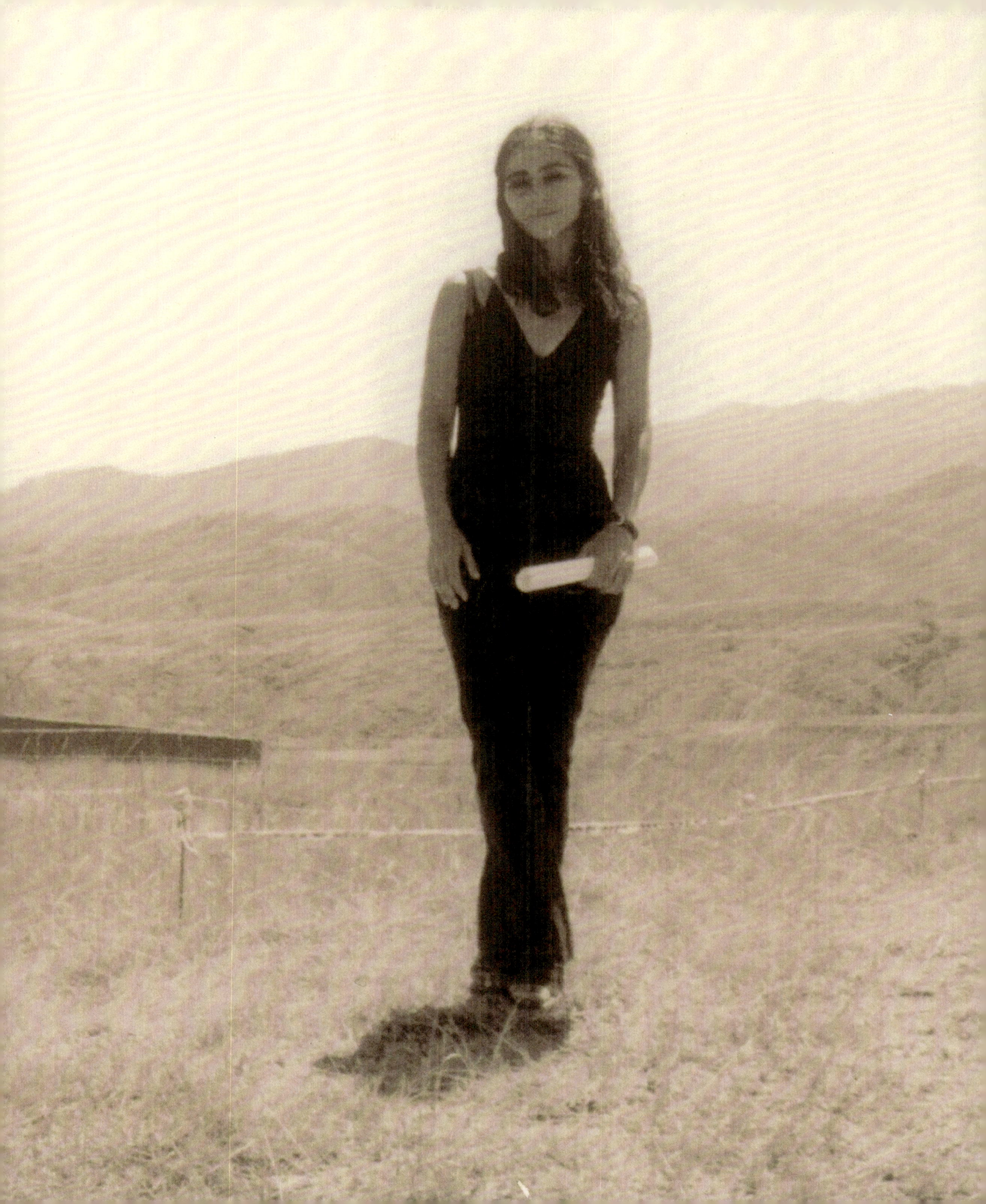

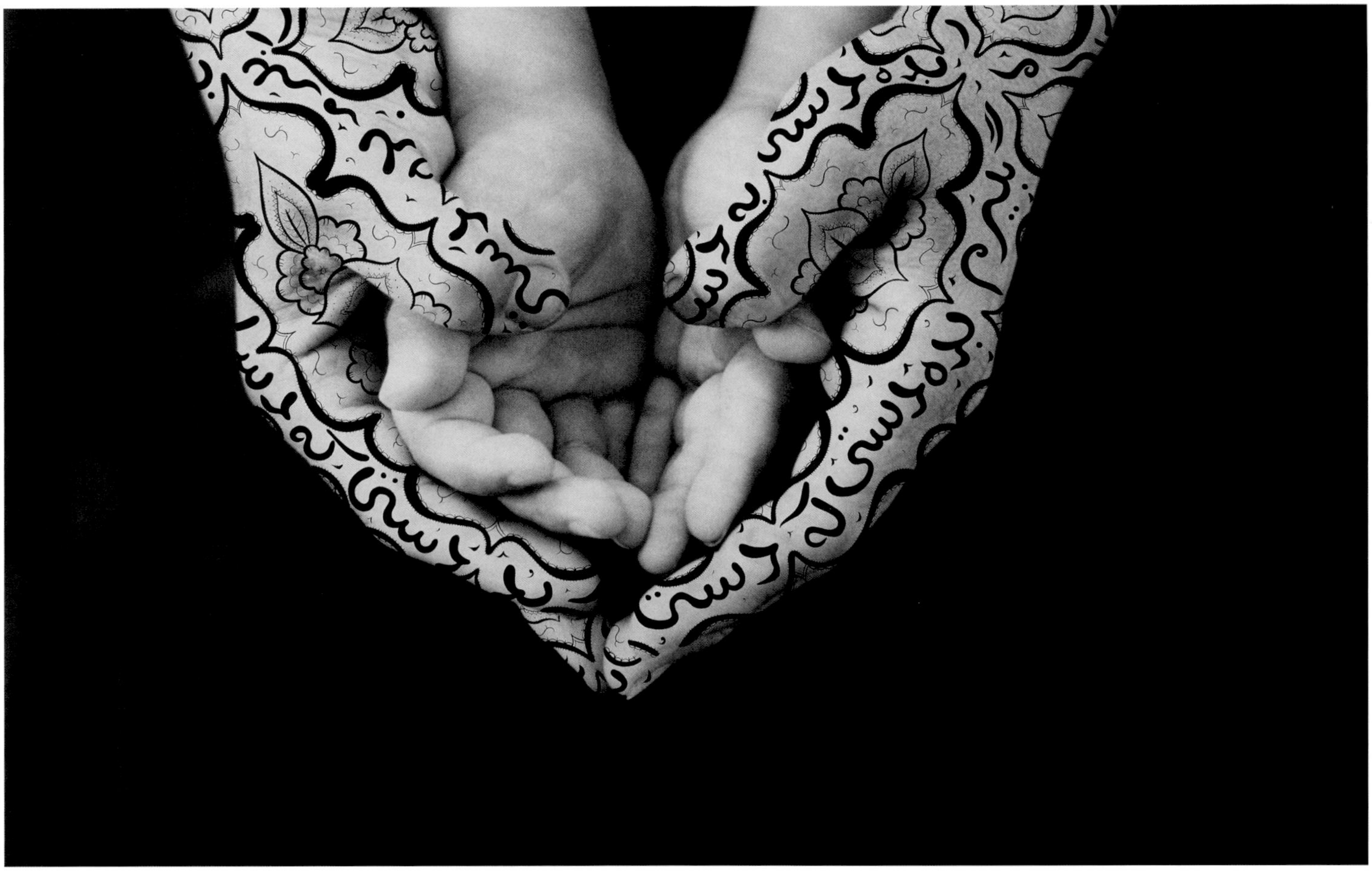

1

THOUSANDS AND THOUSANDS OF BRANCHES: SHIRIN NESHAT'S JOURNEY FROM IRAN TO PERSIA

ED SCHAD

In Shirin Neshat's early photograph *Bonding* (1995, fig. 1), the universally recognizable connection between a mother and child lovingly resides in a union of hands. The larger pair of hands belongs to Neshat. The smaller pair, cupped within the mother's hands, belongs to her five-year-old son Cyrus. The photograph was made in New York, Neshat's residence, but is about Iran, the home that she was forced to leave in 1975. She and Cyrus traveled to Iran together twice in the 1990s before uniting in *Bonding*. Iran was the country where Neshat was born and spent her childhood, the country that she had been away from due to the political turbulence of the Islamic Revolution in 1979, when Iran dethroned its king and became a theocracy.

Neshat's motherhood and her Iranian heritage interlace in the photo. On top of her hands, she inscribed floral patterns and punctuation marks found in Farsi and Arabic script, patterns that can be described as Persian, Islamic, Iranian, or Middle Eastern. In Iran, these designs are found everywhere, on decorative objects like carpets and dishes, on Nowruz tables celebrating the new year at the vernal equinox, and on illuminated copies of the Qur'an. In *Bonding*, Neshat seemingly offers the layered identity represented by these designs to her son. Birth forms the essential "bond" between mother and son, but Neshat suggests that additional bonds tie a mother to her child, from history, from art, from religion, from politics. They are wrapped into and through our lives and bodies. Cyrus' hands are open as though to receive a gift. In the background, the velvety black fabric of an Islamic veil shines just into view.

Neshat's photographs, videos, and feature films evoke the large and small bonds that become the destinies of individuals. These bonds are the root of identity; they can be universal like motherhood, but they are also delineated and often regulated by history and nations. These structures can empower, be sought as sanctuaries. They can also oppress, resulting in violence and xenophobia between or within peoples. The nature of cultural, political, and historical bonds and their relationship to the bonds that everyone on earth shares is at the heart of Neshat's life and art.

When she took up the camera in the 1990s, Neshat sought to show the fullness and paradoxes of her bonds with the legislative, religious, and political realities of an Iran she left as a teenager, from the point of view of an artist living and working in New York. Her earliest photos, *Women of Allah* (of which *Bonding* is a part), are beautiful articulations of empathy and identification, saturated in a visual language learned in New York and applied to an examination of contemporary Iran. These photos echo the voices of women whose freedom balances precariously on the fault line of an Iran caught between modernizing and conservative forces.

Expanding her practice to include video, film, and performance after 1997, Neshat began to mine an older and even mystical history that underlay the (often local to Iran) realities of her earlier photographs. In work teeming with lush metaphors, texts, and influences from 5,000 years of Persian tradition, Neshat began to look for larger frames of identity, to relate both to Iran and other cultures from her vantage point as an artist in exile. Especially in her most recent projects, national and political borders are found to be porous and pliable, often functioning according to the logic of poetry and dreams.

The exhibition *Shirin Neshat: I Will Greet the Sun Again*, describes this important shift in Neshat's

Fig. 1 *Bonding*, 1995, from *Women of Allah*. Ink on RC print, 34⅜ x 56⅞ x 1¾ inches (87.3 x 144.5 x 4.4 cm). Photograph taken by Kyong Park

Previous spread
Neshat on the set of *Tooba*, 2002. Photo by Dariush Khondji

2

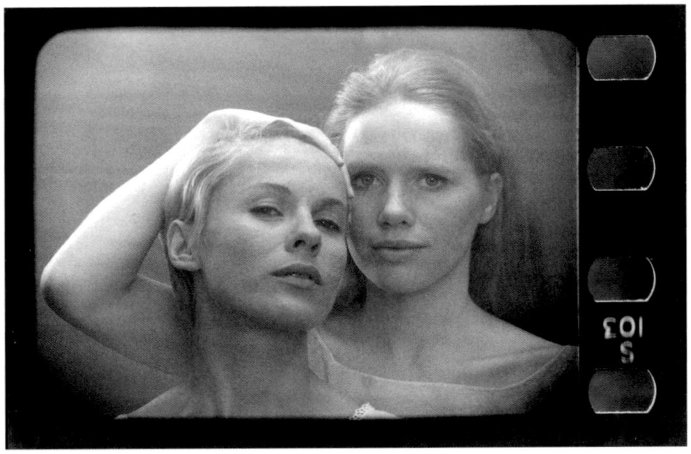

career, offering a cultural plot line for studying it. Like previous surveys of her work, there are anchor points in recent history: Iran's 1979 Islamic Revolution, which occurred during her teenage years in California; its aftermath in her visits to Iran; her life in exile from her native country; the destruction of September 11, 2001; Iran's Green Movement of 2009; the Arab Spring revolts that occurred throughout the Middle East; and even the presidency of Donald Trump.

Neshat's work is informed by history, sometimes speaks to it directly, but is not entirely disclosed by it. Especially in recent projects never before seen in U.S. museums—*The Home of My Eyes* (2015), *Roja* (2016), *Land of Dreams* (2019)—she seeks the historical, physical, and psychological frameworks that often leave people powerless or trapped by nationalistic discourses or shifting political winds. This exhibition offers an account of how Neshat handles these "frames," how she examines them through the bonds that define her personally—Iran and the larger umbrella of Persia that contains it, as well as many other cultures and identities. The bonds are Neshat's heritage. They speak of rootedness, exile, and borders, of things carried on the inside that will never and can never be harnessed by bureaucratic systems.

* * *

As we planned this exhibition, I asked Neshat about specific films that influenced her earliest photographs of the 1990s, *Women of Allah*. I considered it a useful starting point, for even the briefest overview of her career shows an artist actively involved in a dialogue between photography, video, and film. Neshat constantly shifts back and forth between these mediums, between single frames of photography and shifting frames of video, which she deploys often in large installations with multiple screens of projection.

She spoke of Alfred Hitchcock, Ingmar Bergman, and Luis Buñuel, comparing their imagery to the "sculptural quality" and "the simplicity and shaping of . . . women's bodies, always wearing dark clothing, and the focus . . . on faces and hands" found throughout *Women of Allah*.[1] These are but a few of her sources, the fullness of which film critic Godfrey Cheshire skillfully describes in this volume. To these European and American directors, one can add Iranian master filmmakers like Abbas Kiarostami, Mohsen Makhmalbaf, and Dariush Mehrjui.

Neshat pointed to one film specifically: Bergman's *Persona* (1966), in which two very different women—an actress, Elisabeth, who has taken to silence (played by Liv Ullmann), and her nurse, Anna (played by Bibi Andersson)—live together in an isolated beach house on the Baltic Sea (fig. 2). Bergman's camera neutrally observes the women as their intimacy grows through conflict, empathy, and often

Fig. 2 Still from Ingmar Bergman's *Persona*, 1966, featuring actresses Liv Ullmann and Bibi Andersson. © AB Svensk Filmindustri, Photo: Sven Nykvist

3

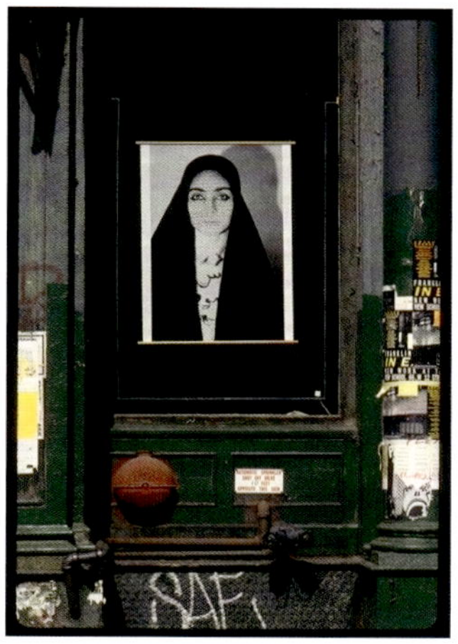

4

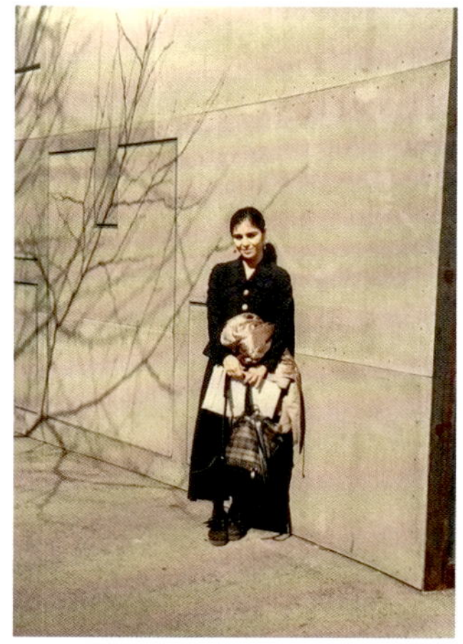

absolute cruelty to each other. In one of cinema's single most famous frames, the women merge, their faces spliced together into an image so remarkably fused that it takes a careful eye to distinguish their identities.

I can think of no better analogy to the forces operating inside of Neshat's *Women of Allah*. As the identities of Elisabeth and Anna meld in the crucible of the beach house, so does Neshat merge her point of view as a displaced person with the divergent voices and concerns of an Iran leading up to and in the wake of the Islamic Revolution. These voices fuse in her photographs, under the political pressures of revolution, war, and exile, but also through the joys of heritage. The *Women of Allah* are images of breathtaking empathy, expressions of bonds with Iran so intimate that it can be hard to parse the particulars.

The photographs openly wear paradoxes and what seem like contradictory points of view. *Bonding* is a tender image, full of ritual and beauty, but in *Identified* (1995, p. 41), Neshat uses the same decorative designs with an overt political edge, found on hands that cover a woman's mouth, thus her voice. The woman's white veil has an allover pattern of tulips, a symbol of the Islamic Revolution. In *My Beloved* (1995, p. 42), Neshat again embraces her son, however this time in a protective posture, holding him within her veil as though it were a refuge from harm. The poem "Let Us Believe in the Dawn of the Cold Season" by Forugh Farrokhzad, an Iranian feminist poet known for her candor in describing and accepting her sexual desire (fig. 12), lines the fabric of the veil. This woman is not silent. She has the words to express her desires, desires often regulated by the Islamic Republic, and the ability and agency to protect her son. A gun holds vigil against the wall.

The *Women of Allah* images were made in three successive waves. The first wave, called *Unveiling* and invoking Farrokhzad's poetry, presents the personal struggles of women (staged and performed by Neshat herself) caught between religiously rooted social codes and the force of their desires. *Unveiling* (1993, fig. 3, p. 46) is part of the wave, as is *Offered Eyes* (1993, p. 45). The second wave finds its main voice in the poet Tahereh Saffarzadeh. The women in these photographs navigate Iran's changing concept of martyrdom, a concept overly simplified and stereotyped in the West. Some of these photos, like *Rebellious Silence* (1994, p. 40), feature a Remington rifle or a pistol and present the call to arms as one of many competing demands in post-revolution Iran. The final wave of *Women of Allah* was shot during Neshat's last trip to Iran in 1995, and is analyzed thoroughly by art historian Layla S. Diba in this volume.

The series began in New York in the early 1990s. Since leaving Iran in 1975, New York was the first place in the U.S. where Neshat felt relatively at ease. Previously, she had lived for eight years in

Fig. 3 Poster of Neshat's photo *Unveiling*, 1993, hanging in the window at Franklin Furnace, New York, in April 1993, during her first public exhibition, *Unveiling*. Photo: Marty Heitner, Courtesy of Franklin Furnace Archive

Fig. 4 Neshat at the Storefront for Art and Architecture in downtown New York, 1990s

5

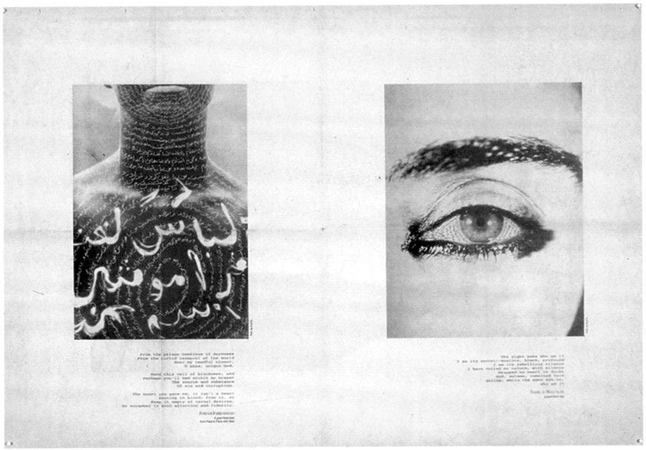

6

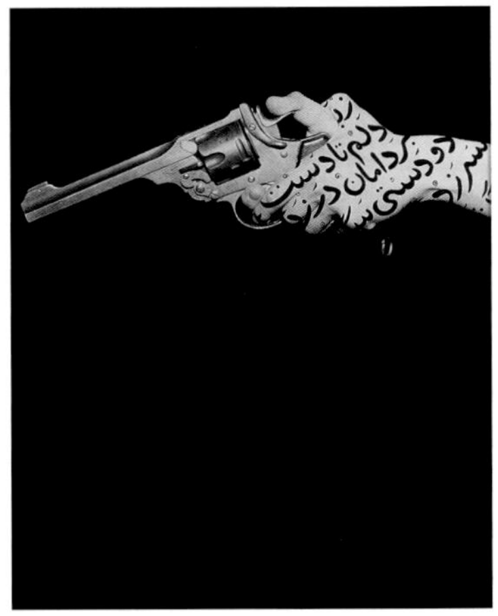

Fig. 5 Early works by Neshat on display at Franklin Furnace, New York, in April 1993, featuring poetry by Forugh Farrokhzad and Nazik Al-Malaika. Photo: Marty Heitner, Courtesy of Franklin Furnace Archive

Fig. 6 *Grace Under Duty*, 1994, from *Women of Allah*. Ink on LE silver gelatin print, 50 x 41¼ x 1⅞ inches (127.6 x 104.8 cm). Photograph taken by Robert Wesler

California, first in Los Angeles, from which she observed the Islamic Revolution at a distance, then in Berkeley, where she attended university. Neshat's California years were the toughest of her life, marked by periods of depression partially caused by being separated from her family in Iran. She endured distrust of and outright hostility toward Iranian émigrés during the hostage crisis of late 1979, including anti-Iran protests at Berkeley. The hostage crisis was pivotal to the 1980 presidential election that brought Ronald Reagan into office. When Neshat arrived in New York in 1983, however, she found a welcoming community. After a few years, along with then-husband Kyong Park, she co-directed the Storefront for Art and Architecture (fig. 4), a wonderfully international incubator of ideas that worked with artists and architects as diverse as Mel Chin, Vito Acconci, Zaha Hadid, Jean Nouvel, and Steven Holl.

Storefront was Neshat's training ground for her future art career. The filmmakers that she mentions as formative influences were being sourced by many Pictures Generation artists like Cindy Sherman, Robert Longo, and Laurie Simmons. Neshat's life overlapped with and absorbed a vibrant art scene, and she has noted Andy Warhol, Keith Haring, and Jean-Michel Basquiat as outsized presences in her early career. She has also spoken of the influence of Kiki Smith, Alfredo Jaar, Antonio Muntadas, Dan Graham, Nam June Paik, and Mary Miss. When a photographer like Nan Goldin is described as alternating "between a cool detachment and an aggressively confessional style" based in the "recognition that the way one lives life is an inherently political act," the description can equally apply to Neshat.[2] Her first solo exhibition was held in 1993 at Franklin Furnace (fig. 5), a fault line in a New York cultural scene suffering through the AIDS crisis and embroiled in censorship controversies.[3] One can easily find parallels, aesthetic and otherwise, between Neshat's photograph of a gun in *Grace Under Duty* (1994, fig. 6) and Robert Mapplethorpe's *Gun Blast* (1985).

While much of *Women of Allah's* aesthetic incubation occurred in New York, the photographs' direct concerns arose from Neshat's desire to connect with her former home of Iran, specifically the country as she discovered it in May 1991 during a return visit. Iran had experienced colossal change under the Islamic Republic and during the devastating eight-year war with Iraq. Western influences—often associated with commodity culture in the form of clothes, books, music, or movies—were abolished, seen as shah-era threats to both the primacy of Shia Islam and the sovereign rights of the country to its natural resources. Citizens, if found to be askew of the government (politically, socially, religiously), were often jailed without charge, interrogated, tortured, and killed.

Most striking was the presence of the veil. At the beginning, the Islamic Republic avoided outright

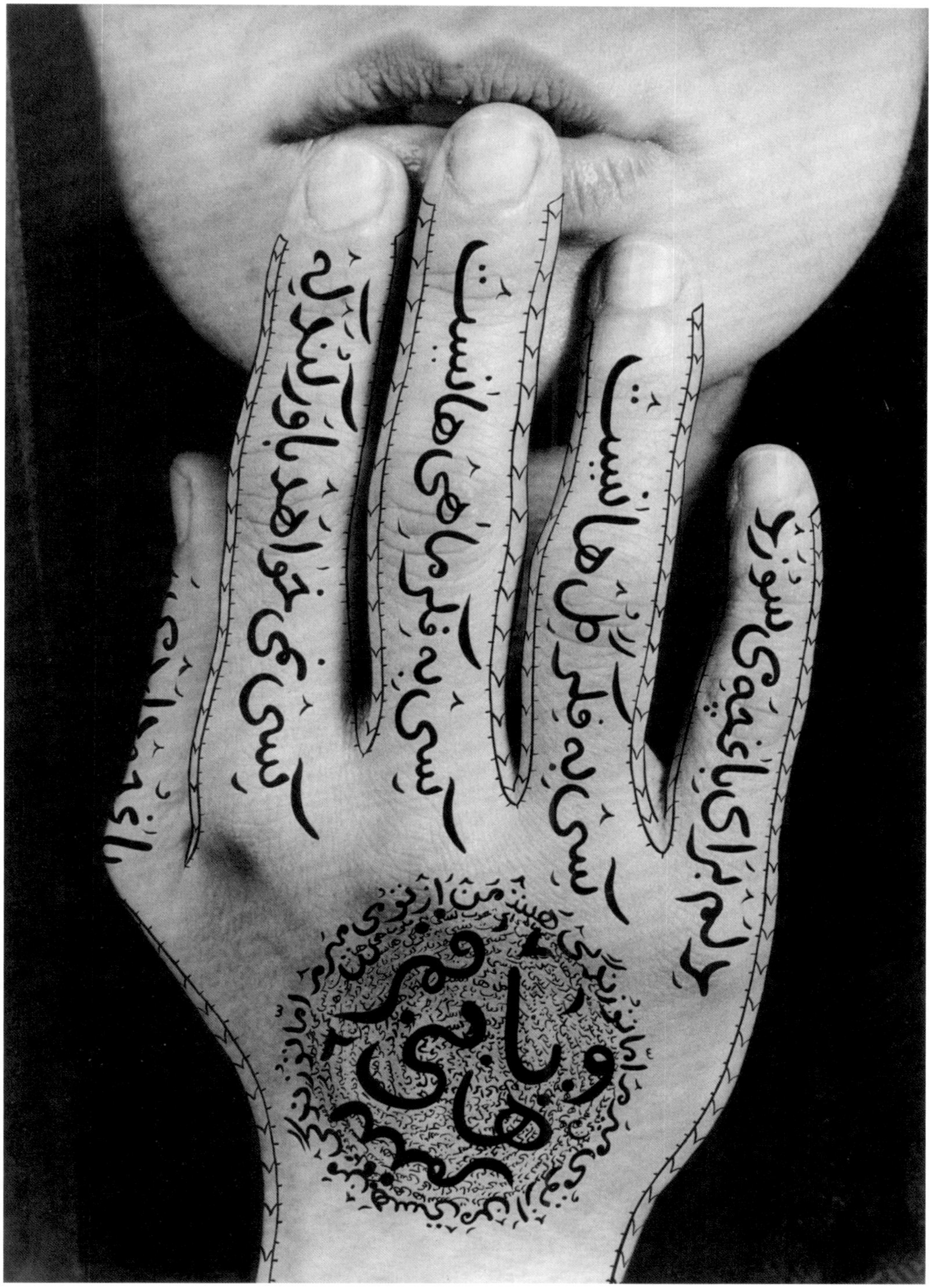

7

Fig. 7 *Untitled*, 1996, from *Women of Allah*. Ink on RC print, 53 x 39¼ x 1⅞ inches (134.6 x 99.7 x 4.8 cm). Photograph taken by Larry Barns

8

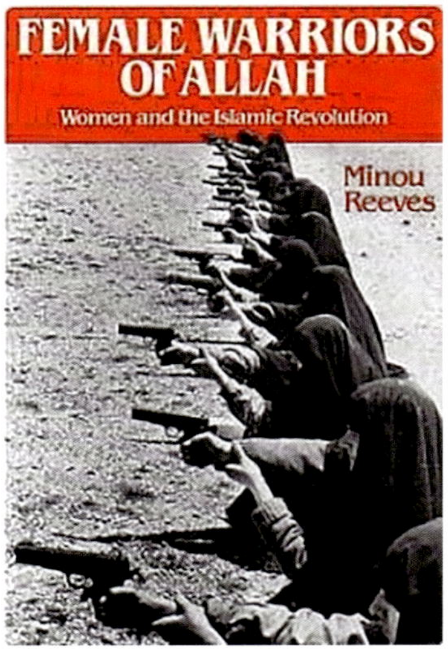
FEMALE WARRIORS OF ALLAH
Women and the Islamic Revolution
Minou Reeves

9

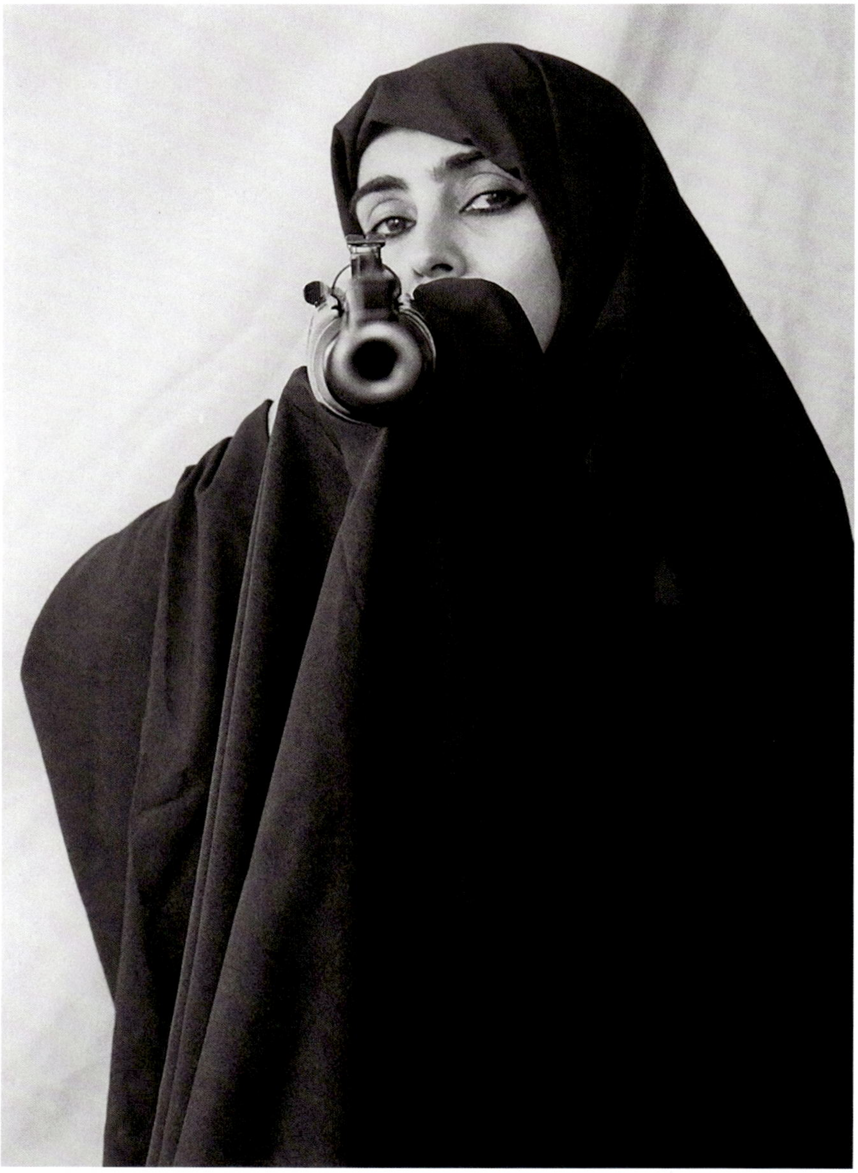

edicts making the veil compulsory, but by 1991, Neshat would see veiled women all around her. Reza Shah had banned the veil in 1936, but it was restored, first through the fervor of religious zealots (the most vicious enforcers were, and often still are, private citizens, even women), and second, by law. For Neshat, the veil was so pervasive as to be atmospheric: "It was as if you lost color and suddenly everything went to black-and-white."[4]

Less well known in the accounts of Neshat's trips to Iran in the early 1990s, however, are the feelings of sympathy and association that she retained with her culture despite the years away. With Cyrus and her mother, she traveled to Kashan, famous for its architecture and the harvesting of rosewater, and visited the cave of Ali Sadr in Hamedan. She enjoyed meeting artists, intellectuals, and all manner of people, discussing recent events and navigating ever-evolving realities: "It was such a wonderful experience to be in these remote towns again, getting to know average Iranians living simple lives after the revolution. I started to get used to being Iranian again, dressing like everyone else in the hijab and enjoying local activities."[5]

When many photographs from *Women of Allah* are installed together (fig. 10), it is striking how they oscillate between themes seemingly focused on a culture that Neshat loves (her identification with motherhood, with family, with eroticism, with the beauty of Iranian art and rituals) and some of the toughest challenges facing Iranian women: the Iran-Iraq War that seemingly empowered women through a call to arms, the mandate of the veil, and the religious and political realities circumscribing their sexuality, expression, and physical freedom.

The Bergmanesque compression of *Women of Allah* can be parsed through two texts that, according to Neshat, formed the conceptual backbone of the series. Surprisingly, it is rare to find references to these central texts in existing literature about the artist. The first is Farzaneh Milani's *Veils and Words* (1992), the first English-language, book-length study of female Iranian writers. The second is Mansoor

10

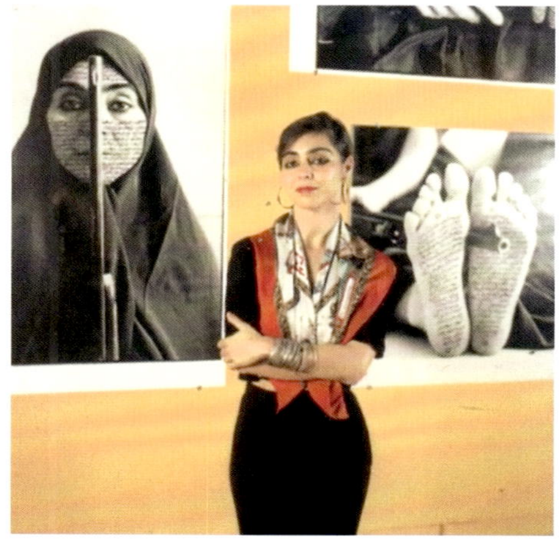

Ehsan's "Politics of Martyrdom in Post-Revolutionary Iran," a doctoral dissertation filed at the University of Oregon in 1992.[6]

Milani demonstrates that the voices of Iran's women were being heard with increasing clarity, power, and recognition. Under the Islamic Republic, Iran continued to modernize. Though controlled by censors, Iranian women were notably publishing at an unprecedented rate in the late 1980s, in Iran as well as in an increasingly large diaspora of Iranian émigrés in the United States, Canada, and Australia. She places feminism as a force in Iran on a par with or even as a rival to Iran's constitutional revolution of 1904 and the Islamic Revolution of 1979, arguing her case to the wider world through the works of writers such as Farrokhzad, Saffarzadeh, Tahereh Qorratol'Ayn, and Simin Behbahani. Milani shows the struggle and empowerment of Iranian women in equal measure, tracking their influence as well as their ongoing repression, dictated structurally by culture, law, and even architecture (evidenced by the segregated layout of Iran's traditional houses).

Ehsan's text addresses perceptions of Iran purveyed by American magazines, newspapers, and scholarship, perceptions that impacted Neshat personally.[7] His central question concerns martyrdom, a concept that he found to constitute a false Iranian "essence" for the West. For example, a *CBS Nightly News* commentator opined that "Shiites have a

Fig. 8 Cover of Minou Reeves' book *Female Warriors of Allah: Women and the Islamic Revolution* (New York: Dutton, 1989)

Fig. 9 *Untitled*, 1994, from *Women of Allah*. RC print, 31 x 46 inches (79 x 118 cm). Photograph taken by Cynthia Preston

Fig. 10. Neshat in front of the display of her work at the Bronx Museum, New York, 1994

11

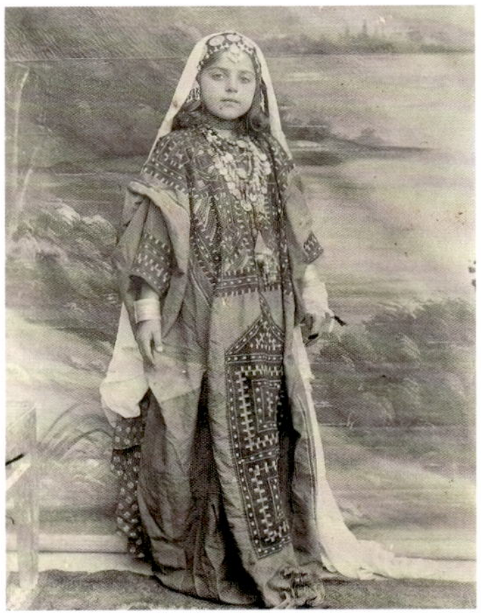

12

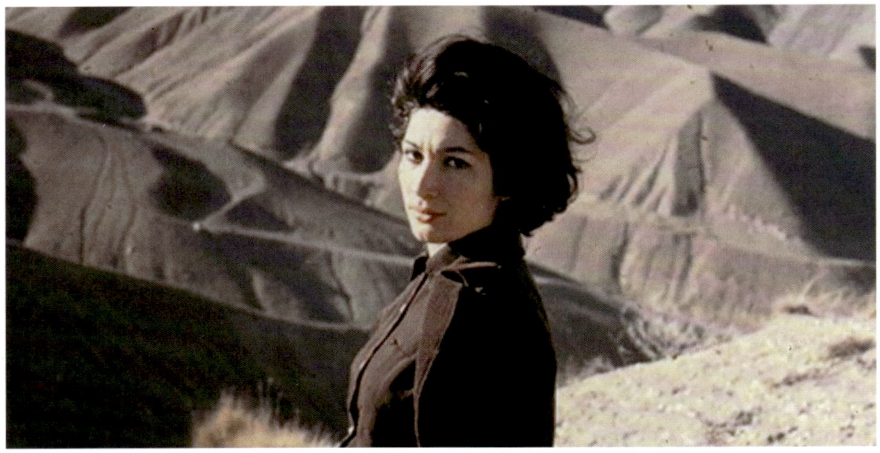

persecution complex, so no wonder they produced a Khomeini." The *Chicago Tribune* similarly editorialized that "People who consider dying to be an honor are, by definition, fanatics. Vengeful blood lust and yearning for martyrdom seem especially pronounced among the Shia Moslems of Iran."[8] Ehsan, on the other hand, found that the "martyrdom complex," though present in Islamic history, gained force in Iran only over the course of a generation; the activation of this "complex" under the Islamic Republic is analogous to the cyclical rise and fall of anti-immigrant violence stoked by isolationist rhetoric in the United States.

In their respective investigations of the spiritual, political, and personal paradoxes of modern Iran, Milani and Ehsan both cite a particular voice, that of Ali Shariati (1933–1977), an Iranian revolutionary and sociologist of religion and a dominant figure in pre-revolution Iran.[9] For Ehsan, Shariati can be credited with reinterpreting and thus revitalizing the notion of martyrdom in Iranian society.[10] For Milani, Shariati's writings and speeches reveal an ambivalence over the role of women in which he promotes both active, modern participation in society and a stringent view of women as domestic, chaste saints.[11]

In *Women of Allah*, one can almost read newspaper headlines, hear the speeches of ayatollahs and polemicists, and feel the conflicting forces of a country caught between modernization and religious conservatism. The two poets whose words appear with the most frequency in Neshat's photos, Farrokhzad and Saffarzadeh, exemplify these conflicts and form an elegant way to unite Milani's and Ehsan's Iran, to which Neshat relates with both longing and a critical stance.

In Neshat's *Untitled* (1996, fig. 7), Farrokhzad's "I Pity the Garden" is written on a woman's fingers and encircles the Abbas ibn Ali, a symbol of the house of Ali and Shia Muslims. The upright position of Neshat's hand mimics the *hamsa*, a popular symbol and good luck charm throughout the Middle East, a talisman against the evil eye, and often a commemoration of the prophet Muhammad's daughter Fatima. Here, Neshat's use of the *hamsa* connects her with one of Shariati's paragons of female saintliness, Fatima, in this case aligned with Ali.

However, the intermingling of Fatima and Farrokhzad's iconoclastic and heroic voice for the expression of female desire visualizes the ambivalence of Shariati's polemics. The antithetical roles offered to the woman literally cover her mouth—that is, her voice. Farrokhzad's poem adds even more layers of meaning:

> The speaker of "I Feel Sorry for the Garden" can be taken as very close to the poet herself, and the family members are stereotypes of educated Tehrānis. The father turns selfishly in old age to the Iranian cultural past, the elitist, masculine

Fig. 11 Childhood photo of Neshat's mother, Mahin, in traditional Persian tribal costume

Fig. 12 Poet Forugh Farrokhzad. Photo courtesy of Ebrahim Golestan

> past of Persian monarchy and mythology. He reads Ferdowsi's epic *Shāhnāmeh* and *Nāsekh ol-Tavārikh*, the famous Qājār Era (1796–1925) general history . . . The mother . . . has substituted religion for living, and religious superstition for thinking . . . The speaker's sister epitomizes the artificiality and superficiality of Tehrān life in the 1960s when many urban Iranians seemed determined to discard their Iranianness and adopt Western ways . . .[12]

Neshat unites a poet very much outside of the usual lines of social demarcation in Iran, and a symbol interlaced with the law and ethos of Shia Iran. The woman in the photo is both rooted in tradition—bound to country, family, and religion—and in sympathy with a voice that is erotic, empowered, and candid.[13]

Farrokhzad, whose life and death long preceded the Islamic Revolution, is a much different symbol than the other dominant voice in *Women of Allah*. Tahereh Saffarzadeh originally lived in the United States but returned to Iran after the revolution to become a supporter, though an outspoken feminist one, inside the regime.[14] President Mahmoud Ahmadinejad spoke at Saffarzadeh's funeral in 2008. As recently as December 2018, on the other hand, the gate to the cemetery containing Farrokhzad's grave was locked to prevent tributes.

Saffarzadeh appears in Neshat's work through poems taken from a collection called *Allegiance with Wakefulness* in three of her most well-known photographs: *Rebellious Silence*, *Faceless*, and *Allegiance with Wakefulness* (all 1994). Saffarzadeh's words are written on images inspired by Islamic Republic propaganda featuring women taking up arms during the Iran-Iraq War and the Islamic Revolution, specifically the cover art of Iranian writer and former politician Minou Reeves' book *Female Warriors of Allah* (published in 1989) (fig. 8).

Neshat's guns shift between power to powerlessness. In *Faceless* (p. 48), she points a barrel at the viewer. Saffarzadeh's poem repeats over and over, taking on increasing textural weight and density as the words move from Neshat's head to her hands, from the seat of the mind to the mind's actor in the world. In a violent action coming to life in the body, the irony of the title *Faceless* and Neshat's choice to place the Farsi word for "darkness" directly on the woman's forehead chillingly hovers over the whole proceeding, as though condemning the act at the very moment of its genesis. The gun in *Speechless* (1996, p. 47), on the other hand, seems all coiled potentiality, all power. The poem saturates the veiled face of Neshat's friend Arita Shahrzad. The title can be read in many ways: as being denied a voice, as being at a loss for words, as being beyond speech.

The torture of martyrdom is visceral in these photos, a navigation of characterizations of her country delivered via America's nightly news, beliefs about Iran seemingly as entrenched as the "complexes" that the commentators claimed to be diagnosing. While Neshat addresses this alternating reality of empowerment and oppression, she also finds Iran to be full of wonders whose paradoxes and complexities she has encountered firsthand. *Women of Allah* represents the Iran that Neshat found after twelve years away, an Iran at odds with its portrayal in the West. All of these realities fuse together in images of remarkable compression.

But the artist's enthusiastic immersion in her native country came to an abrupt halt with an incident at the Tehran airport in 1995. Neshat was carrying contact sheets of photographs that would become the last in the *Women of Allah* series, reminiscent of the royalty portraits of Anton Sevryugin as well as girlhood photos of Neshat's mother (fig. 11, pp. 50, 52–53). Although these images were made through her connection to Bahman Jalali, a photographer on the board of directors of the Akskhaneh Museum of Photography, Neshat had no official permit to make them.

Yet the photographs had nothing to do with her detainment. The truth was that another Shirin

13

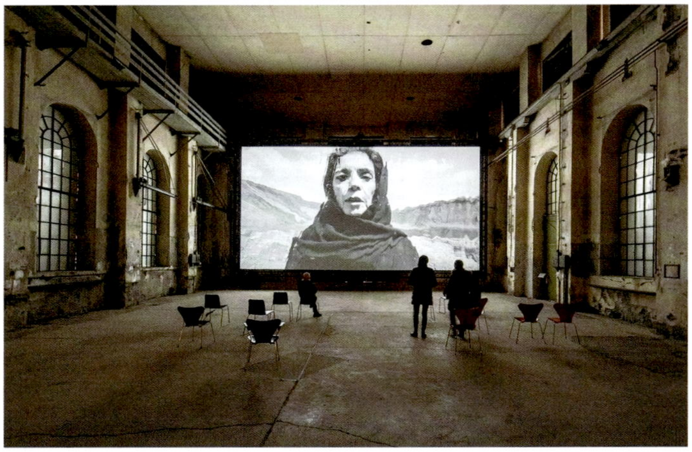

14

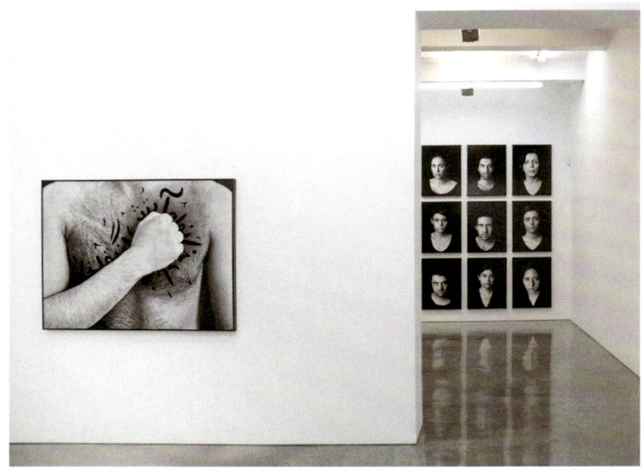

Neshat—with the same birthdate and father's name—was on the Islamic Republic's watch list that day. This Neshat was the daughter of a military general under the last shah and had founded an anti–Islamic Republic movement in Los Angeles called "Sarbazan." The border guards were looking for that Neshat, a royalist marooned in the U.S. and working for the restoration of the shah. Though Neshat was allowed to leave Iran, the interrogation would lead to a self-imposed exile, an exile that, sadly, is increasingly secure, due to the ongoing criticism of her work by the Islamic Republic. How slippery her destiny must have felt when she heard the name of that second Shirin Neshat.

* * *

In the wake of being interrogated, Neshat turned away from photography to video and film, a hiatus that lasted until 2009.[15] Amazingly productive, she directed thirteen video installations between 1996 and 2003 that solidified her status as a major figure in global art. As Eleanor Heartney observed, Neshat found a receptive audience in an art world swept up in an "embrace of otherness" coinciding with "the collapse of various paradigms valorizing straight white European or American males over all other groups."[16] The video *Turbulent* (1998) would lead to Neshat winning the International Prize at the 1999 Venice Biennale. The same year, the Whitney Museum of American Art acquired *Rapture* (1999). The Serpentine Gallery in London staged Neshat's first survey in 2000.

Neshat's transition to the projected image was accompanied by a shift in her thinking about history and politics. The union of her Iranian heritage with New York and European aesthetics in *Women of Allah* gradually turned outward, toward other cultures and other frames of identification that speak across national and political borders, to Mexico, to Egypt, to Laos and beyond. The pliability of these frames is metaphoric, personal, and literal. Pushing the conventions of installation is a defining feature of Neshat's work since 1997, both in terms of video and the photography that would flow from it (figs. 13, 14). From portrait photography, she moved to rooms of multiscreen video projections and, subsequently, to large galleries of portraits that are virtual countries in and of themselves, offering the intimacy of faces and hands and gestures as well as the ability to move inside of large historical constructs. It is the outward-facing nature and cultural bonds carried by these installations that I would like to discuss in the second half of this essay.

Neshat's breakthrough video *Turbulent* (p. 54) is exhilarating to witness. In a dark room with two projections on opposite walls, cameras show a white-shirted man on one screen (white shirts are often a sign of adherence to the Islamic Republic) and a

Fig. 13 Installation of *Roja* at Kunstraum Dornbirn, Austria, 2018. Photo by Stefan Hauer

Fig. 14 Installation view of *The Book of Kings*, Gladstone Gallery, New York, 2012. Photo by David Regen

veiled woman on the other screen. The man sings a poem by Persian poet Rumi to a male audience, brimming with the love, longing, and eroticism of the thirteenth-century lyrics. The woman then sings alone to an empty auditorium. Her song is wordless, full of tonal shifts, breathwork, and tremendous power. Though veiled and unable by law to sing in public, the woman's song seems modern, attuned to avant-garde currents in music, and free, beyond the strictures and bonds of language. The camera swings around her, gliding with the music. The camera on the man remains static.

Turbulent sets into place many of the bedrocks that will concern Neshat after *Women of Allah*. The video splits open the single-frame nature of portraiture, promoting the experience of real space with multiple screens. The viewer's eye is able to shift back and forth between different scenes, genders, architectures, countries—different visions and frames of a divided self. Furthermore, a cultural and political reality (in *Turbulent*, the law prohibiting women from singing in public) is mediated and critiqued through literature and music. Lastly, *Turbulent* is a fable, an allegory, a work of magical realism. Far from an illustration of history, it presents an alternate reality, neither Iran nor the United States nor anywhere. It is political, rooted in topical realism, but doesn't hold history or logic too tightly. The video is a place apart.

Neshat's videos and later photographs plunge the present into the past, into reflections and echoes that cut across time and geography. The work is equally capable of conjuring, for instance, the Persian poet Attar and the filmmaking style of Maya Deren (in her video *Illusions and Mirrors* [2013], both at the same time). This strategy is very much intentional. Neshat calls it an "Iranian point of view," looking outward from personal experiences onto the world, to a sense of universals.[17] "I am foremost interested to make art . . . that transcends politics, religion, the question of feminism, and becomes an important, timeless, universal work of art," Neshat said in her 2010 TEDTalk.[18] This interest is echoed over and over. In interviews and lectures after *Women of Allah*, including her conversation with Glenn Lowry in this volume, the word "universal" is ever-present.

The quest for universals can be hard to grapple with from an art-historical perspective. After all, the business of art history is to make distinctions, to examine specific relationships between aesthetics and history. For this reason, accounts of Neshat's videos and later photographs tend to emphasize their origin points in current affairs. *Turbulent* has its touchstone in laws that veil and limit the ability of women to sing. One can then move to Neshat's take on the 1953 American-aided overthrow of Iranian prime minister Mohammad Mossadegh in her videos *Munis* (2008) and *Farokh Legha* (2009), to the Green Movement protest against Iran's fraudulent 2009 election in *The Book of Kings* (2012, p. 138), and on to the growth of the Green Movement, which flowered into the protests of the Arab Spring in *Our House Is on Fire* (2013, p. 154). Her newest project, *Land of Dreams* (2019, p. 204), posits the theocracy of Iran and the U.S. under Donald Trump as mirror images.

Reading Neshat's career through a direct link to Iran, though often elegantly presented,[19] has its limitations. While contemporary events may serve as a springboard, her intention is often to transcend them entirely, to find their roots and larger structures in ancient history. One gets the sense that this is an ethical choice for Neshat, that going deeper into history is where she hopes to find linkages between cultures and nations, outside of the iron grip of nationalistic discourses. She locates these universal bonds in the elusiveness of poetry, in symbols loose enough to be both political and beyond politics. She moves freely inside the spaces of metaphor much in the same way one moves between the screens and various frames inside of her installations.

A way of thinking about Neshat's use of installation, the mediation of poetry, and a magical realist approach is through the concept of Persia as an expansive expression of Iranian identity. "Persia," by definition, is a shifting frame, a negotiated border, an internal country. Persia is a portable and mystical heritage that from its ancient origins has survived conquest and geographic boundaries. It contains the country of Iran, as well as Azerbaijan and other countries, and can be found all over the world through diasporic communities. It can contain multiple languages, religions, and identities. Its primary language, Farsi, is genderless. Its poetry, famously difficult to translate, is dense with imagery and symbolism.

"Iran" is the official name of the country where Neshat is from. "Iran" is a name that is both ancient and recently imposed. The oldest version of the word refers to kinship, implying "us." The oldest systematic usage is found in the *Shahnameh*, the central poem of the Iranian people written between 977 and 1010 A.C.E., in which "Iran" figures as a political community, a legacy of kings. Contemporary Iran officially received its name in 1935, when its penultimate king, Reza Shah Pahlavi, directed his foreign delegates to use the term in their business dealings with other nations. The spirit of Reza Shah's "Iran" seems to align with the term "Iranshahr," which means "a domain within which the authority of the shah is enforced."[20]

Persia predates Iran. It was an area of the Middle East where competing tribes centralized power through successive dynasties. The name "Persia" has its root in Greek, born as a series of adjectives describing the empire of Cyrus the Great in the fifth century B.C.E. The Persian empire changed hands often, its borders constantly fluctuating, at times extending deep into North Africa and as far east to what is now Pakistan. The word "Persia" was a way for empires like Greece and Rome to account for the people geographically bounded by the walls of the Zagros, Caucasus, and Kopet Dag mountain ranges, as well as the Caspian Sea, the Indus River, and the Persian Gulf. The king of this region mattered little, whether its people practiced Zoroastrianism or Islam, whether the center of power was near Shiraz, closer to Baghdad, or in the shadow of Mount Damavand. The social formations that sprang from this area were called "Persia."

For Neshat, "Persia" plays dual, paradoxical roles: as a source of national pride and tradition, and as a site of subversion and protest.[21] This paradox is, more often than not, represented inside of the indeterminate and magical world of poetic metaphor. Such is the stature of the Persian poet Hafez, for instance, that Shia clerics are compelled to recast his lyrical imagery of wine and intoxication into symbols of ecstatic encounters with God, simultaneously recognizing the poet's status in *Persian* culture—an entity transcending contemporary religion and politics—while affirming the prohibition against alcohol in *Iran*.

The man in the white shirt of the Islamic Republic sings Rumi in *Turbulent*, but in *Pulse* (2001), Rumi's words pour into an enclosed room through a radio. The singer, Sussan Deyhim, ethereally conjures a freedom in the words that bleeds through and beyond walls. These two very different usages of Rumi point to the specific and universal power of Persian poetics.[22] Both within the regime of the Islamic Republic and in resistance to it, the use of "Persian" metaphors and poetry can operate both as a political principle and a means of transcending politics.

The elasticity of Neshat's Persian heritage and its outward-facing spirit can be felt in the entirety of her work. The artist has, at times, even expressed frustration over the inability to grasp this complex nature of her symbolism. Regarding *Tooba* (2002, p. 114), for instance, she observed:

> My feeling is that most Americans don't really get the poetry and symbolism of this piece . . . In *our* culture, metaphoric/poetic language is the only means of expression for most of us, who are not permitted to speak freely. Poetry becomes a political statement, and the public becomes accustomed to reading between the lines.[23]

I suspect this is also true of the lack of attention paid to the videos in which symbolism is not overtly grounded in immediately recognizable current events, such as *Mahdokht* (2004), *Illusions and*

15

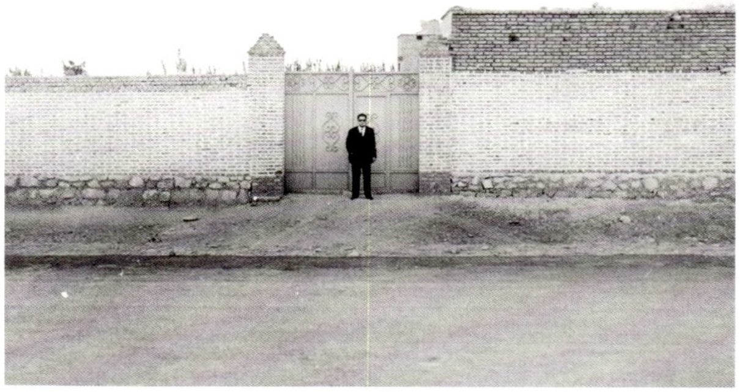

16

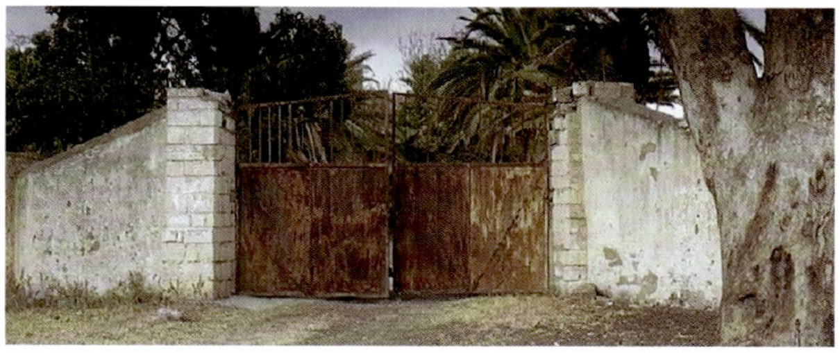

Mirrors, and *Sarah* (2016). These videos shift emphasis away from the events that feature so prominently in *Women of Allah*—the headlines, wars, and traumas emanating from Iran's twentieth century—turning instead to a historical idea of Persia as a generative force in the development of rituals and themes that echo globally. They are among Neshat's most poetic works, each full of the very language that she says her culture uses to speak of, through, and beyond politics.

Tooba addresses collective mourning and grief. Shot on a hillside near Cuilapan de Guerrero in Mexico, the video is, in Neshat's words, "an examination of the symbolic significance of the garden in the mystical traditions of Persian and Islamic cultures, to which it represents the space of spiritual transcendence, freedom, exile, and refuge."[24] In a brick enclosure on a hill, a woman is encased in, and at one with, a tree. A group of women and men journey toward her, dressed in black, while the film cuts to a circle of bearded men resembling religious or governmental figures. The first group of women and men climb the walls of the enclosure and confront the woman/tree. The woman subsequently disappears.

Neshat has tied this video to 9/11 and her ambivalent feelings of being a resident of a country under attack yet held in suspicion by that same country because of her background: "I wondered if it [would get] to the point where we were not so welcome here. Philosophically I felt this new fear over my head. I thought about leaving, but I didn't know where we'd go."[25] However, the choice of Mexico as a location is important. Contrary to the use of Morocco to mirror Iran in works such as *Rapture* and *Turbulent*, Mexico lies in a less stark position in the binary of "East" and "West."

In *Tooba*, Neshat looks for a place outside of her conflicted feelings. The artist has associated *Tooba* with Mexico's central symbol, the Virgin of Guadalupe, and has noted a kinship between that symbol and the legend of a mystical tree in the Qur'an, a tree whose branches extend over the whole world, keeping all Muslims in the welcoming shade of its canopy. The tree is found in the enclosure of a garden, one of the most profound symbols in all of Persian culture, predating Iran and Islam. In *Tooba*, Neshat presents a symbol that is Persian, Iranian, and Islamic, a symbol flexible enough to speak of the ironies and shifting political climate that immigrants often endure in their new countries.[26]

Persia's permeable and mystic borders, its many identities contained within a changing surface, serve Neshat's universalist aims.[27] Persia is both a way of having a frame for one's identity and of dissolving the frame. In Persia, one can be secular or religious, Azerbaijani, Iranian, even American. In Persia, an opponent of the Islamic Revolution has a place in which to reside and share a heritage with a supporter of the current regime.

Fig. 15 Neshat's father, Ali, in front of the gate to their family orchard in Qazvin, Iran, 1970s

Fig 16. Still from Neshat's feature film *Women without Men*, 2009, showing the entrance to the garden outside of Tehran, where the lives of multiple Iranian women converge during the 1950s

17

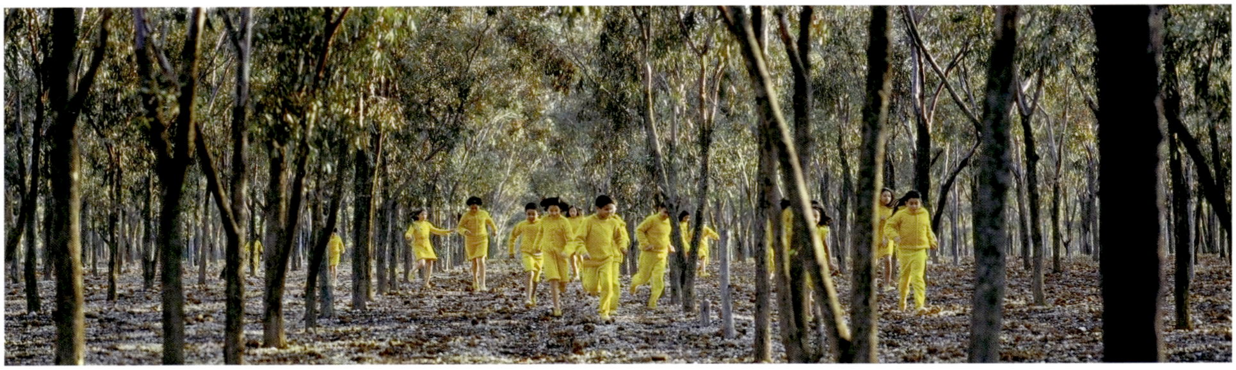

Neshat's most beautiful evocation of "Persia," which to me seems a sort of metaphoric source for her shifting bonds, for her seeking of structures and frames that people share across cultures, is her video *Mahdokht,* saturated in images recalling the orchard of her childhood in Qazvin (figs. 15–18).[28] The character of Mahdokht comes from the novel *Women without Men* by Shahrnush Parsipur, which Neshat made into a feature film. Parispur is a kindred spirit to Neshat, a writer who also uses the power of magical realism and the evocation of deep Persia to find the freedom to critique as well as transcend contemporary events. *Mahdokht* reverberates with Persian culture, speaking directly to Neshat's border-crossing, universalist impulses. Parsipur describes the character in this way:

> She would become thousands and thousands of branches. She would cover the entire world. Americans would buy her shoots and take them to California. They would call the forest of Mahdokht the forest of Mahdekat. Gradually they would pronounce her name so many times until it would become Maduk in some places and Maaduk in others. Then four hundred years later the linguists, with their veins standing out in their foreheads like twigs, would debate over her and prove that the two words come from the root Madeek which is of African origin.[29]

Children run through the garden around the figure of Mahdokht, who sews her golden threads in a seemingly mad frenzy of creative output. The threads are dispersed across the ground, extending in all directions.

This sense of Persia, which Neshat continues to explore, is the virtual and dreamlike world that she creates, a paradise lost, a garden of deep historical identification from which she can connect to the world.

* * *

In an early conversation with Neshat, we discussed how in 1979 many people who had fled the revolutionary upheaval in Iran for the United States adopted the identity of "Persian" rather than "Iranian."[30] This was, I discovered later, a way to assign one's own identity, of choosing a deeper heritage. Identifying as "Persian" can be a way of sidestepping association with the Islamic Republic, but also an assertion of a common bond, a heritage not confined to Iran. To be "Iranian" during the hostage crisis, during cycles of saber rattling and thaw between Iran and the United States over the past forty years, is to assert a label that cannot contain the full reality of one's heritage, to open oneself up to stereotypes and ignorance found in both countries, whose destinies have been intertwined for almost a century.

While I would not claim that all of Neshat's recent work can be contained within the metaphoric

Fig. 17 Still from *Mahdokht*, 2004

frames of Persia, the concept certainly allows a poetic way of thinking about how one can find Farsi written on the faces of Egyptians in *Our House Is on Fire* (p. 154), or, in the portraits of *Games of Desire*, Laotians. For *The Home of My Eyes* series (2015, fig. 19, p. 162), Azerbaijanis—people whose heritage is "Persian" but whose passports say "Azerbaijan"—were asked by the artist to define what home means to them. Their answers are written on their faces in the portraits, along with words from *Khosrow and Shirin*, a poem by the Persian poet Nizami Ganjavi (1141–1209), recounting the love of an Iranian king and an Armenian princess thwarted by politics, borders, and internal moral codes. A way of thinking about such border crossings and shared identities, a way of looking beyond politics and nationalism, is to define oneself as Persian. *The Home of My Eyes* is a proxy family album for Neshat, a way of looking into Iran through the eyes and faces of those who share its Persian heritage.

In Neshat's newest project, *Land of Dreams* (p. 204), this reality comes full circle, this time in the United States. *Land of Dreams* features photography and video, presenting the journey of a woman of Iranian heritage crossing the United States photographing everyday rural Americans. Many of the visuals of the film take their inspiration from Orson Welles' *The Trial* (1963). Neshat is currently developing the project into a feature film. Returning to her earliest influences, she collaborated on the screenplay with Jean-Claude Carrière, longtime writer of Luis Buñuel's films, a master of the shifting nature of identity inside of dreams as well as how reality itself can rip identity apart.

The woman does not define these Americans solely by their faces or where they live. She is more interested in their dreams, what exists beyond the terms that typically define them. She collects these dreams and writes them onto her sitters' portraits. In a world of nations and religions and labels that delineate and circumscribe the lands and peoples of the world, the woman's interest in these dreams is presented as both liberating and sinister. She takes the dreams and logs them in an Iranian colony in the desert, into a bureaucratic, Kafkaesque nightmare.

Border crossing, the dissolution of boundaries, living universally, can only be a partial reality. Instead, societal pressures and all sorts of irony-laden myths build the land of dreams. Borders always rise to meet you. The essential bonds that you seek, in the embrace of the garden, in the woman in the tree, always vanish when the census begins.

Ed Schad is Curator and Publications Manager at The Broad.

18

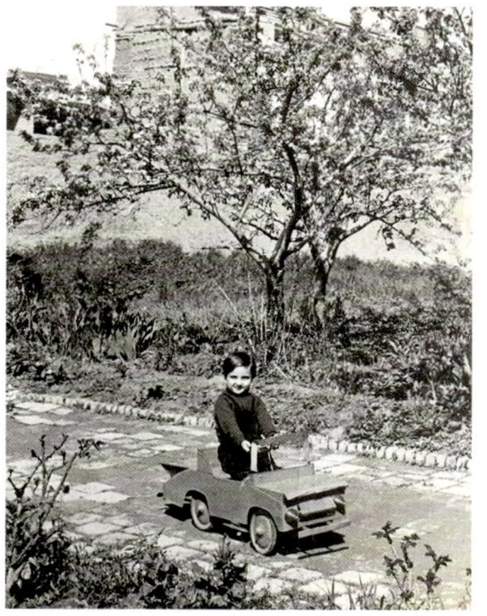

Fig. 18. Neshat's brother, Amir, in the family orchard in Qazvin, Iran, 1970s

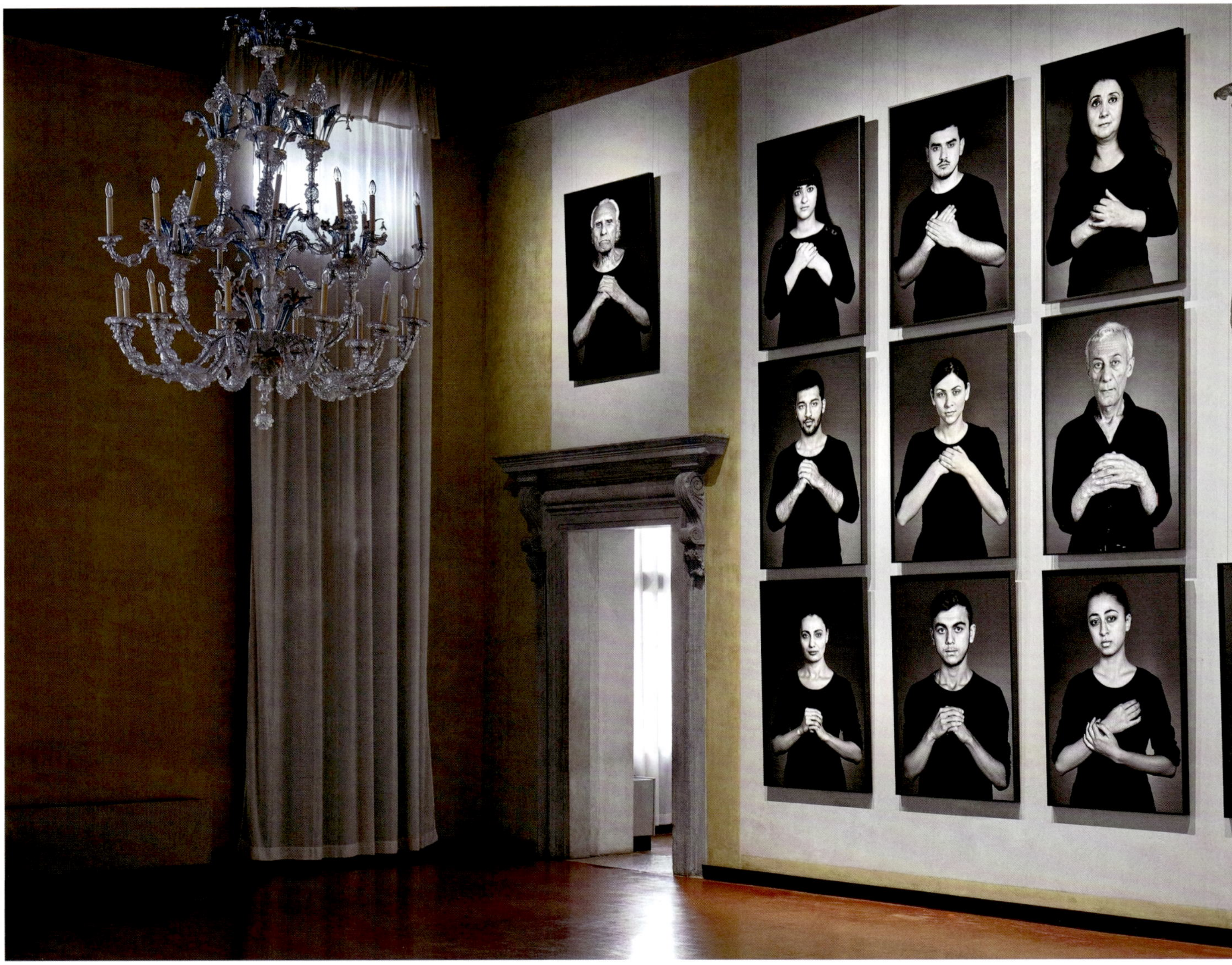

19

NOTES

I thank Shirin Neshat, Layla S. Diba, Sarah Loyer, and Philomena Mariani for reading and proofing my curatorial essay at various intervals throughout editing, as well as Katayoun Bahrami, David Raskin, Peter Mendenhall, Tyler Green, and Jarrett Earnest, who read and gave feedback on previous drafts.

1 Shirin Neshat, interview with the author, December 27, 2018.

2 Douglas Eklund, "Art and Photography: The 1980s," *Heilbrunn Timeline of Art History*, October 2004, at https://www.metmuseum.org/toah/hd/ap80/hd_ap80.htm.

3 Habitués of Franklin Furnace would have seen Neshat's *Unveiling* series in a context of other risk-taking exhibitions. The National Endowment for the Arts rescinded its grant to the organization due to a performance by Scarlet O. in 1991. At the request of Senator Jesse Helms, Franklin Furnace was audited by the IRS and the state comptroller of New York in 1990, investigated for its staging of Karen Finley's installation *A Woman's Life Isn't Worth Much*. See http://franklinfurnace.org/research/organizational_timeline/timeline.php.

4 Shirin Neshat quoted in Lauren Collins, "Voice of the Veil," *The New Yorker*, October 15, 2007, p. 91.

5 Neshat, interview with the author, December 27, 2018.

6 Neshat knew Ehsan when she lived in Los Angeles and reconnected with him on her visits to Iran. On one of those visits, he gave her a copy of his dissertation. Ibid.

7 Ehsan "beautifully wrote about the psychological, philosophical yet ideological and religious mindsets of those who chose to become martyrs. That intersection of love, devotion, self-sacrifice, yet cruelty, violence and ultimately death was a fascinating paradox for me." Ibid.

8 Mansoor Ehsan, "Politics of Martyrdom in Post-Revolutionary Iran," PhD diss., University of Oregon, 1992, pp. 16, 17.

9 For further reading about Ali Shariati, see Laura Secor, *Children of Paradise: The Struggle for the Soul of Iran* (New York: Riverhead Books, 2016), pp. 3–21.

10 This reactivation centers on the reinterpretation of the Battle of Karbala on October 10, 680, and the death of Muhammad's grandson Husain. By stressing Husain as a martyr, discourse in post-revolutionary Iran replaced a "quietist" or peaceful anticipation of Shia Islam's hidden Iman with an active call for a struggle to bring the Iman about in history. Ehsan, "Politics of Martyrdom in Post-Revolutionary Iran."

11 Farzaneh Milani, *Veils and Words: The Emerging Voices of Iranian Women Writers* (Syracuse, N.Y.: Syracuse University Press, 1992), pp. 128–30.

12 Michael C. Hillmann, *A Lonely Woman: Forugh Farrokhzad and Her Poetry* (Washington, D.C.: Three Continents Press, 1987), p. 122.

13 The words of Farrokhzad appear throughout Neshat's career, arising and changing under different circumstances. "I Will Greet the Sun Again," "I Pity the Garden," "Another Birth," and "Rebellion" repeat throughout her photographs in the 1990s, as words spiraling on top of eyes, twisting around dancing arms, tattooed on fingers, and, notably, on both the outside and interior of chadors. In the film *Rapture*, Farrokhzad's "Let Us Believe in the Beginning of the Cold Season" is revealed on the hands of a group of women, who, shortly after singing and chanting in tension with a group of men, set sail on an empty and turbulent sea. Recitation of "The Window" stops an interrogation in its tracks in *The Last Word*, and "The Gift," "Later On," and litany of selections from Farrokhzad can be found among words of protest from Iran's young people, both in photographs from the Masses and the Patriots in *The Book of Kings*. The feet of corpses in a morgue, memorializing the dead in Egypt's Arab Spring protests, are marked with "Another Birth," "Escape and Pain," and "The Wall."

14 "After voicing the concerns of a woman who strove to free herself from social restrictions and then leaving Iran in 1963 to study in the United States, when she returned to the country in the seventies she dedicated herself entirely to Khomeini's revolution, became a devout fundamentalist and a spokeswoman for the Islamic republic." Octavio Zaya, "An Exteriority of the Inward," in *Shirin Neshat: La última palabra / The Last Word* (Milan: Charta, 2005), p. 19.

15 Photography would take a backseat to video as Neshat's primary form of making art. From 1997 to 2009, she would continue to make photographs inspired by the images in her films. In terms of installation of any given series, the artist prefers to show either the film *or* the photographs.

16 Eleanor Heartney et al., *After the Revolution: Women Who Transformed Contemporary Art*, 2d ed. (New York: Prestel, 2013), p. 248.

17 Shirin Neshat, lecture for Harvard University Graduate School of Design, November 27, 2018, at https://www.gsd.harvard.edu/event/shirin-neshat/.

18 Shirin Neshat, "Art and Exile," TEDWomen 2010, December 2010, at https://www.ted.com/talks/shirin_neshat_art_in_exile?language=en.

19 For instance, see Melissa Ho, "A State of In-Between: Shirin Neshat's Iran," in *Shirin Neshat: Facing History* (Washington, D.C.: Smithsonian Books, 2015), pp. 10–25.

20 Abbas Amanat, *Iran: A Modern History* (New Haven: Yale University Press, 2017), p. 10. Amanat's introduction is a brilliant discussion of the legacy and nuance of the terms "Iran" and "Persia." Sussan Babaie, "Visual Recitations: Neshat's 'Persian Arts,'" in *Shirin Neshat* (Detroit: Detroit Institute of Arts, 2013), also discusses the complexity of the term "Persia," leading into a focused study on Neshat's 2009 photography series, *The Book of Kings*.

21 Azar Nafisi, "Foreword," in *Shahnameh: The Persian Book of Kings* (New York: Penguin, 2016), pp. x–xi: "Against the brutality of time and politics, against the threat of constant invasions and destructions imposed on them by enemies alien and domestic, against a reality they had little or no control over, they crafted magnificent monuments in words, they reasserted both their own worth and the best achievements of mankind through a work like *Shahnameh*, the golden thread that links one Persian to the other, connecting the past to the present."

22 Amanat, *Iran: A Modern History*, p. 21: "The liberating space that was Persian poetry . . . allowed subversive—indeed, heretical—expressions forbidden in any other media." One finds this phenomenon in other cultures, notably in the poetry and literature of former Soviet bloc countries as well as in the magical realism of Latin America, but in Iran its legacy is undeniable. Neshat, in collaboration with Shoja Azari, Deyhim, and Ghasem Ebrahimian, notably used both the specific and universal power of Persian poetics in 2001, reinterpreting Attar's *Conference of the Birds* (a poem that is, among many other things, a spiritual manual for the mystical school of Islam called Sufism) as a feminist narrative. Azari described the project, titled *The Logic of the Birds*, in this way: "Persian culture is 5,000 years old, and the Islamic invasion only happened 1,500 years ago. The history of Iran is resistance to domination through a mystical approach to Islam. Basically, what we are doing is trying to make sense of this confused identity, to go back to our roots and translate them into a universal language." Shoja Azari quoted in Amei Wallace, "Theater; An Islamic Culture In All Its Beauty," *The New York Times*, September 30, 2001.

23 Scott MacDonald, "Between Two Worlds: An Interview with Shirin Neshat," *Feminist Studies* 30 (Fall 2004), reprinted in *A Critical Cinema 4: Interviews with Independent Filmmakers* (Berkeley: University of California Press, 2005), pp. 340–41.

24 Shirin Neshat quoted in Arthur C. Danto, *Shirin Neshat* (New York: Rizzoli, 2010), p. 131.

25 Shirin Neshat in conversation with Tyler Green, Modern Art Notes Podcast, April 4, 2013.

26 For an account of the association between *Tooba*, Persian gardens, 9/11, and immigration, see Tyler Green, "Shirin Neshat's Tooba," *Modern Art Notes*, April 30, 2005.

27 "We keep going back to Attar, Rumi because we need to reflect back on all humanity. After exile, you see there is no boundary, that the world, like [the poet] Nima Yooshij said, is your home," as Neshat's longtime director of photography Ghasem Ebrahimian puts it. "You feel empathy for people you didn't know . . . that's why we keep repeating that all these borders, all these languages, all these religions, all these costumes, and all these cultures are under the one umbrella." Ghasem Ebrahimian, interview with the author, October 8, 2018.

28 Neshat speaks with great nostalgia of her original home in Iran, of her family's orchard, house, and garden in Qazvin, medieval capital of the Safavid dynasty of Persia. There is wonderful resonance to the story she tells of her orchard, full of cherries, olives, and pomegranates, and it is easy to extend the sense of this place as a sanctuary beyond the experiences of her family. The city of Qazvin is surrounded by orchards and, since the seventh century, has used its orchards as an absorptive barrier against floodwaters flowing from the surrounding mountains into the Qazvin plain. Neshat left Qazvin in 1975; a few years later, her orchard was confiscated by the Islamic Republic. As Neshat moved from Los Angeles to Berkeley and eventually to New York, the physical and existential question of the orchard's fate was in the background. Neshat's sister would eventually win the orchard back in court, only to sell it off piece by piece.

29 Shahrnush Parsipur, *Women without Men* (New York: Feminist Press at CUNY, 2010), p. 11.

30 Shoku Amirani, "Tehrangeles: How Iranians Made Part of LA Their Own," *BBC News*, September 29, 2012, at https://www.bbc.com/news/magazine-19751370.

Fig. 19 Installation view of *The Home of My Eyes*, Museo Correr, Venice, 2017. Photo by Philipp Ottendörfer

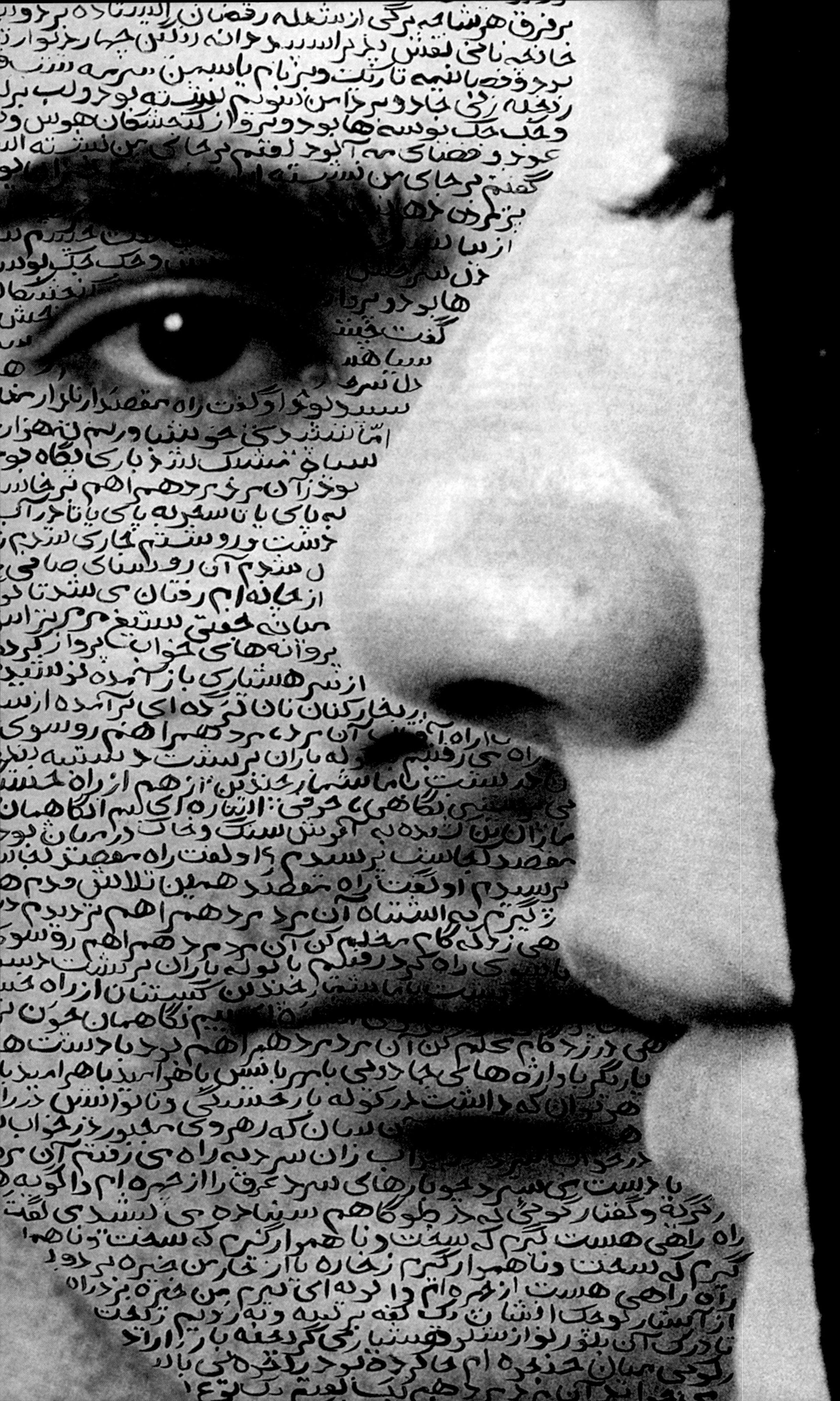

WOMEN OF ALLAH, TURBULENT, RAPTURE

From 1993 to 1997, Neshat's work largely consisted of photography, primarily portraits of women shown navigating an Iranian society often defined physically, politically, and intellectually by gender dynamics, imposed by cultural custom and religious mandate. The women in these photos, collectively called "Women of Allah," are nameless, often veiled, but also full of agency, engaged in acts of tenderness, self-protection, prayer, and self-identification. The words of poets and writers in Farsi, as well as decorative patterns commonly found in Persian manuscript illumination, are inscribed on their bodies. As Neshat has explained, the inscriptions give voice to her subjects, expressing their inner desires and beliefs. These inscriptions are a device that defines Neshat's practice to this day.

Women of Allah, inspired by the artist's trips to Iran in the early 1990s as well as her life and work in New York, are discussed extensively in this volume. Within the series are three subsets. The first, called *Unveiling*, features the poems of Forugh Farrokhzad, well known in Iran for her revolutionary and unapologetic expressions of female desire. The second set revolves around the words of poet Tahereh Saffarzadeh as well as the novelist Moniru Ravanipur and explores the nature of martyrdom in Iran during the country's war with Iraq from 1980 to 1988. The final photographs of *Women of Allah* were taken in Iran in 1995, a trip that ended with the artist's interrogation by police at Tehran airport, resulting in her ongoing exile from the country.

Soon after, Neshat turned from photography to film and video. Her photographic images had been made in collaboration with Plauto, Cynthia Preston, Kyong Park, Larry Barns, and Bahman Jalali, and this spirit of collaboration would explode in her films. *Turbulent* (1998) proved transformative in many ways. It earned Neshat the International Prize at the 1999 Venice Biennale. It featured the acting of Shoja Azari (Neshat's future partner), the acting and music of Sussan Deyhim, and the cinematography of Ghasem Ebrahimian, each of whom would continue to influence Neshat's work. And it ushered in decades of creative partnerships with diverse

Previous spread
Whispers (detail), 1997

numbers of international voices, including Philip Glass, Ryuichi Sakamoto, Mohsen Namjoo, Markus Hinterhäuser, and Shahrnush Parispur.

A viewer cannot experience the entirety of Neshat's early films as one would a film projected in a movie theater. Her works split open what Andrei Tarkovsky called the "time-thrust, or the flow of time within the frame."[2] The installations, whose structures are determined by content and theme, force viewers to focus on one screen or another, to move back and forth between screens, as though physically embodying the dualities of place, gender, and society explored in the films. In *Turbulent*, rooted in the fact that women are not legally allowed to sing in public in Iran, two screens depict a male singer in front of a crowd and a female singer in front of an empty auditorium. The camera shows a man (voiced by Shahram Nazeri and played by Azari) singing a poem by Rumi, then shifts to the woman (played by Deyhim), who sings a series of escalating and cascading sounds expressive of a personal freedom that transcends social prohibitions.

Shot in Essaouira, Morocco, *Rapture*'s (1999) location was partially inspired by its use in Orson Welles' *Othello* (1952). In the video, two screens manifest the male/female divide as conveyed through cultural metaphors that link men with the city and women with nature. According to Neshat, the groups of men and women depicted here engage in an "allegorical duel." White-shirted men march together through the streets of a fortress, finally looking out from its walls, as though bound to the city itself. On the other screen, women congregate in nature, singing and praying, until some of them sail away on the open sea.

Rapture has been regarded as a critique of cultural traditions and laws that delineate and define access to physical space according to gender. Its final image has also been tied to "political migrations in recent history, including the precarious seafaring attempts by refugees from Cambodia, Cuba, Haiti, and Vietnam to reach freedom in other countries."[1] These themes—how access to space and movement are regulated by politics, tradition, and identity—interlace through Neshat's work from her earliest videos to the present.

NOTES

1 James Rondeau, "Rapture," in *Shirin Neshat* (Paris: Galerie Jérôme de Noirmont, 1999), p. 16.

2 See Shoja Azari, "Perceptual Dislocation," in *Shirin Neshat: Women without Men* (Milan: Charta, 2011), p. 9.

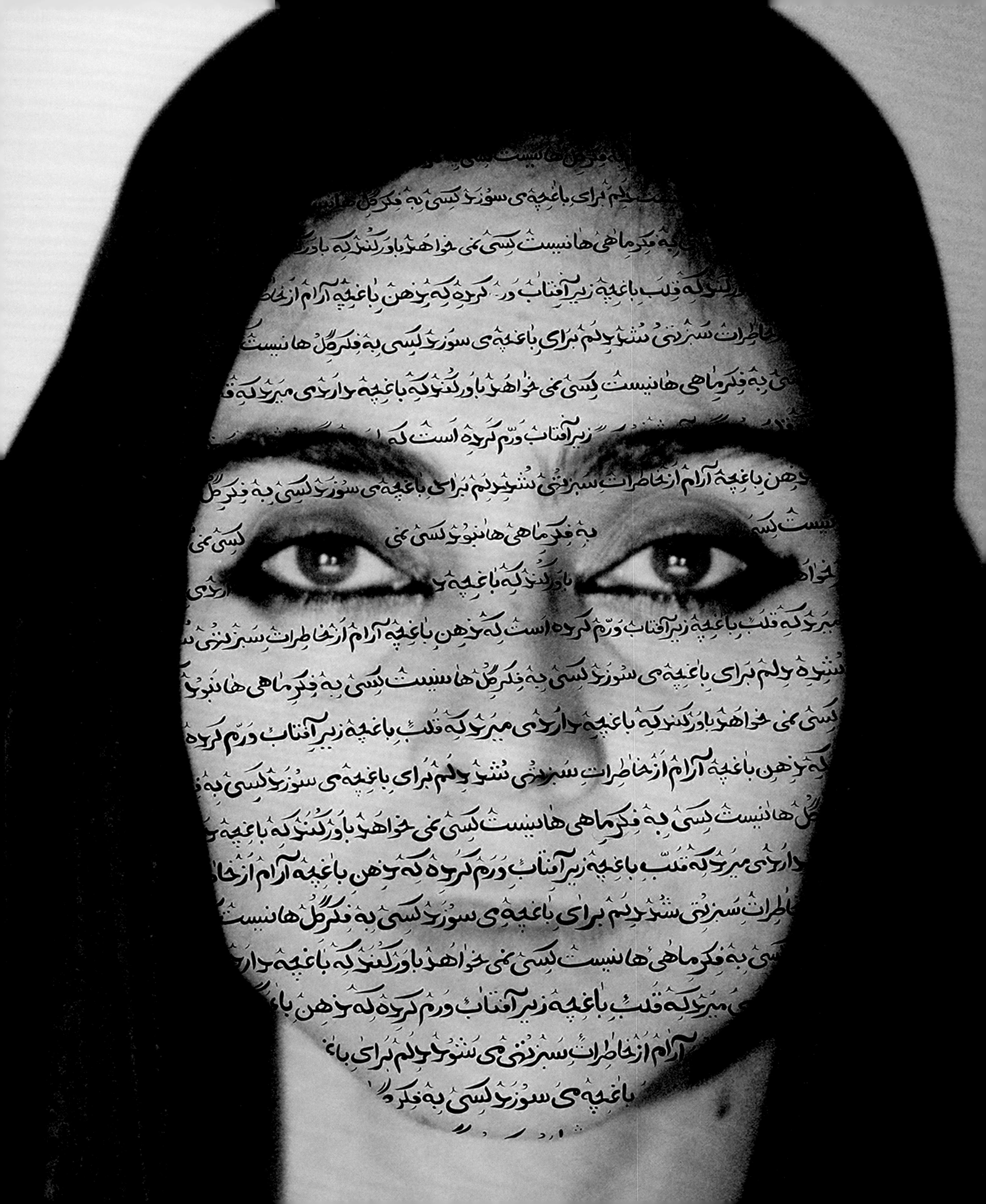

I PITY THE GARDEN
Forugh Farrokhzad

No one thinks of the flowers.
No one thinks of the fish.
No one wants to believe the garden is dying,
that its heart has swollen in the heat of this sun,
that its mind drains slowly of its lush memories.

Our garden is forlorn.
It yawns waiting
for rain from a stray cloud,
and our pond sits empty.
Callow stars bite the dust
from atop tall trees
and from the pale home of the fish
comes the hack of coughing every night.

Our garden is forlorn.

Father says: *My time is past, my time is past.*
I've carried my burden.
I'm done with my work.
He stays in his room from dawn to dusk,
reads *History of Histories* or Ferdowsi's *Epic of Kings*.

Father says to Mother:
Damn every fish and every bird!
When I'm dead, what will it matter
if the garden lives or dies.
My pension is all that counts.

Mother's life is a rolled out prayer rug.
She lives in terror of Hell,
always seeks Sin's footprints in every corner,
imagines the garden sullied
by the sin of a wayward plant.

Mother is a sinner by nature. She prays
all day, then with her "consecrated" breath
blows on all the flowers, all the fish
and all over her own body.
She awaits the Promised One
and the forgiveness He is to bring.

My brother calls the garden a graveyard.
He laughs at the plight of the grass
and ruthlessly counts the corpses of the fish
rotting beneath shallow water's dead skin.
My brother is addicted to philosophy.
He sees the healing of the garden in its death.
Drunk, he beats his fists on doors and walls,
says he is tired, pained, and despondent.
He carries his despair everywhere,
just as he carries his birth certificate,
diary, napkin, lighter, and pen.

But his despair is so small that each night
it is lost in crowded taverns.

My sister was a friend to flowers.
She would take her simple heart's words
—when mother beat her—
to their kind and silent gathering,
and sometimes she would treat the family
of fish to sunshine and cake crumbs.

She now lives on the other side of town
in her artificial home, and in the arms
of her artificial husband she makes natural children.
Each time she visits us, if her skirt is sullied
with the poverty of our garden
she bathes herself in perfume.
Every time she visits she is with child.

Our garden is forlorn.
Our garden is forlorn.

All day from behind the door
come sounds of cuts and tears,
sounds of blasts.
Instead of flowers, our neighbors plant
bombs and machine guns in their garden soil.
They cover their ponds, hiding bags of gunpowder.
The school children fill their backpacks
with tiny bombs.

Our garden is dizzy.

I fear the age that has lost its heart,
the idleness of so many hands
the alienation in so many faces.

I am like a schoolchild madly in love
with her geometry books.
I am forlorn
and imagine it is possible to take the garden to a hospital.
I imagine   I imagine
And the garden's heart has swollen in the heat
of this sun, its mind slowly drains of its lush memories.

Translation by Sholeh Wolpé

Unveiling (detail), 1993

Selections from ALLEGIANCE WITH WAKEFULNESS
Tahereh Saffarzadeh

From "The Journey of the Awakened"

O, you martyr
hold my hands
with your hands
cut from earthly means.
Hold my hands,
I am your poet,
with an inflicted body,
I've come to be with you
and on the promised day
we shall rise again.

From "The Height of Wakefulness"

O Guard
in the heart of night's cold
you watch as if from outside
the house of your own body
with tired eyelids
a night nurse
so that the wounded city can rest
from the plunder of death.
Your wakefulness comes from earnest faith,
your sincerity and Al-Asr.
Stories of your martyrdom
like martyrdom of the people
remain unheard
they have no voice, no image, no date,
they are unannounced.
O light of the eyes
O good
O my brother
O watchful one
as your bullets in the air
break my sleep,
as if by reflex, I pray for you,
guardian of the liberating Revolution
O lonely hero,
watching against the nightly enemy
let God safeguard you from calamity.

Translation by Farzaneh Milani

Rebellious Silence (detail), 1994

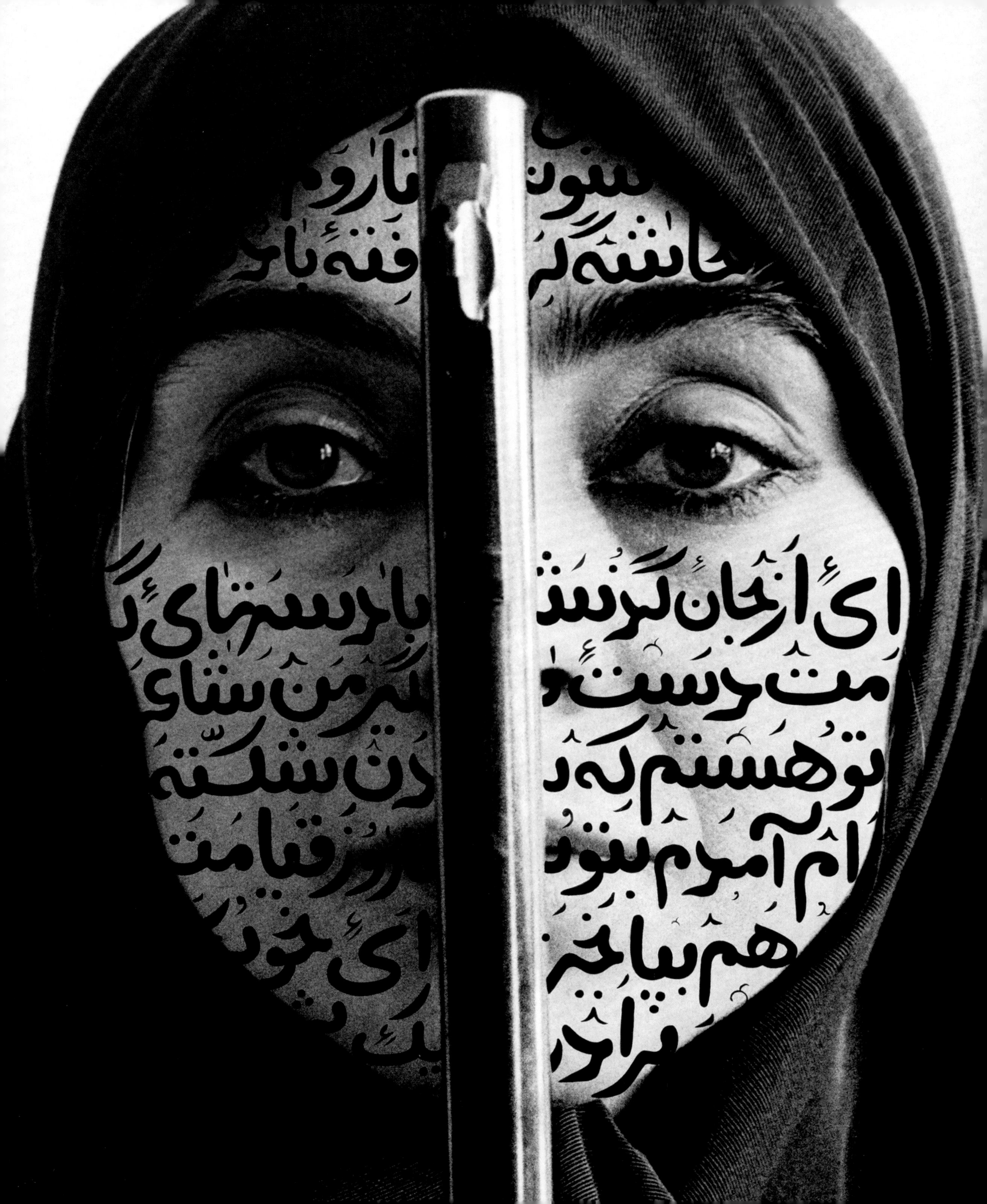

WOMEN OF ALLAH

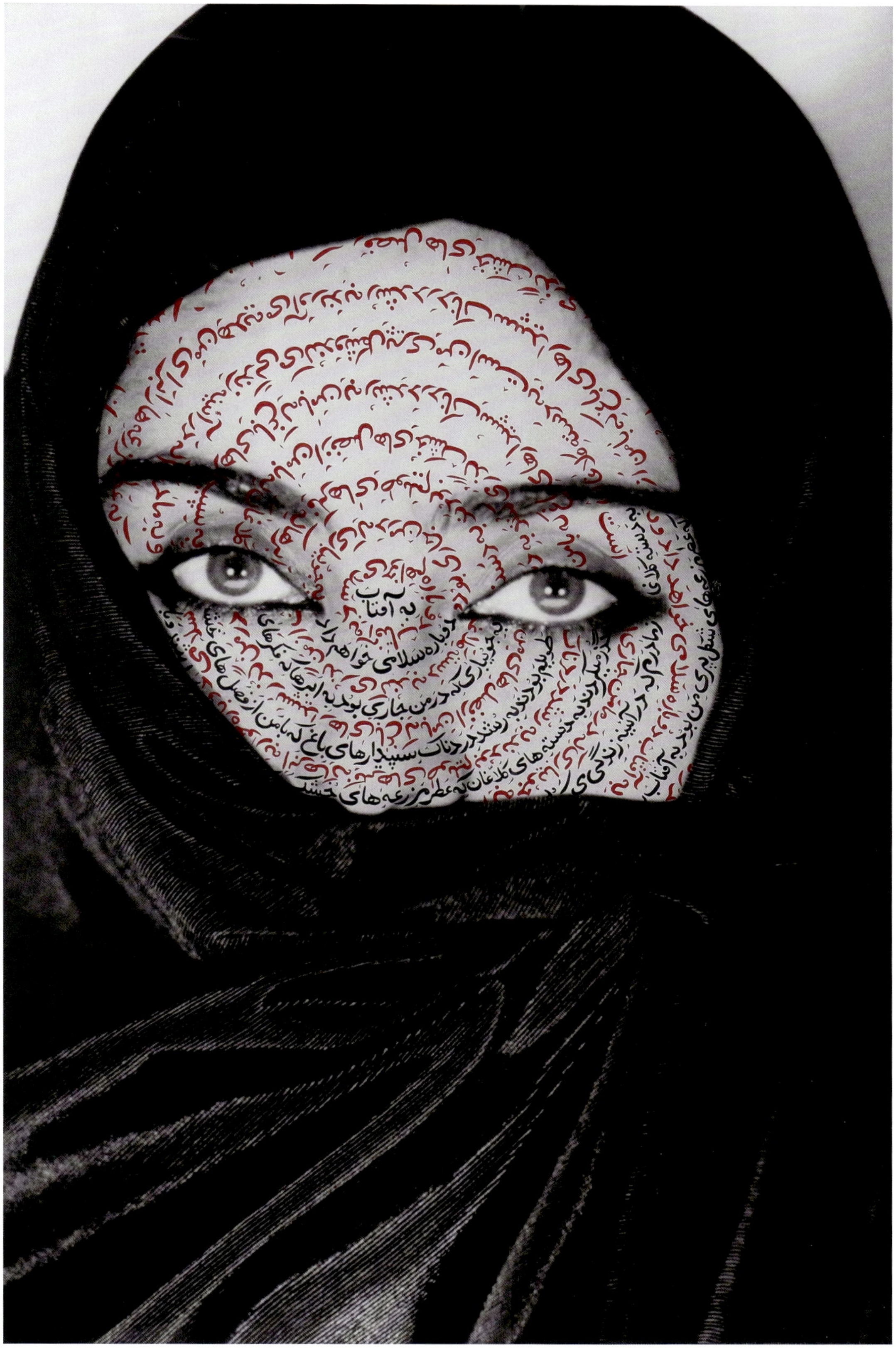

I AM ITS SECRET, 1993

Ink on RC print, 54⅞ x 39⅛ x 1⅞ inches (139.4 x 99.4 x 4.8 cm).
Photograph taken by Plauto

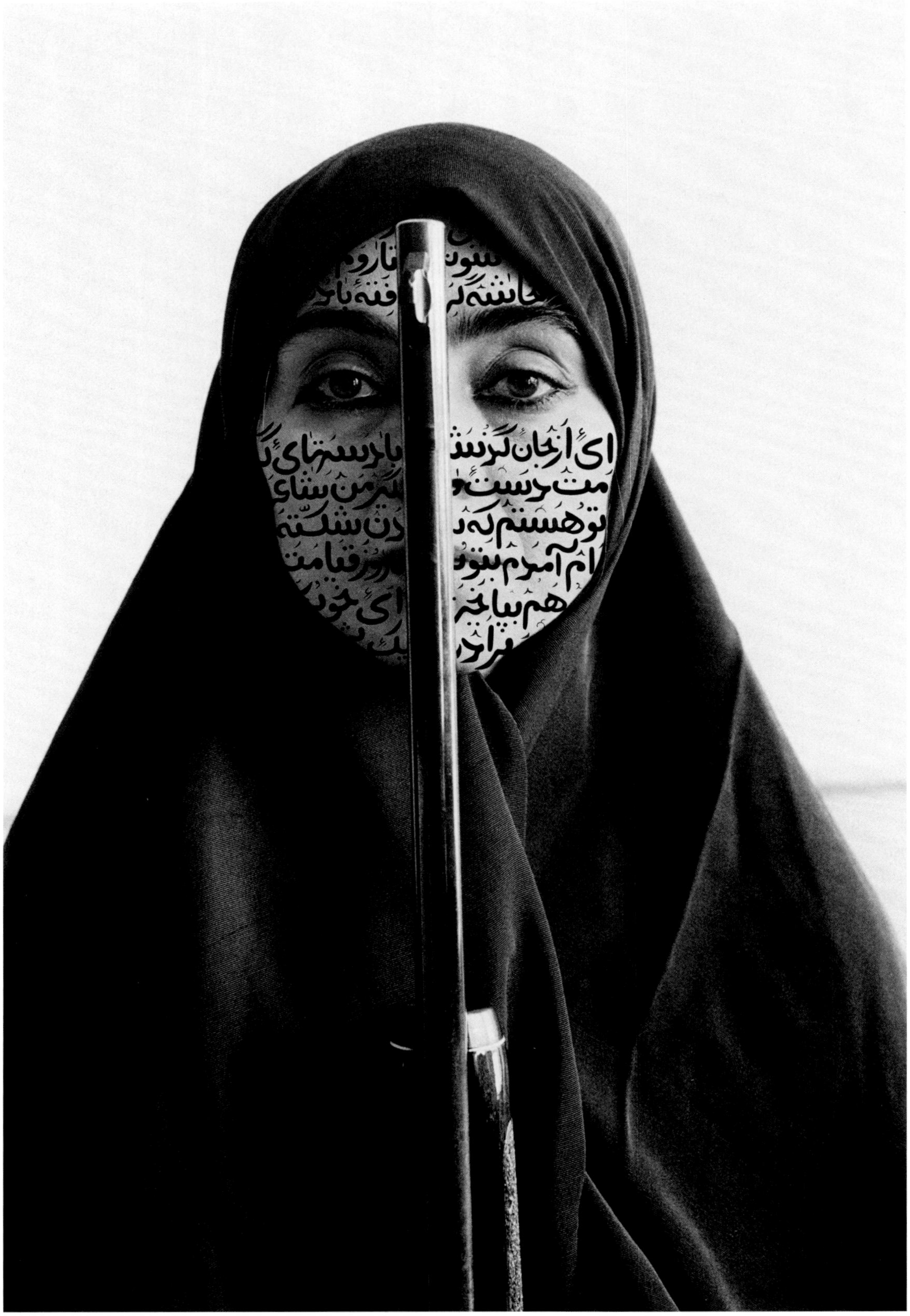

REBELLIOUS SILENCE, 1994

Ink on LE silver gelatin print, 51⅞ x 36½ x 1⅞ inches (131.8 x 92.7 x 4.8 cm). Photograph taken by Cynthia Preston

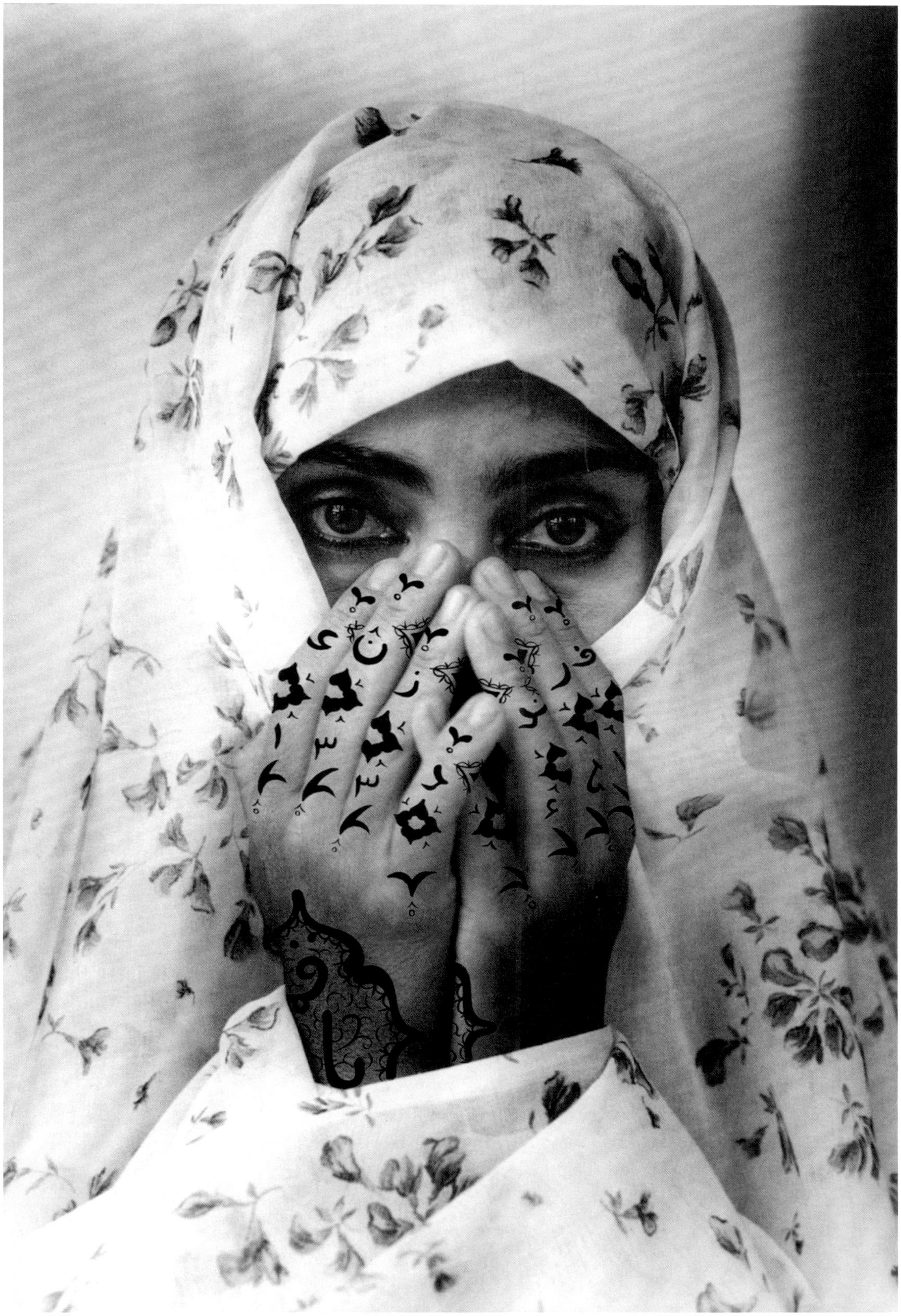

IDENTIFIED, 1995

Ink on RC print, 58¾ x 43¼ x 1⅞ inches (149.2 x 109.9 x 4.8 cm).
Photograph taken by Cynthia Preston

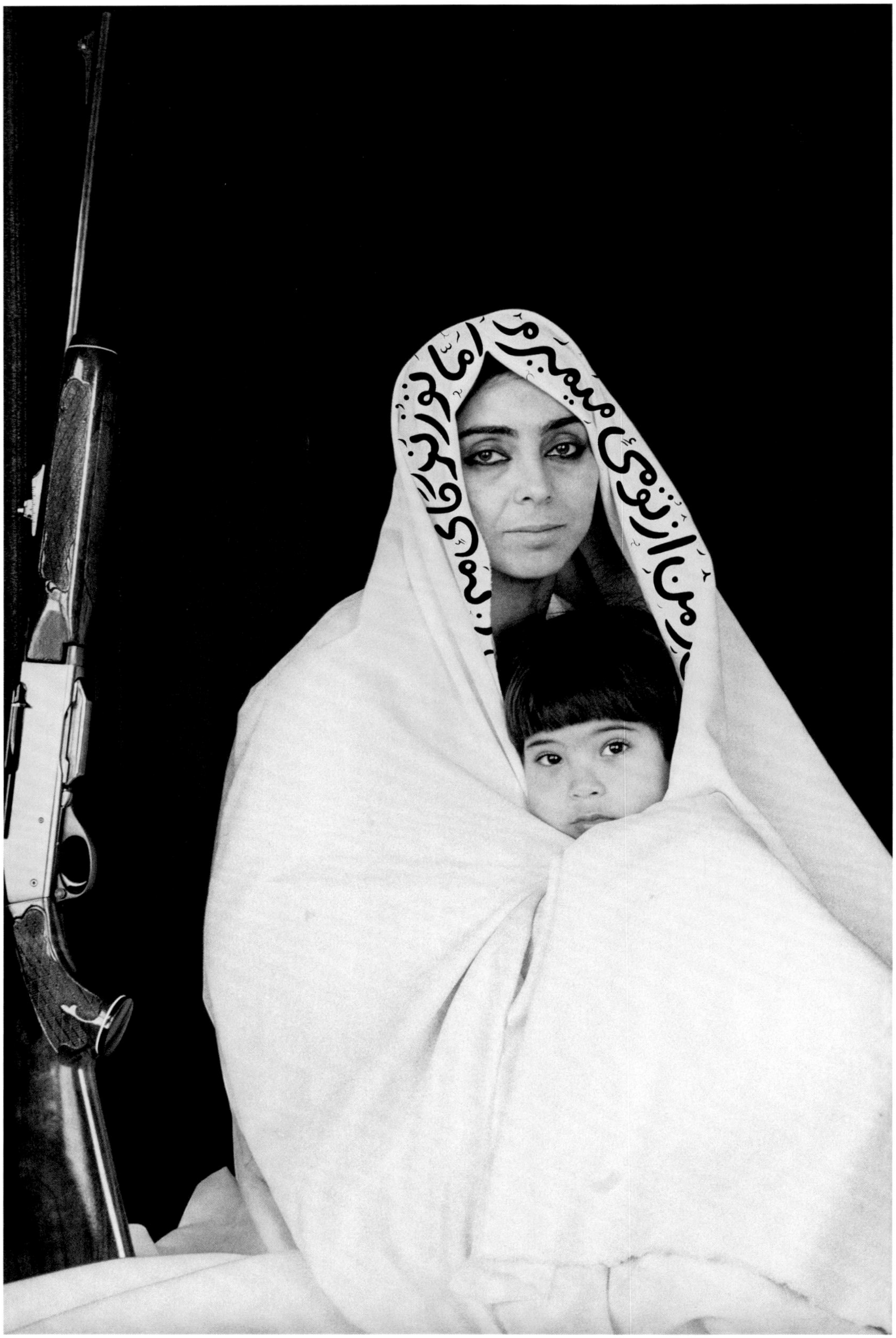

MY BELOVED, 1995

Ink on LE silver gelatin print, 65⅜ x 47⅜ x 2 inches (166.1 x 120.3 x 5.1 cm). Photograph taken by Cynthia Preston. Courtesy of Goodman Gallery, Johannesburg, Capetown, and London

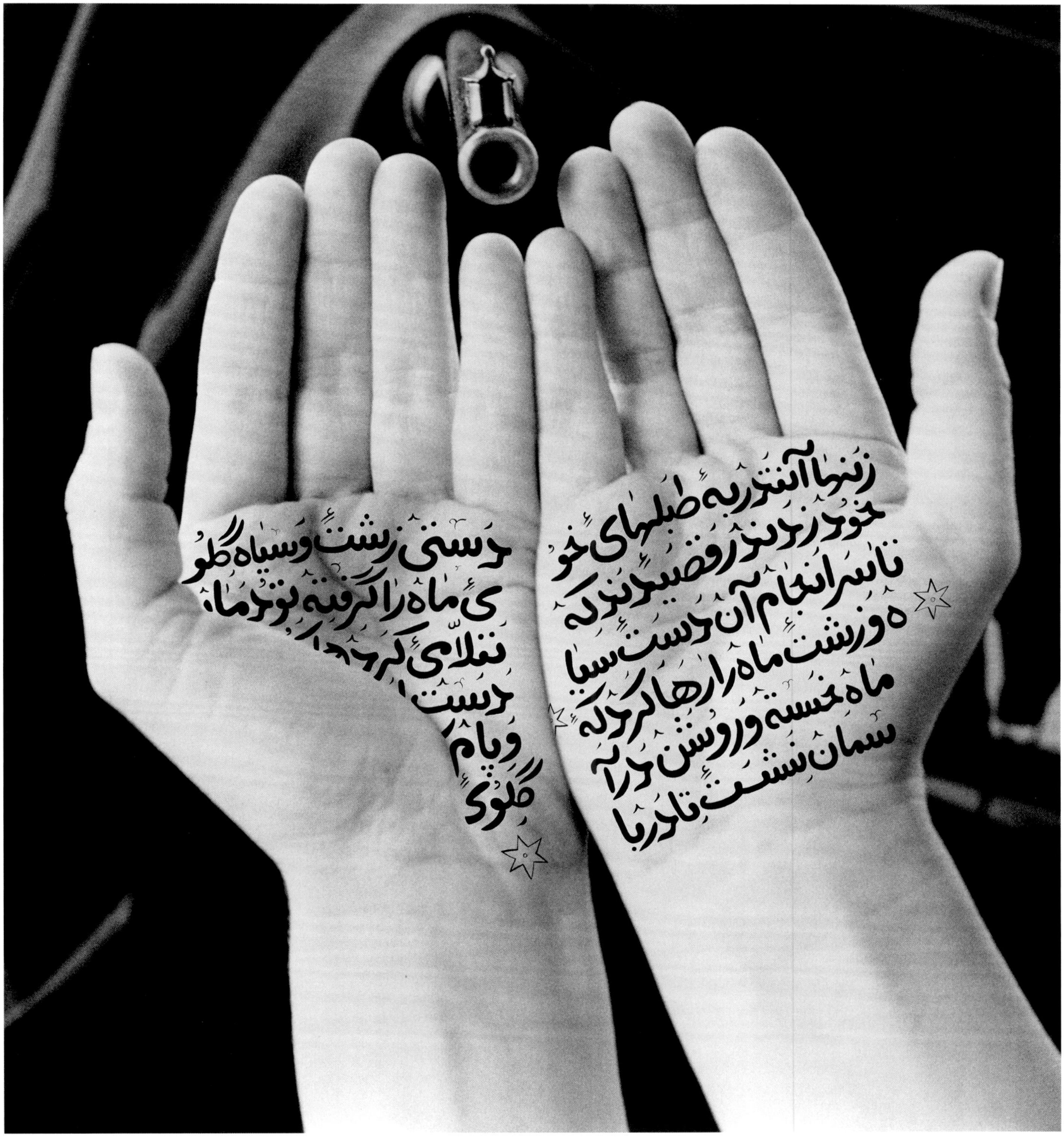

GUARDIANS OF REVOLUTION, 1994

Ink on LE silver gelatin print, 47½ x 43¾ x 1⅞ inches (120.7 x 111.1 x 4.8 cm).
Photograph taken by Cynthia Preston

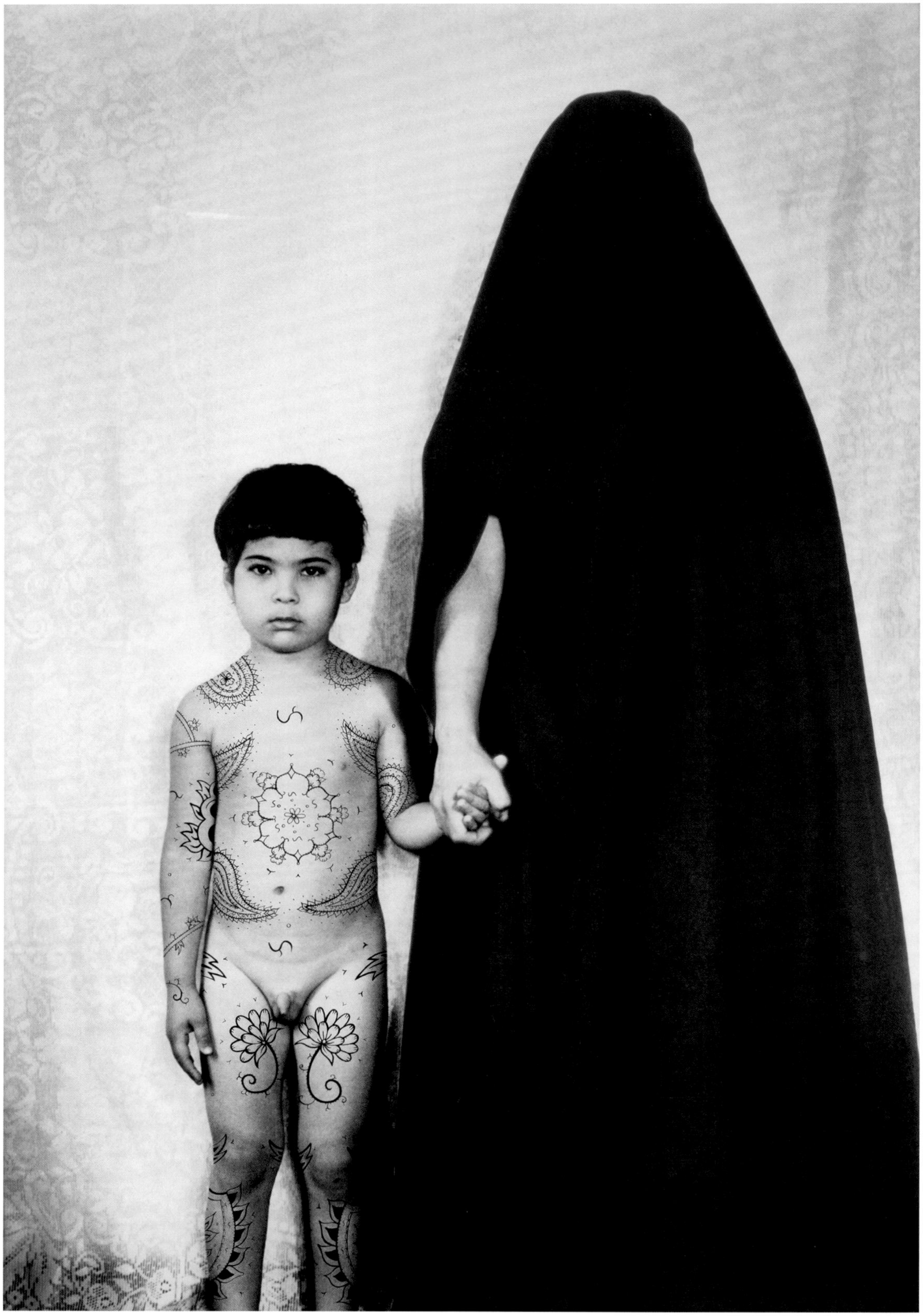

UNTITLED, 1996

Ink on RC print, 58½ x 43 x 1⅞ inches (148.6 x 109.2 x 4.8 cm).
Photograph taken by Kyong Park

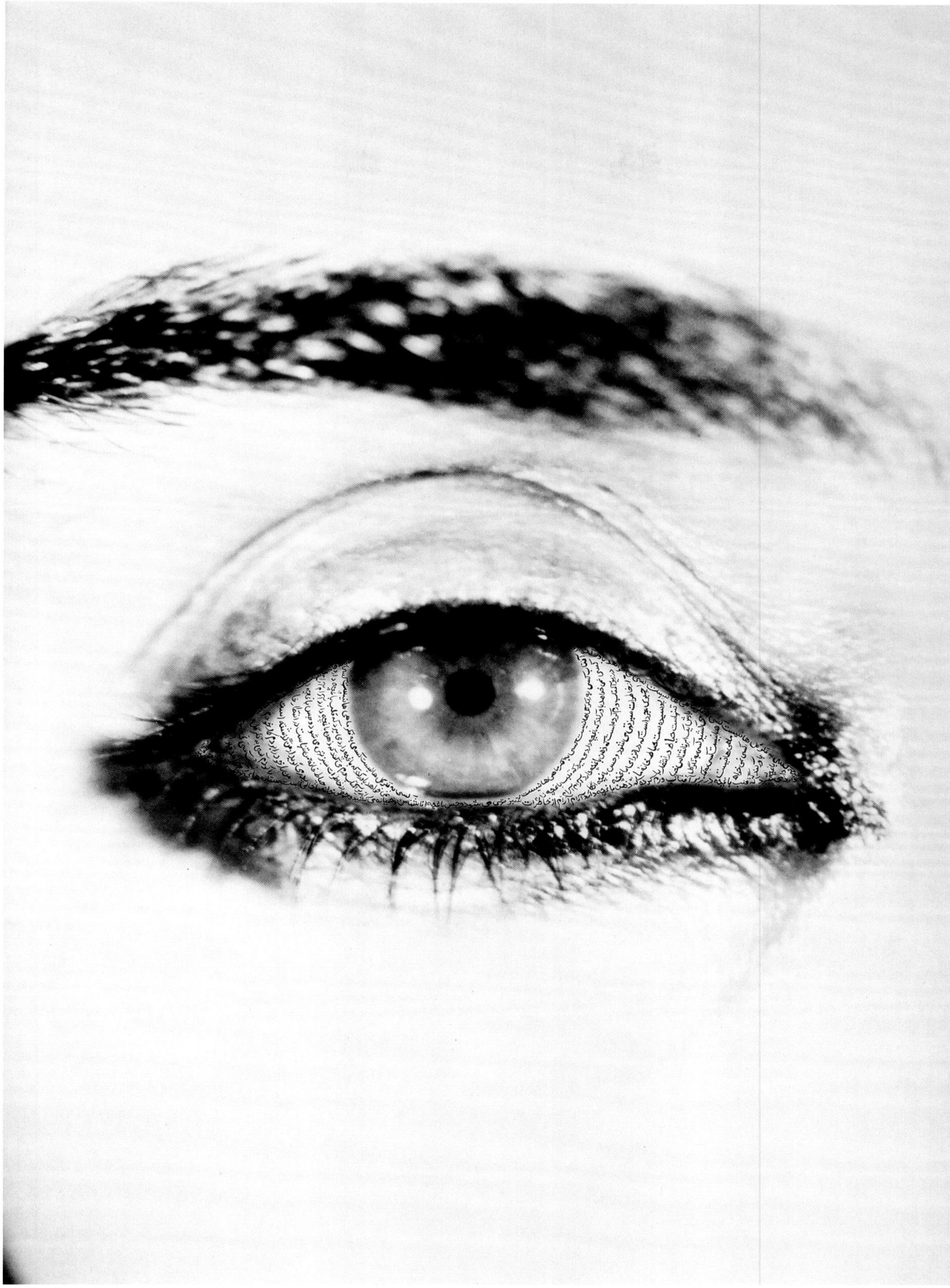

OFFERED EYES, 1993

Ink on RC print, 52⅜ x 36¼ x 1⅞ inches (133 x 92.1 x 4.8 cm). Photograph taken by Plauto

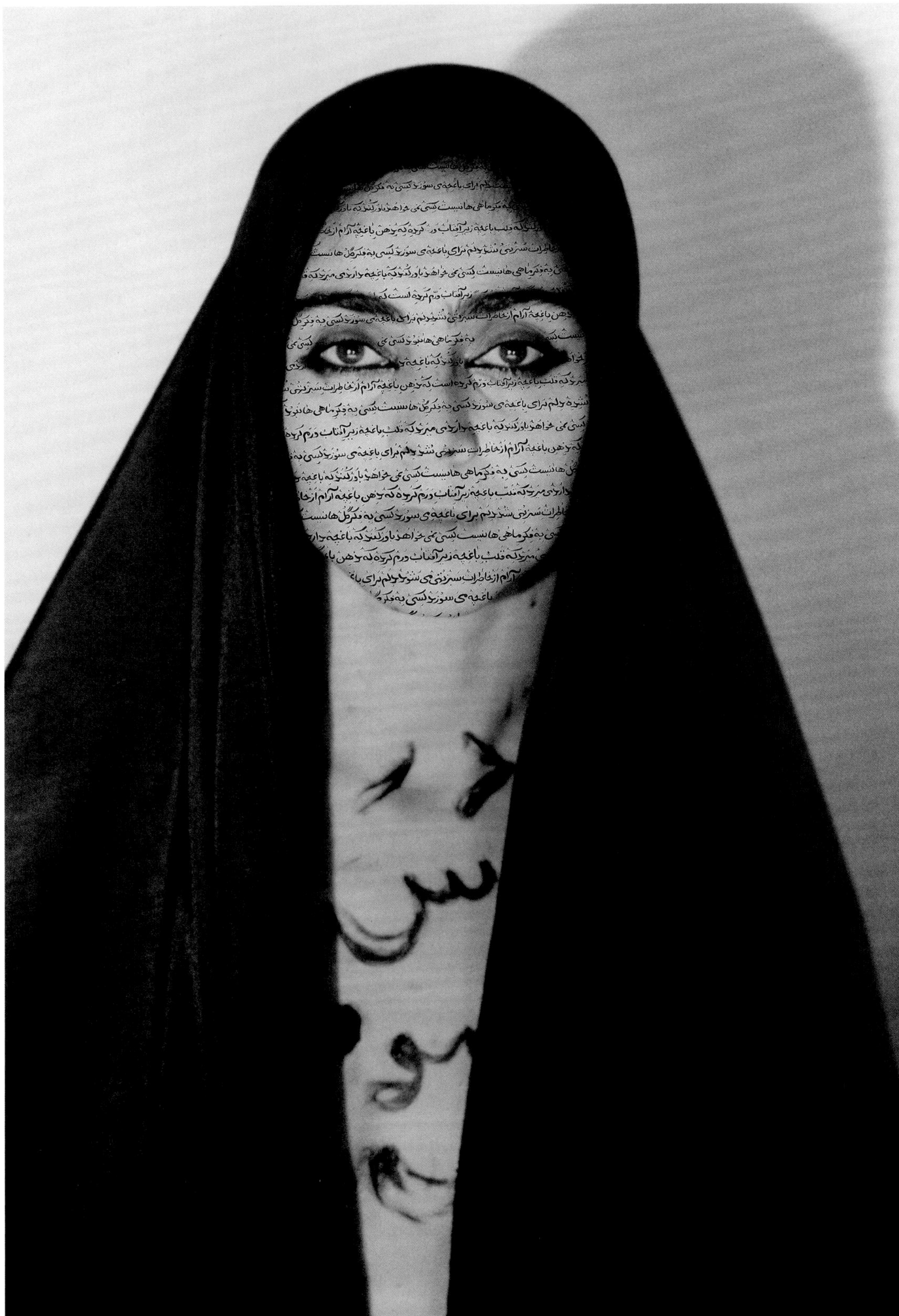

UNVEILING, 1993

Ink on LE gelatin silver print, 59¾ x 39¾ inches (151.8 x 101 cm).
Photograph taken by Plauto. Purchase, with funds from the Photography Committee.
Inv. N.: 2000.267. Whitney Museum of American Art, New York, NY, U.S.A.

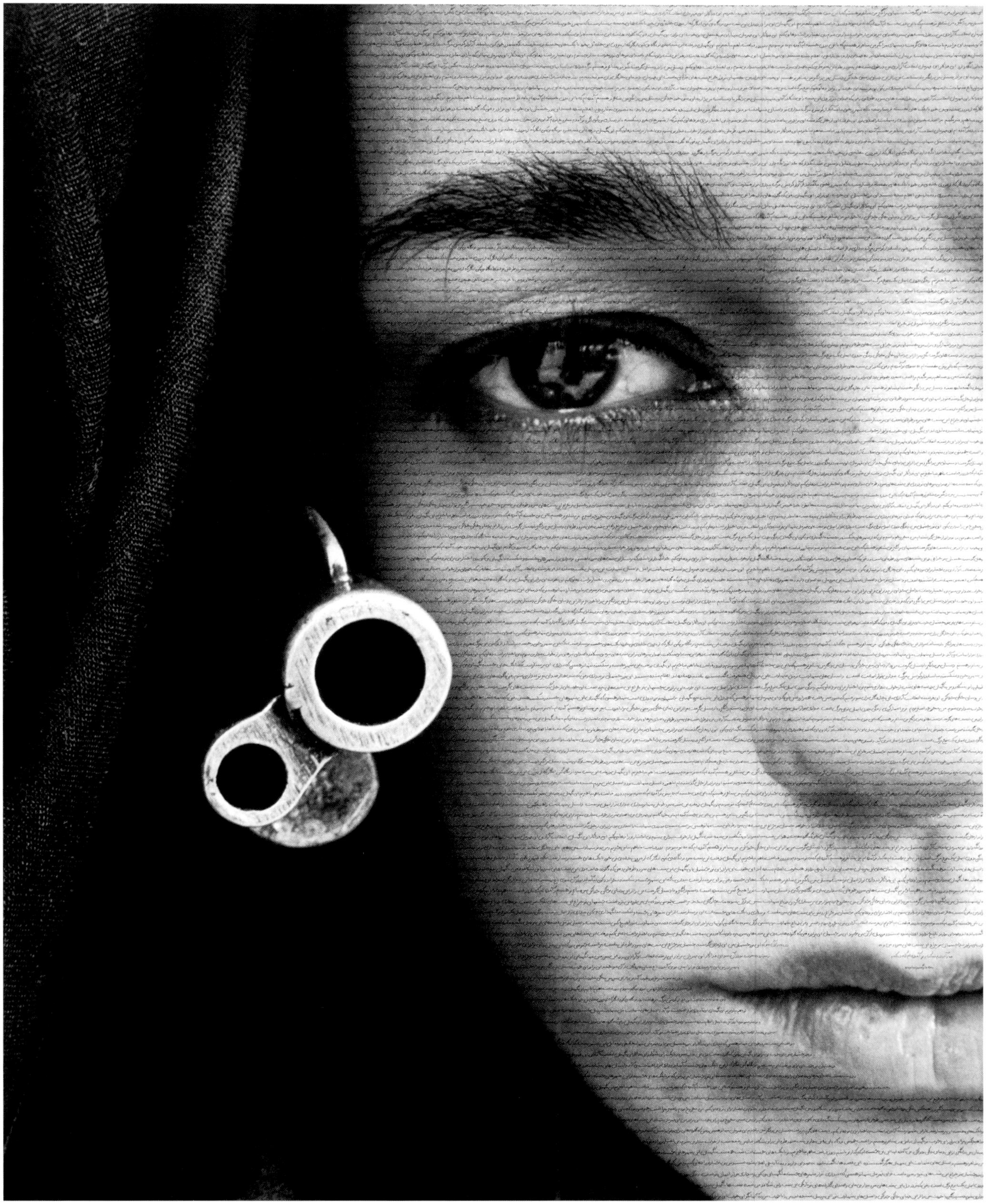

SPEECHLESS, 1996

Ink on RC print, 52 x 39¼ x 1⅞ inches (132.1 x 99.7 x 4.8 cm).
Photograph taken by Larry Barns

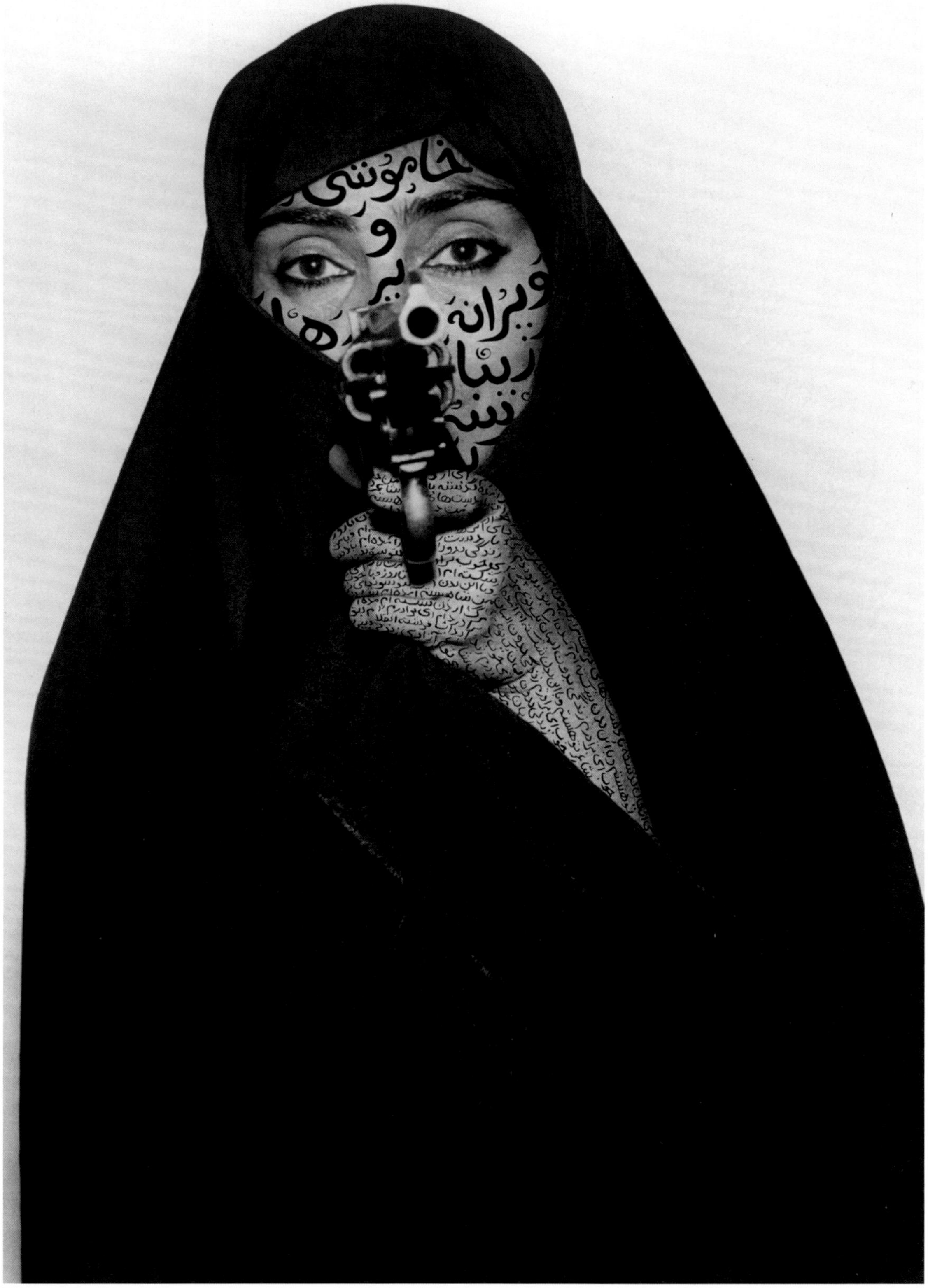

FACELESS, 1994

Ink on RC print, 56½ x 37 x 2 inches (143.5 x 94 x 5.1 cm).
Photograph taken by Cynthia Preston

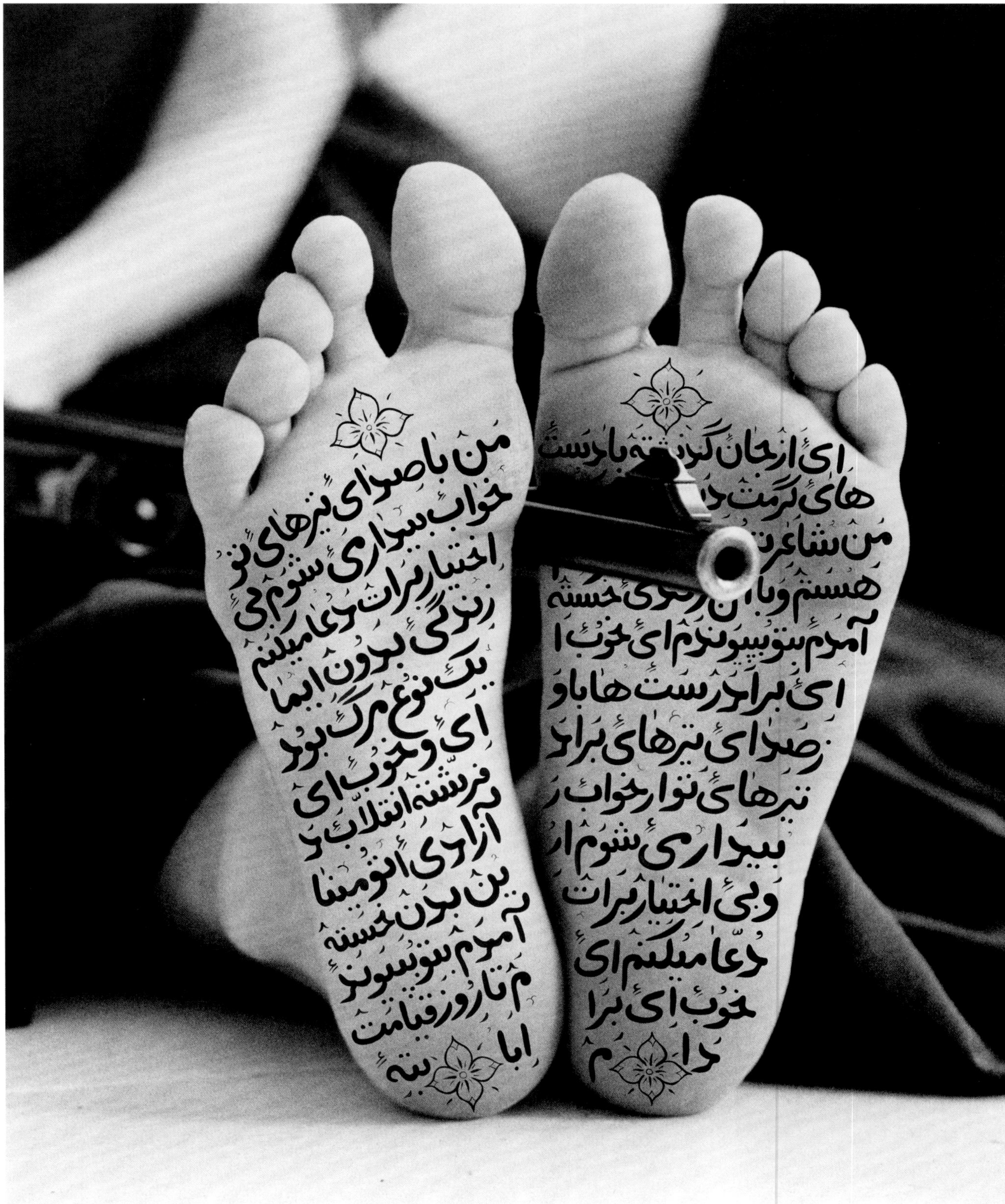

ALLEGIANCE WITH WAKEFULNESS, 1994

Ink on LE silver gelatin print, 52 x 42⅜ x 1⅞ inches (132.1 x 107.6 x 4.8 cm).
Photograph taken by Cynthia Preston

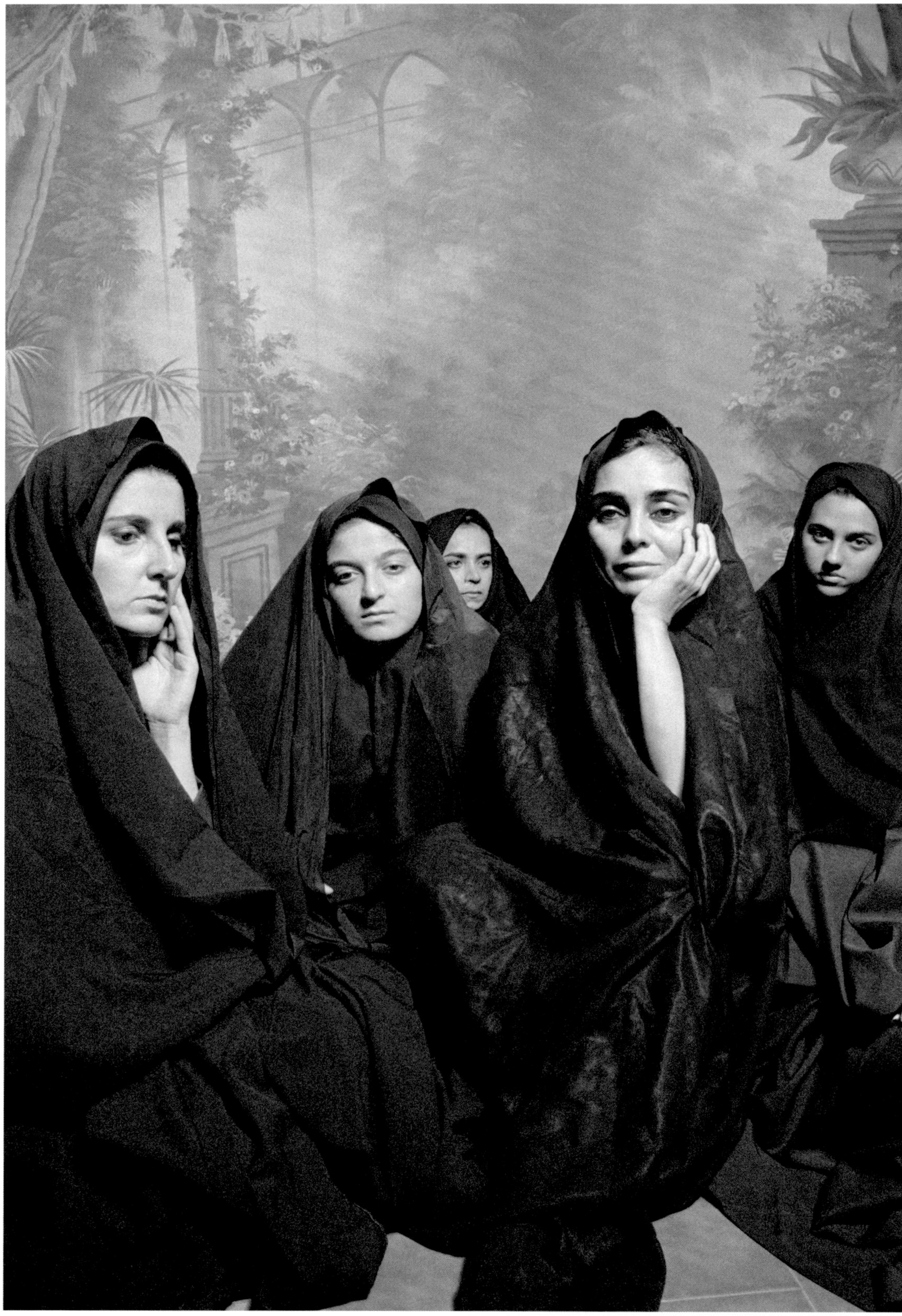

UNTITLED, 1995

LE silver gelatin print, 65½ x 45½ x 2 inches (166.4 x 115.6 x 5.1 cm).
Photograph taken by Bahman Jalali

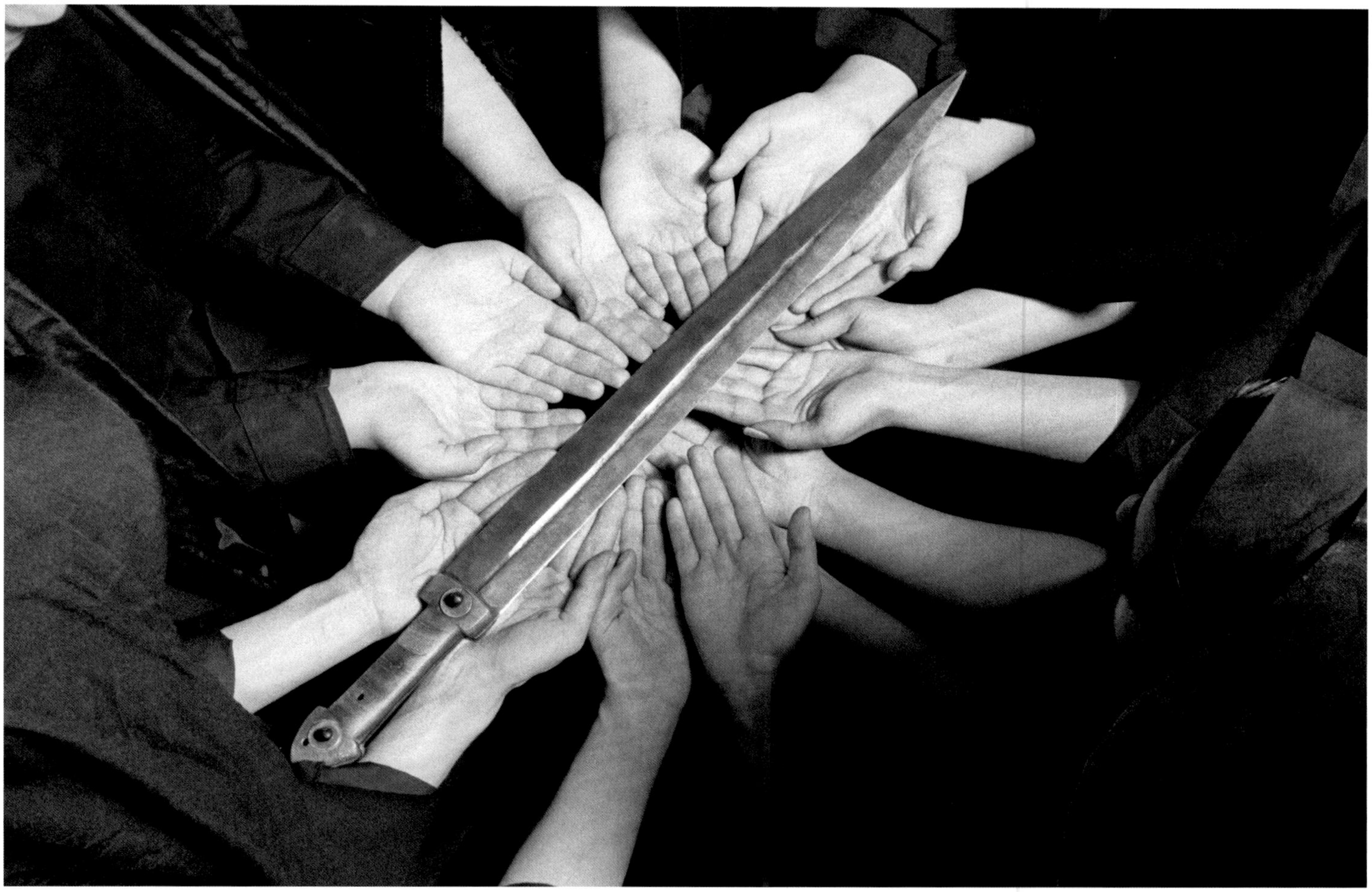

ALL DEMONS FLEE, 1995

LE silver gelatin print, 45½ x 65½ x 1⅞ inches (115.6 x 166.4 x 4.8 cm).
Photograph taken by Bahman Jalali

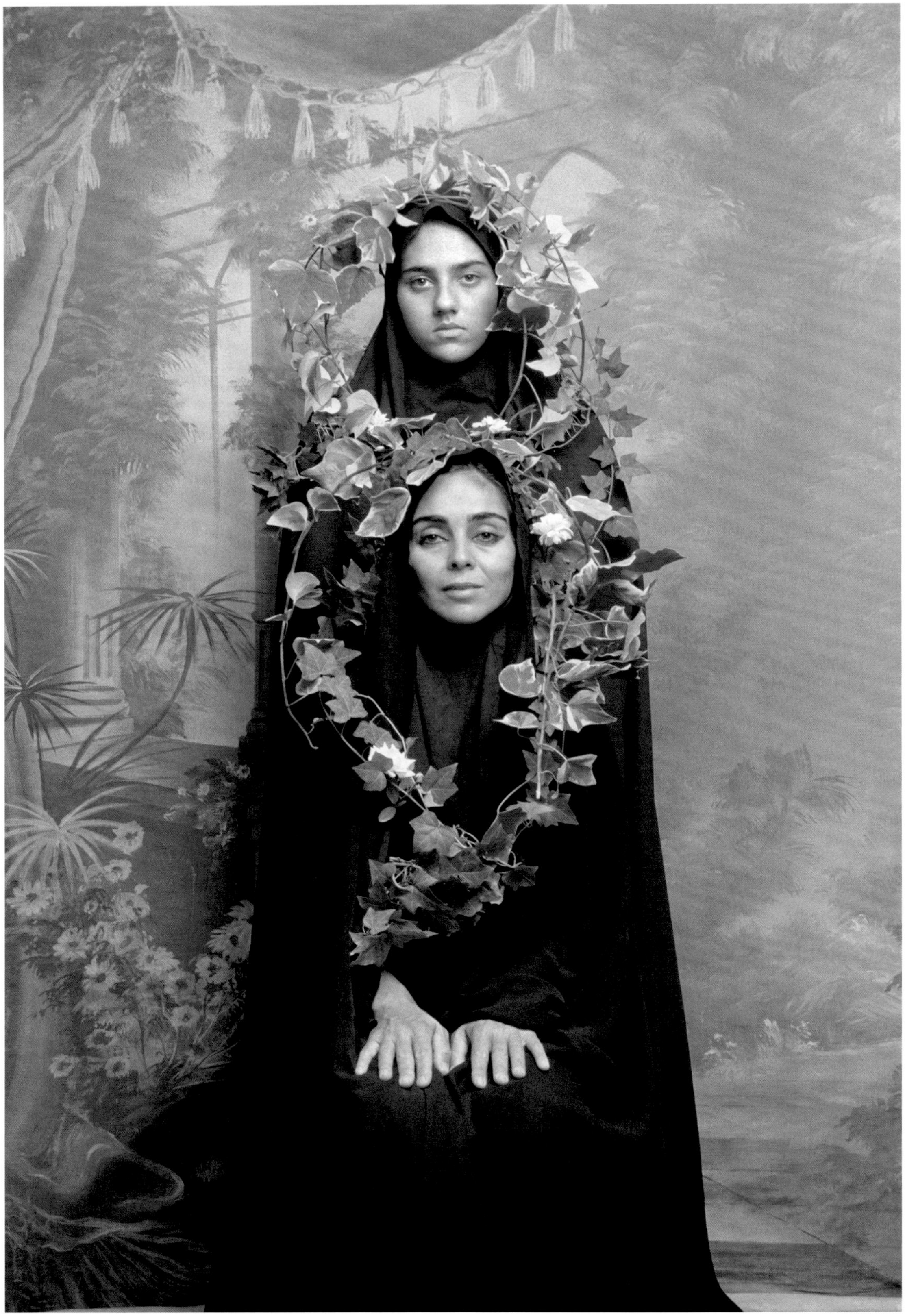

UNTITLED, 1995

LE silver gelatin print, 65½ x 45½ x 2 inches (166.4 x 115.6 x 5.1 cm). Photograph taken by Bahman Jalali

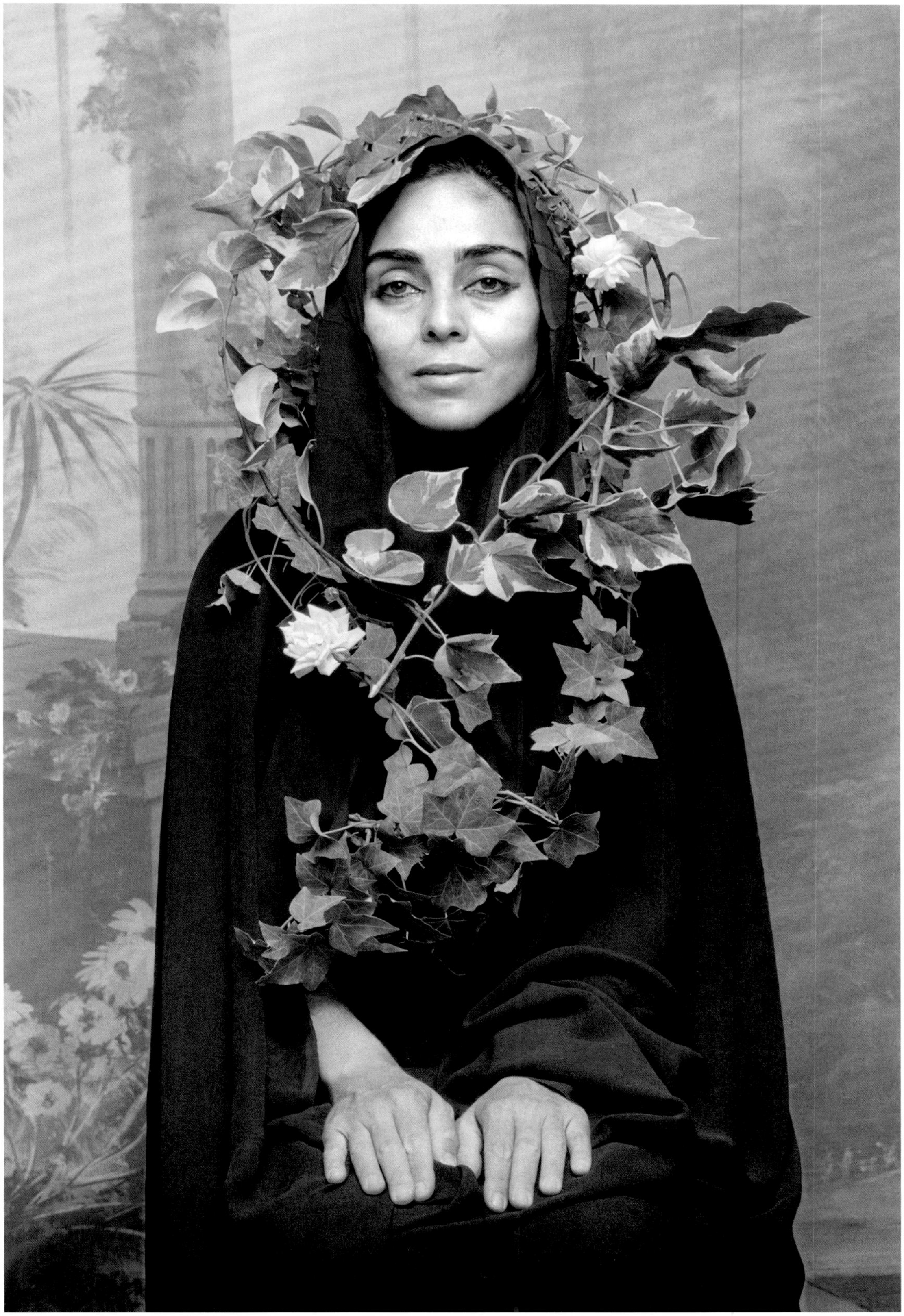

UNTITLED, 1995

LE silver gelatin print, 65½ x 45½ x 2 inches (166.4 x 115.6 x 5.1 cm).
Photograph taken by Bahman Jalali

TURBULENT

1998
TWO-CHANNEL VIDEO INSTALLATION
16MM BLACK-AND-WHITE FILM TRANSFERRED TO VIDEO
DURATION: 10 MINUTES
FILMED IN NEW YORK CITY

DIRECTOR: SHIRIN NESHAT
DIRECTOR OF PHOTOGRAPHY: GHASEM EBRAHIMIAN
FEMALE PERFORMER, VOCALIST, COMPOSER: SUSSAN DEYHIM
MALE PERFORMER: SHOJA AZARI
VOCALIST FOR MALE PERFORMER: SHAHRAM NAZERI
POETRY BY: JALAL AL-DIN RUMI
PRODUCTION MANAGER: BAHMAN SOLTANI
PRODUCER: MARCO NOIRE CONTEMPORARY ART

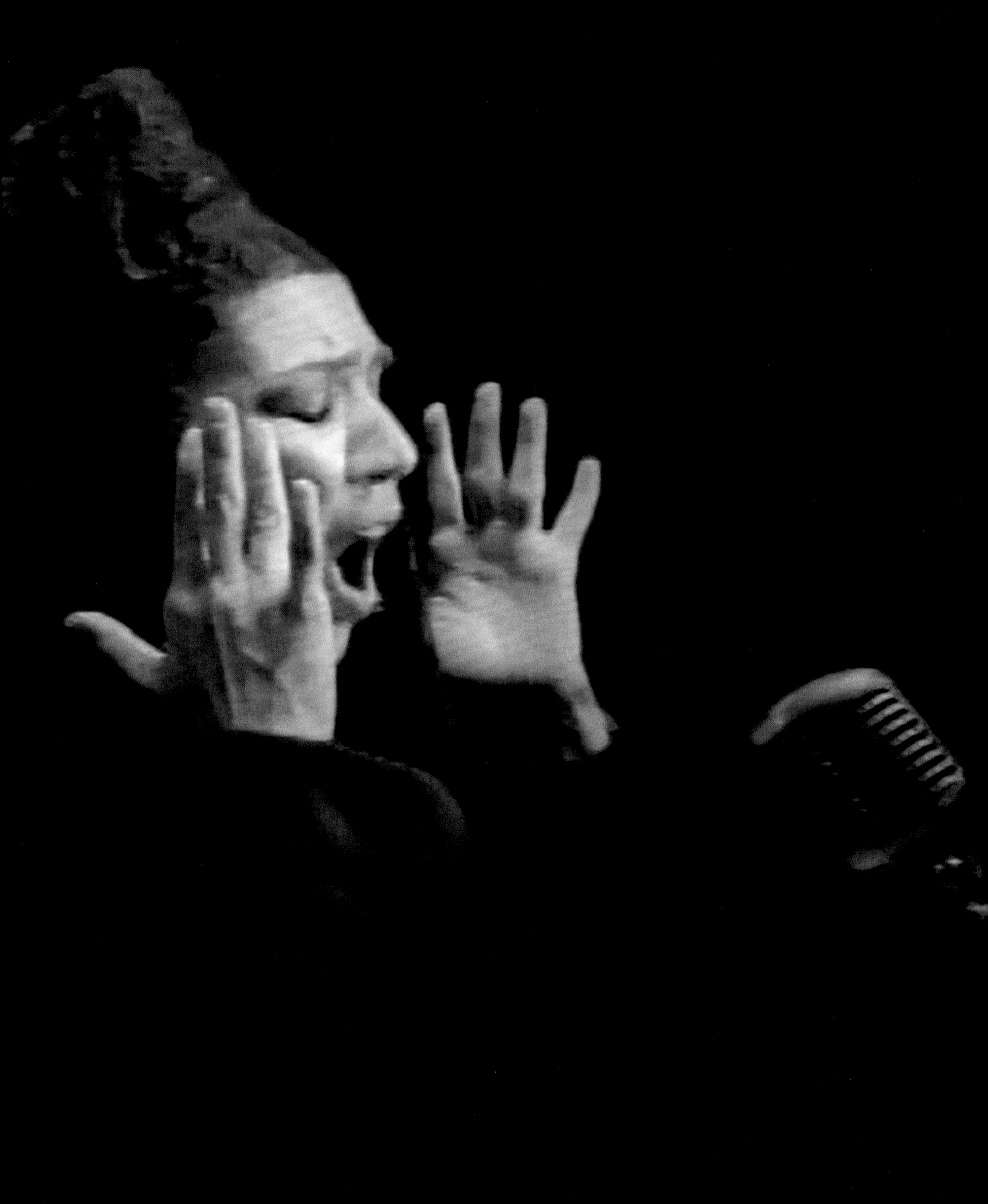

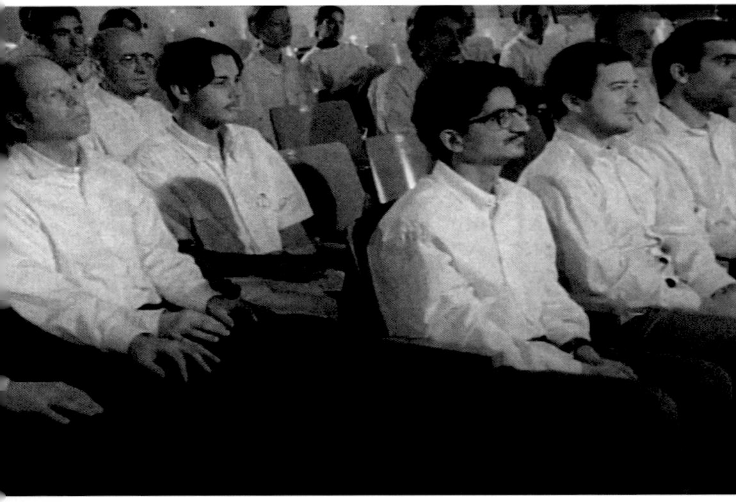

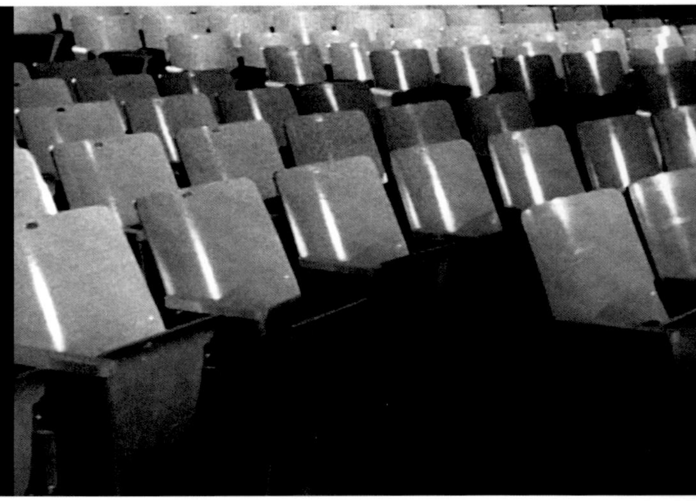

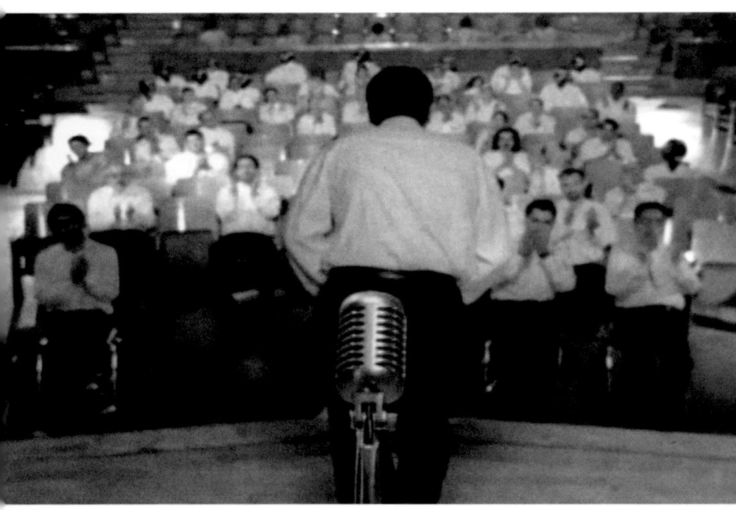

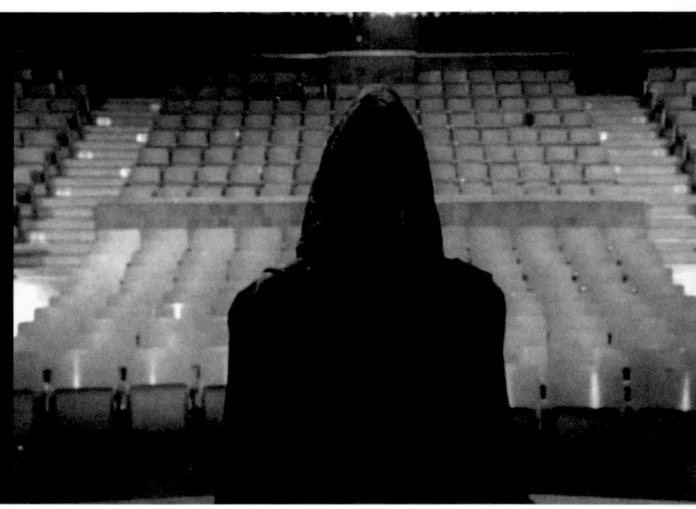

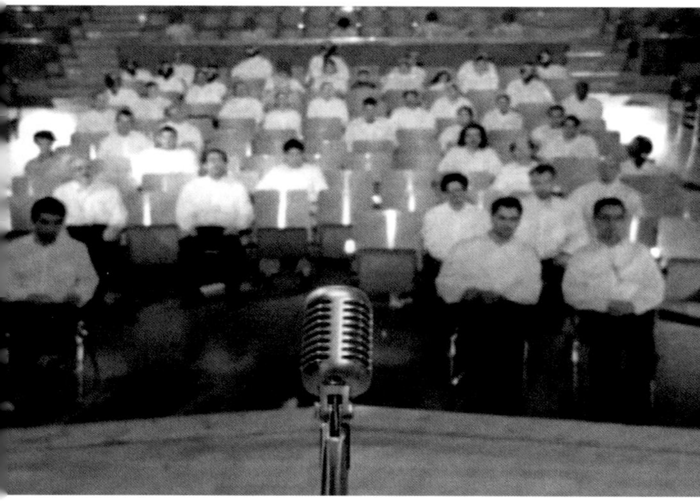

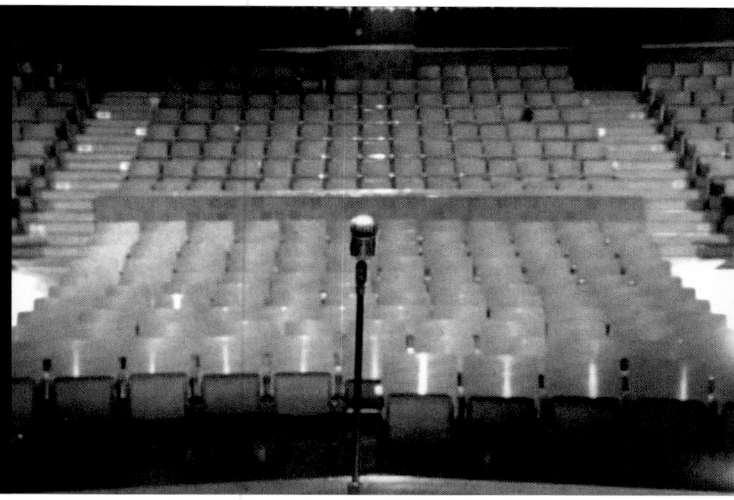

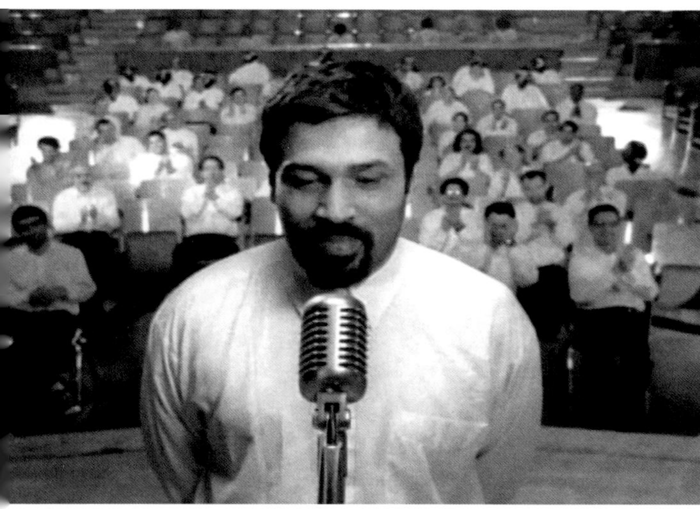

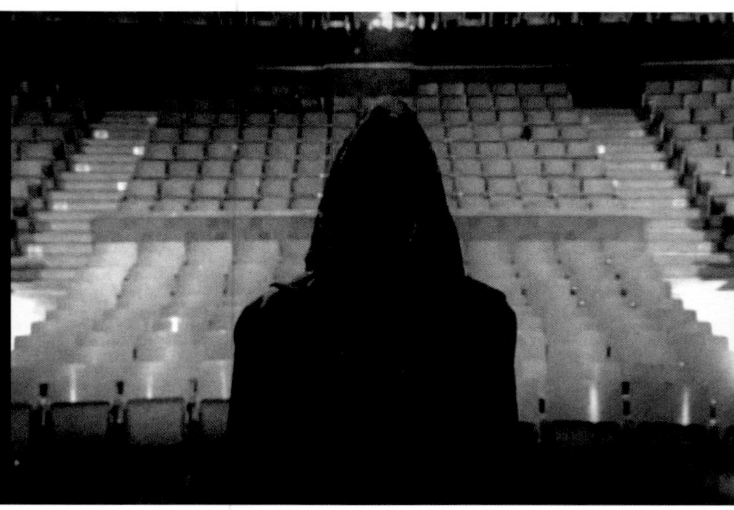

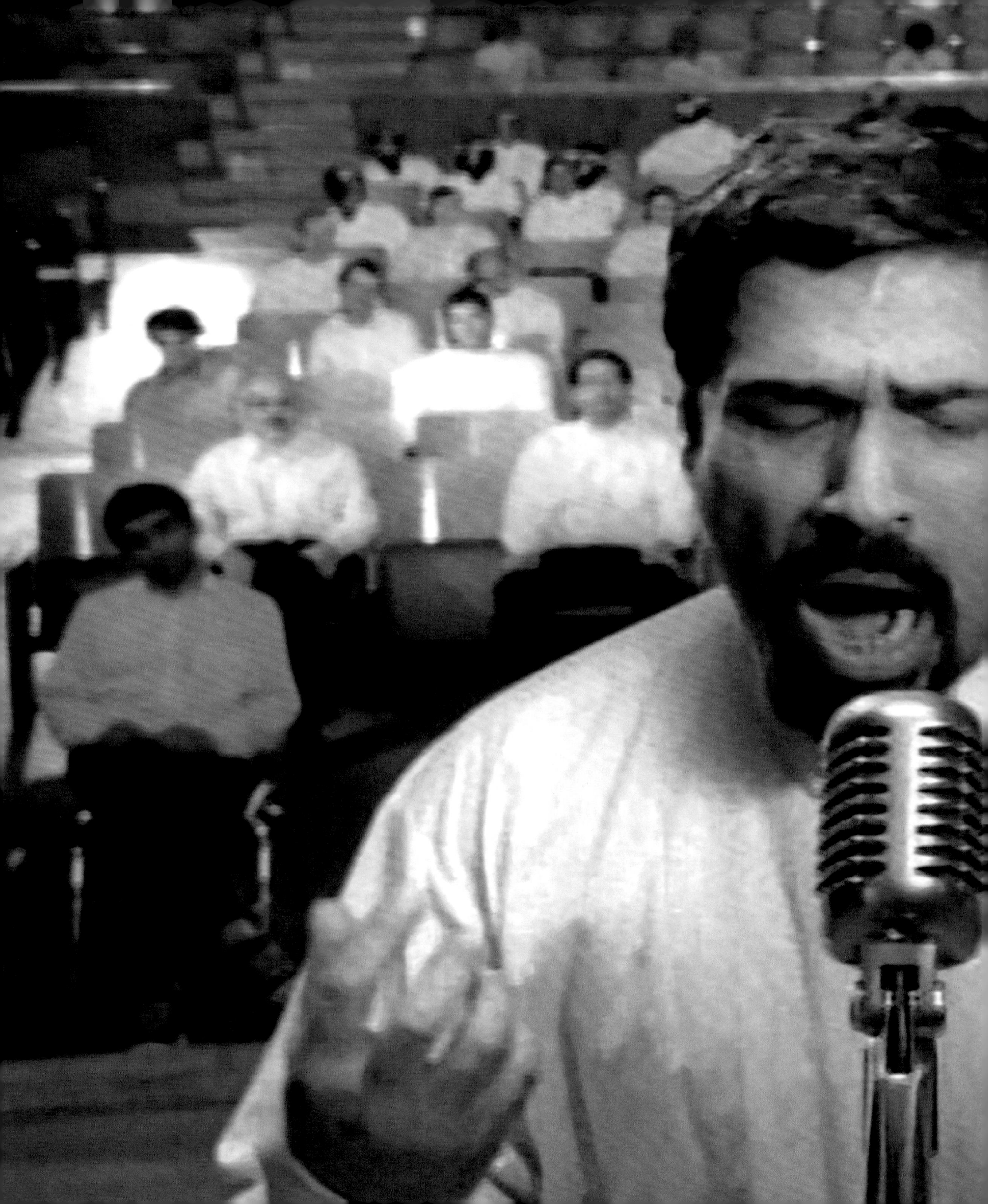

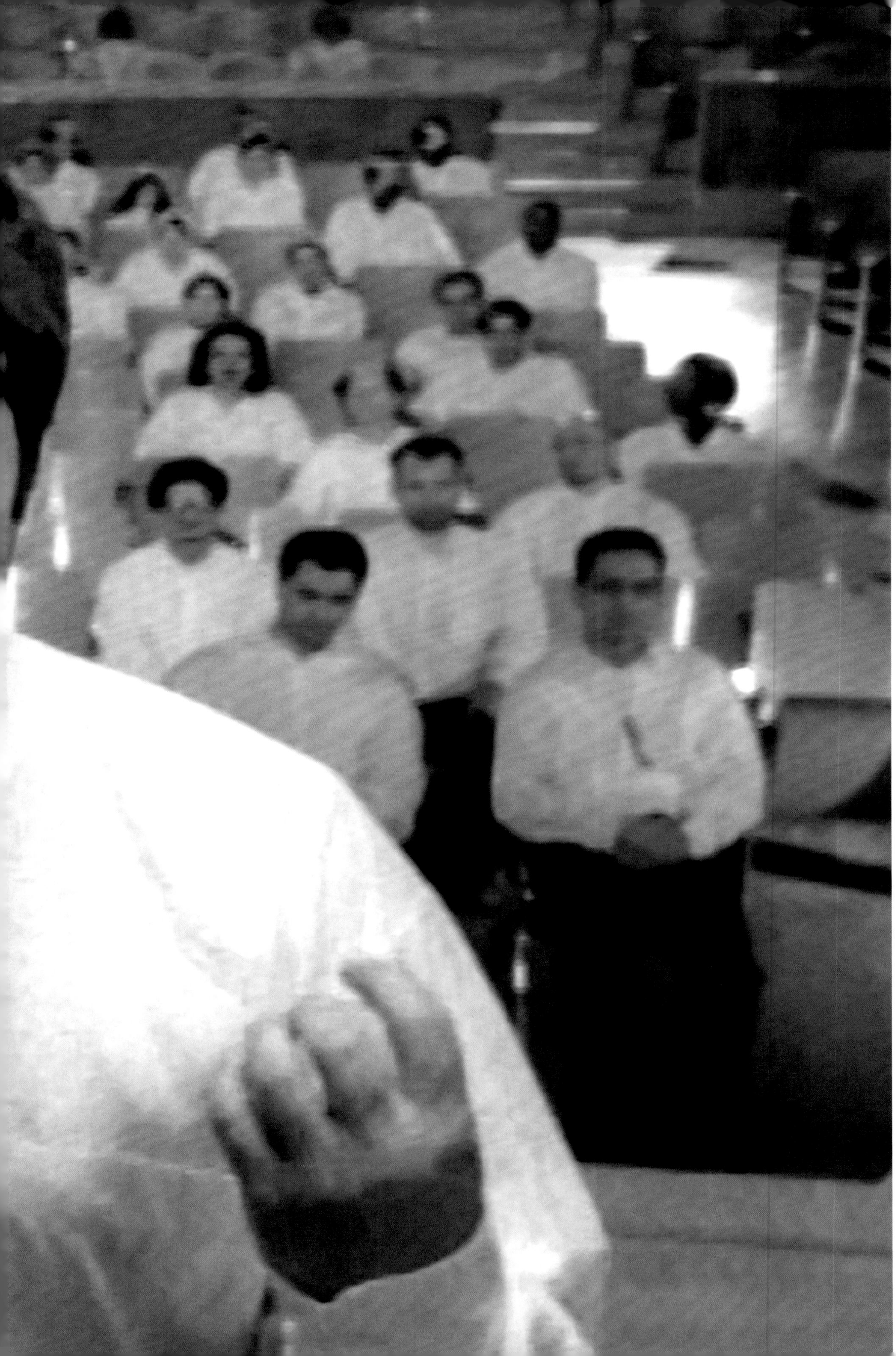

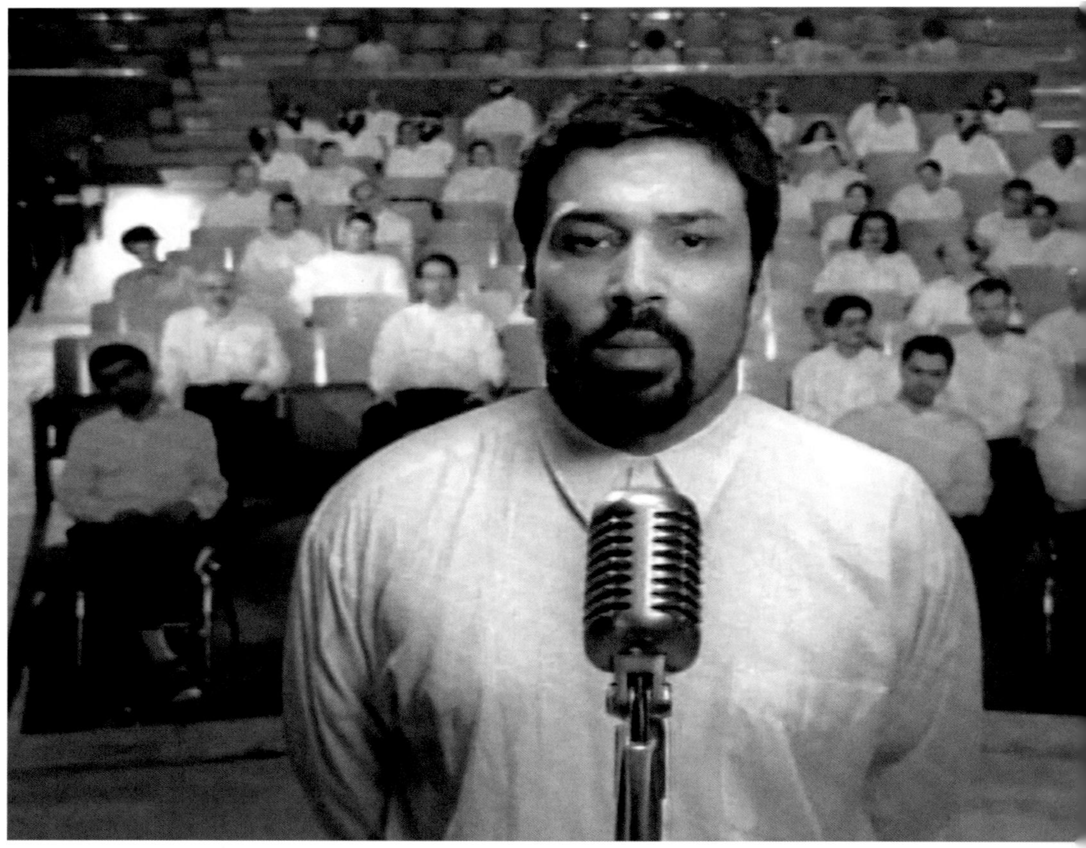

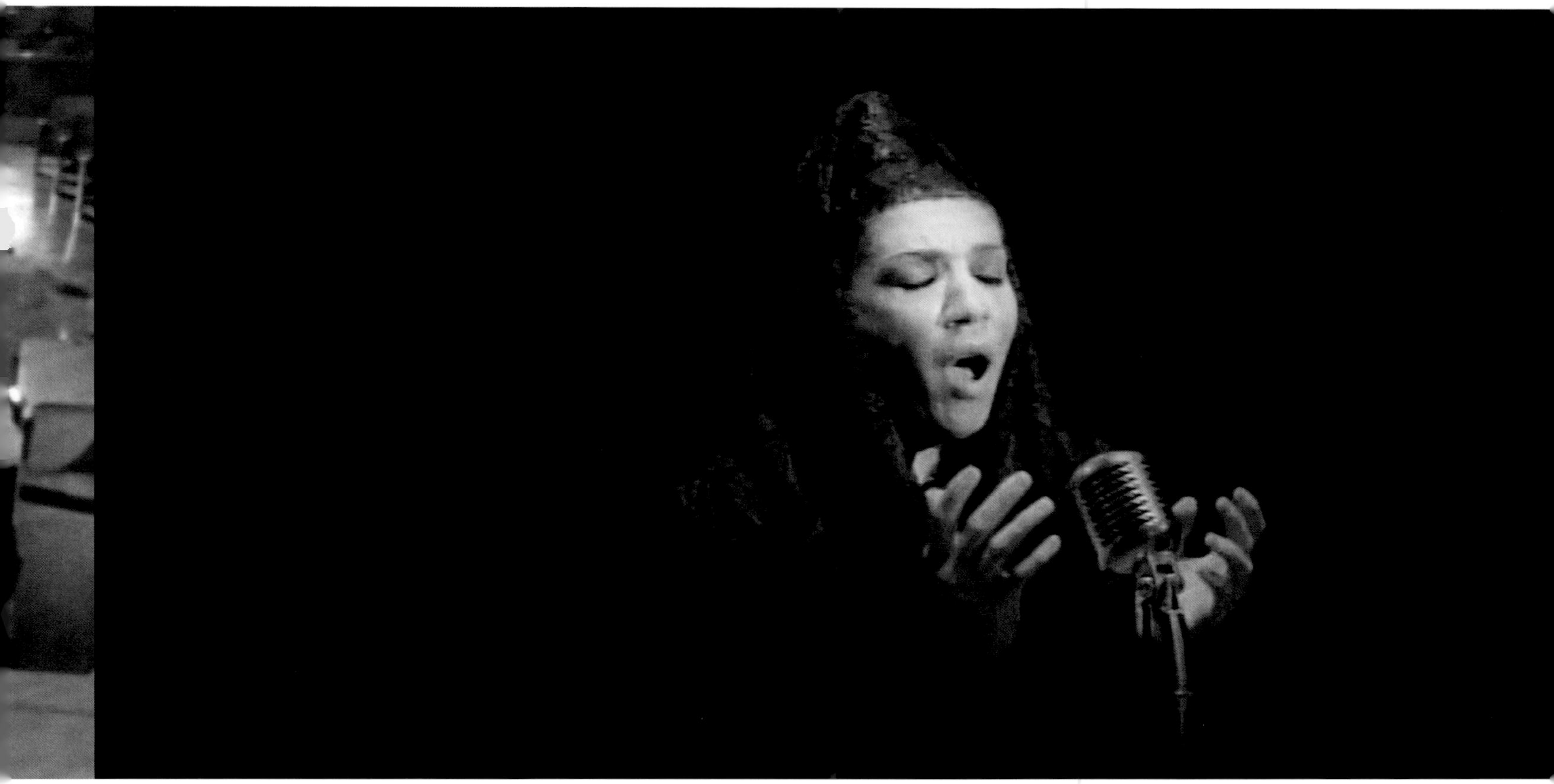

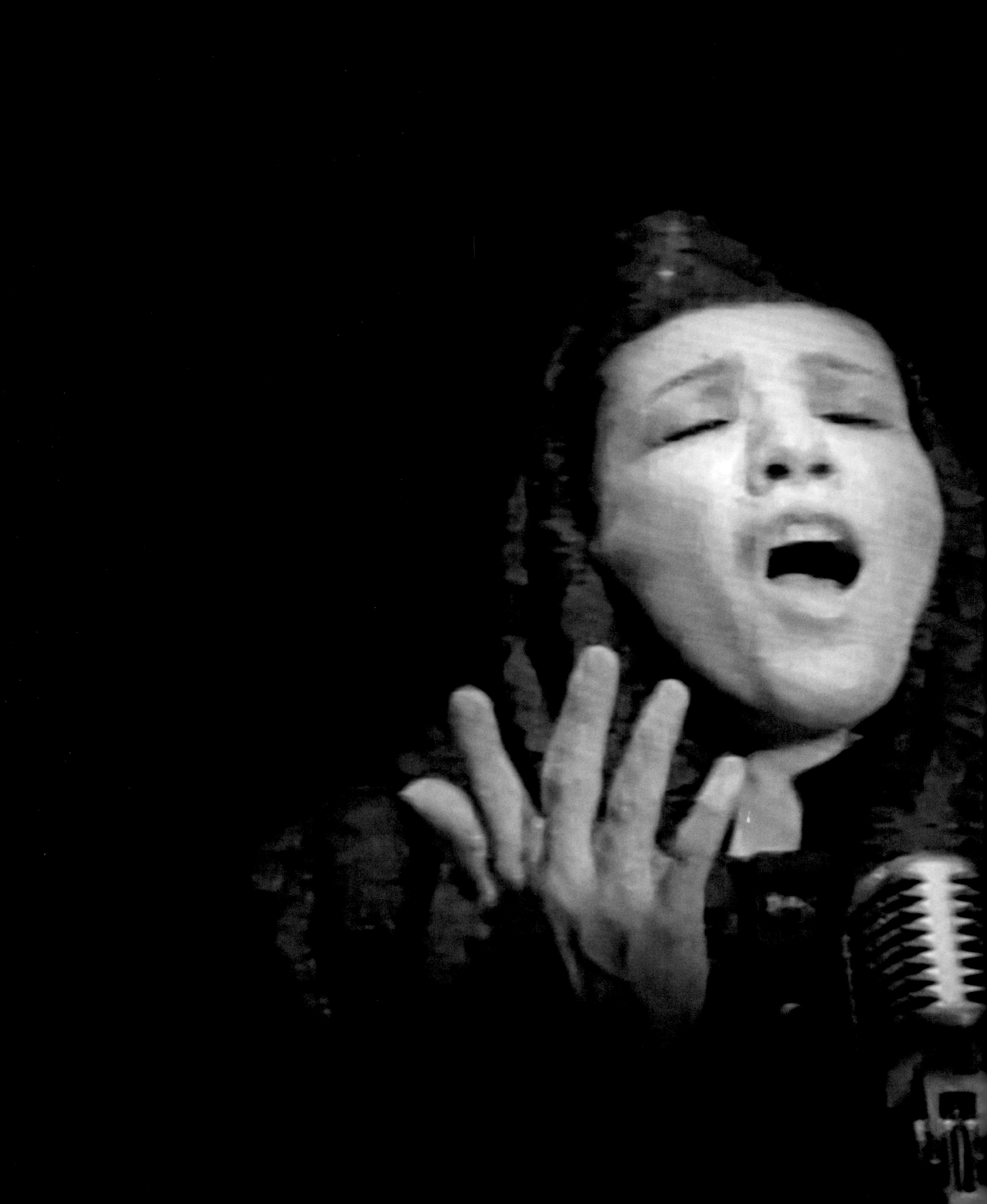

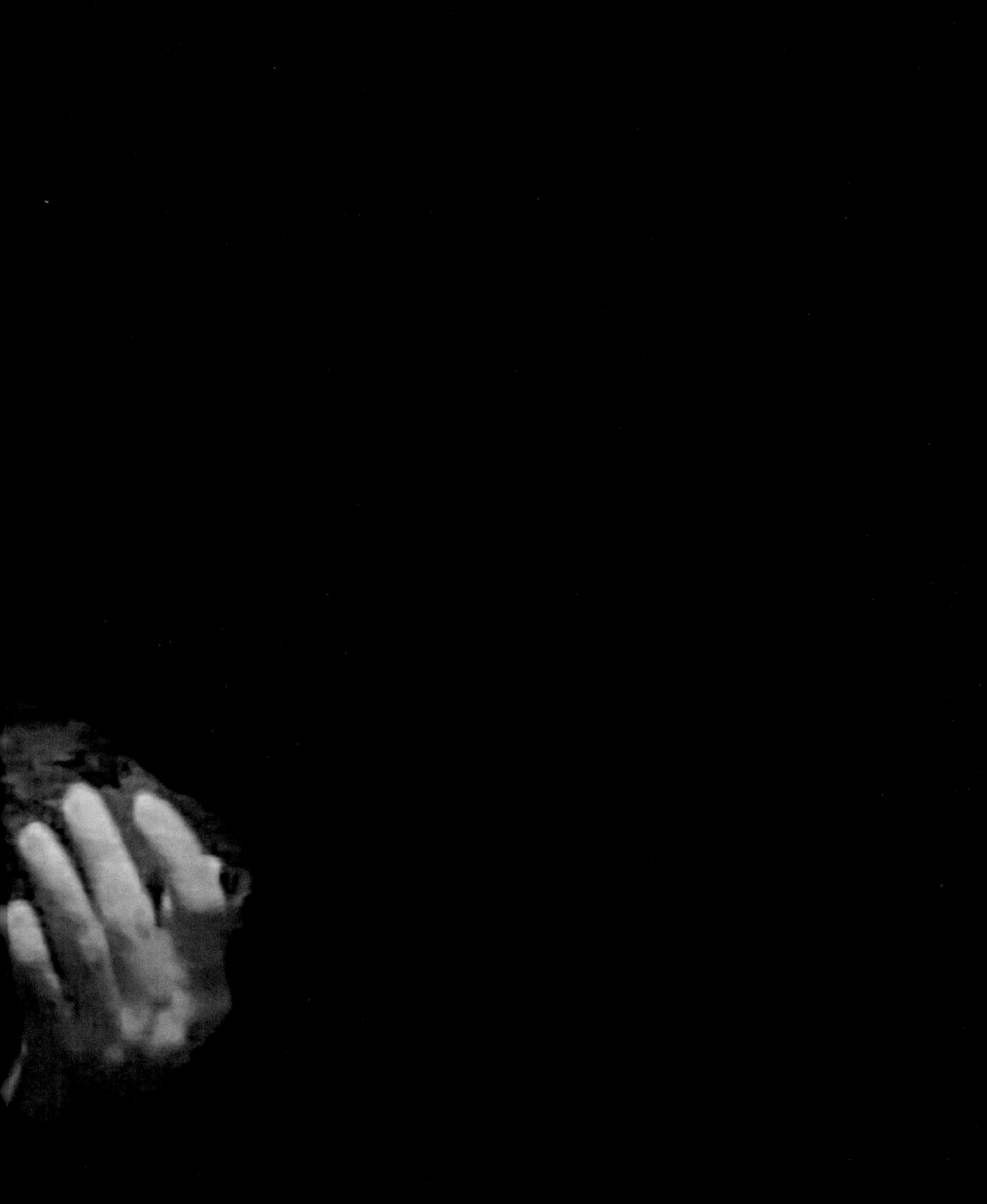

RAPTURE

1999
TWO-CHANNEL VIDEO INSTALLATION
16MM BLACK-AND-WHITE FILM TRANSFERRED TO VIDEO
DURATION: 13 MINUTES
FILMED IN MOROCCO

DIRECTOR: SHIRIN NESHAT
IN COLLABORATION WITH: SHOJA AZARI
DIRECTOR OF PHOTOGRAPHY: GHASEM EBRAHIMIAN
MUSIC AND SOUND DESIGN: SUSSAN DEYHIM
PRODUCTION MANAGERS: HAMID FARDJAD AND BAHMAN SOLTANI
COSTUME DESIGNER: NOUREDDINE AMIR
PRODUCER: GALERIE JÉRÔME DE NOIRMONT

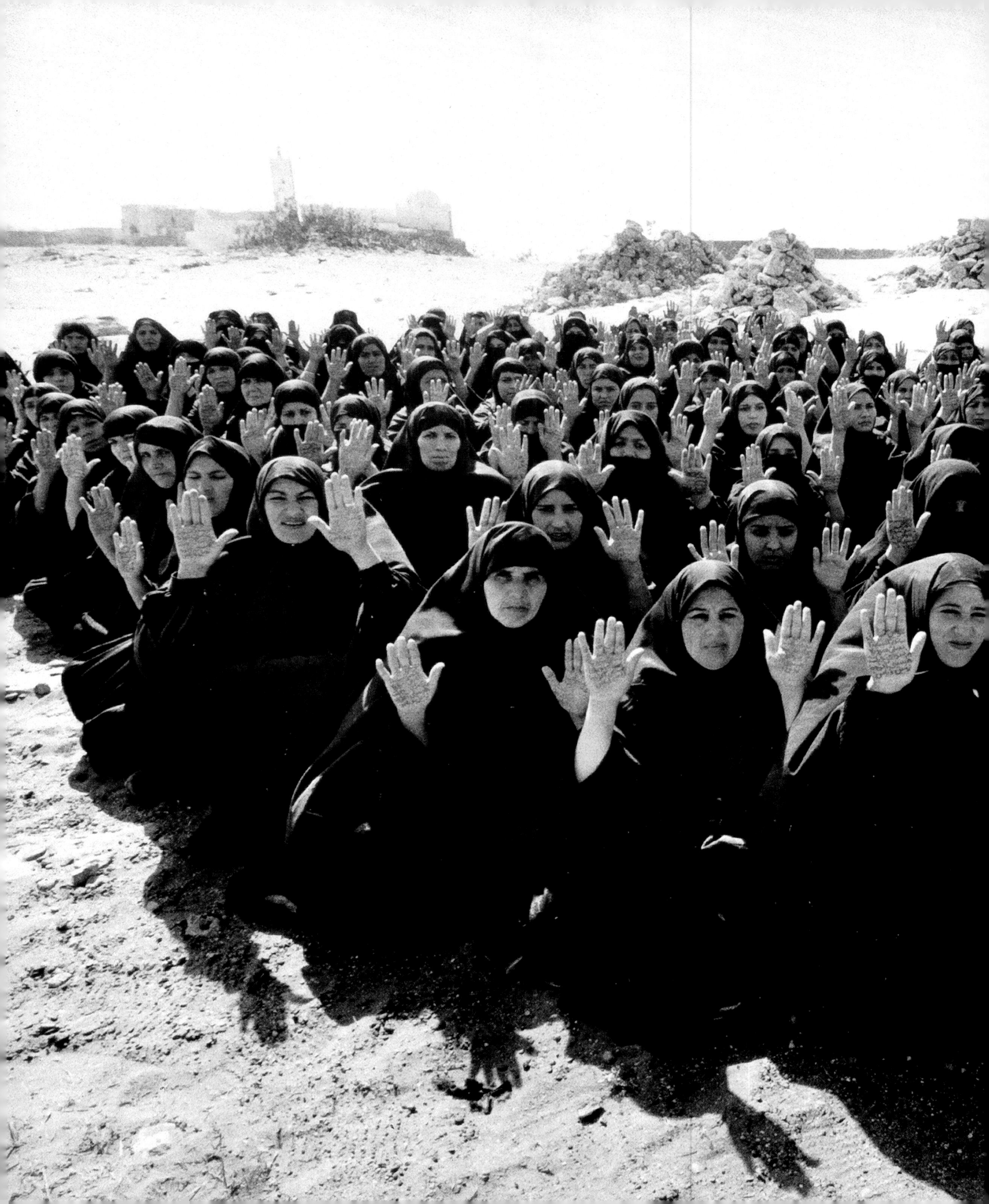

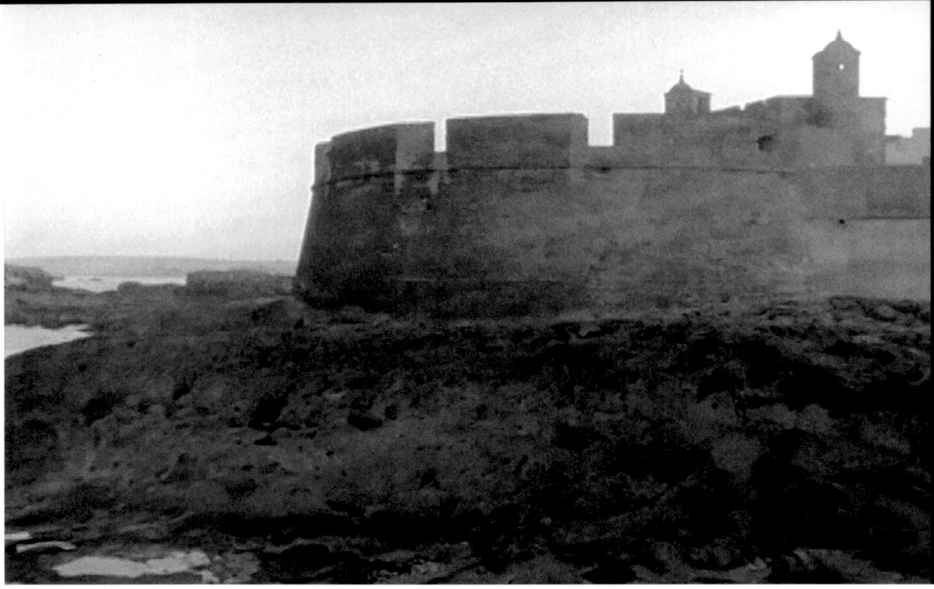

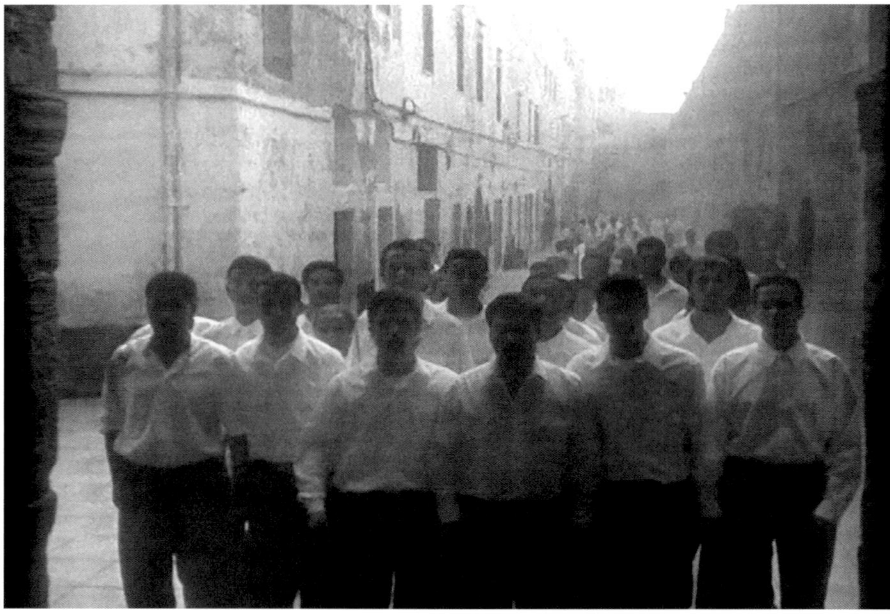

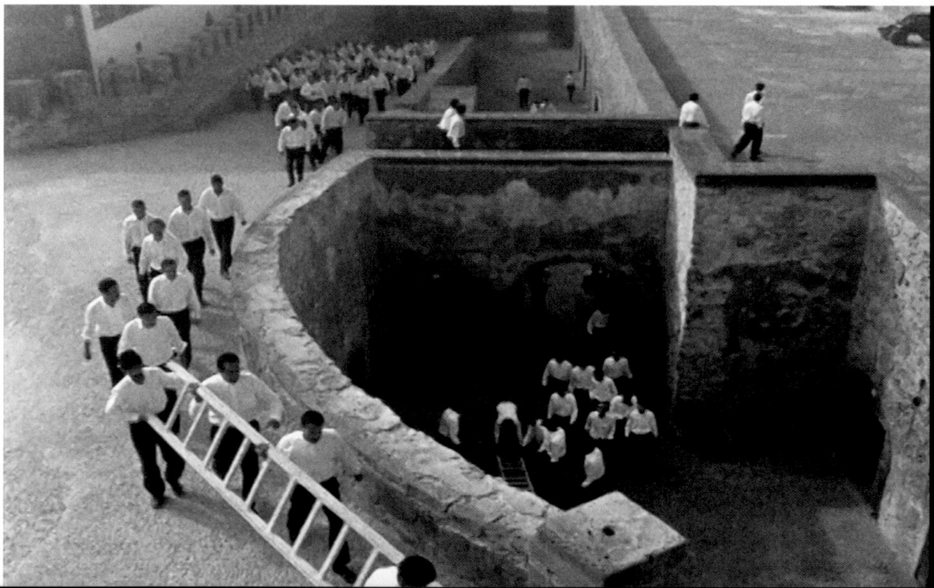

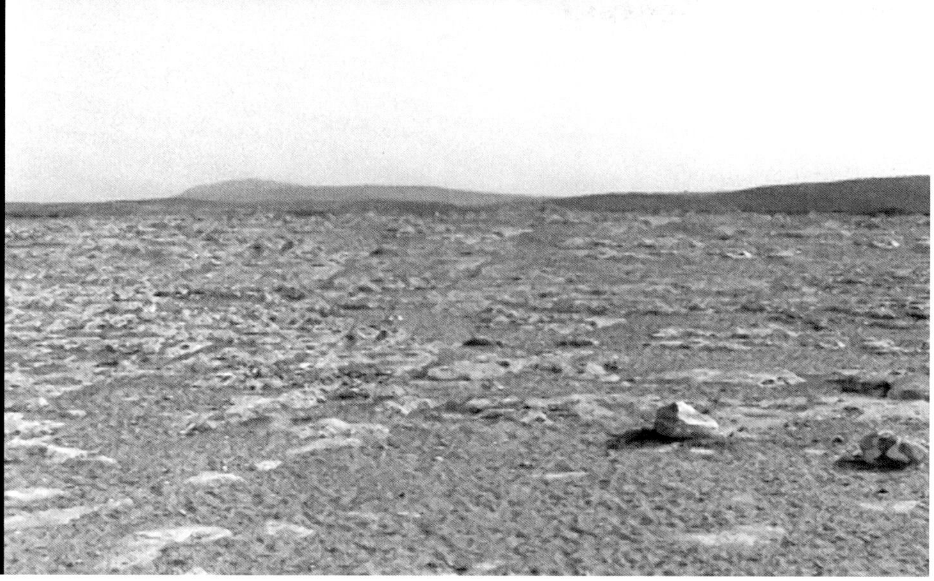

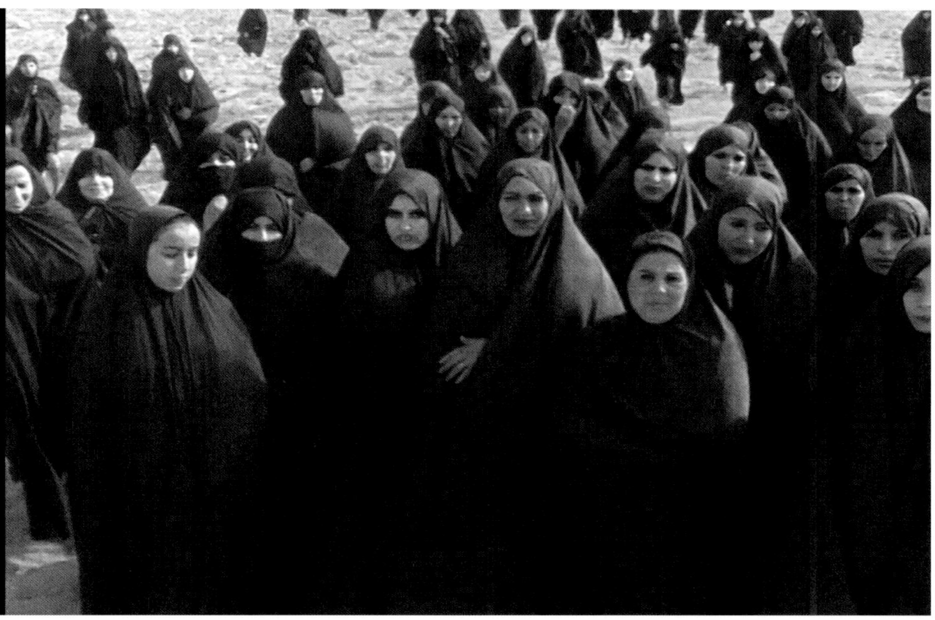

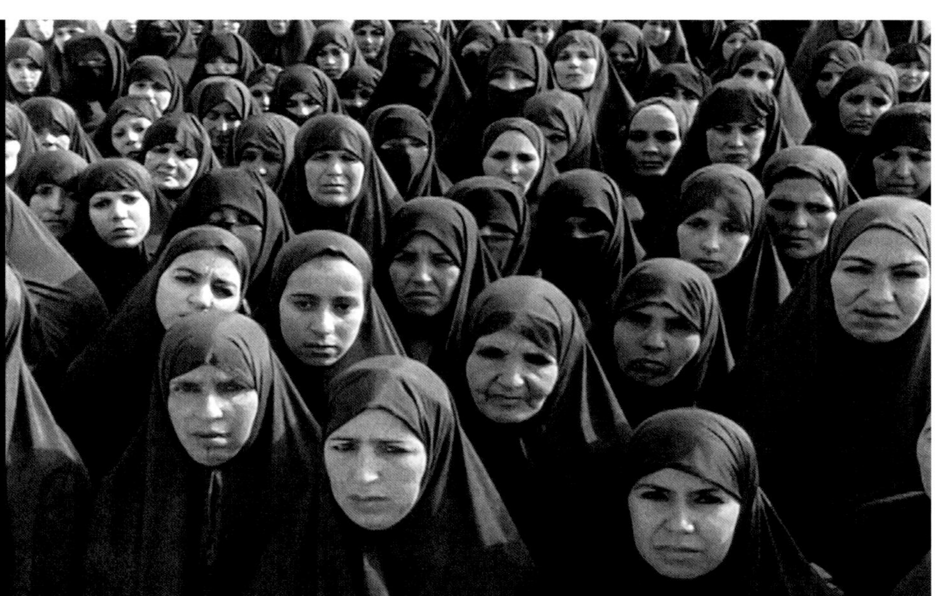

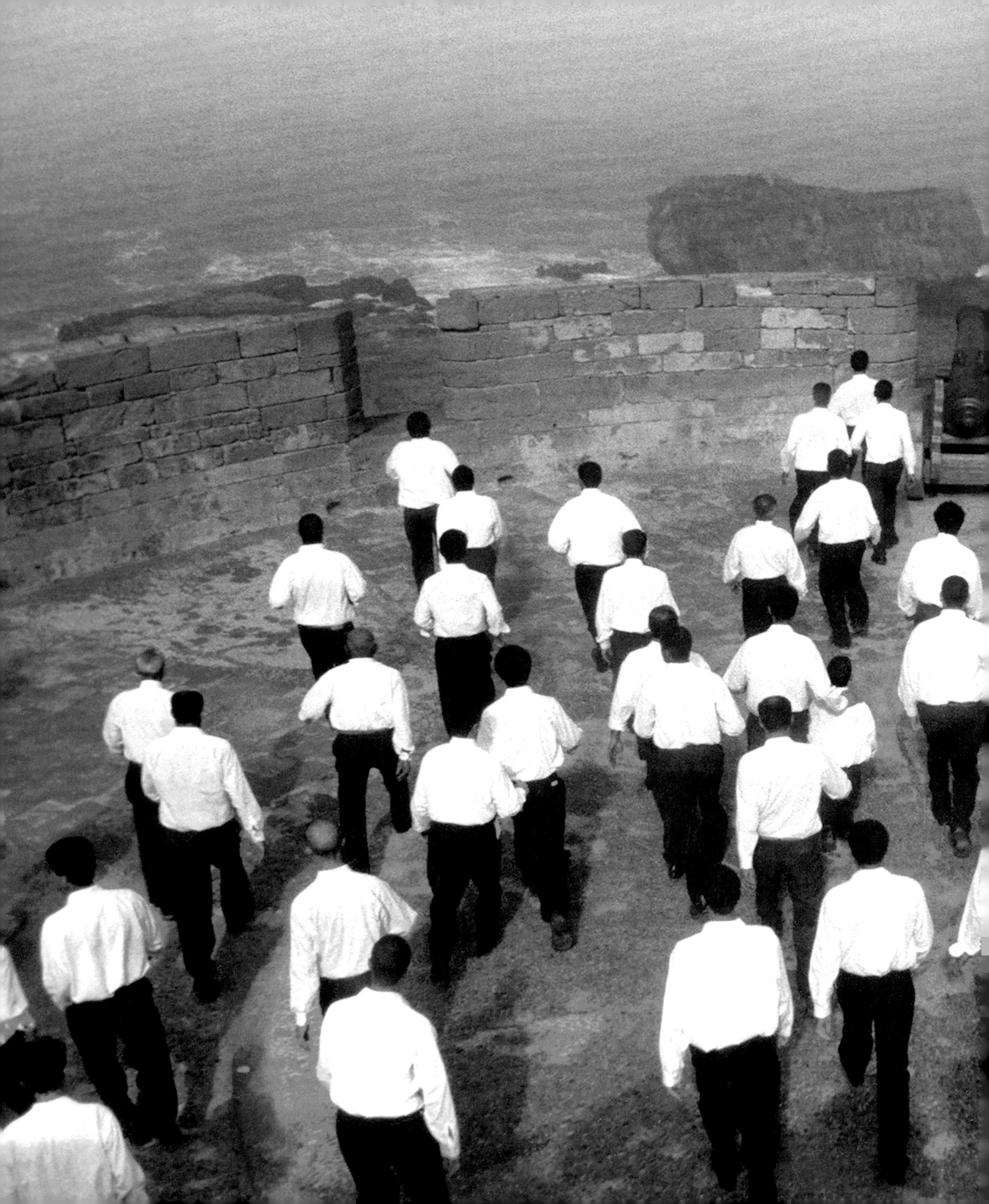

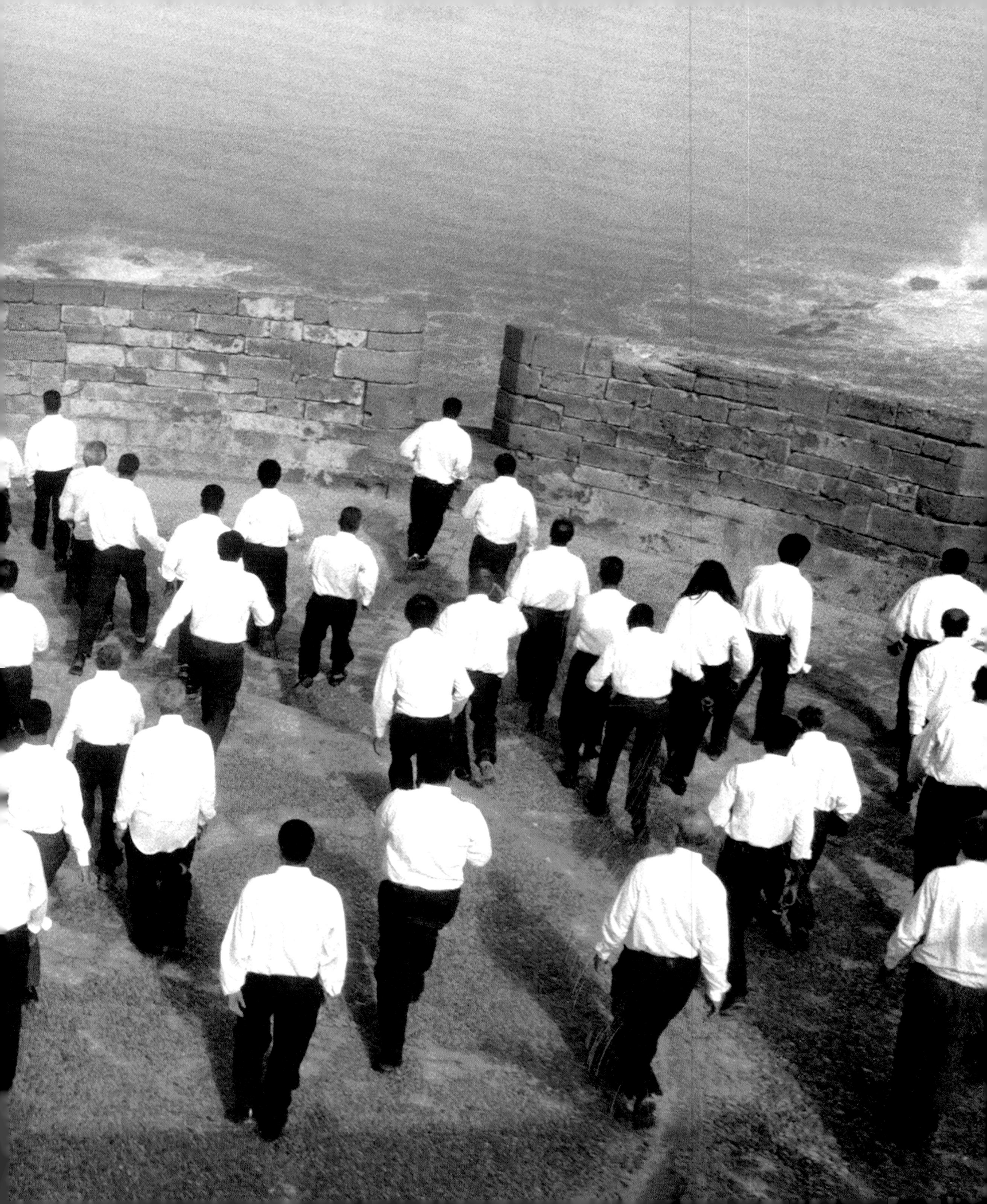

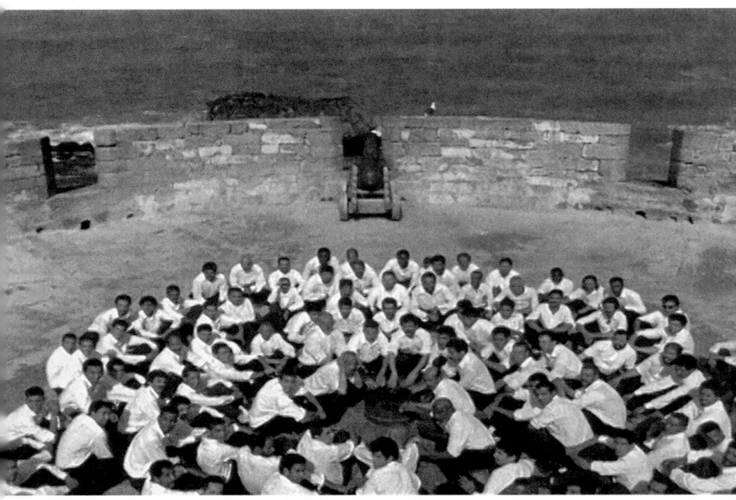

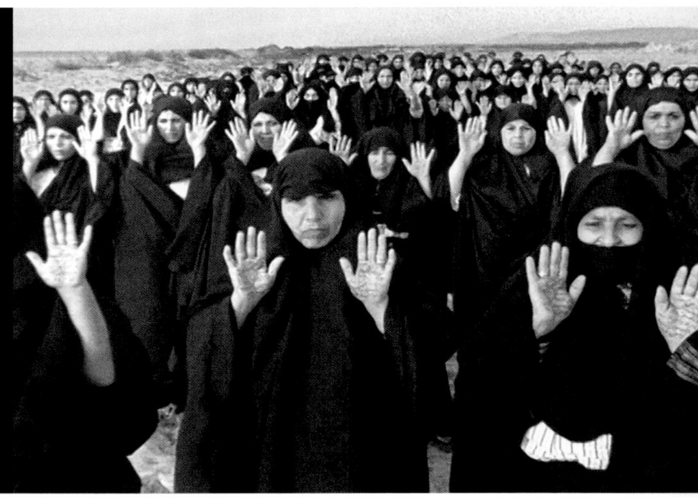

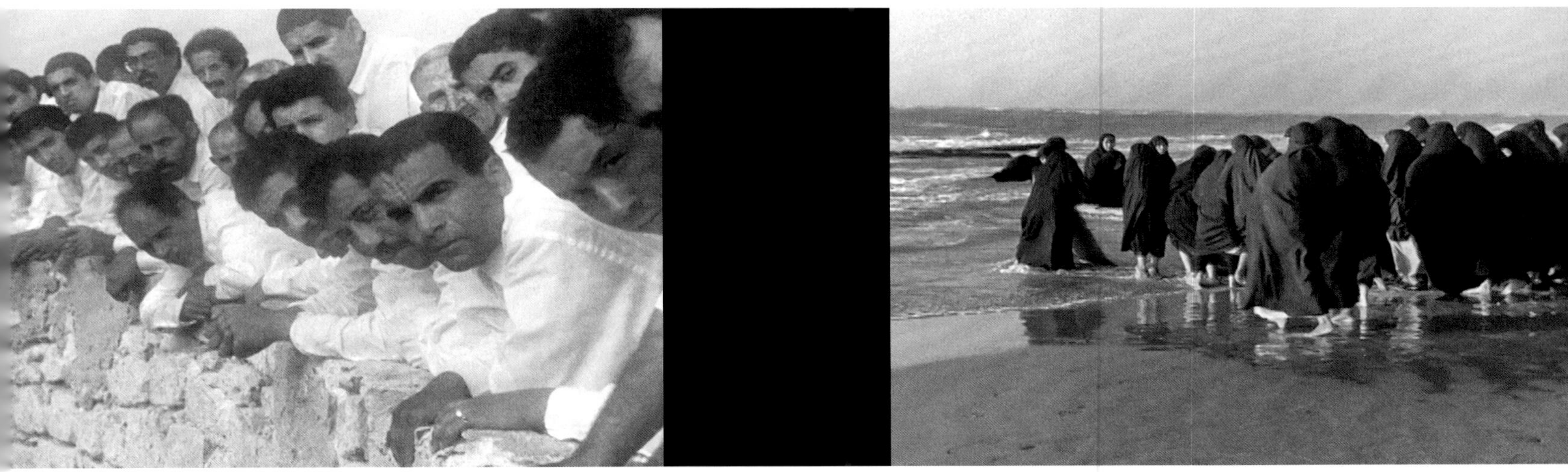

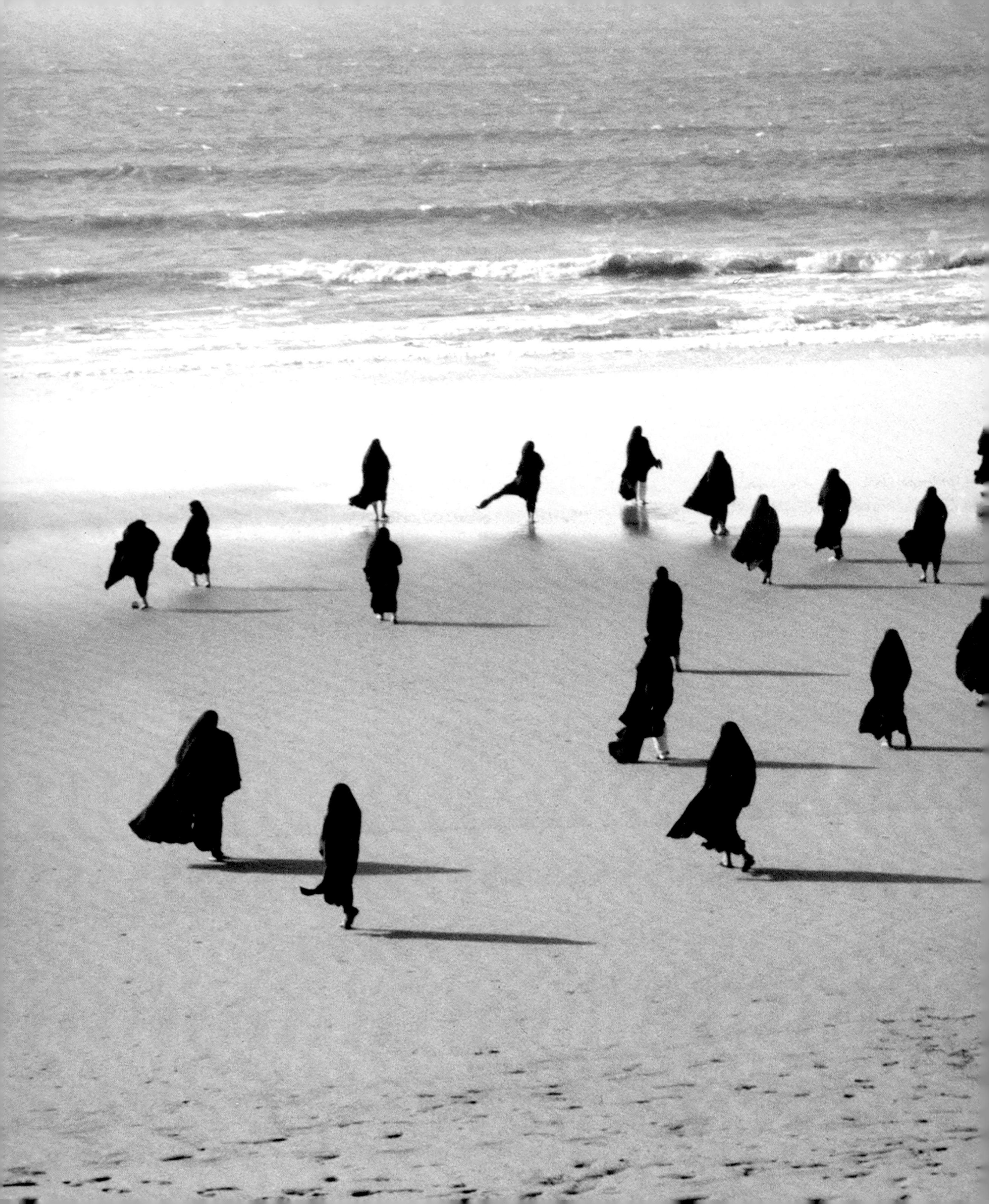

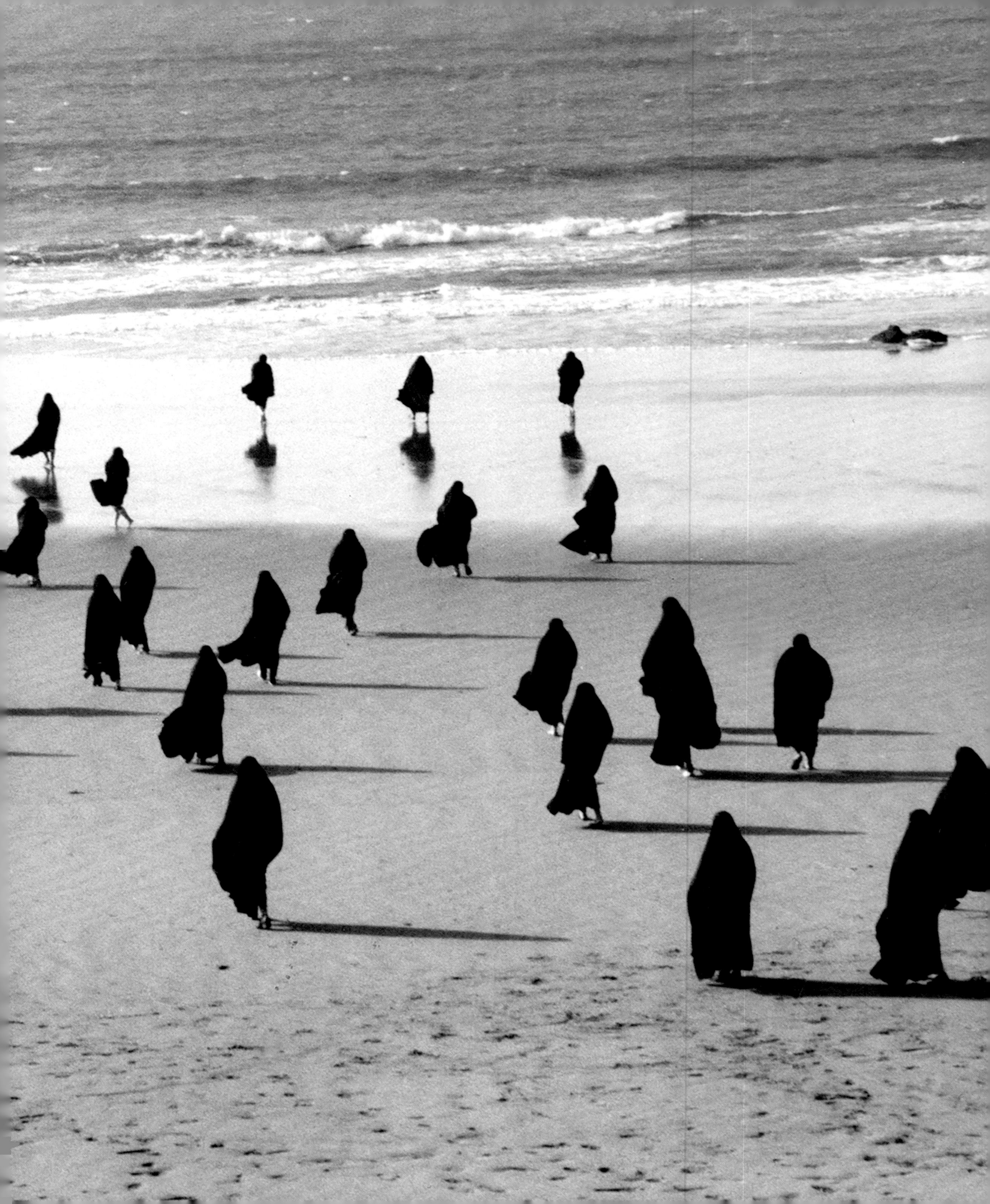

COLLECTING DREAMS: SHIRIN NESHAT IN CONVERSATION WITH GLENN LOWRY

GLENN LOWRY: Why don't we start, Shirin, with your arrival in the United States. How old were you at that time?

SHIRIN NESHAT: I was seventeen. We grew up imagining the best of everything in the U.S. Hollywood was our imagination. We didn't have television at the time, but my father had this expectation that his children should study abroad, and then return one day to Iran. He had the highest aspirations in terms of how his children should be educated in the West, but when I arrived in Los Angeles, I remember vividly, even at that young age, I was pretty devastated by what I saw, and of course by the idea of separating from family.

LOWRY: Did you come alone?

NESHAT: I came with my older sister, who unfortunately had lost her husband in an accident, so I was sent along to keep her company. But she returned to Iran very quickly, and I found myself alone in this country. This was in the late 1970s.

LOWRY: Before or after the Islamic Revolution?

NESHAT: It was just before. It was 1975, and the revolution happened in 1979. I was in high school and didn't speak a word of English. We were living in very generic, ugly modern apartments, a drastic change from the beautiful house in which I had grown up in Iran, with a big garden, and in a city where I knew everybody. The first few years in Los Angeles proved to be very difficult for me. Once, when my father came for a short visit, I begged him to take me back, but he wouldn't and insisted America was a better place to be than Iran! In the meanwhile, I visited Iran several times, until the revolution, which then caused eleven years of separation from my family.

LOWRY: Did you communicate by writing or phone?

NESHAT: Soon after the revolution, especially after the hostage crisis, there was no more diplomatic relationship between Iran and the U.S., so no postal service existed. Phone connections were also very sporadic. In addition, the Iran-Iraq War broke out, which further complicated the situation, forcing Iranian borders to close.

The next decade in Iran proved to be one of the most brutal and bloody periods in Iran's modern history, both by the war with Iraq, and the aftermath of the revolution by the new regime. A dark period indeed for all Iranian people whether living inside or isolated outside of Iran. In my case, I found myself alone at a young age in a foreign country without any guidance or family member. Meanwhile, at UC Berkeley, a huge anti-Iranian sentiment grew on the campus after the hostage crisis, with massive demonstrations targeting Iranian students. This was a tough period.

LOWRY: Can you describe your sense of the alienation and dislocation?

NESHAT: I felt psychologically and emotionally destabilized to the degree that I could no longer focus on my studies at school. I was one of the worst students at art school and barely made it to graduate school!

LOWRY: Did you study film?

NESHAT: No, I studied at the art department. I was not only politically affected by the revolution, but also financially. My father's support was suddenly cut by the sanctions, so my education took a back seat.

LOWRY: So what did you do?

NESHAT: I worked part-time at a flower store and took other small jobs to get by. Meanwhile, I started to feel physically ill. I thought there was something seriously wrong with my health, so I started to visit various types of doctors, but it proved to be psychological. By now, I was too emotionally and physically traumatized to participate in school or to make art in the way that was expected from me.

LOWRY: You moved to New York in the 1980s?

1

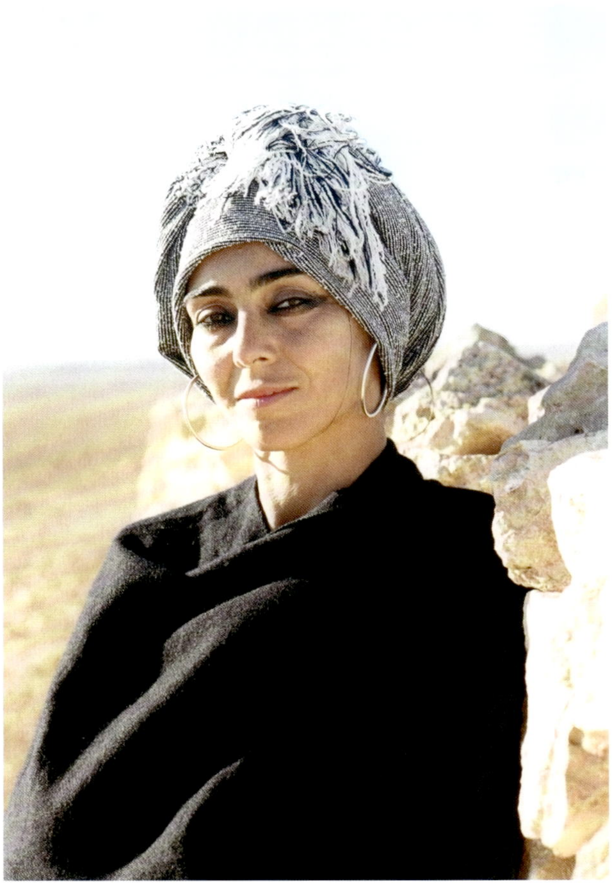

NESHAT: I moved here in 1983, mainly because I had reached a dead end in California. I wasn't making art. School was finished. I was not happy. I went to New York with another student from Berkeley and we tried to start over again. I met Kyong Park, who was the director of Storefront for Art and Architecture, and we ended up getting married and having a child. We worked for the next ten years at Storefront together, and that's when I began to feel anchored. Kyong is Korean and had immigrated to the United States as a child; we shared many cultural values—neither of us is Western, but we are both educated and live and work in the West. He had founded a not-for-profit experimental organization that operated on a meager budget, but it was one of the most exciting alternative spaces in New York City. Meanwhile, having stopped making art, I had no focus at the time, so instead of working in meaningless jobs, I decided to join Kyong in running Storefront. This proved to be my true education, as opposed to art school, where I was trained to be a studio artist and work intuitively. I was now exposed to amazing minds, artists, architects, cultural critics, with knowledge and research as central to their process.

LOWRY: By which time you were a mother. When do you think of yourself as having been clear about being an artist, and is there a work that you think of as your first mature work?

NESHAT: Ironically, I became professionally active as an artist after I became a mother, and after I finally returned to Iran in 1991. I remember vividly how shaken I was emotionally and politically on that trip and the visits that followed. I was simultaneously exhilarated and petrified by the changes I was witnessing in the country after the Islamic Revolution. When I returned to New York, for the first time in a long time I felt compelled to make art that somehow reflected what I had experienced in Iran, but mainly to find a way to frame my own questions regarding the foundation of the Islamic Revolution and how it had impacted the lives of Iranian people, particularly women. Once the process started, everything grew organically, my visual aesthetic as well as the concepts and narratives. In my spare time at Storefront, I would scribble drawings of my hands and feet, then would write on them, and suddenly I thought, I should photograph my body instead of drawing. Then, in 1993, I had an exhibition at a small but wonderful alternative space, Franklin Furnace.

LOWRY: The photographs that constitute the core of *Women of Allah* (p. 38) identify themes that stay with you for decades. The question of identity, the question of location, and perspective. The shifting nature of women in society, the undercurrent of violence, and above all, politics. Your own life, the way you live it, and your work strike me as being deeply and profoundly political, and I wonder if you think of them that way?

NESHAT: I am the product of a revolution, therefore the political and personal always seem to run parallel in my life and work. However, while my work is driven from a personal perspective, I have never been interested in making autobiographical art. I have always approached my subjects like a sociologist would, framing the issues but never providing any answers.

When I started, only a decade after the Islamic Revolution, there seemed to be a wealth of subjects to explore, for example how the revolution had transformed the country from Persian culture to a heavily Islamized society; how the new regime had done everything in its power to eradicate Iran's past history, by imposing its backward ideology, which had taken the country back to the Middle Ages.

Fig. 1 Neshat on the set of *Passage*, 2001

I decided to focus on the controversial concept of "martyrdom" that had become so popular and even institutionalized during the revolution by the government, when innocent Iranians' lives were put at risk with the promise of life after death.

Looking back at the *Women of Allah* series, I understand how the work has a nostalgic, even slightly romantic point of view. But my intention at the time was sincere and clear, a need to reconnect with the country and to create a dialogue.

LOWRY: Do you feel that you were able to reconnect? Do you think of yourself as an Iranian who lives in exile? Or do you think of yourself as an American who was born in Iran? Where do you locate yourself in this range of possibilities?

NESHAT: My political situation has changed drastically both in respect to Iran and to America over the span of time. Sometimes I miss the earlier phase of my life, when I was able to freely travel back and forth to Iran and visit my family before I became known as an artist. Of course, the Iranian government's treatment of me has been totally unjustified, since I don't believe I am political, but nevertheless my name and work continue to be a problem in Iran. And ever since 1995, after my last unfortunate experience leaving Tehran's airport, I have not returned to Iran.

Back in the U.S., it has not been that easy, as I explained earlier, adapting to a foreign culture at a young age, then later the move to New York in my early twenties proved to be challenging as I tried to build a new life and identity as an artist. I often felt intimidated and misunderstood here. In my first exhibition at Annina Nosei Gallery (1995) with *Women of Allah*, a reviewer from *The New York Times* complained that my work was too confusing—Where was I coming from? Was this a case of radical chic, or a way to romanticize violence? From the start, my work has generally drawn mixed reactions from Western art critics and the Iranian regime. Today, after so many years of working, I see how my art will always remain controversial and will be interpreted differently by people of different cultures.

LOWRY: I was always struck by the impact that *Turbulent* (p. 54) had on the larger art world. To me, it felt like a breakthrough where suddenly your perspective as an Iranian connects with larger questions about identity and the tension between male and female roles. Did you feel it in a similar way as a kind of defining moment?

NESHAT: Absolutely. By 1997, after years of making the *Women of Allah* photographs, I felt a certain exhaustion with the medium of photography, the labor of writing calligraphy on their surfaces, but most of all by the range of misinterpretations and judgments that came because of the work's overtly political nature. So in 1997, I made the bold decision to take a break from photography and make video installations. Part of me was excited by how with the moving picture I could build more mystery, enigma, and sense of timelessness, while referencing sociopolitical realities. *Turbulent* marked the beginning of a major shift in my work—I was able to venture outside of the studio into the world, and collaborate with skilled artists, and most importantly I learned to direct, to incorporate music, drama, urban and natural landscapes, and choreography into my work. Finally, *Turbulent* became a very sculptural piece, where the viewers were seated between two opposing projections and had to navigate their attention back and forth between the male and female singers, so they became literally participants in the piece, creating an interesting physical and emotional experience.

LOWRY: And then *Rapture* (p. 64) follows on very quickly.

NESHAT: Yes, *Rapture* followed in *Turbulent*'s footsteps, also highly stylized and choreographed and based on the similar notion of opposites, black/white, masculine/feminine, nature/culture. But for *Rapture*, we traveled to Morocco and worked with over 200 Moroccans. It was a tremendous experience and lesson in filmmaking. What distinguished *Rapture* from *Turbulent* was that in *Rapture* the camera never once came to a close up on one character: the narrative always evolved around groups, never on a single protagonist. With *Rapture*, I felt that I was transitioning into cinema, from conceptual art into storytelling.

LOWRY: You choose to work almost uniquely in black and white. Why?

NESHAT: There is a severity in black and white that I like, and generally I find color dangerously seductive and distracting. In the case of the *Turbulent*, *Rapture*, and *Fervor* video installations, as they were essentially constructed around the notion of opposites, the use of black and white became central in the meaning of the work. But in the case of *Women without Men*, for example, it was clear from the start that we would not shoot the film in black and white, as so many nuances of the settings—the central orchard and the look of 1953 Tehran—would have been lost.

LOWRY: I want to shift to your filmic work, which isn't binary, which is so layered and complicated. *Women without Men* is of course a profoundly political story, but it's really hard to understand all the perspectives because each character comes at it differently, and there is such an emotional charge that runs through the film that you lose the binary clarity of your video, it collapses. Is that intentional?

NESHAT: *Women without Men* was a cinematic challenge, taking a magical realist novel, one of the most difficult types of literature to turn into a screenplay, and directing it as a visual artist who had never studied filmmaking before. However, I took my usual binary approach. If the orchard where the four women took refuge represented a magical, otherworldly, and timeless space, the city of Tehran represented the realm of reality as it underwent a coup d'état in 1953. Our team developed visual and audio strategies that helped distinguish these different realms. Even the nature of the four female characters was distinct; Munis and Zarin were allegorical characters, while Farokh Legha and Faezeh were fully realistic. Symbolically, the film was meant to make an allegorical link between the plight of the four women characters as they looked for an idea of freedom, and the country of Iran fighting for independence from imperialist powers.

LOWRY: Your more recent work moves away from being set in Iran.

NESHAT: Yes, perhaps because I have lost all interest in going back to Iran.

LOWRY: To live?

NESHAT: To live, or to visit. By now, I had made a large body of work all related to Iran, but in 2011, something had changed in me. I felt that I had reached the end of my tolerance for nostalgia, and had lost hope in returning to Iran, so I turned my attention to other cultures. It helped that I already had practice in working like a nomad, in places such in Mexico, Morocco, Turkey, Egypt, and Azerbaijan. Also, I knew that while my new subjects might no longer be about Iran, they would always be from an Iranian perspective. In the film *Looking for Oum Kulthum*, for example, the film is a parallel story between the iconic Egyptian singer and an Iranian woman filmmaker who is attempting to make a biopic about her.

LOWRY: Who's never really present.

NESHAT: Yes, precisely.

LOWRY: Can you explore that a bit, because that's the part that I love so much about that work.

NESHAT: It seems like subconsciously every work that I've made so far has been somewhat personal, or at least driven by subjects that have related to my own personal dilemma, anxieties, experiences as a human being. Making the film *Looking for Oum Kulthum* was of that nature. It stemmed from my long obsession with this mythical, larger-than-life icon, easily considered the most important Middle Eastern artist of the twentieth century, who happened to be a woman. I was mesmerized by Oum Kulthum's timeless popularity; how as an artist she was worshipped by the poor, rich, men, women, secular, nonsecular, Christians, Jews, and Muslims; how, unlike most iconic Western female singers, she didn't have a tragic ending; and how, when she died, four million Egyptians poured into the streets of Cairo to mourn her death.

So the film is a series of questions. How did she do it? How did she succeed as a woman artist in male-dominated societies? Is it possible for women to balance a personal life and a successful career? These were the questions asked by the character of the Iranian director.

LOWRY: And a woman artist in exile.

NESHAT: Yes, indeed. Another big theme of the film was the issue of failure, and how the Iranian director was puzzled by Oum Kulthum's flawless career, while battling with her own vulnerabilities and failures as a mother and as an artist.

LOWRY: Do you worry about failure?

NESHAT: I often fail in my work, not always meeting the standards that I have set for myself. I also struggle in the competitive, male-dominated Western culture including the art world and the film industry, but I think failures and struggles are what have kept me on my toes.

LOWRY: Who are the artists and writers that you think about? Who are the thinkers and artists that inhabit your mind?

NESHAT: My influences are very broad, ranging from filmmakers to visual artists. I have many favorite filmmakers, including the Russian Andrei Tarkovsky, who has been hugely influential in my film work. I absolutely love his dreamy, poetic, philosophical, and highly politically charged narratives and visual style. The Iranian filmmaker Abbas Kiarostami has been a long-time idol of mine, and I was lucky to become his friend. I'm blown away by his clever yet simple approach to social realism, which on the surface seemed to capture the malice of Iranian culture, but in reality, his vision was grander than his own country. I'm also deeply inspired by Scandinavian cinema, master filmmakers such as Ingmar Bergman, Roy Andersson, and Lars von Trier.

At art school, I was obsessed with Frida Kahlo—her paintings, her persona, her style, her relationship to Diego Rivera, her political life and friendship with Russian intellectuals. Among contemporary artists, Cindy Sherman continues to inspire me as an artist and as a human being. Marina Abramović is another artist I respect and look up to for her art, and endurance, for maintaining a fascinating and long career. I am a huge fan of William Kentridge, who never ceases to amaze me for his depth, poetry, and intelligence.

LOWRY: As you've moved away from Iran as the immediate subject of your work to perhaps a reverberation of Iran, does it feel different? Do you see new directions for your work?

NESHAT: Yes, as my palette has become bigger, and I navigate between many different cultures, I have gained a broader audience, but I also feel a greater pressure and responsibility.

My new plan to finally make work about America is a decision that I delayed for years, because although I have lived in this country for so many years, I never felt qualified. But now, in light of the current political situation in America and my own position as a Muslim immigrant, I feel that it is time for me to make a work that offers my perspectives as an Iranian/American artist about this country.

LOWRY: And do you think it's possible for Americans to understand Iran and Iranian culture? Do you think that the trauma of the revolution and the hostage-taking is so pervasive that we as a nation simply are incapable of bridging some social or cultural divide, or do you feel that the episodic anti-Iranian rhetoric that bubbles up doesn't properly reflect how Americans feel and understand another place?

NESHAT: I get the impression that in the eyes of most Americans, Iran remains the same country as it was during the hostage crisis back in 1979, but Iran's internal politics and contemporary culture are so extremely complex and have changed so much, that even I, as an Iranian, with a family living in Iran, and connected with Iranians on a daily basis, have a hard time fully grasping the situation. What has not changed, however, is the government's continuing anti-American antagonism.

In my next project, *Land of Dreams* (p. 204), I hope to touch on some of the historical tensions between the two countries which are escalating as we speak, but with the use of absurdity and satire. I find it ironic that my past work was sort of a critique of Iranian society, the Islamic fundamentalism and fanaticism that was prompted by the regime, and now the American administration is starting to look more and more like the Iranian government.

LOWRY: That's the irony, isn't it?

NESHAT: Precisely. Who would have thought that one day, an American president would share values with Iranian spiritual leaders?

LOWRY: It's also interesting how the binary dimensions of your work capture this, how we need enemies.

NESHAT: It seems that by identifying and focusing on "enemies," all governments distract from internal crisis and create a sense of unity among their citizens. I know for a fact that the Iranian regime profits each time political tensions between Iran, the U.S., and Israel escalate. The same seems to go for the American government, where with the tremendous social and economic problems at home and in the world, the administration thrives by focusing on nonthreatening issues such as Mexican and Muslim immigrants.

I'm hoping that in my film *Land of Dreams*, I will be able to touch on some of these absurdities. The story revolves around an Iranian woman who works as a census taker for the American administration in a small working-class town. The administration has added an additional question to the census questionnaire, which is: What is your latest dream? She goes door-to-door, collecting people's dreams. In the meanwhile, there is an Iranian colony where Iranians are kept like refugees, but actually they are receiving, selecting, and interpreting American people's dreams.

LOWRY: This issue of dreaming seems to me another central dimension of your work. For instance, you can look at *Turbulent* as a dream. There's a dimension to it where you're not sure whether you're witnessing something that's happening in real time, in real space, or something that's being imagined. And *Women without Men* is a dream sequence in a way. It talks about real events and tragedy and coups, but it also unfolds like a dream. Do you see the world as a dream? Do you distinguish between fact and fiction?

NESHAT: We all dream. Dreams are innocent and dreams cannot be judged. And it's through dreams that we find a shared humanity, where we're completely naked, free, vulnerable, and where we face our worst fears and anxieties. What I also like about dreams is that they are like magical realism—there are always references to reality, places we have visited, people we know. In *Land of Dreams*, as the Iranian woman collects people's dreams, she realizes that despite cultural differences, her dreams and nightmares are not that different from those of Americans.

LOWRY: That's almost a sense of reconciliation.

NESHAT: Exactly.

LOWRY: Which has been absent, I think, from so much of your earlier work.

NESHAT: I think for me the moment has come for this notion of reconciliation, of bridging my past with the present, issues related to my native country with my host country; understanding the profound differences yet immense similarities.

LOWRY: And I think you have shown yourself to be this extraordinarily acute observer of these complex social and political conditions always through the lens of a feminist perspective, but not limited to that. You address universal issues even if you ground them in something that's either very familiar to you or something that you wish to recover. You used the word nostalgic. I don't know whether I think of your work as nostalgic necessarily, so much as about a longing.

NESHAT: That is very true. In many ways, had not this sense of longing been with me since young adulthood, I would never have been an artist. As I said, my issue as a human being is no longer a question of nostalgia, but about my unresolved relationship with my homeland. Ironically, what has helped me throughout is a form of reflection that arises in Persian poetry and history of mysticism, where the notion of longing and melancholy is an essential form of philosophical guidance.

LOWRY: But it's also about another form of knowledge. Mysticism is a way of acquiring knowledge through other than direct means, and that's why Oum Kulthum is so interesting. We get to know her without ever really meeting her.

NESHAT: Exactly.

LOWRY: Whether it's the kind of dreamlike sequences that you build, or because your work is actually ultimately about a dream, you have a way of creating knowledge that's visually immediate but also always slippery. You think you've grasped it and then it moves.

NESHAT: On one hand, everything I make is grounded in history yet is created in a surrealistic manner, which helps take the narrative to a different level, deviating from the specificities of place and time. My work is always about mediating between knowledge, facts, and the imaginary and unbelievable.

At the end, I would like to be remembered as an artist who became a narrator of history in fictional form. There is something in me that gravitates toward history, maybe because history tends to repeat itself.

Glenn Lowry is The David Rockefeller Director of the Museum of Modern Art, New York.

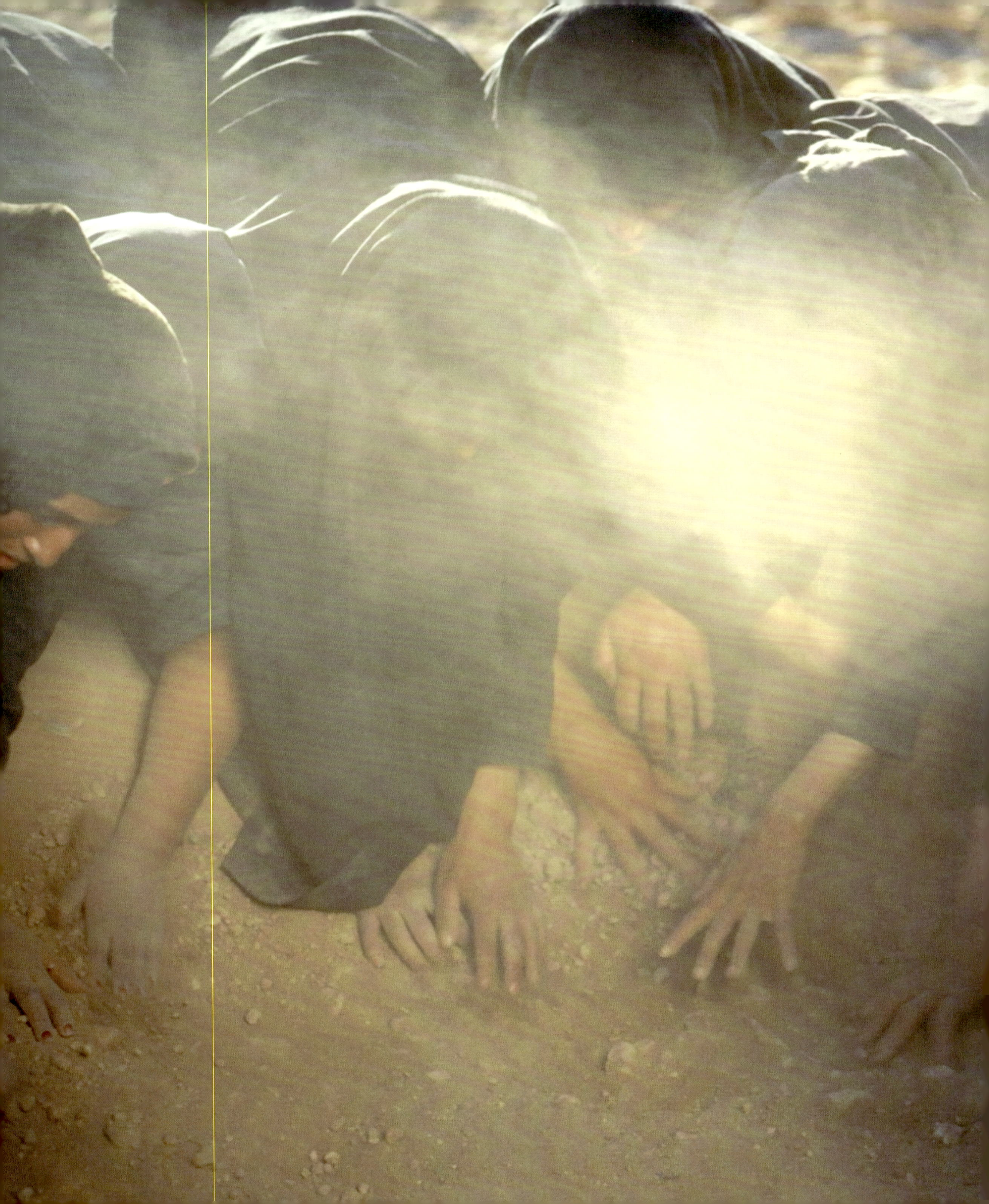

SOLILOQUY, PASSAGE, POSSESSED, TOOBA

In 1999, Neshat made a series of photographs and a video called *Soliloquy*, her most personal exploration of the psychological, temporal, and physical divisions experienced by people living in exile. Projected on two channels, the video alternates between black-and-white and color, showing Neshat moving through and inhabiting both modernist buildings in New York—including The Egg Center for the Performing Arts in Albany, and St. Ann's Church and the World Trade Center in Manhattan—and schools, mosques, and other buildings in Mardin, Turkey. "Through the opposition of East and West, modern and traditional, displacement and memory, biography and history," Neshat wrote, "*Soliloquy* aims to offer a glimpse into the experience of a divided self in need of repair . . . standing at the threshold of two worlds, apparently tormented in one but excluded from the other."[1]

Neshat often produces photographs in conjunction with her videos and films, choosing to exhibit either the still images or the moving pictures in her exhibitions. With its arresting locations and stark dichotomies between cultures, which Neshat attempts to navigate and find a place in, *Soliloquy*'s photographs (made in collaboration with Larry Barns) are among her most striking. Somewhat ironically, after the project she will increasingly describe her practice as grounded in universalist impulses, expressing a desire to dissolve, break, or transcend the very boundaries asserted in *Soliloquy*.

This push toward universals is perhaps clearest in *Passage* (2001) and *Tooba* (2002), videos that travel farthest from a direct representation of Neshat's native country. The first depicts a burial ceremony inspired by images of funeral processions resulting from the Israeli/Palestinian conflict. The second was made in the wake of September 11, 2001. *Passage* and *Tooba* shift emphasis away from the contemporary events that feature so prominently in *Women of Allah*—the headlines, wars, and traumas of Iran's revolutions—to rituals and themes that resonate globally.

Passage was commissioned by Philip Glass as part of a series of films/musical compositions that would become his work *Film Shorts* (2001). The

Previous spread
Still from *Passage*, 2001

video shows two groups of people—one male, one female—coming together to bury a body in the desert. The men carry the body across a beach, while the women dig a hole in the sand. Also present is a young girl who builds a small ring of rocks for a fire. The viewer discovers that the girl's ring is a smaller version of a much larger ring of rocks that will serve to enclose the men, women, and girl. At the end of the film, this larger ring is lit on fire. "Passage does not exile death and decay to the realm of the private or the personal," Farzaneh Milani observed. "These are depicted as shared social experiences, integral parts of life and collective consciousness."[2]

Tooba was shot in Mexico with Mexican actors. Grappling with the destruction of the Twin Towers, the work, in Neshat's words, "aims to capture a profound sense of collective anxiety and vulnerability by depicting the dynamic interaction of three different images: the sacred garden with the tree of Tooba at its center (a story taken from the Qur'an), a mass of men and women desperately rushing toward the garden, and a circle of bearded men that resembles a gathering of religious or governmental figures."[3] *Tooba* depicts a quest for sanctuary through shared traditions of paradise found in multiple cultures, from the Garden of Eden in Christianity to Persian gardens.

As she worked on *Passage* and *Tooba*, Neshat was introduced to Shahrnush Parsipur's novel *Women without Men*, leading to frequent communication with the author as she began to work on the book as a potential feature film. These encounters spurred reflection on the toll that creative work takes on the psychology of artists, specifically the suffering and perceptions of female artists and writers living in Iran. The lives of Parsipur and poet Forugh Farrokhzad inspired the video installation *Possessed* (2001).

The camera follows a woman without a hijab wandering the alleyways, shops, and squares of a city. This video implies that the woman's "madness," or her creative energies, allow her the freedom to break societal codes of dress and behavior. She occupies a place apart from the people she encounters, and over the course of the film becomes increasingly expressive and frenzied. "I wanted to show how one woman's madness disturbs the public," Neshat has said of the work, "which becomes divided in whether madness should be a way to be freed from social religious norms."[4]

NOTES

1 Shirin Neshat quoted in Arthur C. Danto, *Shirin Neshat* (New York: Rizzoli, 2010), p. 95.

2 Farzaneh Milani, "The Visual Poetry of Shirin Neshat," in *Shirin Neshat* (Milan: Charta, 2001), p. 12.

3 Shirin Neshat quoted in Arthur C. Danto, *Shirin Neshat* (New York: Rizzoli, 2010), p. 131.

4 Shirin Neshat, interview with the author, December 27, 2018.

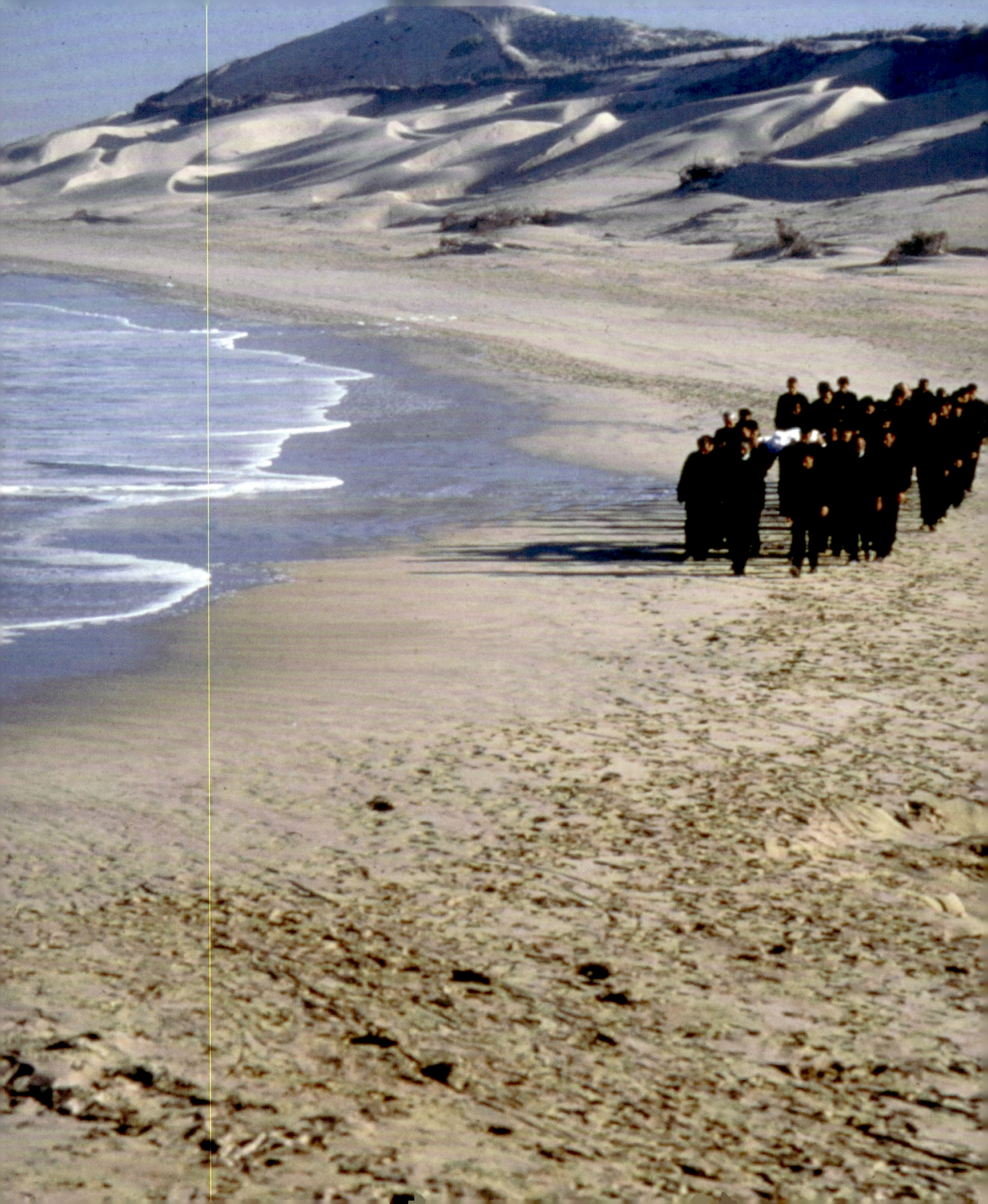

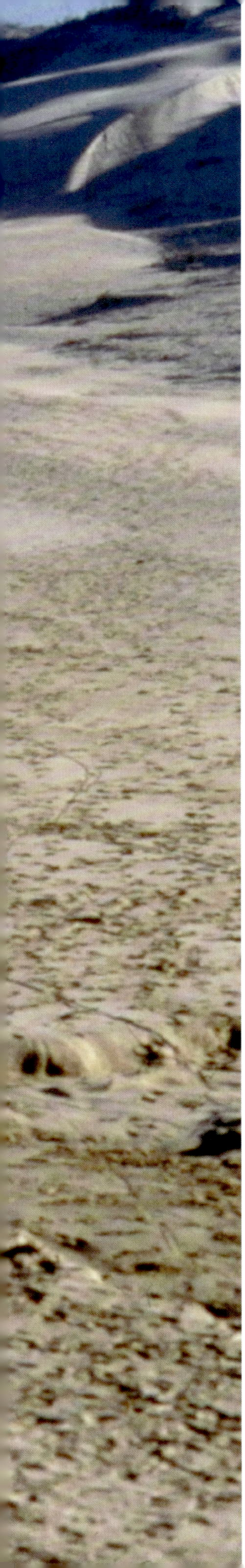

LAMENT

Mehdi Akhavan-Sales

Our dear martyr's body
is left unburied
left upon our hands, left upon our hearts
like the dumb gaze of disbelief,
our chieftain he was, this noble warrior
crusader of our cause, leader of our host
with his message of purity
with his divine nobility, he bade us to go forth
and with him we came
          to this holy war
and he cried out,
"Tomorrow no doubt
is a better day,
no doubt it is ours."

But
now
for many a day
his dear body
is left unburied
left upon our hands, like sighs in our hearts
and
ours are evil days.

Today
we are broken, and we are weary
and instead of us you are the victors
may this defeat and this victory be wholesome to you
however you mock our cause
whoever you capture, whoever you torture
whatever you pillage, whatever you plunder
is yours by your might, may it be wholesome
but at least bury this noble body.

Translation by Ahmad Karimi-Hakkak

Still from *Passage*, 2001

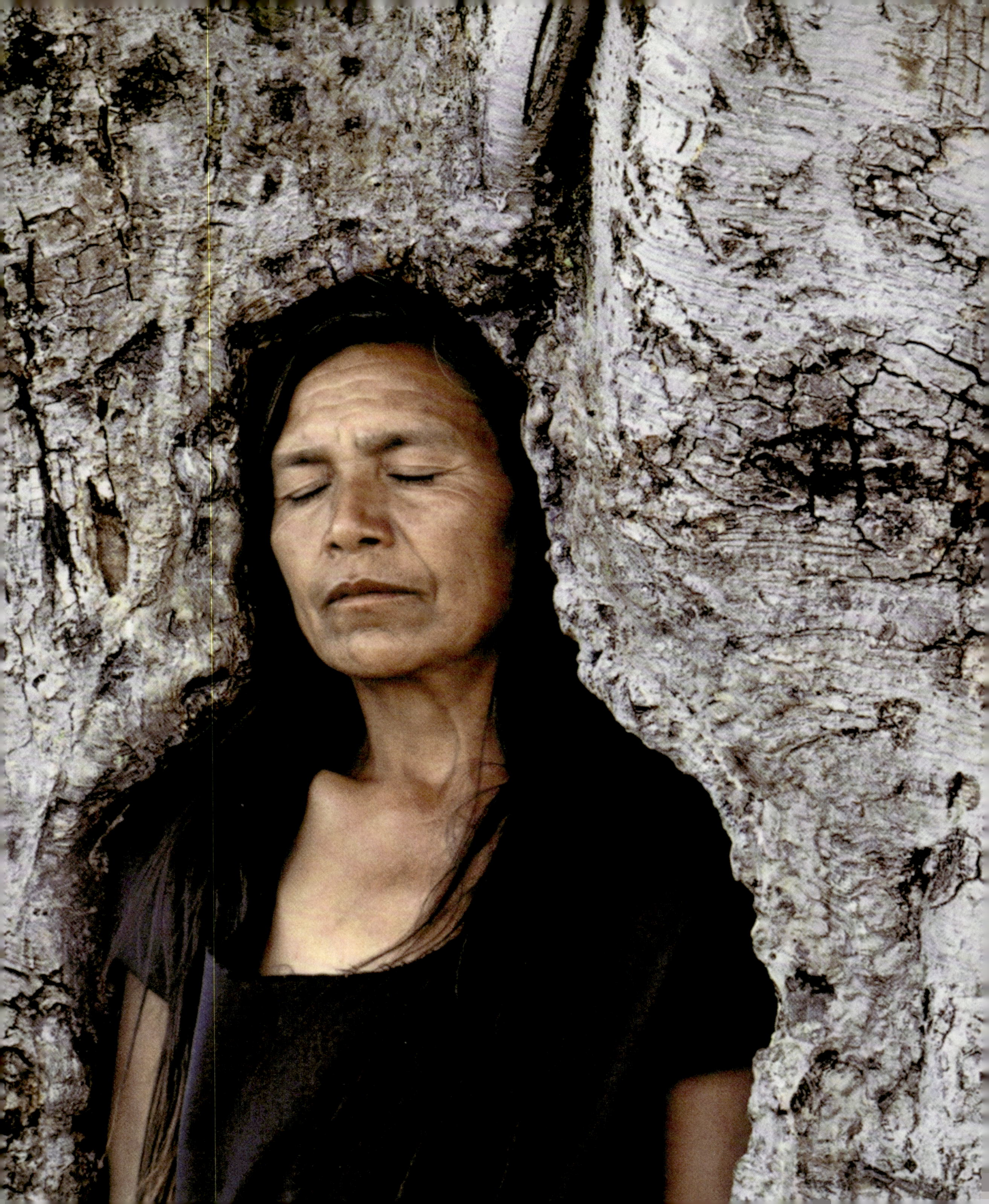

Selection from WOMEN WITHOUT MEN
Shahrnush Parsipur

Well, there was no alternative. Mahdokht decided to stay in the garden and plant herself at the beginning of winter. She had to ask the gardeners what was the best time for planting. She didn't know, but it wasn't important. She would stay and plant herself. Perhaps she would turn into a tree. She wanted to grow on the riverbank with leaves greener than the slime, and fight the battle of shades of green in the pool. If she became a tree, she would sprout new leaves. She would be covered with new leaves. She would give her new leaves to the wind, a garden full of Mahdokhts. They would have to cut down all the sour and sweet cherry trees so that Mahdokht could grow. Mahdokht would grow.

She would become thousands and thousands of branches. She would cover the entire world. Americans would buy her shoots and take them to California. They would call the forest of Mahdokht the forest of Mahdekat. Gradually they would pronounce her name so many times until it would become Maduk in some place and Maaduk in others. Then four hundred years later the linguists, with their veins standing out in their foreheads like twigs, would debate over her and prove that the two words come from the root Madeek which is of Africa origin. Then the biologist would object that a tree that grows in cold climates could not grow in Africa.

Translation by Kamran Talattof and Jocelyn Sharlet

Still from *Tooba*, 2002

SOLILOQUY

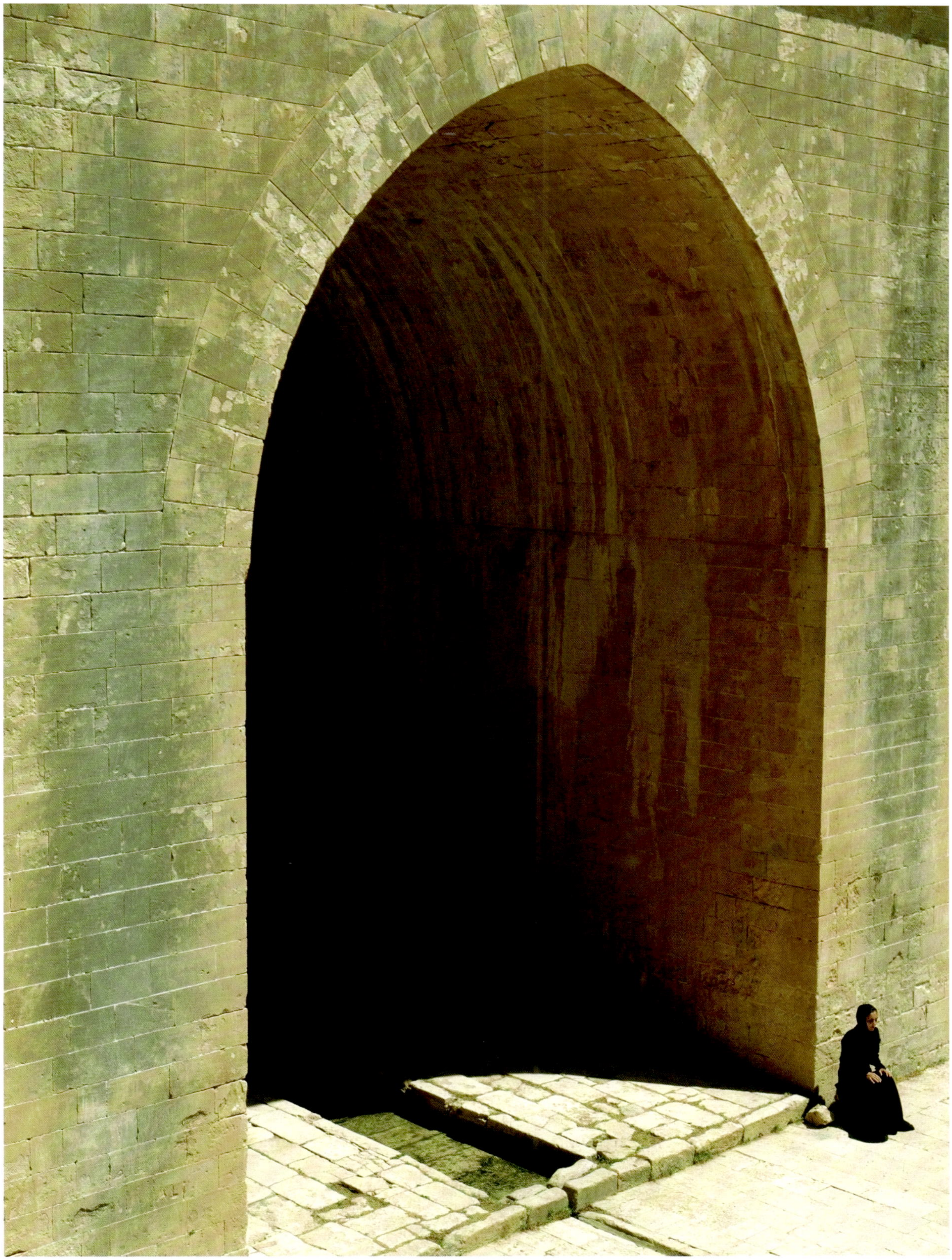

SOLILOQUY SERIES, 2000

Chromogenic print, 63½ x 47½ x 2 inches (161.3 x 120.7 x 5.1 cm).
Photograph taken by Larry Barns

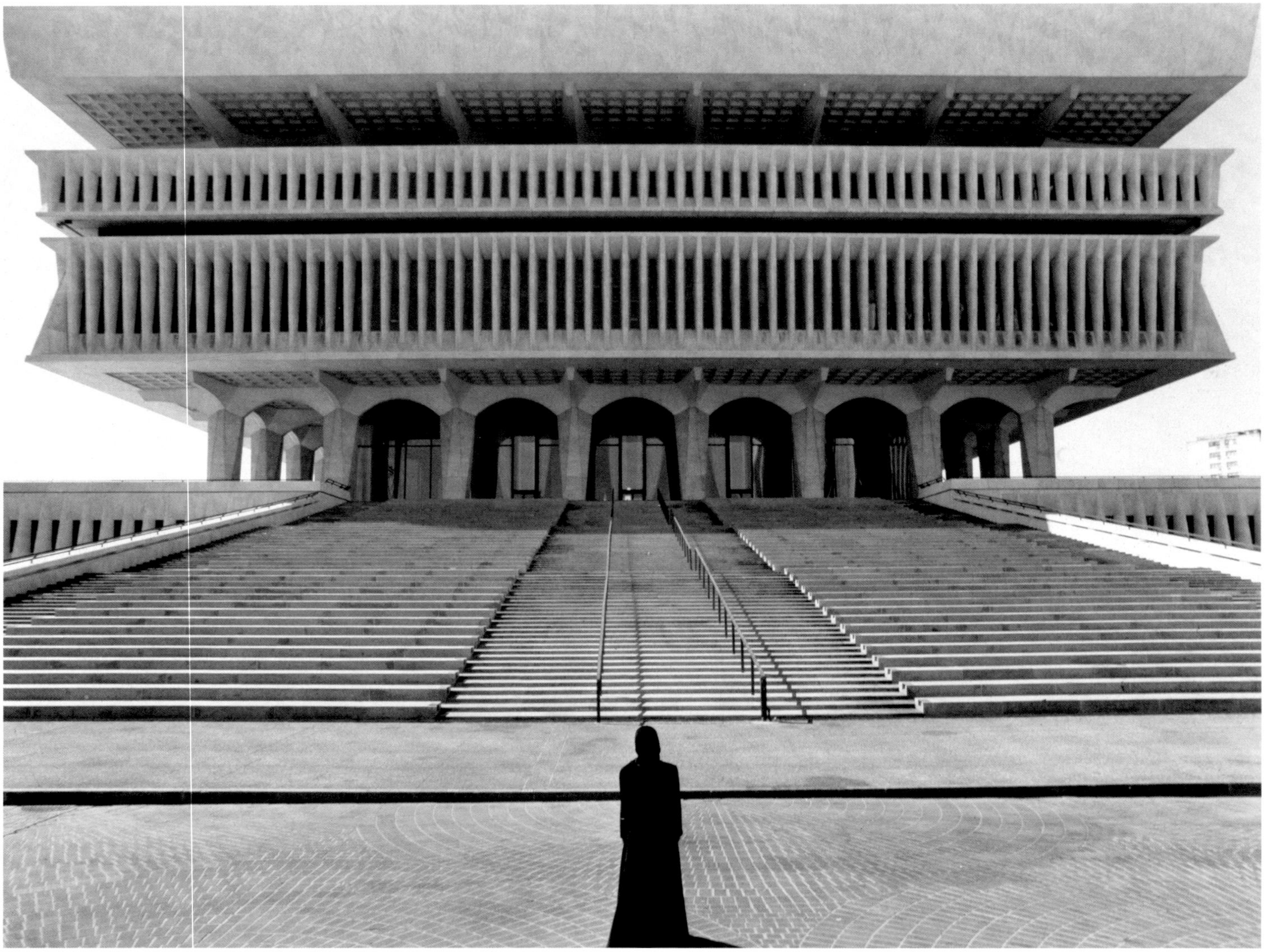

SOLILOQUY SERIES, 1999

LE silver gelatin print, 50⅝ x 66 x 2 inches (128.6 x 167.6 x 5.1 cm).
Photograph taken by Larry Barns

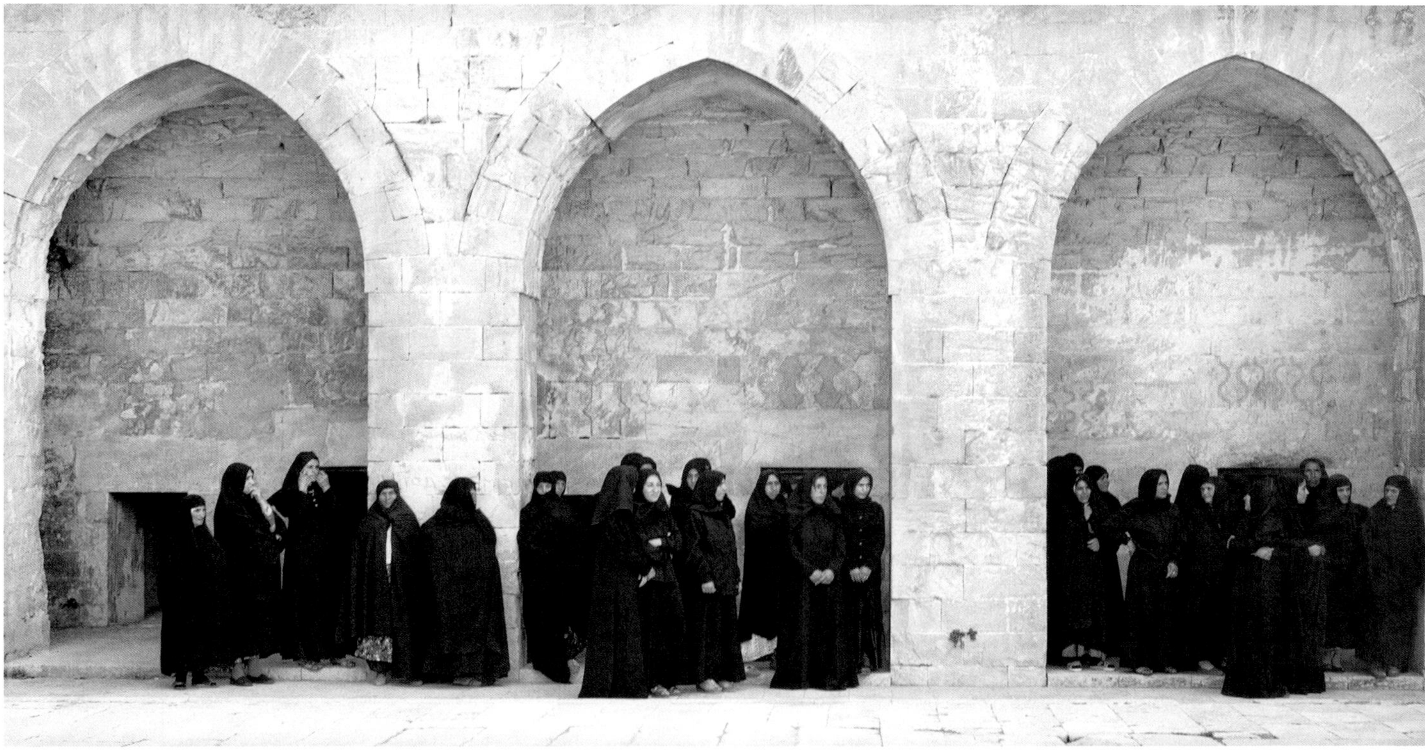

SOLILOQUY SERIES, 1999

LE silver gelatin print, 43¾ x 79¼ x 2¼ inches (111.1 x 201.3 x 5.7 cm). Photograph taken by Larry Barns. Courtesy of Goodman Gallery, Johannesburg, Capetown, and London

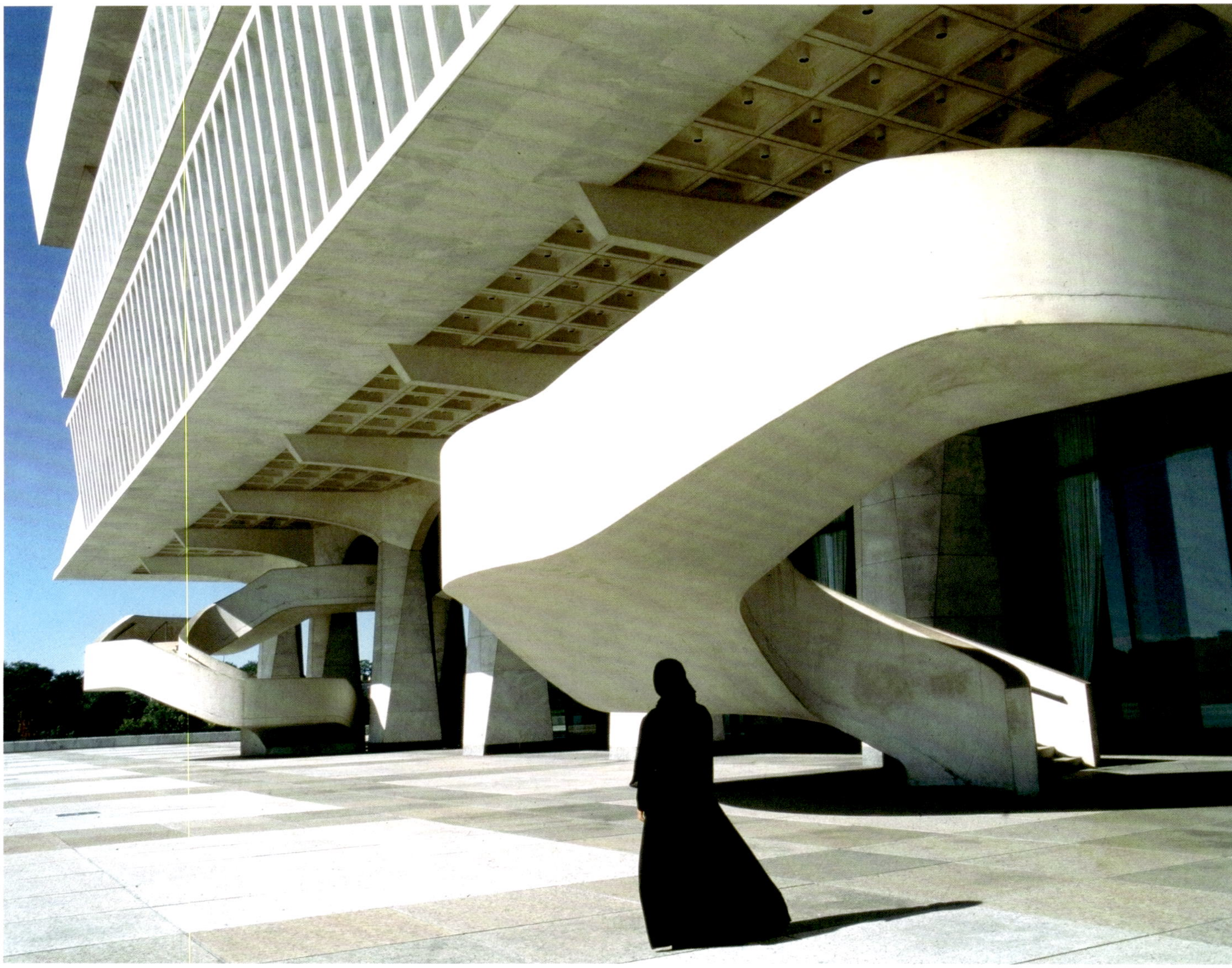

SOLILOQUY SERIES, 2000

Chromogenic print, 48¼ x 60¼ inches (122.6 x 153 cm).
Photograph taken by Larry Barns
The Broad Art Foundation, Los Angeles

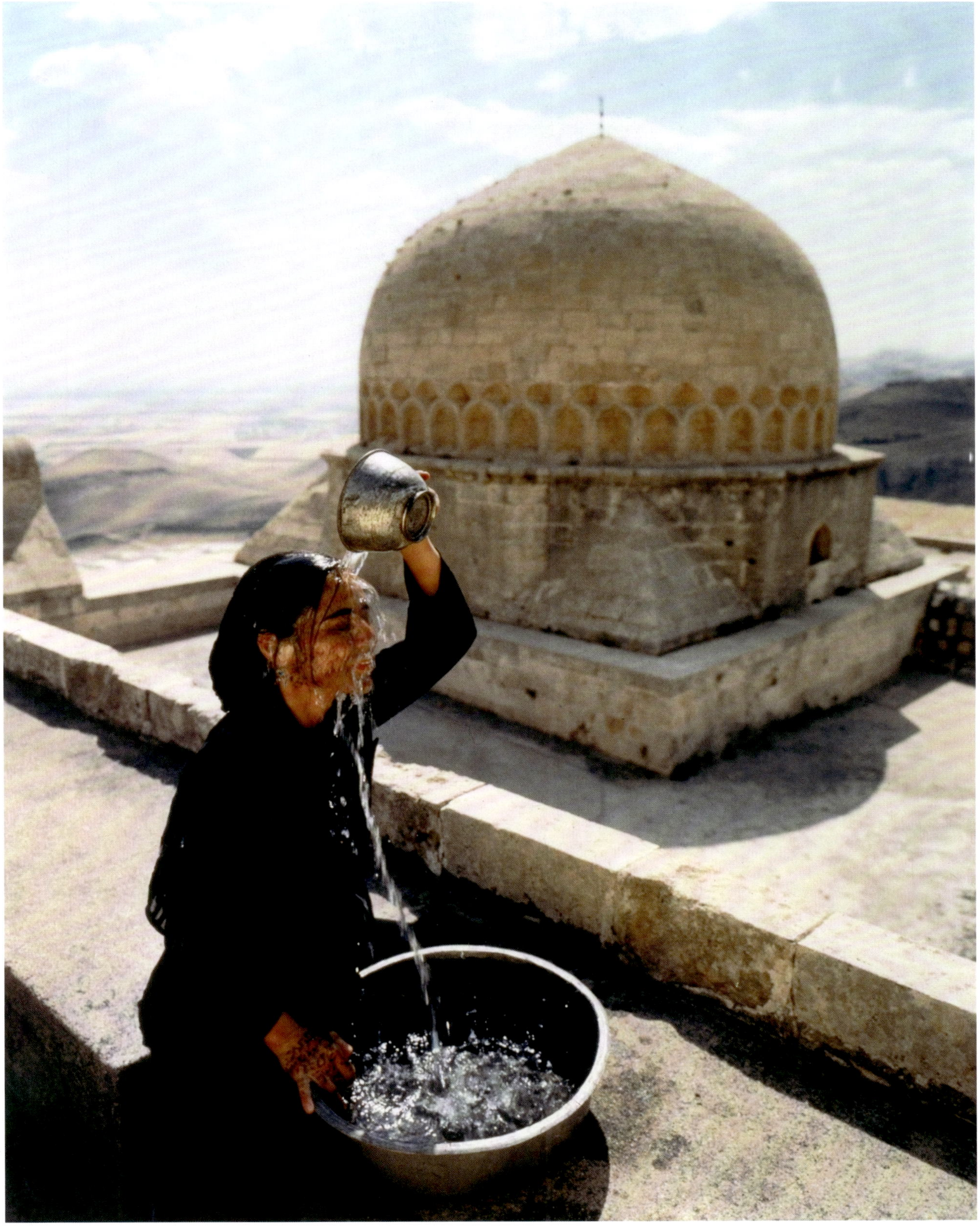

SOLILOQUY SERIES, 2000

Chromogenic print, 60¼ x 48¼ inches (153 x 122.6 cm).
Photograph taken by Larry Barns
The Broad Art Foundation, Los Angeles

PASSAGE

2001
SINGLE-CHANNEL VIDEO INSTALLATION
35MM COLOR FILM TRANSFERRED TO VIDEO
DURATION: 11 MINUTES, 30 SECONDS
FILMED IN MOROCCO

DIRECTOR: SHIRIN NESHAT
IN COLLABORATION WITH: SHOJA AZARI
MUSIC COMPOSITION: PHILIP GLASS
DIRECTOR OF PHOTOGRAPHY: GHASEM EBRAHIMIAN
PRODUCTION DESIGNER: SHAHRAM KARIMI
COSTUME DESIGNER: NOUREDDINE AMIR
LINE PRODUCER: HAMID FARDJAD
PRODUCER: BARBARA GLADSTONE

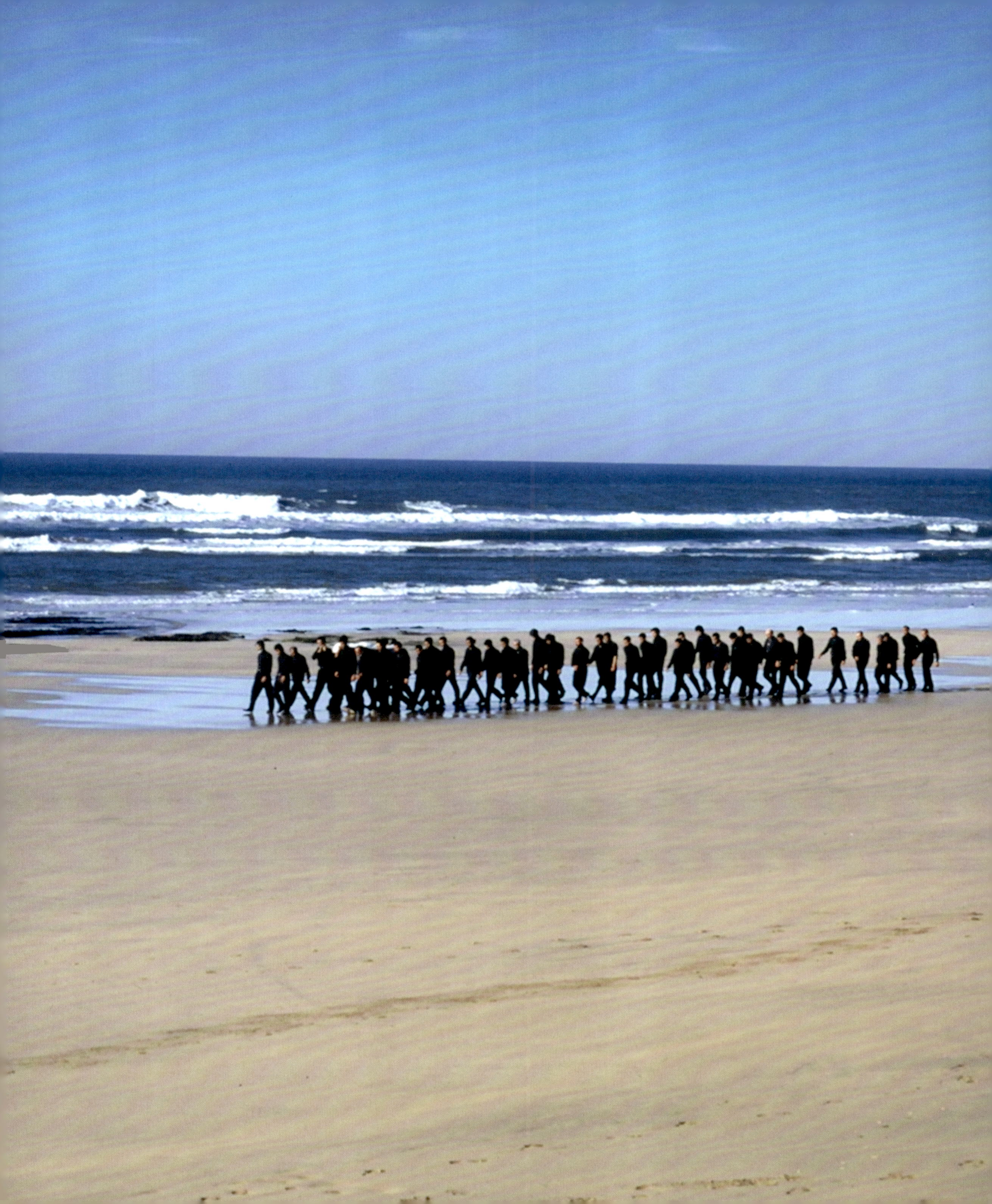

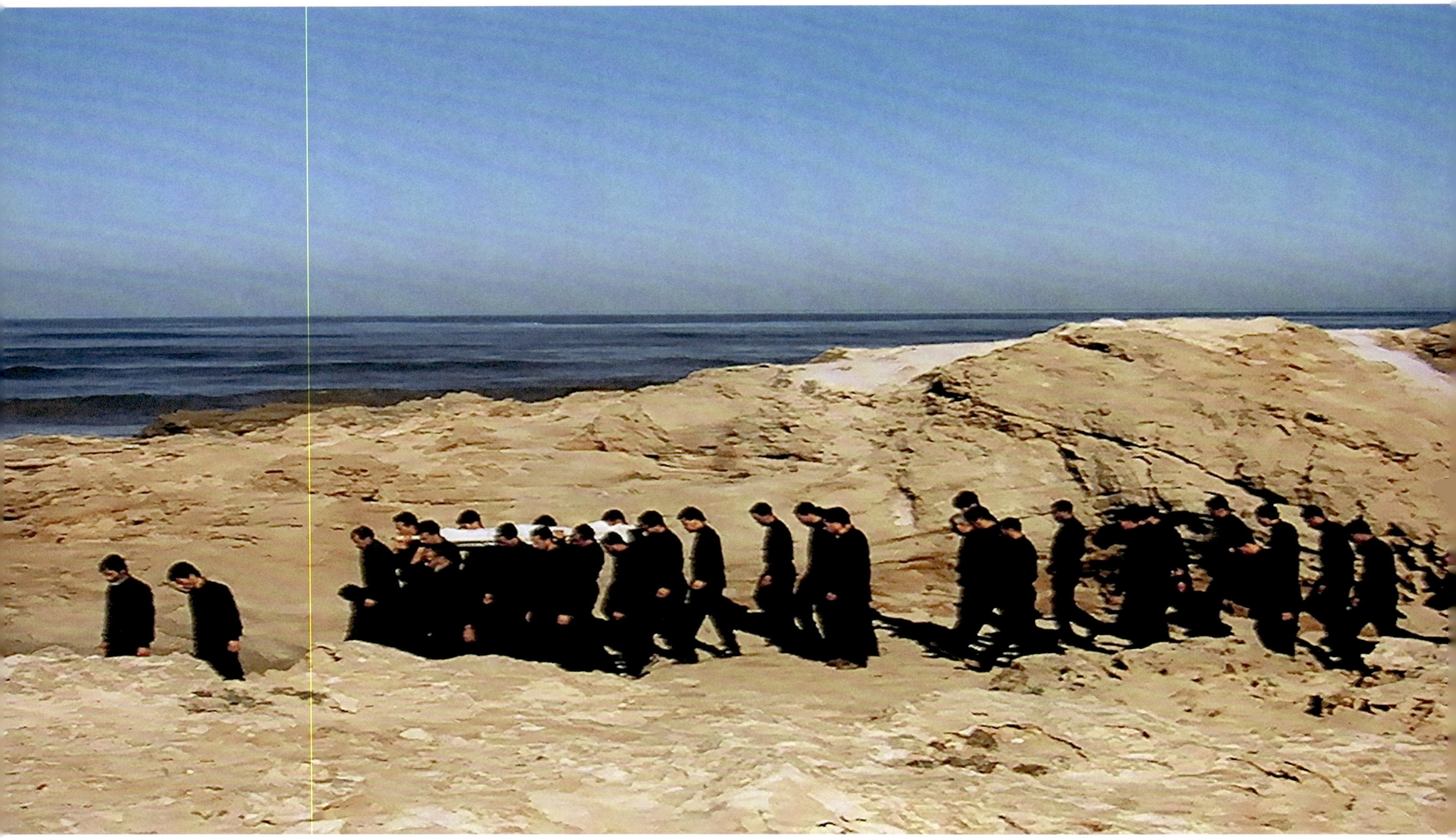

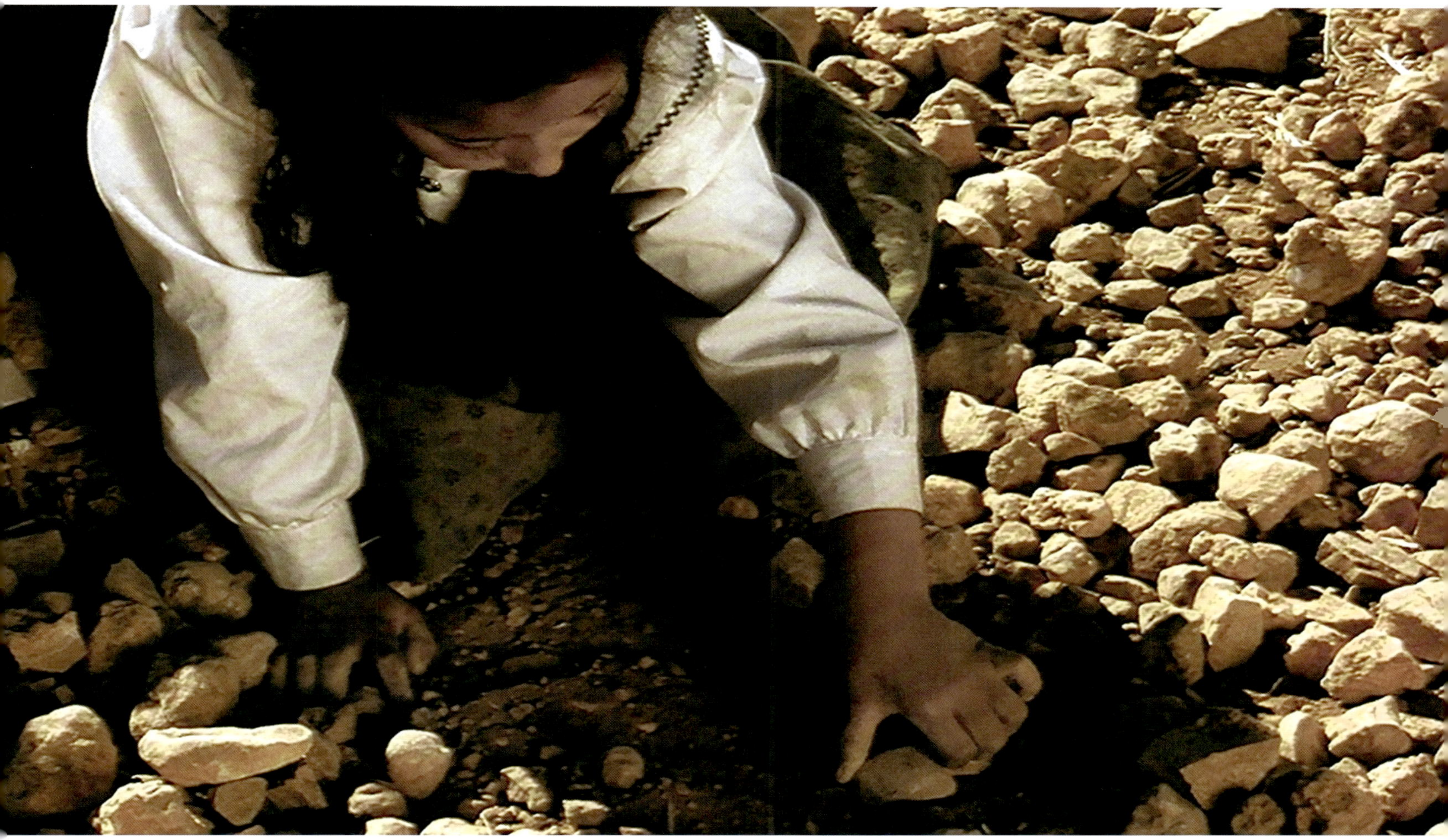

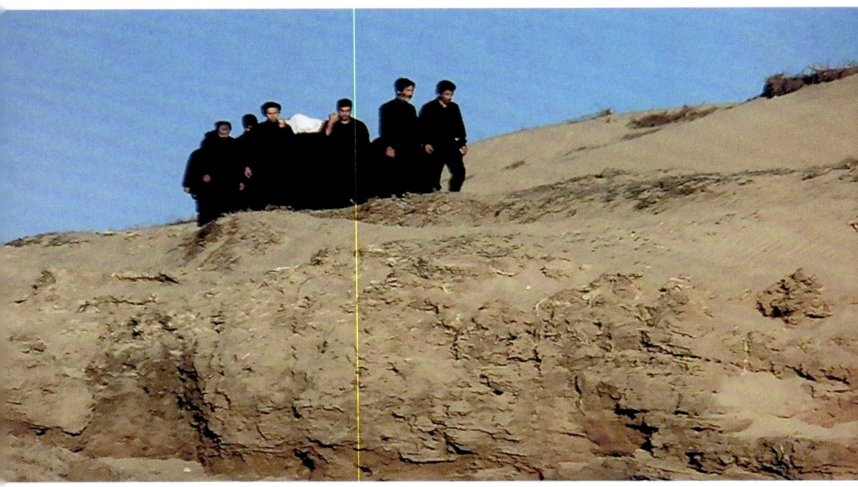

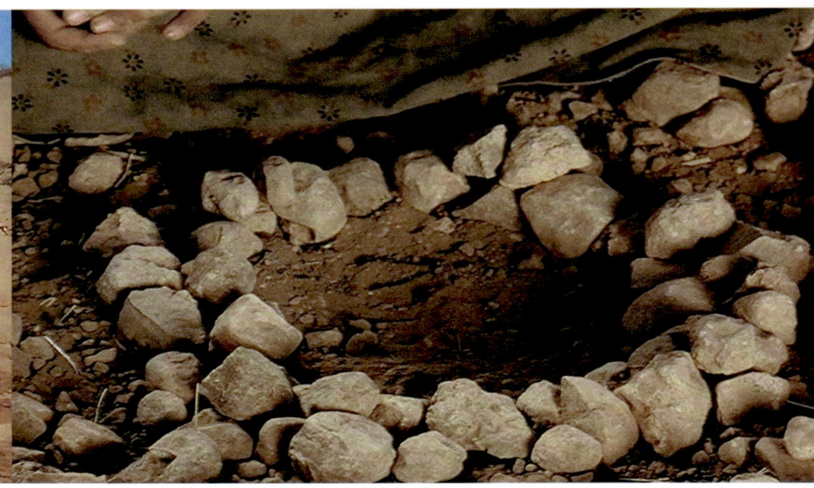

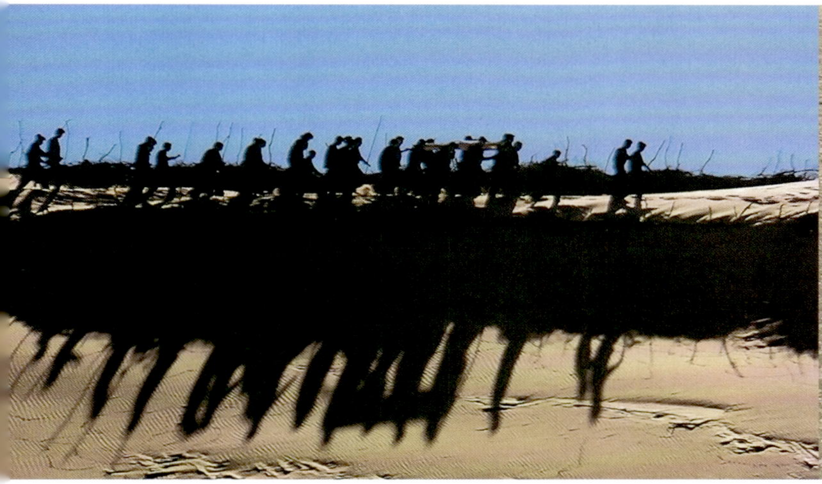

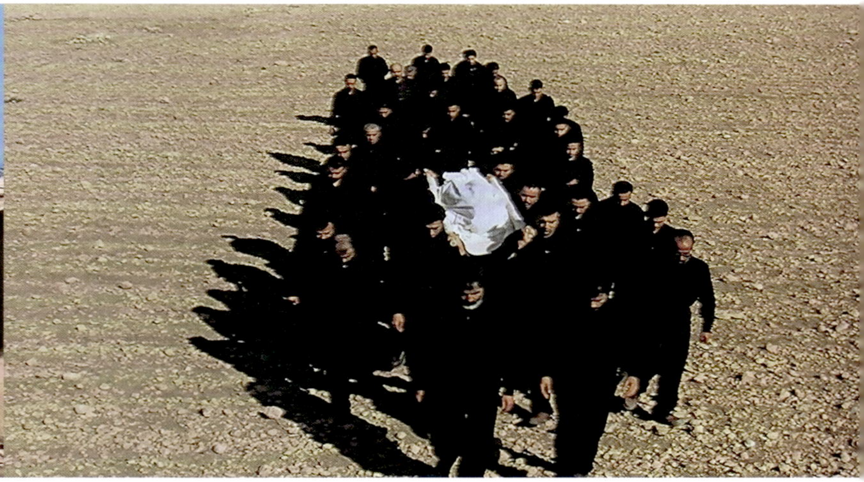

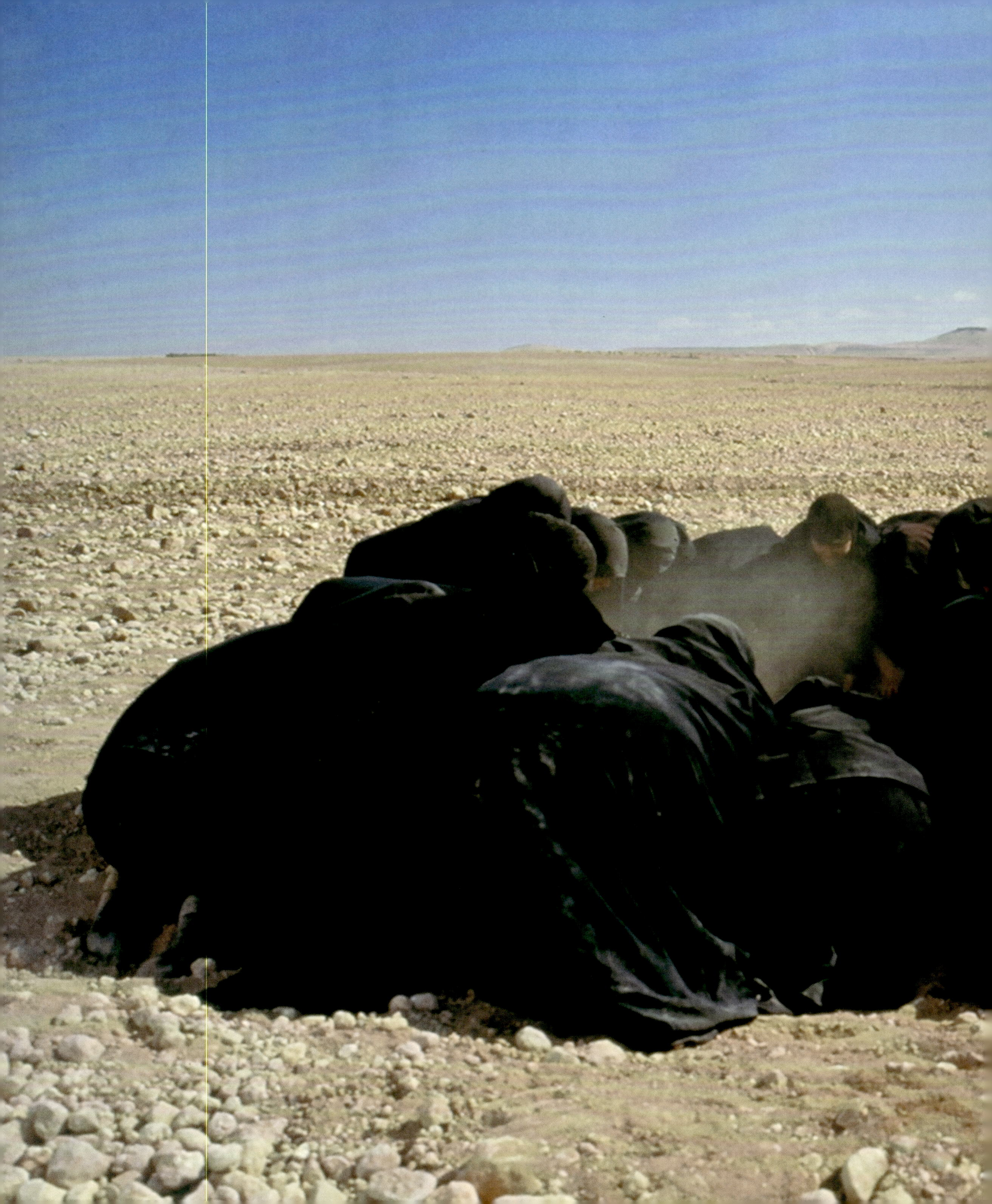

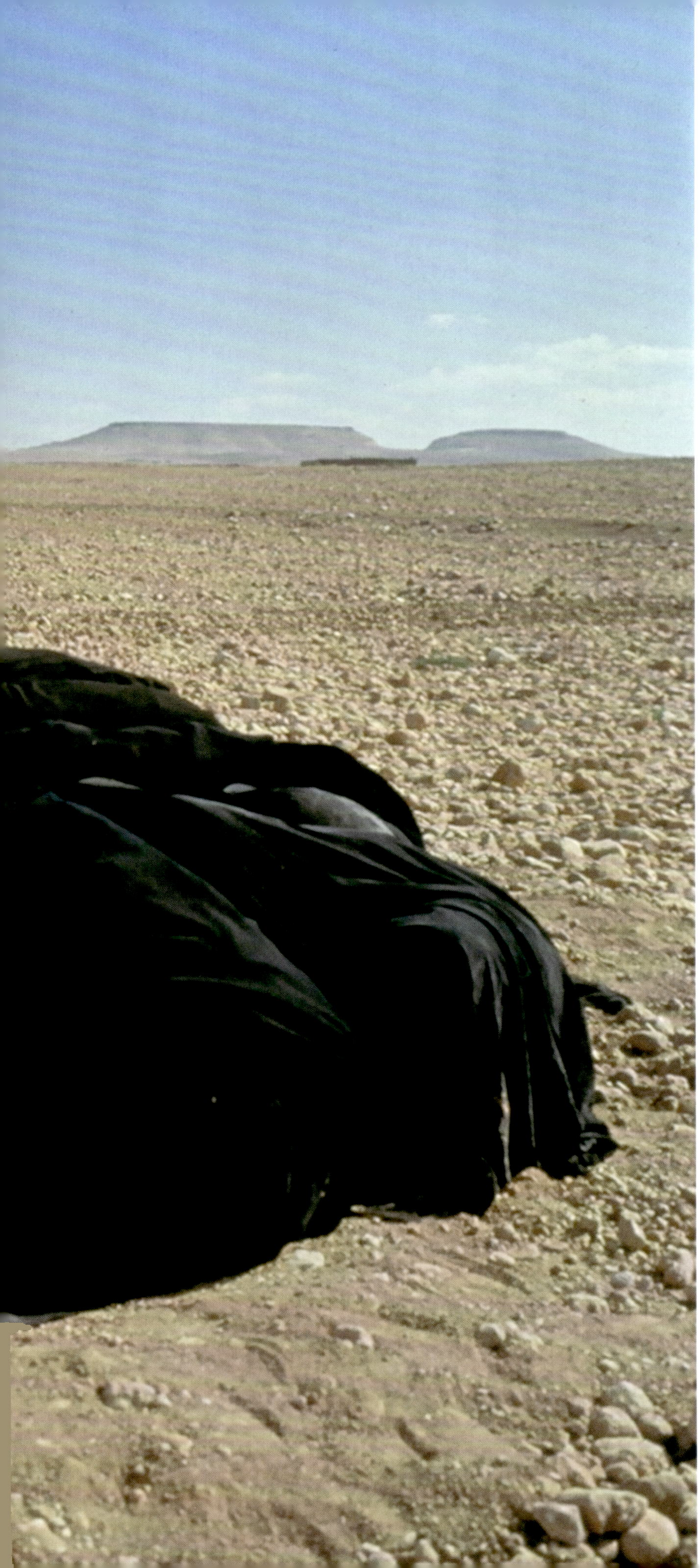

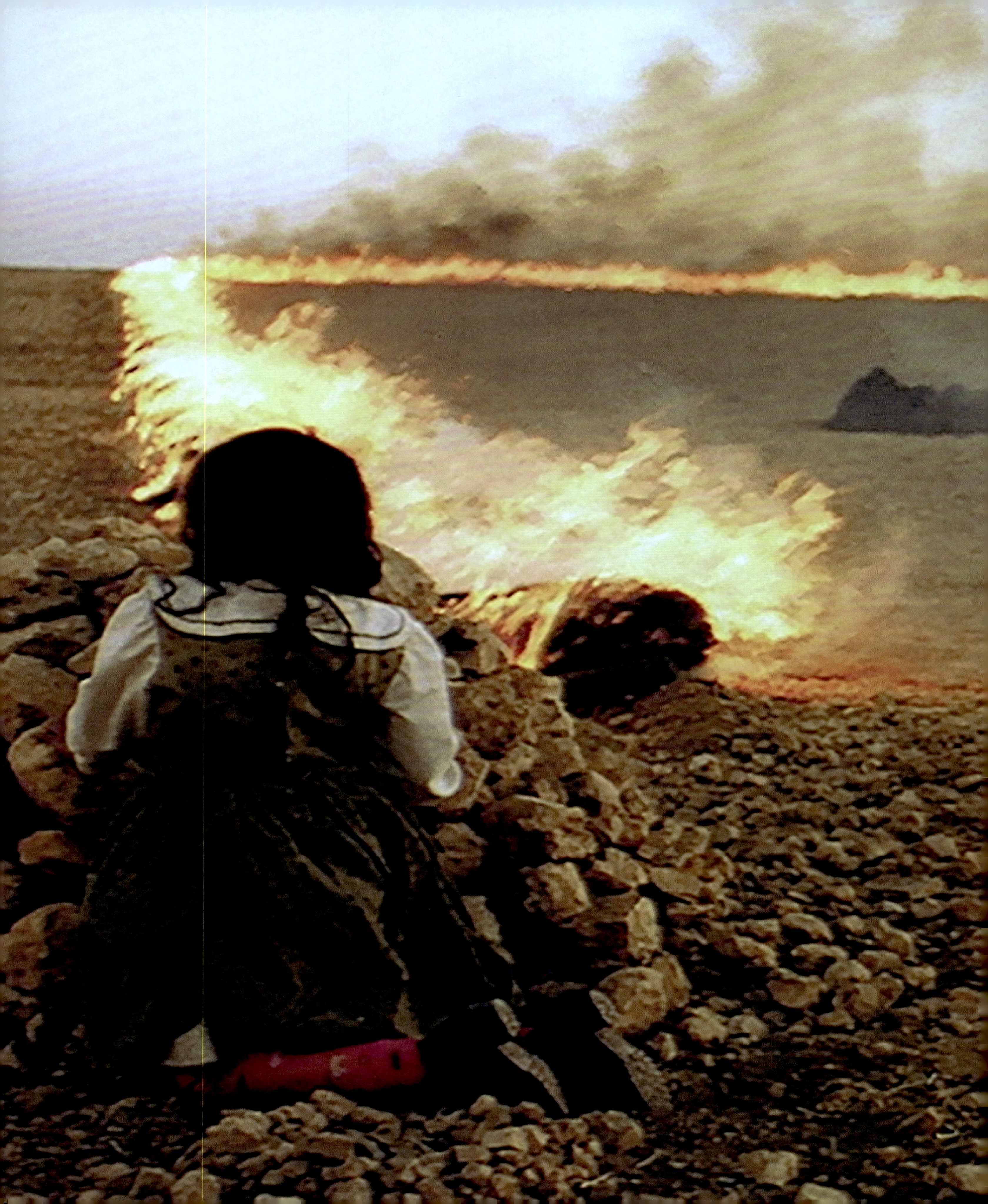

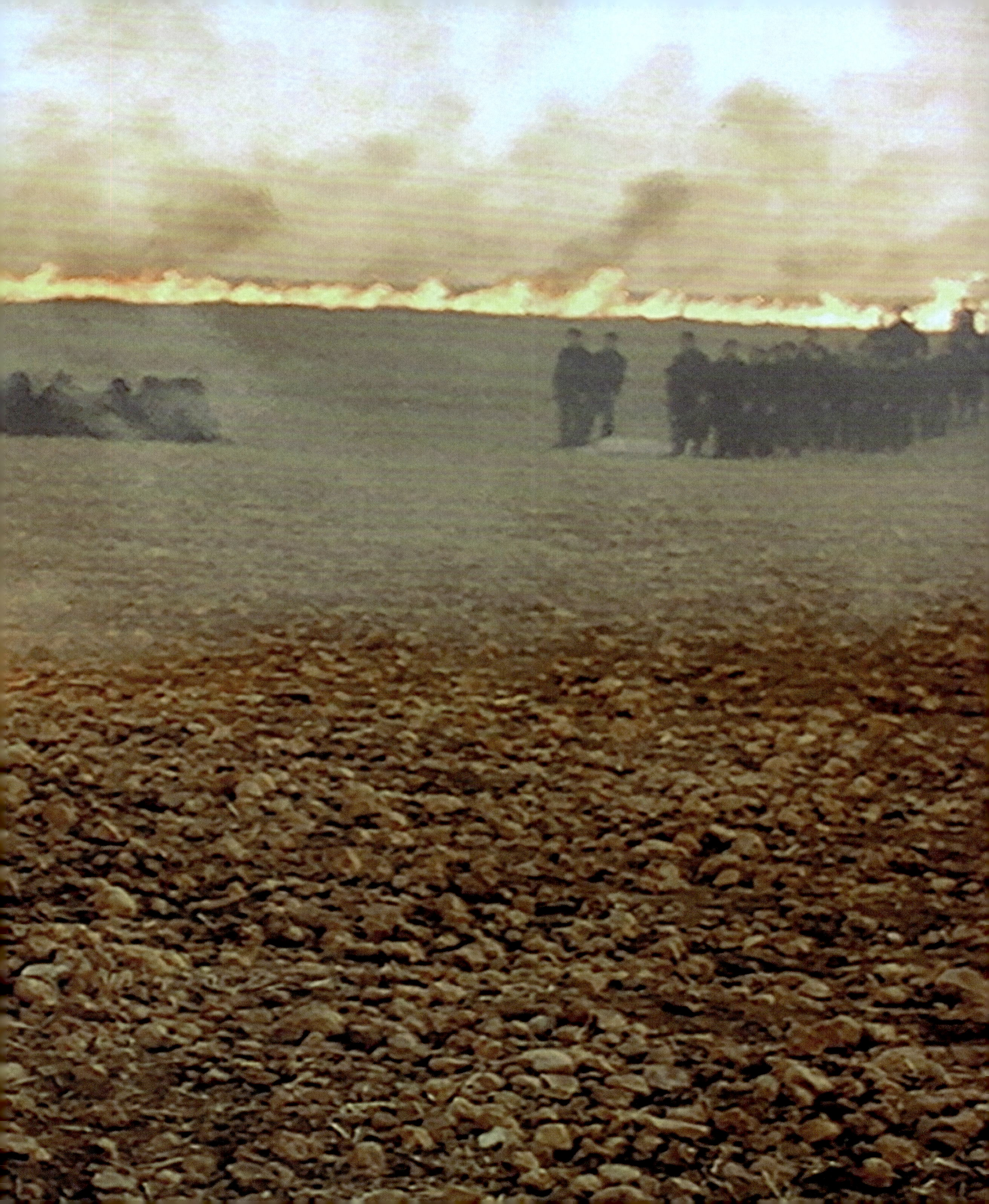

POSSESSED

2001
SINGLE-CHANNEL VIDEO INSTALLATION
16MM AND 35MM BLACK-AND-WHITE FILM TRANSFERRED TO VIDEO
DURATION: 9 MINUTES, 30 SECONDS
FILMED IN MOROCCO

DIRECTOR: SHIRIN NESHAT
IN COLLABORATION WITH: SHOJA AZARI
DIRECTOR OF PHOTOGRAPHY: GHASEM EBRAHIMIAN
MUSIC: SUSSAN DEYHIM
ACTRESS: SHOHREH AGHDASHLOO
LINE PRODUCER: HAMID FARDJAD
ART DIRECTOR: SHAHRAM KARIMI
COSTUME DESIGNER: NOUREDDINE AMIR
PRODUCER: BARBARA GLADSTONE

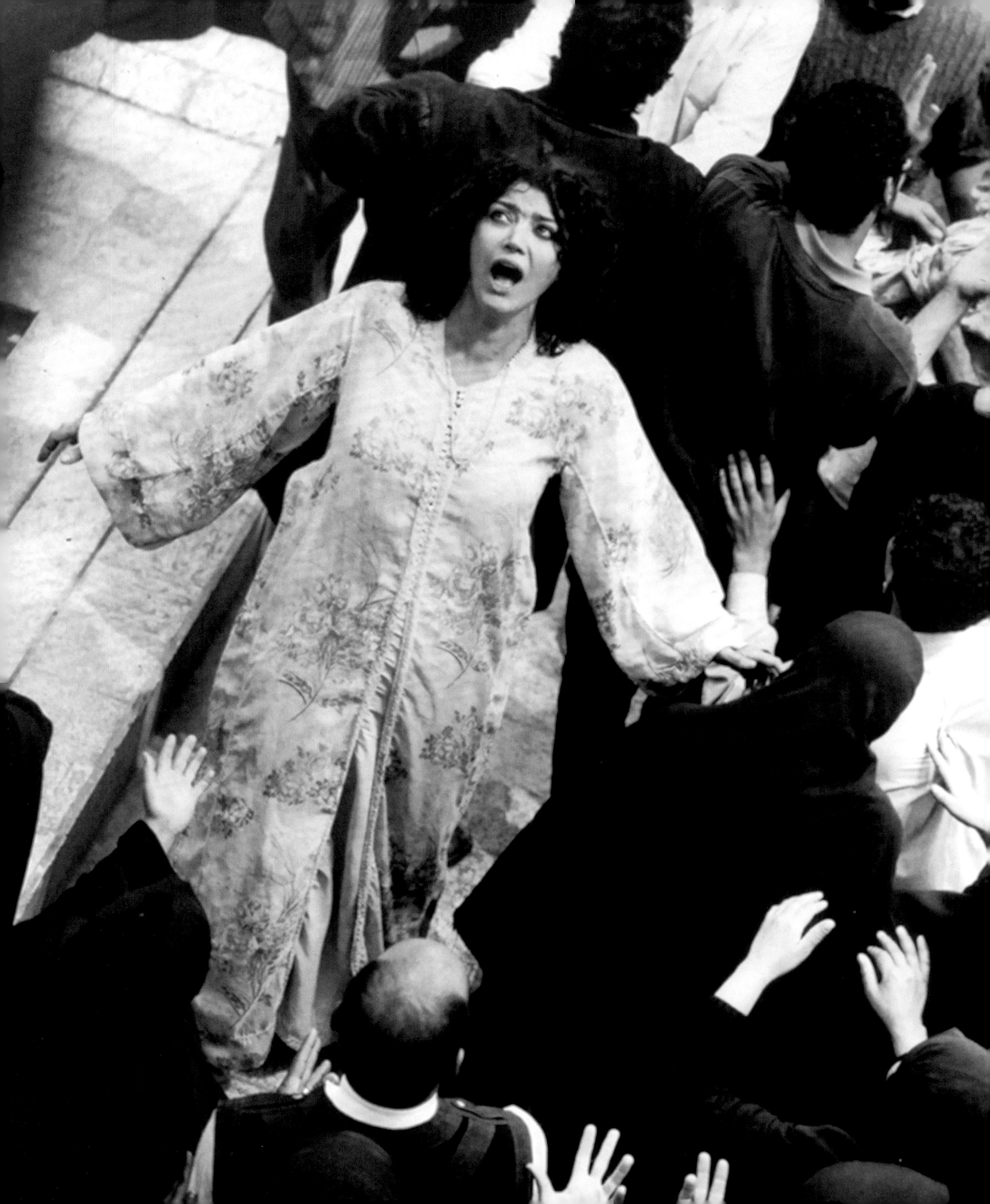

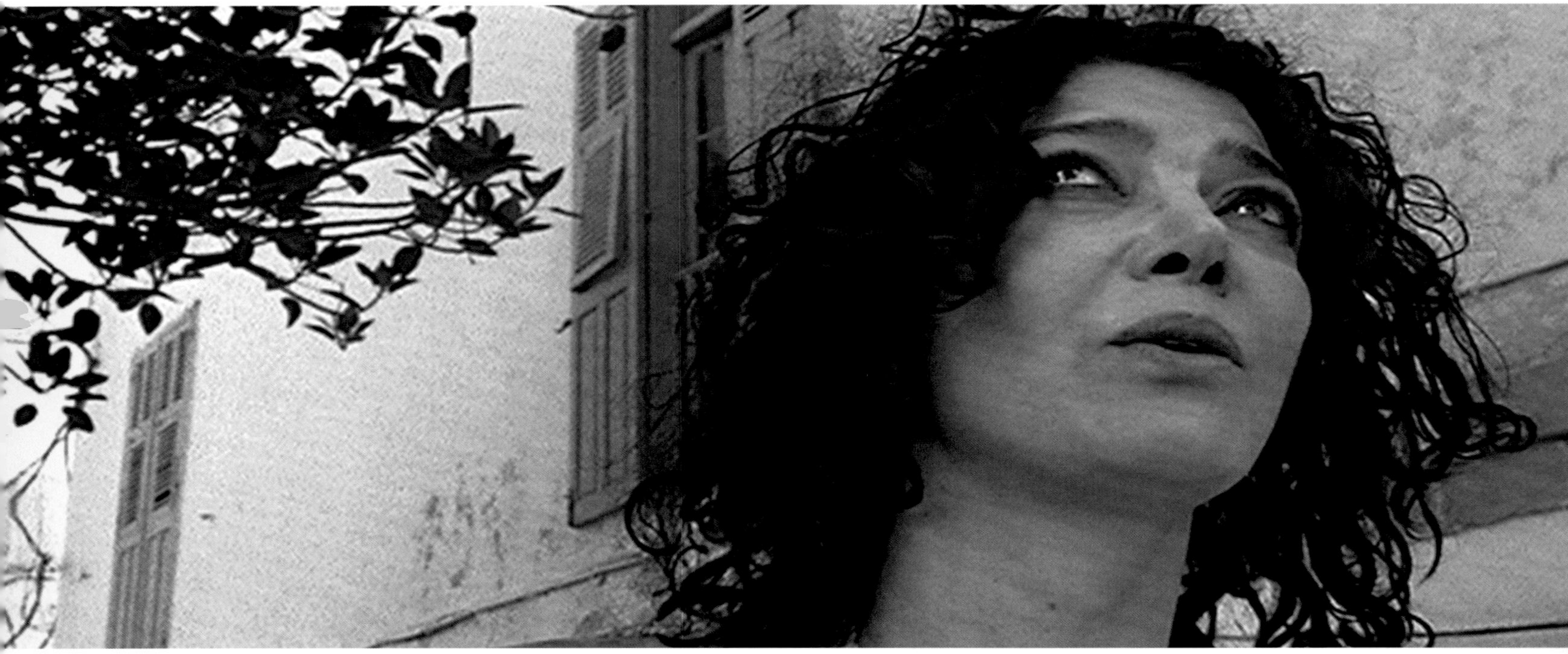

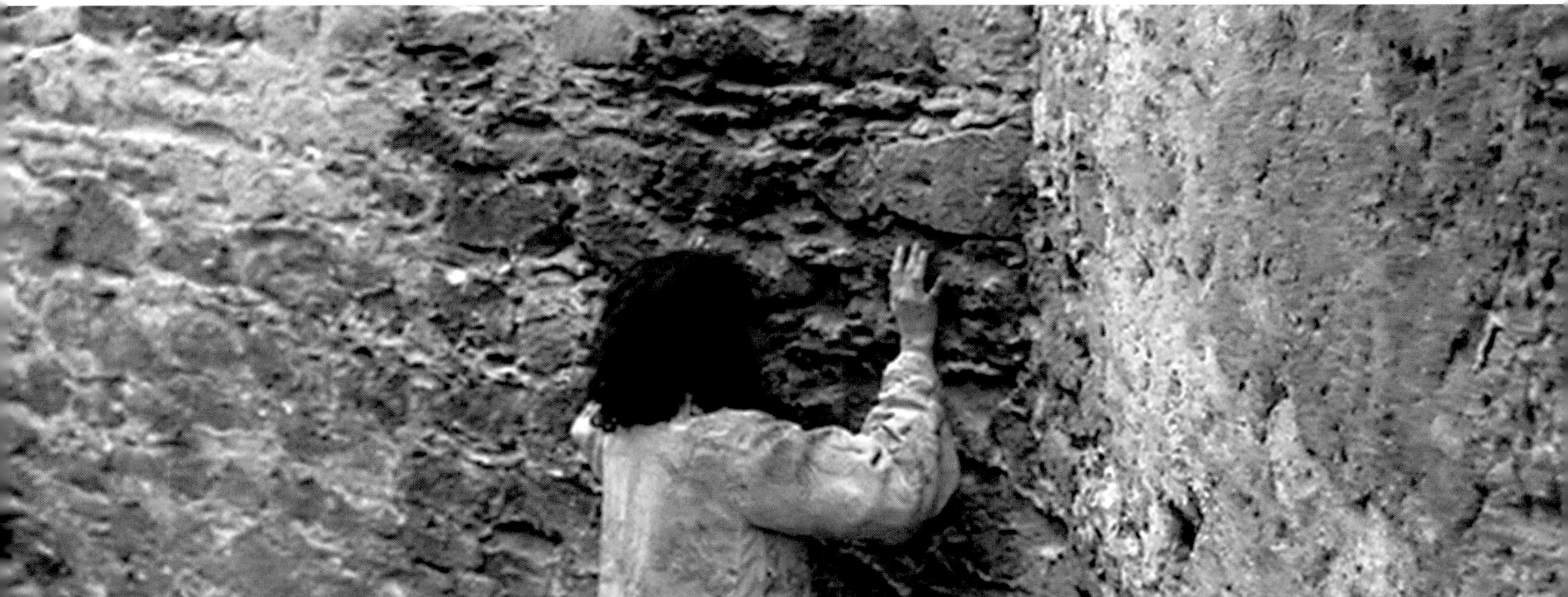

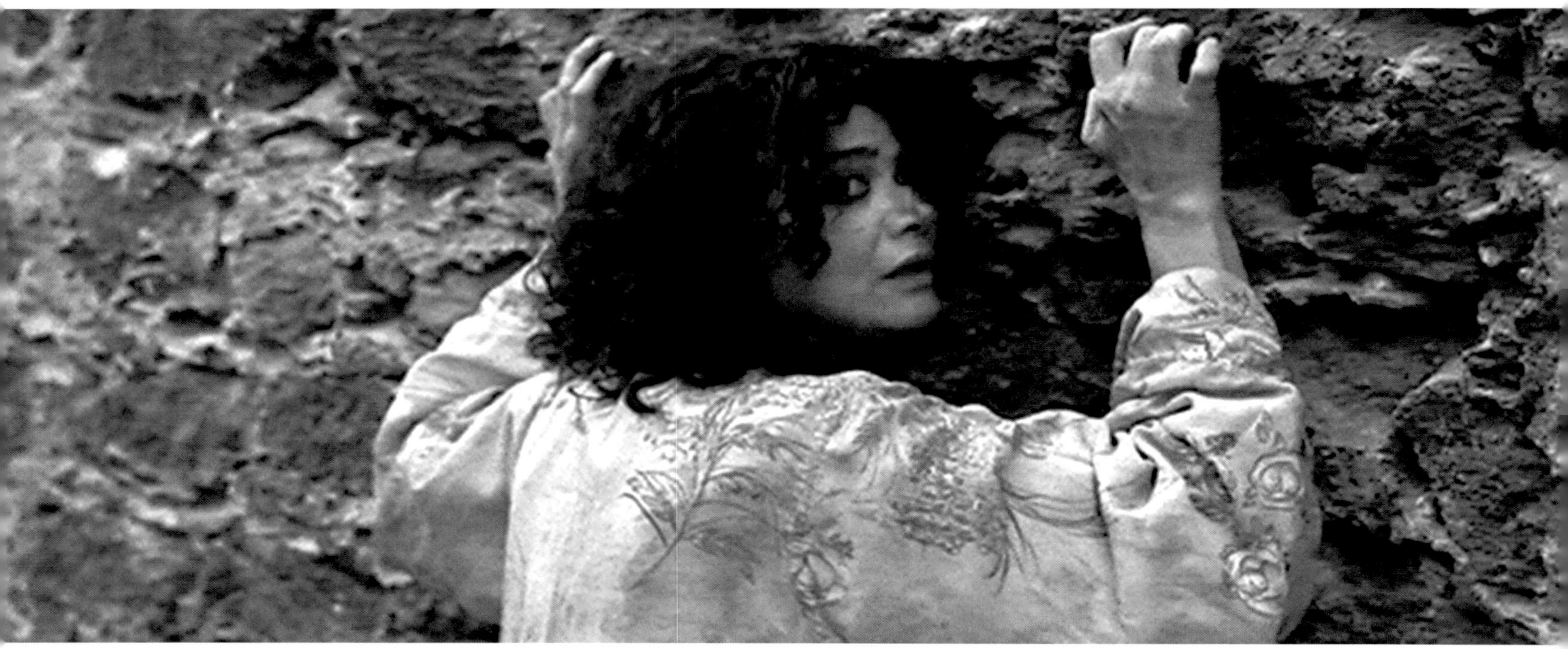

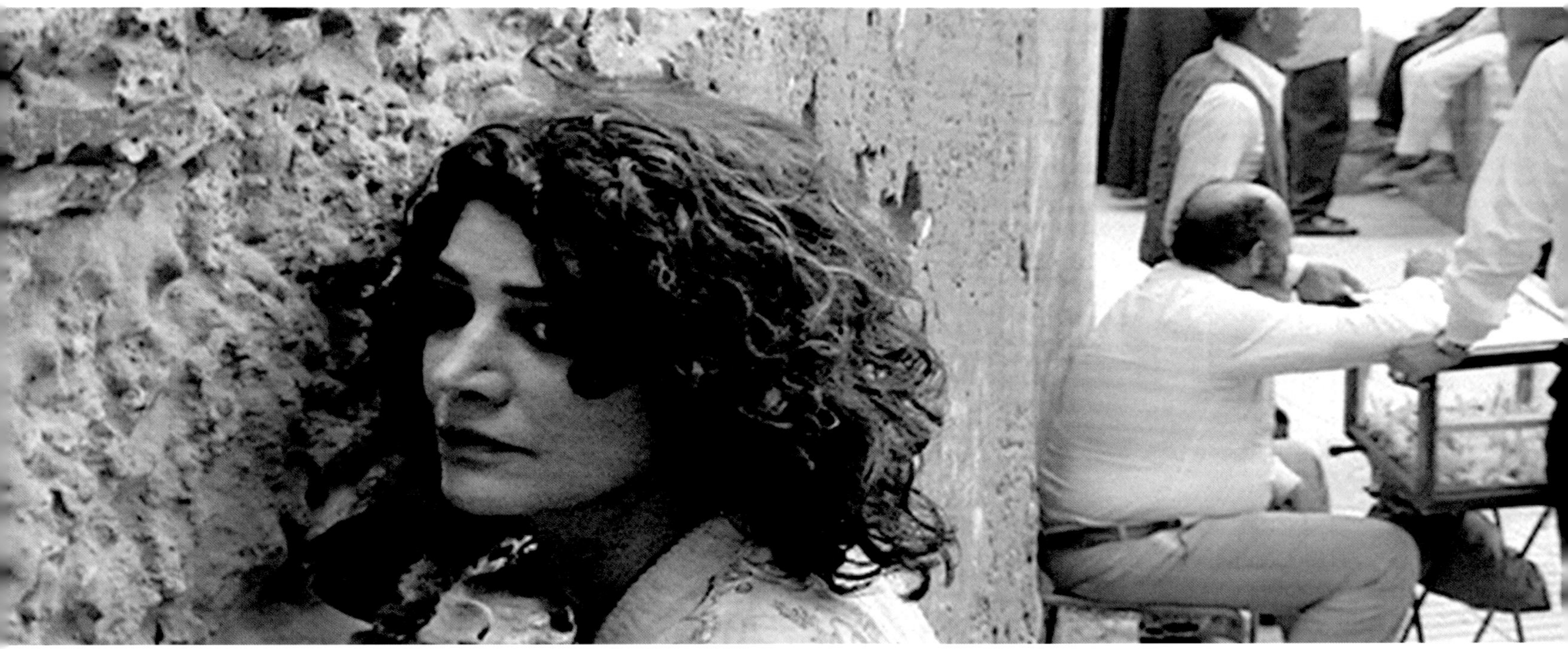

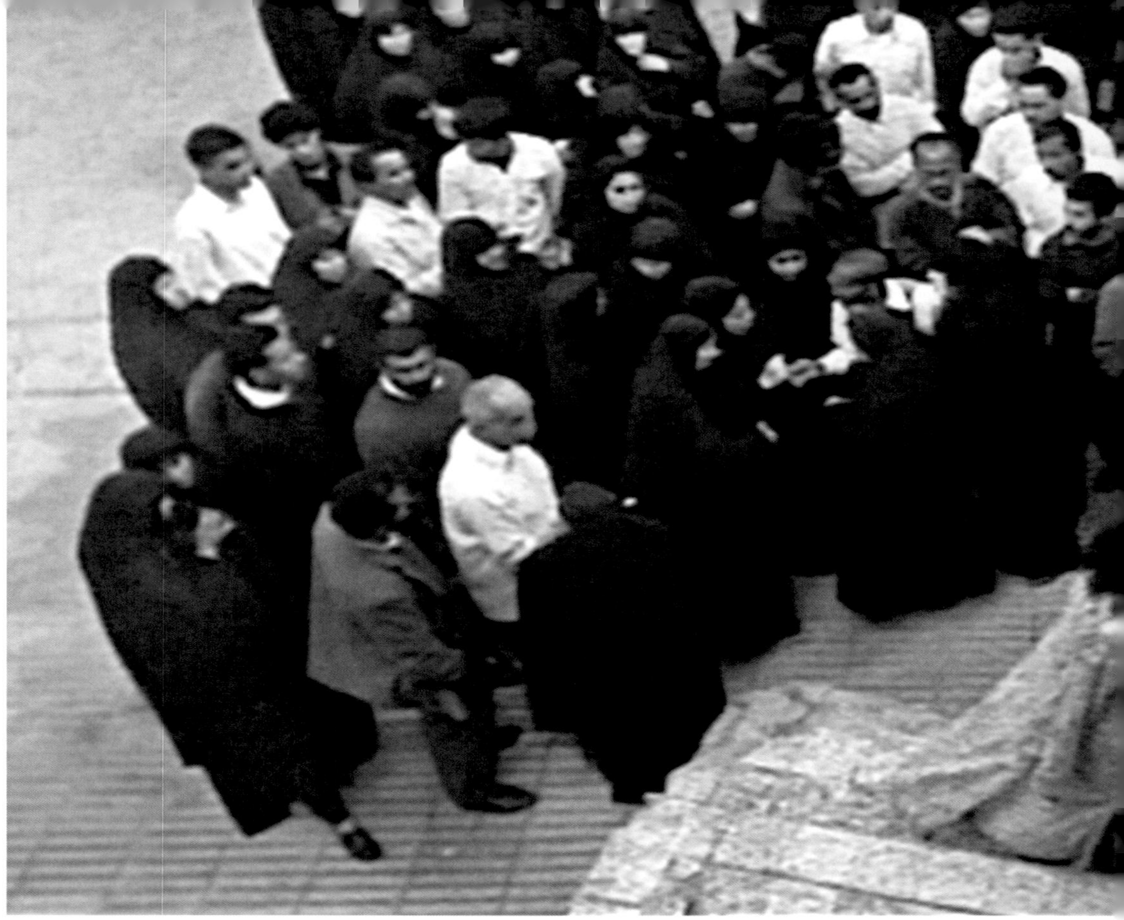

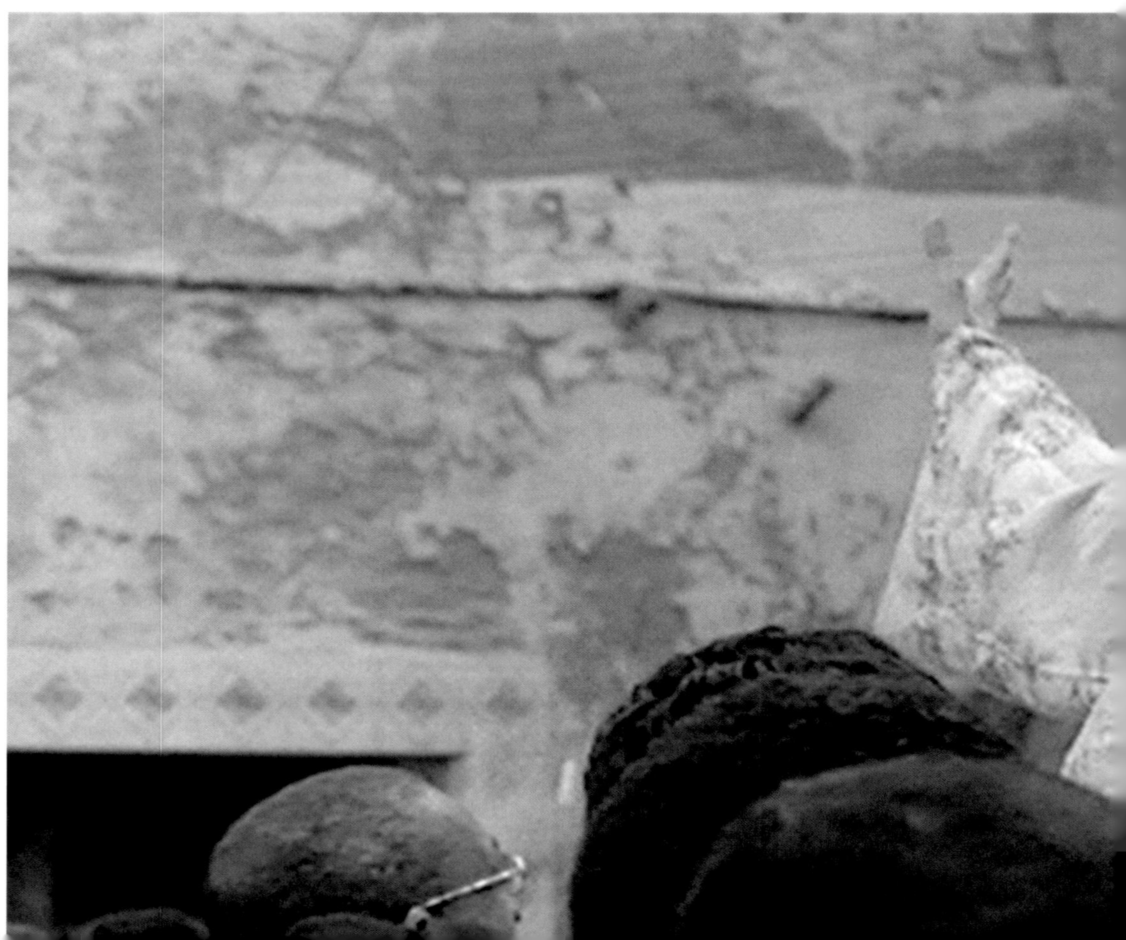

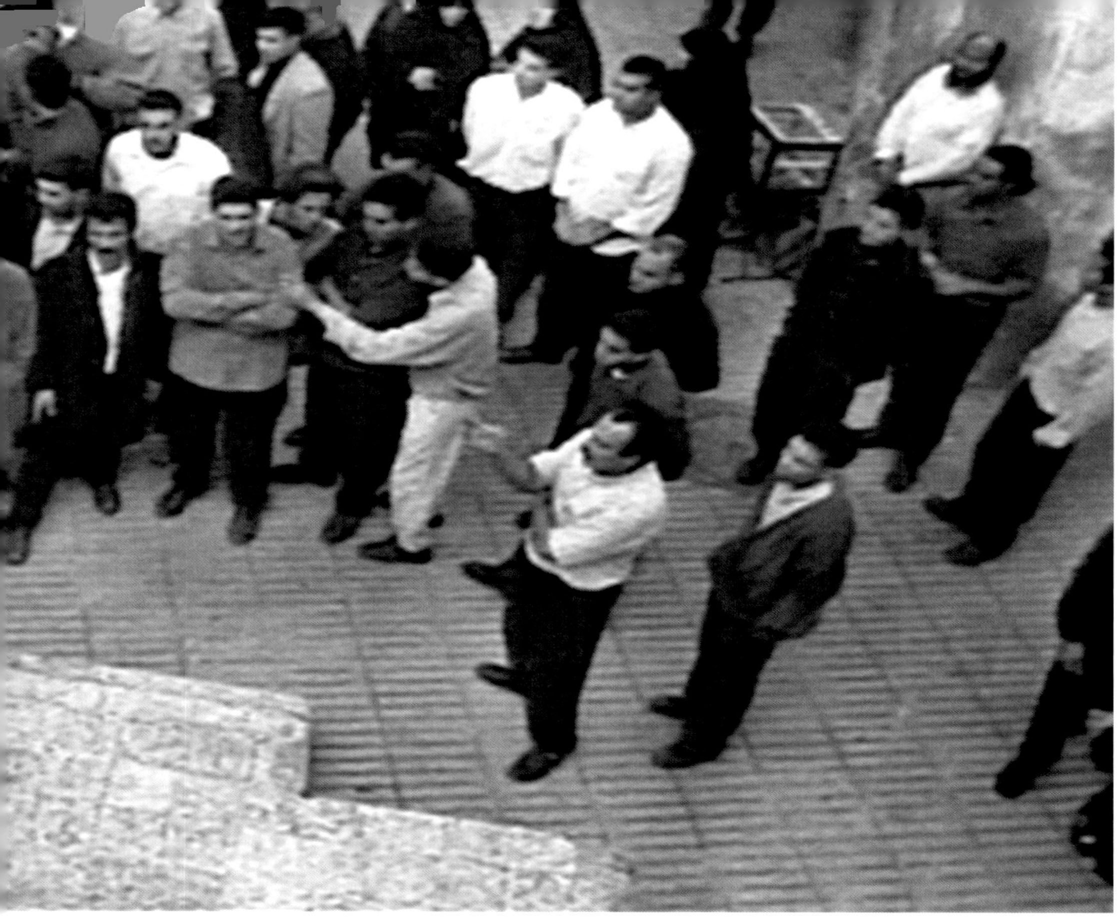

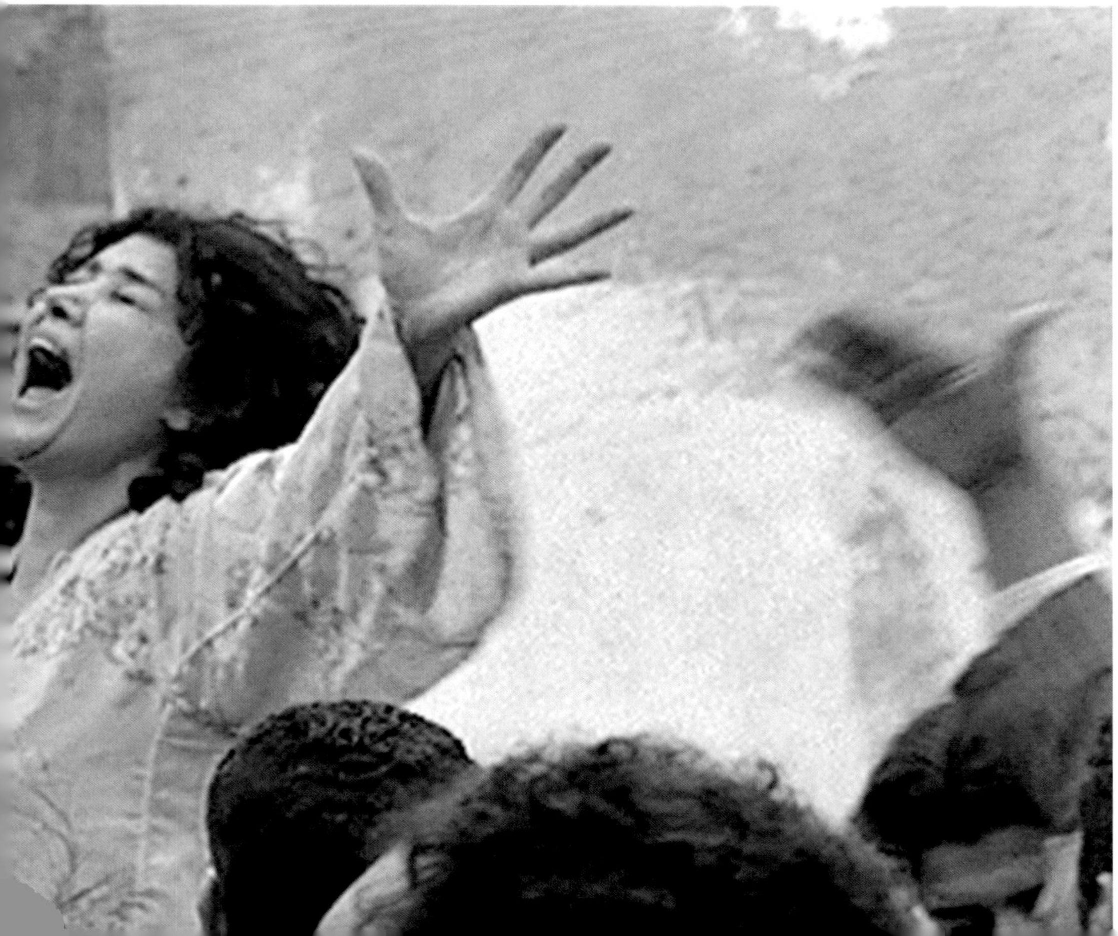

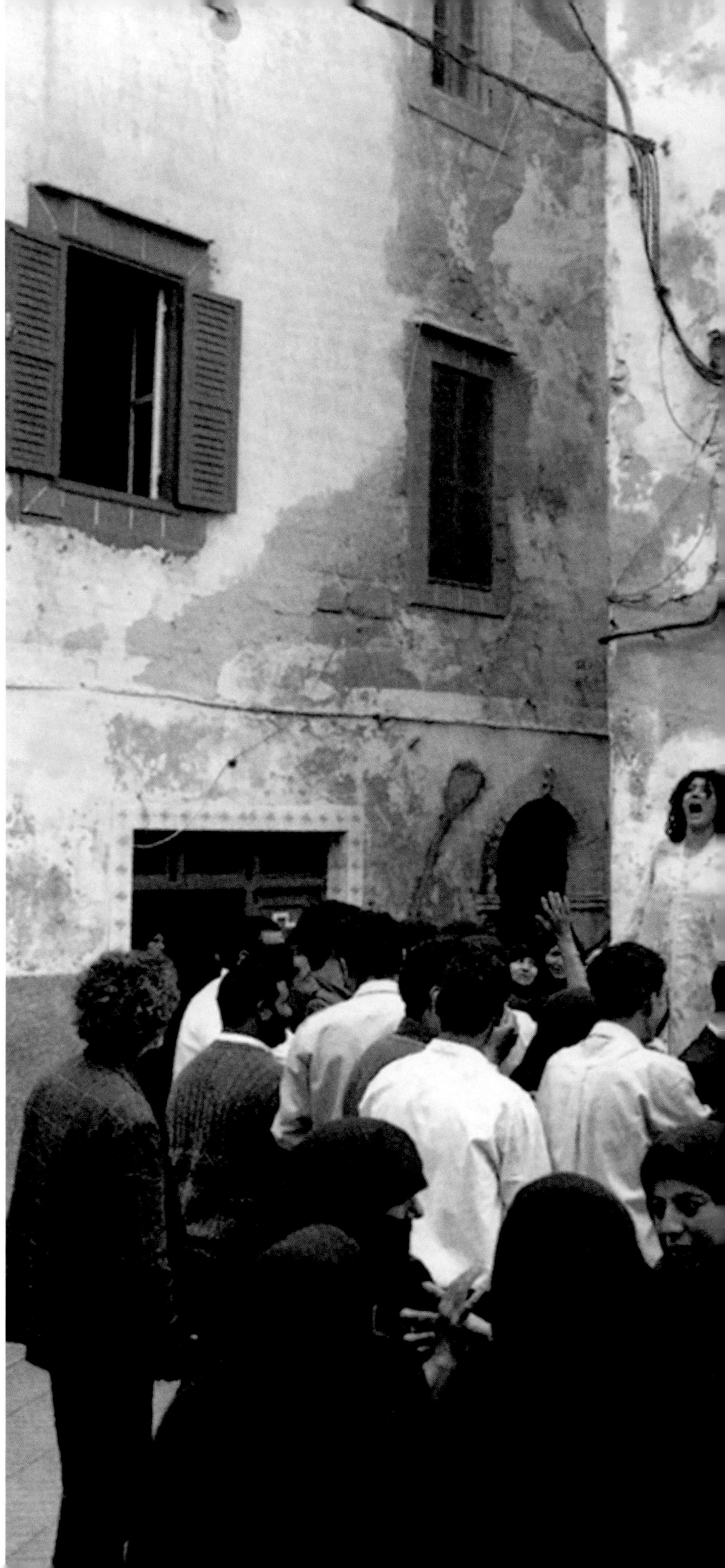

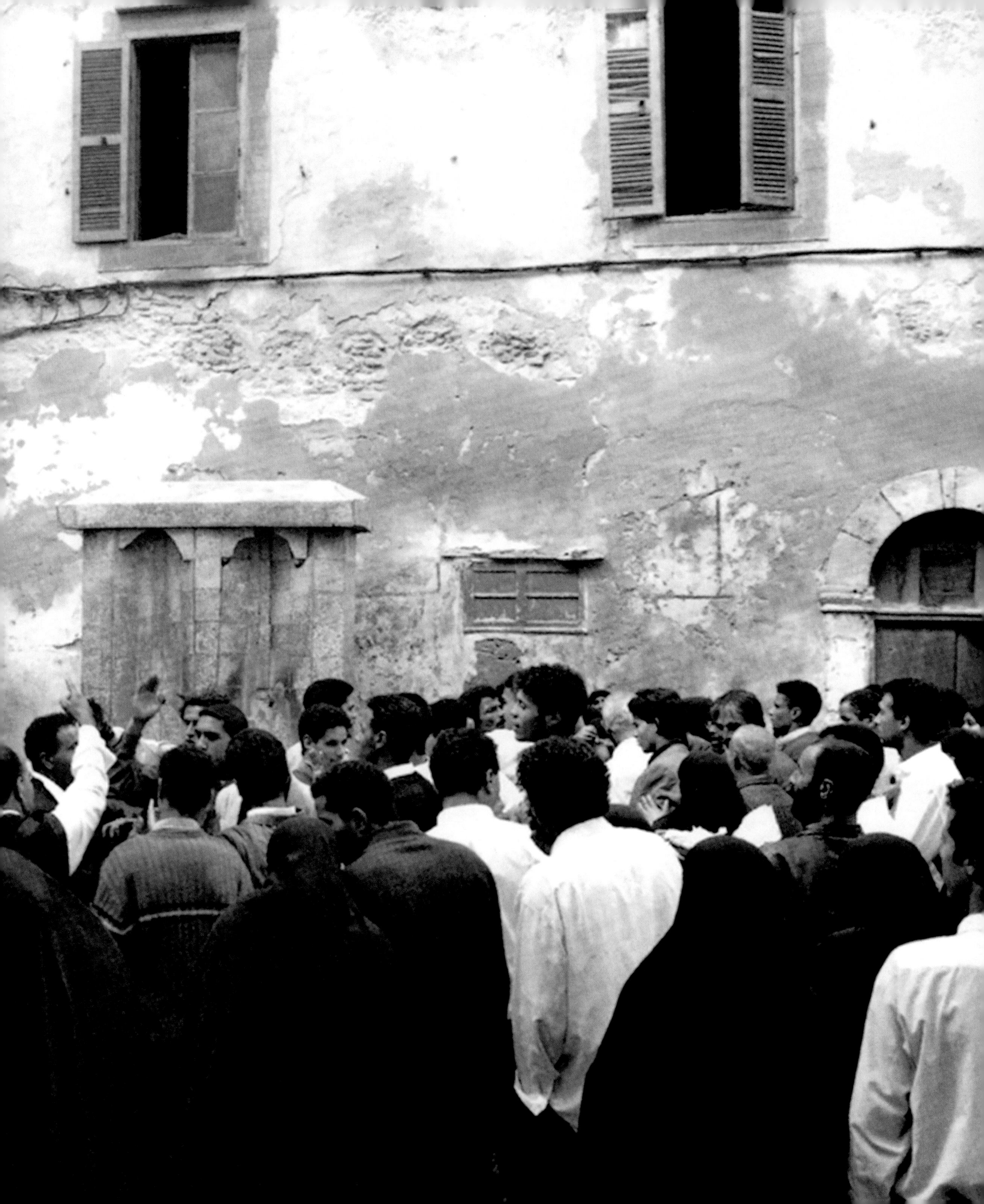

TOOBA

2002
TWO-CHANNEL VIDEO INSTALLATION
35MM COLOR FILM TRANSFERRED TO VIDEO
DURATION: 12 MINUTES, 43 SECONDS
FILMED IN MEXICO

DIRECTOR: SHIRIN NESHAT
IN COLLABORATION WITH: SHOJA AZARI
CAST: MARÍA DE LOS ÁNGELES
DIRECTOR OF PHOTOGRAPHY: DARIUS KHONDJI
MUSIC AND SOUND DESIGN: SUSSAN DEYHIM
PRODUCTION DESIGNER: SHAHRAM KARIMI
EDITOR: SAM NEAVE
PRODUCTION MANAGER/ASSISTANT DIRECTOR: SOL TRYON
LINE PRODUCER: ALICE CHRISTOV-MOORE
PRODUCER: BARBARA GLADSTONE

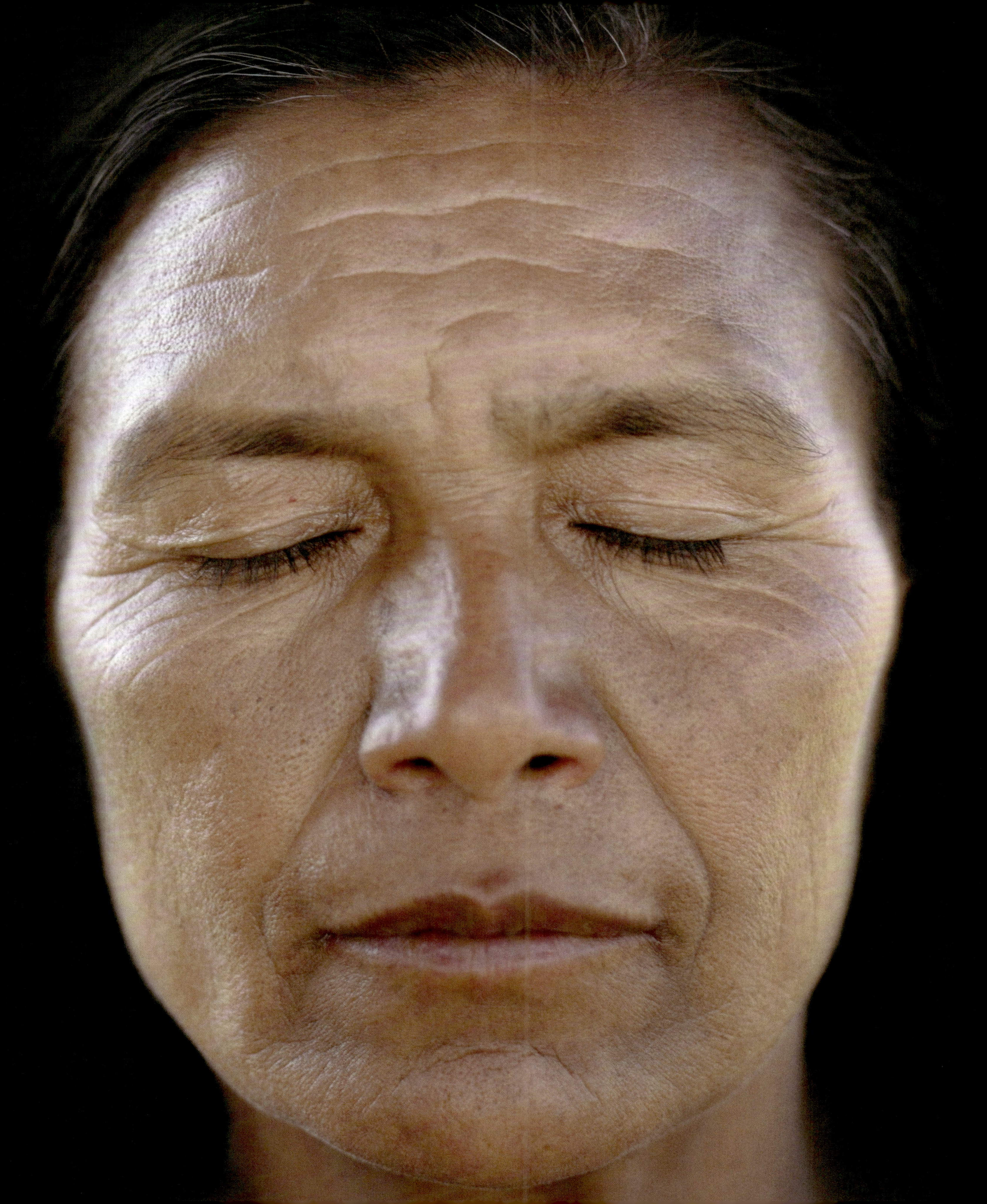

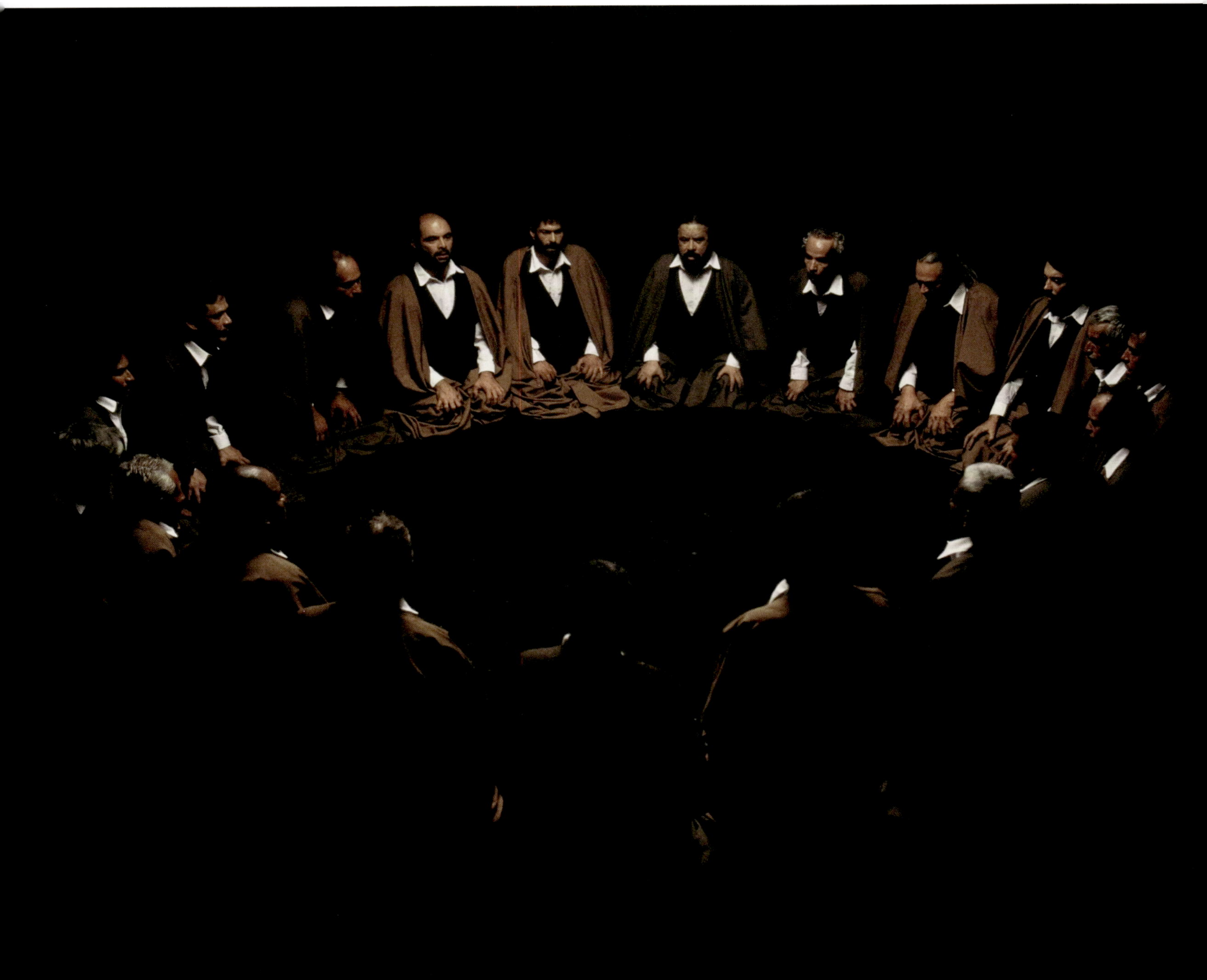

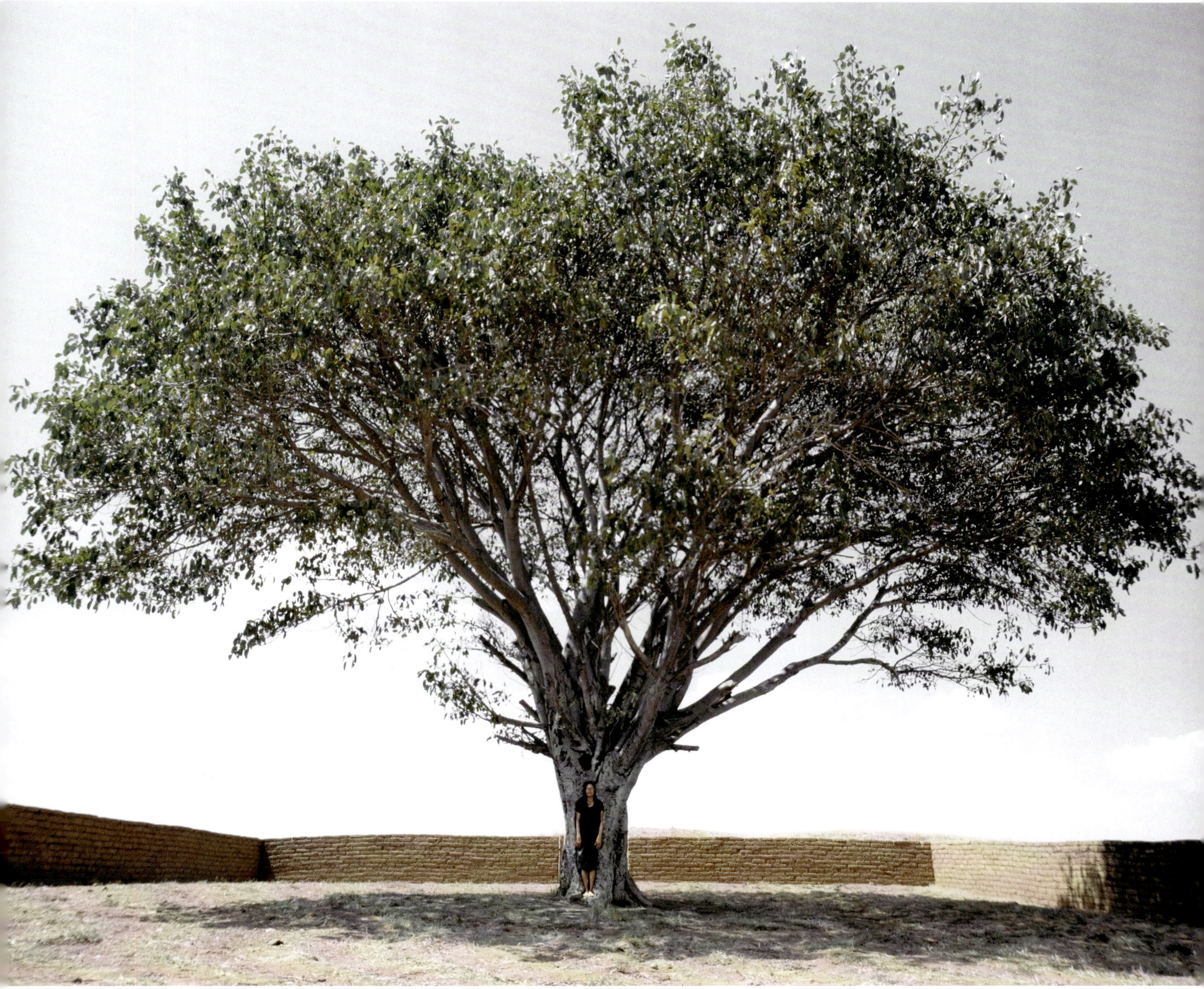

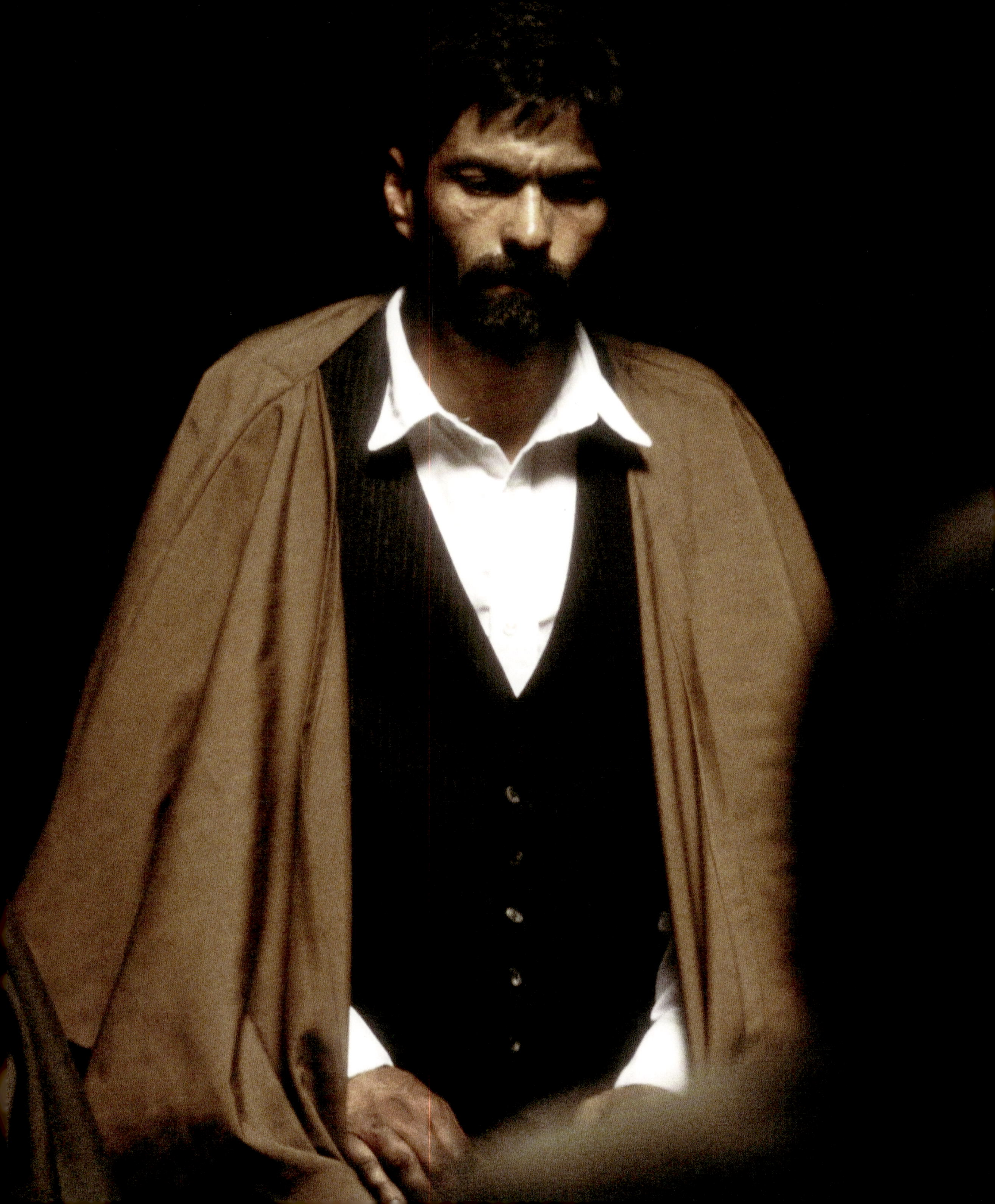

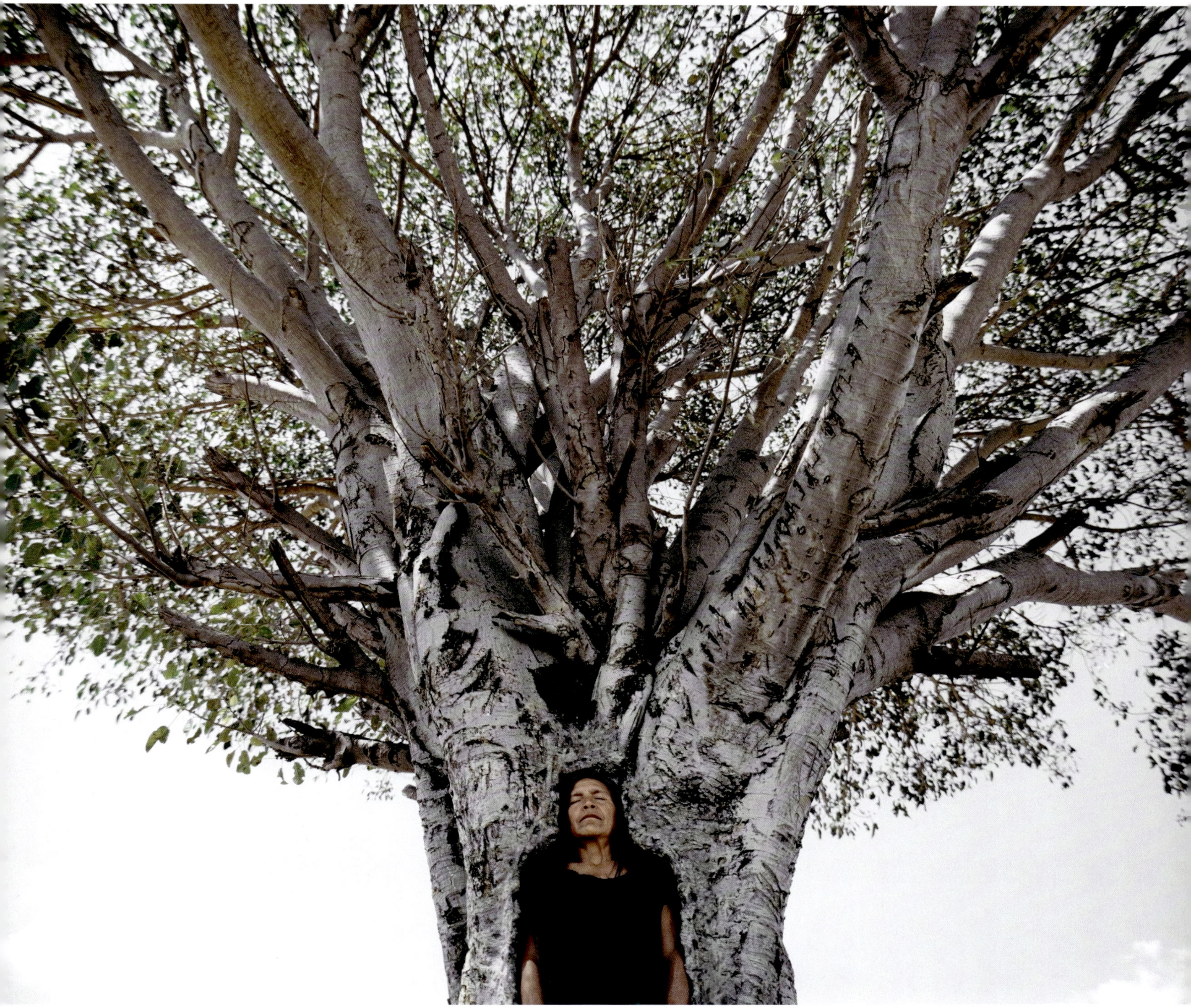

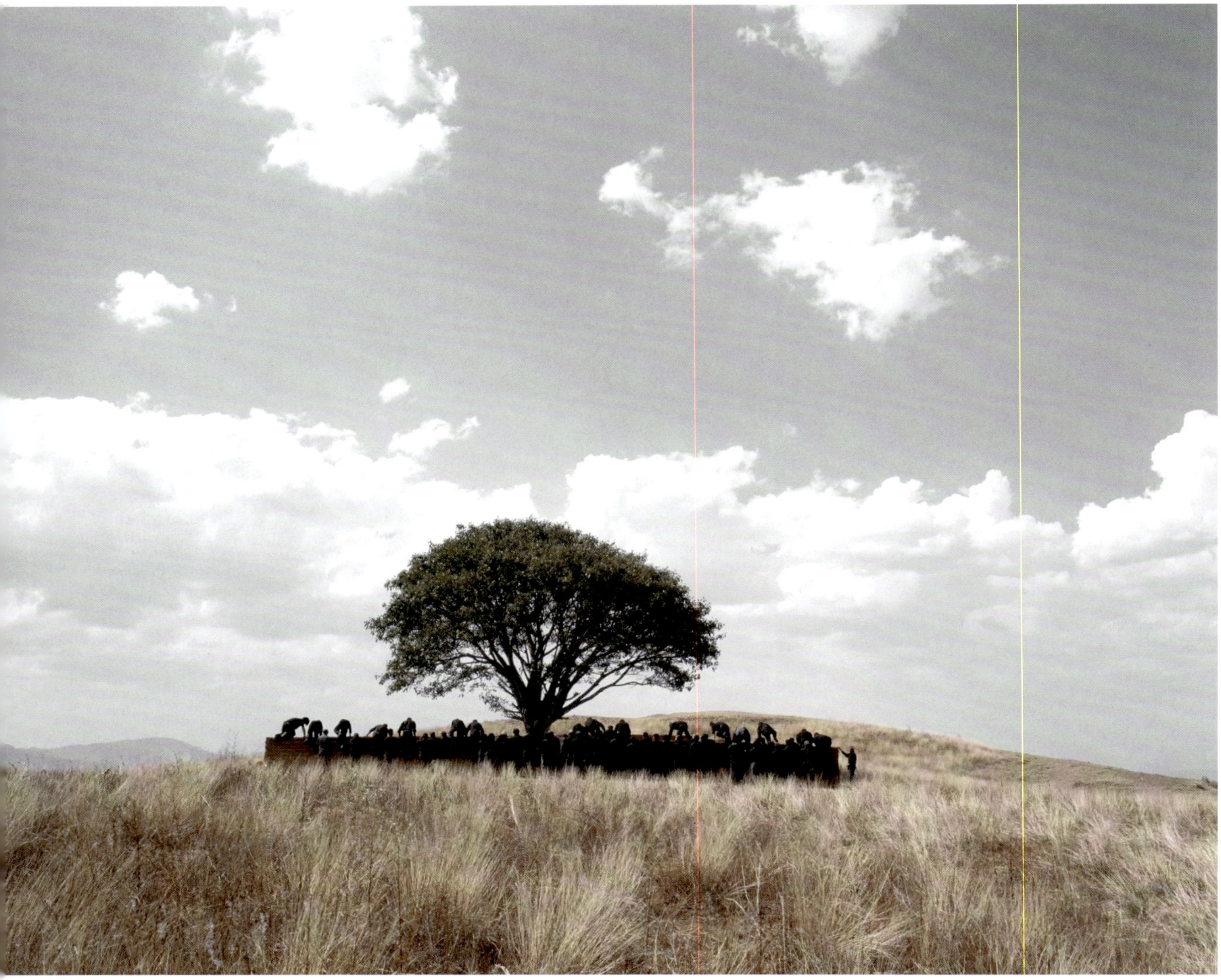

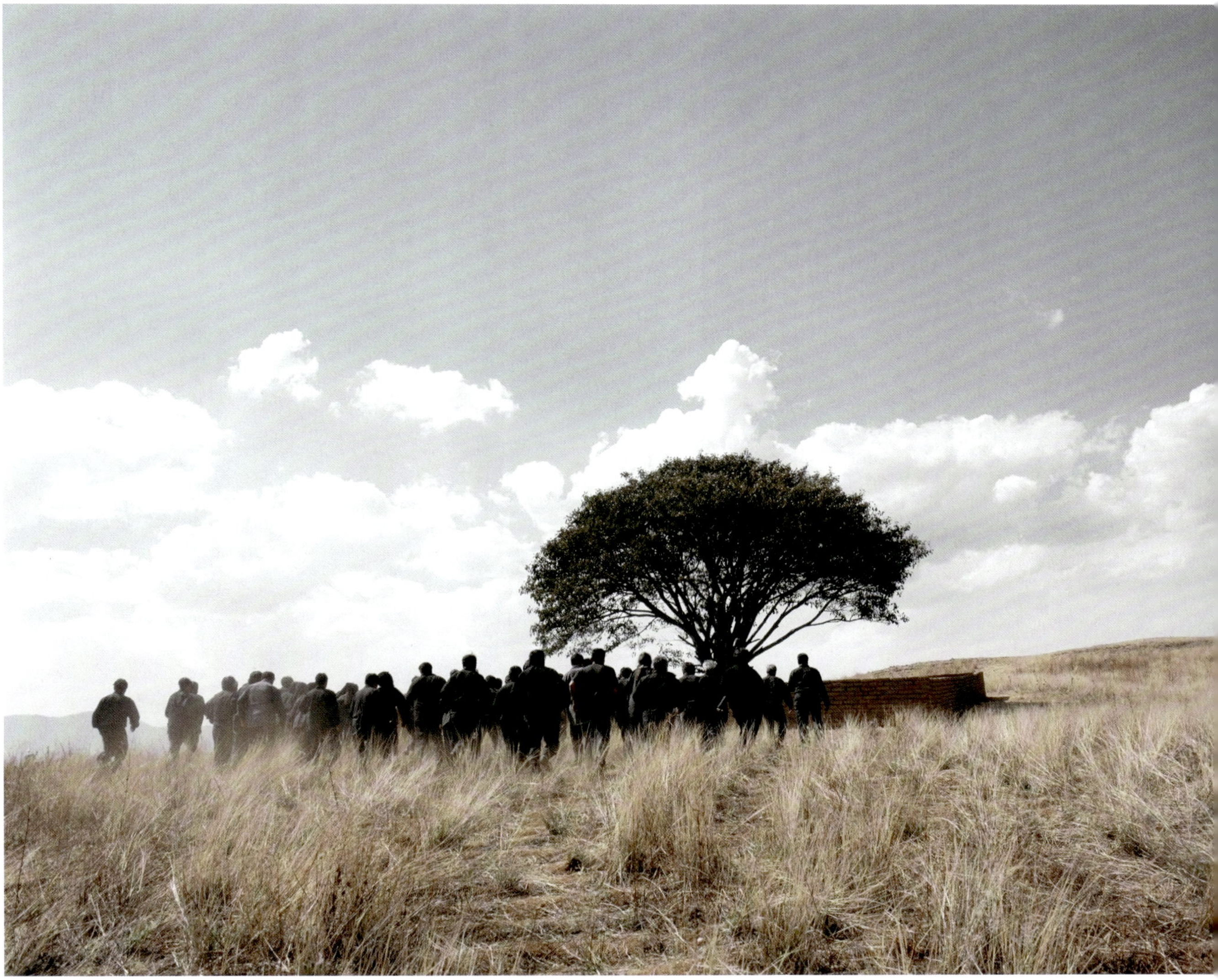

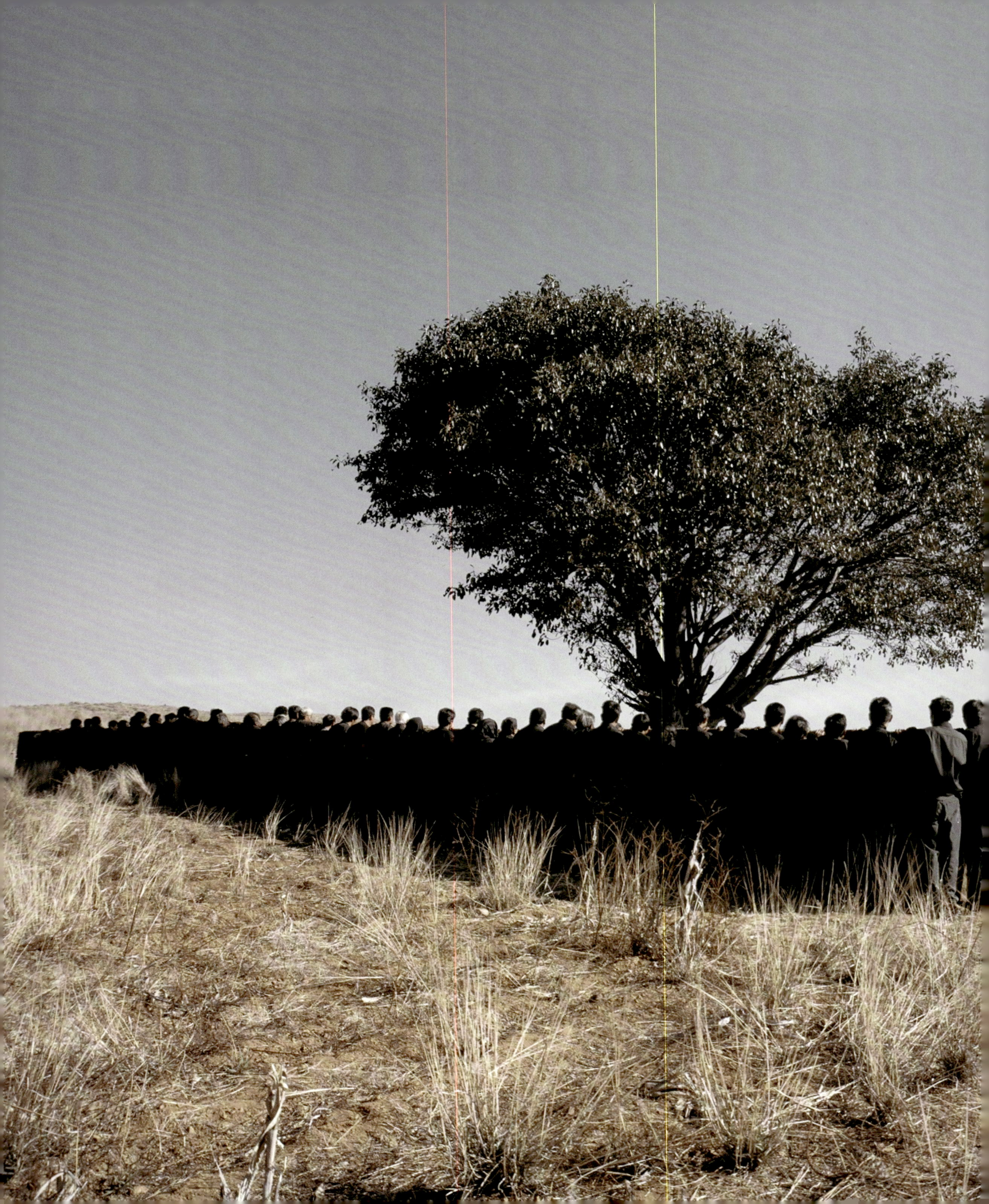

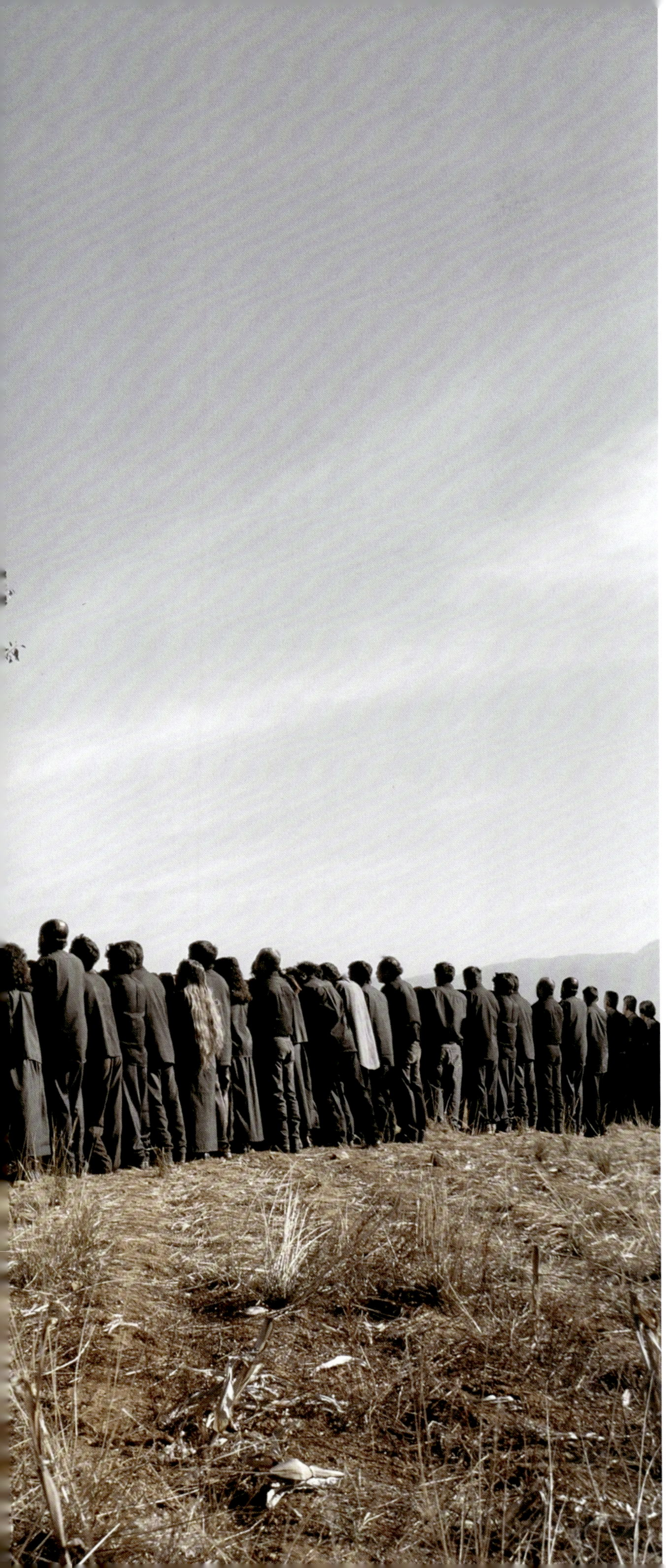

SHIRIN NESHAT: NEW YORK ARTIST

LAYLA S. DIBA

New York has arguably been the epicenter of artistic freedom and creativity for diasporic artists since World War II: from the 1960s through the 1990s, artists such as Ai Wei Wei (in New York City 1983–93) and Yayoi Kusama (in New York City 1957–72) led anonymous creative lives on the edges of the avant-garde on the Lower East Side. Shirin Neshat not only lived in New York at that time, but eventually became an American citizen. When she returned to Iran, it was only for three visits (1991, 1993, 1995), which ended with the artist becoming *persona non grata* there.

By the late 1990s, she rode the waves of feminism, multiculturalism, Conceptual and Minimal art to international art-world acclaim. Her work produced during the 1990s has generally been discussed from postcolonial and Islamic/Iranian cultural perspectives,[1] but over time began to be appreciated for its aesthetic value and universal appeal.[2] However, Neshat was practically unknown in her homeland, where she received conflicting reviews from the Iranian intelligentsia and confounded the authorities. In reality, she was as much a mystery to Iranians as to Americans.

More than forty years have passed since the Iranian revolution and Neshat's early career. It therefore seems appropriate at this juncture to consider the question of her identity as an American, specifically, a New York artist. A new generation of scholars and critics, children of the revolution, have begun to question the labels of "Irano-Islamic" gender and identity applied to her practice.[3]

By imagining her formative years in New York art spaces and think tanks, her reception in galleries and museums of the United States and Europe, and the transformative visits to Iran together, I will argue that a defining feature of Neshat's work of the 1990s is a New York–Tehran axis of creativity. I will then test this theory against what is generally considered the most "Iranian" of her works, the three-part *Women of Allah* series (1992–97). The first two groups, while inspired by the culture shock induced by her return to her homeland, were entirely shot in New York; only the last was actually staged in Tehran (1995). Although the first two parts have been extensively published and exhibited, the group of seven prints in the last series, which will be the focus of my remarks, have remained relatively unknown except to a few initiates.

BECOMING SHIRIN NESHAT: THE NEW YORK ART SCENE REVISITED

Neshat left Iran at the age of seventeen to study in the U.S., graduating in 1983 from the University of California at Berkeley. In the aftermath of the Islamic Revolution in Iran and the American hostage crisis, it was a difficult time to be an émigré of Iranian origin in the United States. For Neshat, it was a period of failure as a painter, isolation, and penury. She could only have had minimal contact with Iran and her family, and probably was not at home with the Iranian diaspora community in California, which was politically conservative and hostile to the new Islamic Republic. Nevertheless, she would have had contact with revolutionary Iran through California television programs and American media images. An Iranian perspective on the revolution would have been provided by her fellow Iranian student Mansoor Ehsan, whose understanding of martyrdom in Islamic Iran would inform much of her early work.[4]

Neshat decided to try her chances in New York and soon became co-director with then-husband Kyong Park of the arts organization Storefront for Art and Architecture, a nonprofit alternative space known for engaging with urban issues such as homelessness and pollution. Other avant-garde (not-for-profit) institutions she collaborated with at that time included Exit Art, Artists Space, Creative Times, and Franklin Furnace, which laid the foundations for her later work with Performa and the Robert Rauschenberg Foundation.

Neshat has described the exciting mix of clubs and alternative spaces and the sense of community among artists in New York.[5] She did not make art for ten years, but rather learned her craft at Storefront and absorbed the ideas coming out of performance and experimental art that were percolating in the downtown arts scene "below Canal."[6] As a rebellious young feminist and activist, she was also committed to humanist causes and social activism, a commitment that has remained with her throughout her career.

This was the era when multiculturalism became fashionable: Neshat remembers the influence of post-colonial cultural historians such as Homi K. Bhabha and the emergence of "nonwhite" artists.[7] At Storefront and Exit Art, she interacted with African American artists such as David Hammons, Kerry James Marshall, and Nari Ward, curator Thelma Golden, and later Lorna Simmons. Commonalities between the experiences of African American and Iranian diaspora artists encouraged Neshat to make art based on her identity as a strong Iranian woman. As Neshat herself has recalled, she did not know of any other Iranian artists doing this, so she felt rather unique.[8]

This was also the era of feminist art, a revolution in which Neshat would play a significant role. She has been recognized for her refusal to be defined or limited by a single ethnic identity.[9] Other ideas she shared with the feminist movement include the use of a female perspective, the female body as a subject, and celebrating female intellectual and emotional power.

After returning from her first visit to Iran, Neshat exhibited new photographic work at two cutting-edge art spaces: Exit Art (1992) and Franklin Furnace (1993). Photography has been described as a gateway medium for women in the arts, and it became the ideal vehicle for Neshat.[10] Archival photos of these installations reveal her awareness of Minimalism and Conceptual art.[11] The stark conceptual photographic portraits that emerged out of the fusion of her New York and Tehran identities were a disturbing blend of figuration, feminism, and text. The pictures questioned the role of Iranian women and the Islamic Revolution. They also invite a reading related to both the appropriation aesthetic of artists of the Pictures Generation such as Cindy Sherman (fig. 1), and the subversive imagery blending image and text of Barbara Kruger and African American feminist photographer Lorna Simpson.[12]

Belonging to the community of New York artists contributed to Neshat's swift rise in the art world, first showing with the Annina Nosei Gallery in 1995 and 1998—largely responsible for crafting her image—and by 2001 joining Barbara Gladstone. Consecrating her status as a major New York visual artist and filmmaker were the presentation of her video *Turbulent* at the Whitney Museum in 1998 and her inclusion in the 2000 Whitney Biennial, arguably the major platform for the most significant postwar American art. As noted in the curators' introduction to the catalogue, this was the most international Biennial ever mounted: the majority of the artists were either immigrants or art nomads, reflecting the global creative center New York had become.[13]

1

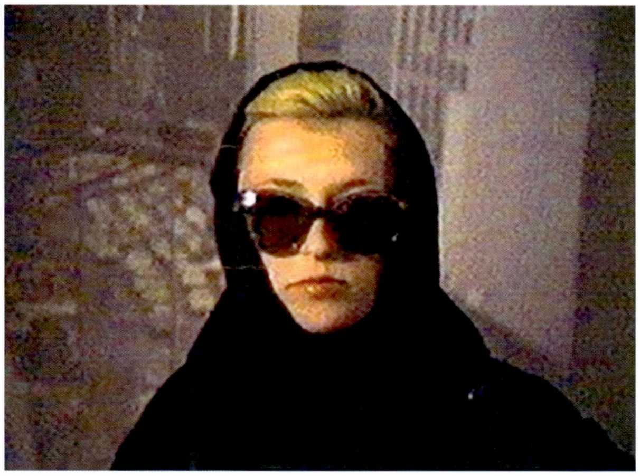

Fig. 1 Cindy Sherman and MICA-TV (Carole Ann Klonarides and Michael Owen), *Cindy Sherman: An Interview*, 1980–81. Video, 10 minutes, 20 seconds, color, sound. Courtesy of Electronic Arts Intermix (EAI), New York

TEHRAN JOURNEYS: DARKNESS AND LIGHT

When Neshat returned to Iran in 1991, it had changed inexorably from the country of her childhood. Iranians were just emerging from the chaos of the Iran-Iraq War (1980–88), with its estimated one million dead martyrs to the revolutionary cause. They were still in the throes of Islamic revolutionary anti-American ideology, and often viewed diasporic artists and intellectuals with suspicion.[14]

All memories of the Pahlavi era had been expunged from the urban landscape and all the street names changed—which must have been a particularly disorienting experience for returning visitors. Women wore the mandatory chador as a sign of allegiance to the new ideology, were separated from men in most public spaces, and forbidden to perform on the stage. Many Iranians—especially the former bourgeoisie—lived schizophrenic social lives, following Islamic mores in public and Westernized lifestyles in private.

The streets were lined with gigantic political murals depicting incidents of the Iran-Iraq War and portraying the leaders of the revolution in a "macho" hybrid style mixing surrealism with Mexican revolutionary social realism. The imagery was highly patriarchal, although women had been very visible in the revolutionary cause, especially in the media.[15]

By 1991, the country was encouraging exiles to return. Neshat was driven by a strong sense of nostalgia to reconnect with her family and to understand the Islamic Revolution. Reflecting on her formative years in the freedom of downtown New York, she recalls the jarring experience on this first visit to Iran of having to don the veil and adapt to an ideological culture foreign to her.[16] However, the darkness of Iranian society would be illuminated for Neshat by rediscovering her country, seeing its shrines, gardens, countryside, and bazaars, and searching for popular art forms inscribed with texts such as amulets and rugs. Her interactions were private, as for most of the returning exiles, meeting with family members and friends among the intelligentsia. Unlike New York, there was little or no avant-garde art scene. She rediscovered her homeland's great women poets and writers, but did not engage with artists, most of whom had emigrated.[17]

Yet the photographers, graphic artists, and filmmakers who *had* stayed, such as Abbas Kiarostami, flourished and were to influence the formal and intellectual concerns of Neshat's work. By her third visit, she was looking for a collaborator to photograph images of her male and female family members and friends in a studio setting. The photojournalist Kaveh Golestan introduced her to Bahman Jalali and his wife Rana Javadi: all three were celebrated for their images of the brutal Iran-Iraq War but were also moving in new directions as artists, teachers, and writers.

Jalali had discovered Iranian photography of the late Qajar era (1785–1925), an age balanced between modernity and tradition and defined by its Westernized, hybrid court culture. He collected old albums and studio materials and established the Museum of Photography in Tehran (the Akskhaneh Shahr), published a journal, and hosted students, including the future art photographer Shadi Ghadirian.

Photography had been introduced to Iran in 1842 and was immediately adopted by the Qajar court. Thousands of albums and glass plates were kept in the Golestan Palace Museum library but were largely inaccessible to the public. The royal albums featured official court photographs as well as private images of the harem taken by the ruler, mainly in the palace studio. Jalali, however, collected unusual "unofficial" photographs of court jesters, women, and marginalized figures from the end of the Qajar era and early twentieth century, an alternative history to the earlier, official narrative.[18]

The rediscovery of Qajar photography occurred in tandem with intellectual discourses current since the late Pahlavi era on Western influence and the search for an authentic Iranian identity.[19] In the realm of visual culture, this took the form of promoting

2

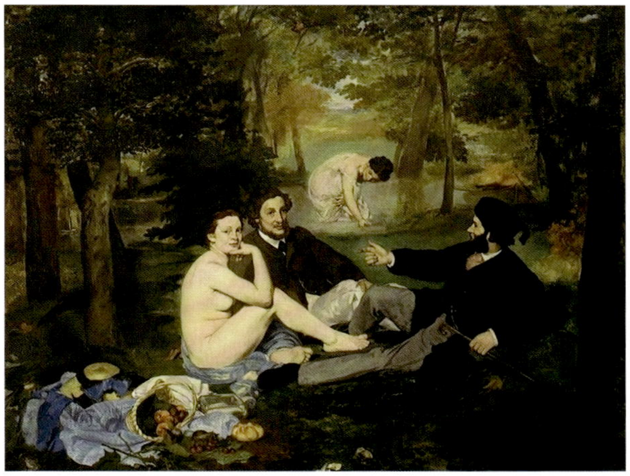

3

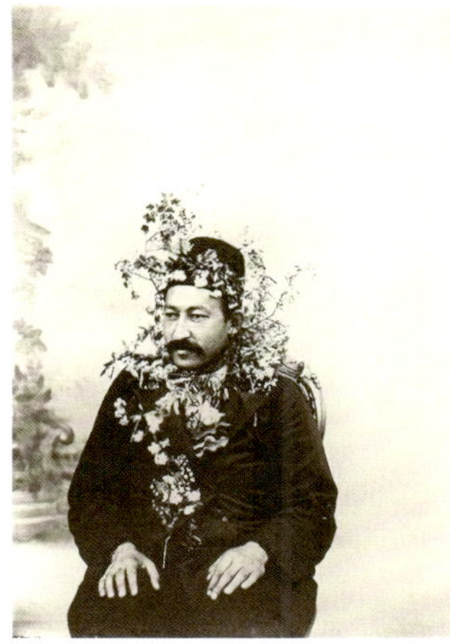

calligraphy, popular art forms, and nineteenth- and early twentieth-century Iranian photography. Paradoxically, contemporary Iranian and French intellectuals perceived Iranian photography as "pure art" untouched by Orientalism or colonialism, contrary to its perception as a "hybrid" form in the West.[20]

Jalali shared his discoveries with Neshat, who was excited by the surrealistic and stylized images she encountered and which she probably understood as authentically Iranian. After examining the photographs amid numerous discussions together, Jalali selected the props—primarily original painted nineteenth-century backdrops of European-style gardens and garden architecture—and took the photographs, while Neshat staged the compositions. Yet the vision is entirely hers: Neshat remembers thinking about people picnicking in gardens as an art-historical theme, most specifically Manet's *Dejeuner sur l'herbe* (fig. 2), which depicted a group of two nude women with clothed male companions—a scandalous painting when shown at the Salon des Refusés in Paris in 1863 and still provocative today.[21]

THE GARDEN PICTURES

The *Women of Allah* series ends with four prints of large massed groups of female family members and three prints of Neshat alone or with one or two women enframed by ivy wreaths, foregrounding the borrowed studio backdrops (pp. 50, 52–53).[22] Two themes are developed simultaneously in multilayered compositions infused with a minimalist aesthetic: the idea of the garden and the relationship between the past and the present.

In the first group of this last series, the flat, black, almost abstract mass in the foreground contrasts with the atmospheric, grayish backdrop of floral decorative forms. Observing the strictures of Islamic dress, only the faces, hands, and feet of Neshat's subjects are visible (p. 50). The facial expressions of the women are impassive and questioning—portals to their inner thoughts. Their melancholy gaze evokes the many paradoxes of what has been termed modern Islamic culture. Indeed, Neshat's visit coincided with Iranians beginning to negotiate a new "modern" identity situated between Islamic fundamentalism and the West. The chador these women wear is that of the modern Iranian woman—not that of the women of the Qajar era—and is intended to contrast with the Western-style garden imagery of the Qajar era.[23] Past and present do not overlap, yet they exist in the same space.

Neshat develops these ideas further in the second group: whether returning to the self-portrait or group images, the sitters are posed with floral wreaths, both grasping them with their hands and encircled by them (pp. 52, 53). Although the floral motif does refer to the columns in the backdrop

Fig. 2 Édouard Manet, *Déjeuner sur l'herbe*, 1863. Oil on canvas, 82 x 104 inches (208 x 264.5 cm). Musée d'Orsay, Paris (RF 1668)

Fig. 3 Unidentified photographer, *Courtier with floral wreath*, late 19th–early 20th century. Albumen print. From Catherine David and Hamid Dabashi, *Bahman Jalali* (Barcelona: Fundació Antoni Tàpies, 2007), p. 50

4

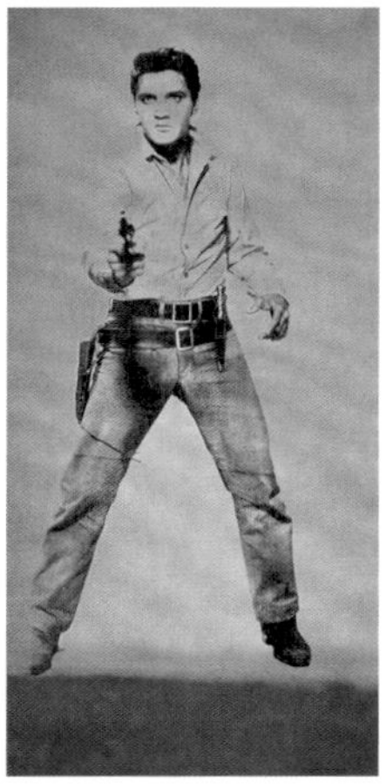

entwined with flowering bushes, there is convincing evidence that Iranian sitters were portrayed in similar guise by local nineteenth-century photographers (fig. 3).[24] The whole group subtly yet probingly questions the Iranian adoption and fascination with Western technologies, represented by the photographic backdrop and Western aesthetic preferences in the form of the ivy wreaths encircling the subjects, possibly referencing the seduction of Western culture. Neshat asks how the modern Islamic woman relates to Iran's Westernized hybrid past.

Looking from the perspective of the tripartite *Women of Allah* series, one sees constant experimentation and a definite evolution as the work moves from New York to Tehran: in the third group, the gun imagery and writing are noticeably absent, and the gaze is no longer quite so direct and confrontational nor the poses so insistently frontal.

In the first two series, Neshat was working in the open, experimental atmosphere of Soho. She was concerned with creating iconic, monumental images investigating the idea of body and female sexuality and intellect within the boundaries of Islamic culture. Her imagery is drawn from pop culture, from both American and Iranian media. Her American visual references include Andy Warhol's images of death and celebrity (fig. 4), artists of the Picture Generation as previously discussed, and possibly an awareness of the oppositional gaze of African American film and art criticism.[25]

In the prints staged in the more restrictive atmosphere of the Tehran studio, Neshat's voice is more modulated, and the main interest has shifted from contemporary politics to reflections on the passage of time and how "the iconography and look" of women had changed. Situating the garden series in the Tehran context, the pictures are unlike anything being produced at the time in Iran, and they presage by a few years the work of a generation of photographers and artists who would draw their main inspiration from Qajar imagery.[26] Shadi Ghadirian's *Qajar Series* (1998–2001) was received to great acclaim abroad, as was Bahman Jalali's *Image of Imagination* series (2000–2008). Ghadirian's women are costumed in Qajar clothing in a Qajar studio setting interspersed with Western consumer items. The images are ironic and playful. Neshat's women wear the modern uniform of the Islamic chador, and the images are serious and questioning. Jalali superimposes contrasting imagery and texts to create an imaginary world, whereas Neshat clearly separates the two. Neither Ghadirian nor Jalali is concerned with the artistic debates of Western art critics or the history of Western art, concerns so apparent in Neshat's practice.

In conclusion, it is hard to imagine Neshat's critical stance without her formative years in New York, and by comparing her work with Iranian contemporaries, we question just how "Iranian" her early works are. Imagined in America and staged in Iran, the garden pictures, which were almost never shown,[27] can now be read as significant transitional works to her later video and film production, where she moved from black-and-white to color and from the local to the universal: the garden theme with its references to the paradise of Islam, which makes its first appearance here, will reverberate throughout her later work as the sanctuaries and refuges of *Tooba* (2002, p. 114) and *Women without Men* (2009).

Layla S. Diba is an independent scholar and curator of nineteenth-century and modern Iranian art.

Fig. 4 Andy Warhol, *Single Elvis [Ferus Type]*, 1963. The Eli and Edythe Broad Collection

NOTES

Acknowledgments: I wish to express my profound gratitude to Shirin Neshat, Laurence Kardish, Brooke Kamin Rapaport, Bee Medinger, and Pei Si Chao for their assistance in the preparation of this essay.

1 Hamid Dabashi, "The Gun and the Gaze: Shirin Neshat's Photography," and Octavio Zaya, "Bounds of Desire, Zones of Contention (Islam, Women and the Veil)," in *Shirin Neshat: Women of Allah* (Turin: Marco Noire Editore, 1997), n.p.; Iftikhar Dadi, "Shirin Neshat's Photographs as Postcolonial Allegories," *Signs* 34, no. 1 (Autumn 2008), pp. 125–50; Sussan Babaie, "Voices of Authority: Locating the 'Modern' in 'Islamic' Arts," *Getty Research Journal*, no. 3 (2011), pp. 137–38; Layla S. Diba, "Shirin Neshat's Visual Poetics: Translation, Authorship and the Creative Process," in *Shirin Neshat: The Home of My Eyes in Venice Museo Correr* (Cologne: Walther König, 2017), pp. 36–43.

2 Arthur C. Danto, "Shirin Neshat's Rapture," in *The Madonna of the Future* (New York: Farrar, Straus & Giroux, 2000), p. 404; "An Excerpt from a Conversation Between Shirin Neshat and Octavio Zaya," in *Shirin Neshat: Women of Allah*, pp. 11–15; Jerry Saltz, "New Channels," *The Village Voice*, January 5, 1999.

3 Amna Malik, "Dialogues Between 'Orientalism' and Modernism in Shirin Neshat's 'Women of Allah,'" in *Global and Local Art Histories*, ed. Celine Jeffery and Gregory Minissale (Newcastle-upon-Tyne: Cambridge Scholars Publishing, 2007), pp. 145–69; Shahrzad Ehya, "Facing Up to Shirin Neshat's *Women of Allah*," PhD diss., University of California, Berkeley, 2012. For a similar view of writers of Iranian origin as "world writers," see Persis Karim, "Writing Beyond Iran: Reinvention and the Exilic Iranian Writer," *World Literature Today* 89, no. 2 (March 2015), pp. 35–37.

4 As discussed in Ed Schad's essay in this volume, pp. 19–20, Ehsan would later write a doctoral dissertation on the concept of martyrdom in Iran.

5 Laurence Kardish, interview with Layla Diba, March 20, 2019, discussed Neshat's acceptance in the avant-garde arts community and invitations to residencies such as at famed retreat Camp Kippy in Maine.

6 Arthur C. Danto, "Shirin Neshat," *Bomb*, no. 73 (Fall 2000), at https://bombmagazine.org/articles/shirin-neshat/.

7 Shirin Neshat, interview with the author, March 18, 2019.

8 Ibid.

9 Linda Nochlin, "Foreword," in *After the Revolution: Women Who Transformed Contemporary Art*, 2d ed. (New York: Prestel, 2013), pp. 7–27.

10 Eleanor Heartney, "Shirin Neshat: Living between Cultures," in *After the Revolution*, pp. 248–71.

11 Ehya, "Facing Up to Shirin Neshat's Women of Allah," pp. 14, 34, 42, and related illustrations.

12 Affinities with Simpson's work are particularly convincing. See Malik, "Dialogues Between 'Orientalism' and Modernism," pp. 148–49.

13 Maxwell Lincoln Anderson et al., *Whitney Biennial* (New York: Abrams, 2000), p. 29.

14 Neshat, interview with the author, March 18, 2019. One of Iran's most prominent artists has only been shown twice in the Tehran Museum of Contemporary Art, in 2000 and 2002, during the directorship of Alireza Sami-Azar, where her work was enthusiastically received by audiences. She was also asked to write a letter of explanation or apology about her work if she wanted to continue to show in Iran, which she refused to do. See also Ed Schad's essay for the final Kafkaesque episode of Neshat's encounter with the Iranian authorities, p. 21.

15 Rose Issa and Ruyin Pakbaz, *Iranian Contemporary Art* (London: Barbican Art, 2001), pp. 23–25; Talinn Grigor, *Contemporary Iranian Art: From the Street to the Studio* (London: Reaktion Books, 2014), pp. 33, 41–91; Azar Nafisi, *Reading Lolita in Tehran: A Memoir in Books* (New York: Random House, 2003), passim; Peter J. Chelkowski and Hamid Dabashi, *Staging a Revolution: The Art of Persuasion in the Islamic Republic of Iran* (London: Booth-Clibborn Editions, 2000), pp. 88–125; Lila Azam Zanganeh, ed., *My Sister, Guard Your Veil; My Brother, Guard Your Eyes: Uncensored Iranian Voices* (Boston: Beacon Press, 2008), especially a moving interview with Neshat about her memories of the family farm and growing up in a garden, p. 49.

16 Lina Bertucci, "Shirin Neshat: Eastern Values," *Flash Art* 30 (November–December 1997), pp. 86–87.

17 Her visits predated the era of official government support for the arts in the late 1990s, which led to the return of Iranian modernists and the emergence of a vibrant contemporary painting and sculpture scene. Grigor, *Contemporary Iranian Art*, pp. 120–24.

18 Layla S. Diba, "Towards an Alternative Art History: Qajar Photography and Contemporary Iranian Art," Louvre-Lens, forthcoming. For surveys of Qajar and early twentieth-century photography, see a special issue of *History of Photography* 37, no. 1 (February 2013), pp. 126–33, and Muhammad ibn Ali Mishkat al-Mulk et al., *Visible Treasure* (Tehran: Cultural Research Bureau, Cultural Heritage Association, 1998), passim; Parisa Damandan, *Portrait Photographs from Isfahan: Faces in Transition, 1920–1950* (London: Saqi, 2004), passim, a work written by Iranian scholars based entirely on local sources and archives which particularly impressed Neshat.

19 For a discussion of the theoreticians Ali Shariati and Jalal al-e Ahmad, see Chelkowski and Dabashi, *Staging a Revolution*, pp. 90–91; also Dariush Shayegan, "Regained Aura," in *Bahman Jalali* (Cologne: Walther König, 2011), p. 235; and Danto, "Shirin Neshat," for her thoughts on this question.

20 Diba, "Towards an Alternative Art History," forthcoming. For discussions on hybridity and purity, see Frederick N. Bohrer, ed., *Sevruguin and the Persian Image: Photographs of Iran, 1870–1930* (Washington, D.C.: Arthur M. Sackler Gallery, Smithsonian Institution, 1999), pp. 35–53; and Catherine David and Hamid Dabashi, *Bahman Jalali* (Barcelona: Fundació Antoni Tàpies, 2007), pp. 26–29.

21 Neshat, interview with the author, February 2009.

22 See also Ed Schad's essay, p. 20, fig. 11.

23 For the representation and role of women in Qajar photography, see Khadijeh Mohammadi Nameghi and Carmen Pérez González, "From Sitters to Photographers: Women in Photography from the Qajar Era to the 1930s," *History of Photography* 37, no. 1 (February 2013), pp. 48–73; Jennifer Y. Chi, ed., *The Eye of the Shah: Qajar Court Photography and the Persian Past* (New York: Institute for the Study of the Ancient World at New York University, 2015), pp. 46, 47; David and Dabashi, *Bahman Jalali*, pp. 15, 23; Bohrer, *Sevruguin and the Persian Image*, p. 28.

24 Diba, "Towards an Alternative Art History," forthcoming.

25 Neshat's women confront the male and neocolonial gazes through unflinching directness, presenting affinities with the oppositional gaze theory as articulated by bell hooks, "The Oppositional Gaze: Black Female Spectators," in *Movies and Mass Culture*, ed. John Belton (New Brunswick, N.J.: Rutgers University Press, 1996), pp. 247–65.

26 Michket Krifa, *Regards Persans: Iran, une révolution photographique* (Paris: Paris-Musées, 2001), pp. 43–65.

27 Neshat has described Annina Nosei's lack of interest in showing these prints that had no text; her photographs inscribed with words, which had by now become the artist's signature style, were very marketable. Neshat herself was reluctant to show the studio portraits because she wanted to protect the privacy of family members who had posed for her. Neshat, interview with the author, February 2009.

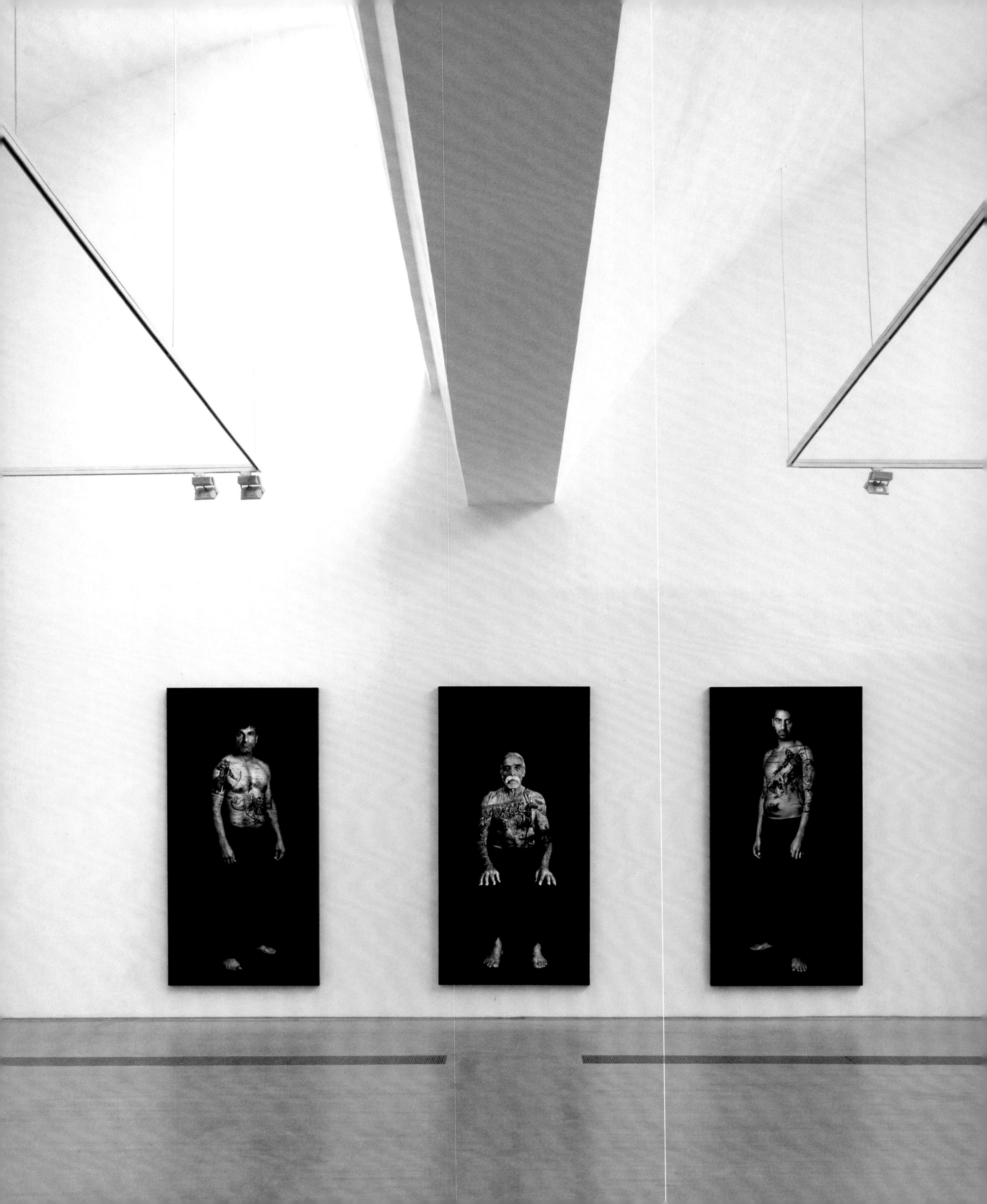

THE BOOK OF KINGS, OUR HOUSE IS ON FIRE, THE HOME OF MY EYES

From 2002 to 2009, Neshat completed her first feature film, *Women without Men*, for which she received a Silver Lion for Best Director at the 66th Venice Film Festival. Based on the book by Shahrnush Parsipur, the film follows the interlocking stories of four Iranian women—politically minded Munis, prostitute Zarin, religiously devout Faezeh, and upper-class socialite Farokh Legna—as they navigate the turbulent time of the 1953 military coup in Tehran. The fates of these characters lead them to a garden in which they enjoy freedoms not available to them in the city.[1]

Women without Men introduced named protagonists to Neshat's work. Whereas previous bodies of work predominantly featured anonymous individuals taking part in allegorical narratives, the subjects of subsequent photographs and videos frequently have proper names and bear personal witness to events as sweeping as the Green Movement in *The Book of Kings* (2012) and the Arab Spring in *Our House Is on Fire* (2013). *The Home of My Eyes* (2015) examines the historical relationship between the people of Azerbaijan and the wider concept of Persia. The installation of these three bodies of work echos their themes—each series uses portraiture to mirror the cultural and historical makeup of countries.

The Book of Kings exudes a martial sensibility. The series was inspired by the notions of "activism" and "patriotism" that permeated the Middle East during the Green Movement and Arab Spring, movements met with violence and tyranny by existing political structures. The installation is ideally introduced with two menacing photographs—*My House Is on Fire* and *Divine Rebellion* (both 2012)—as an advance-guard to a larger gallery featuring portraits of ordinary people. As though organized into military units, some portraits in the larger gallery are part of a group called Masses, others a group called Patriots, and three are designated as Villains. Collectively, the photographs present mythological archetypes of kings and heroes in Persian history, as well as the extension and critique of this tradition in Iran's Green Movement, a wave of protests sparked by the fraudulent reelection of Iranian

Previous spread
Installation view of the exhibition *Shirin Neshat: The Book of Kings*, Faurschou Foundation, Beijing, 2013. Photo by Jonathan Leijonhufvud, © Shirin Neshat & Faurschou Foundation

president Mahmoud Ahmadinejad in 2009. Certain individuals appear in both the Masses and the Patriots, suggesting shifting destinies for subjects caught up in large political movements and events.

For *Our House Is on Fire*, Neshat photographed older Egyptians who were directly impacted by the Arab Spring, a series of protests and demonstrations throughout the Middle East and North Africa that began in 2010. *Our House Is on Fire* has a somber tone, a reflection in part of the death of the twenty-two-year-old daughter of Neshat's collaborator Larry Barns as well as the experiences of the people in the photos, some of whom lost children in the suppression of the protests. The subjects do not play roles or pose. The photos are the only example of a direct, documentary approach thus far in Neshat's work, and are installed as though evidence exhibited for a trial. The faces—inscribed with poetry written so small as to be virtually unreadable—join images of feet and hands photographed in a New York morgue.

The Home of My Eyes is installed in a soaring salon-style manner, recalling the portrait galleries of Beaux-Arts museums or grand houses. The fifty-five portraits in the series were commissioned by the Yarat Contemporary Art Centre in Baku, Azerbaijan, where it debuted in 2015. Featuring ordinary Azerbaijanis, the work is, in Neshat's words, "a portrait of a country that for so long has been a crossroads of many different ethnicities, religions, and languages."[2] The surfaces of the portraits are interlaced with Nizami's epic poem *Khosrow and Shirin*, which recounts the love between a Persian king, Khosrow, and the queen of Armenia, Shirin. In the story, the lovers are separated by many trials, including mountains, political borders and intrigue, family, morality, and rival lovers.

When Nizami's texts are juxtaposed with those taken from interviews conducted by Neshat of her subjects and written in the Azerbaijani dialect of Farsi, the portraits gently reveal a people with whom she feels a close affinity and a country that reminds her of "own childhood home, Iran." Azerbaijan was part of Iran until the Qajar dynasty lost the territory to Russia in 1813. The countries share a common ancestry, many traditions, and a similar language. In her interviews, the artist's main question asked of her subjects was: "What does home mean to you?" In the gestures and words of the Azerbaijanis as well as the stories of Nizami, *The Home of My Eyes* suggests that home is both a political and personal concept rooted in the nuances of recent and ancient history.

NOTES

1 *Women without Men* will be screened as part of this exhibition.

2 Shirin Neshat quoted in *Shirin Neshat: The Home of My Eyes in Venice Museo Correr* (Cologne: Walther König, 2017), p. 11.

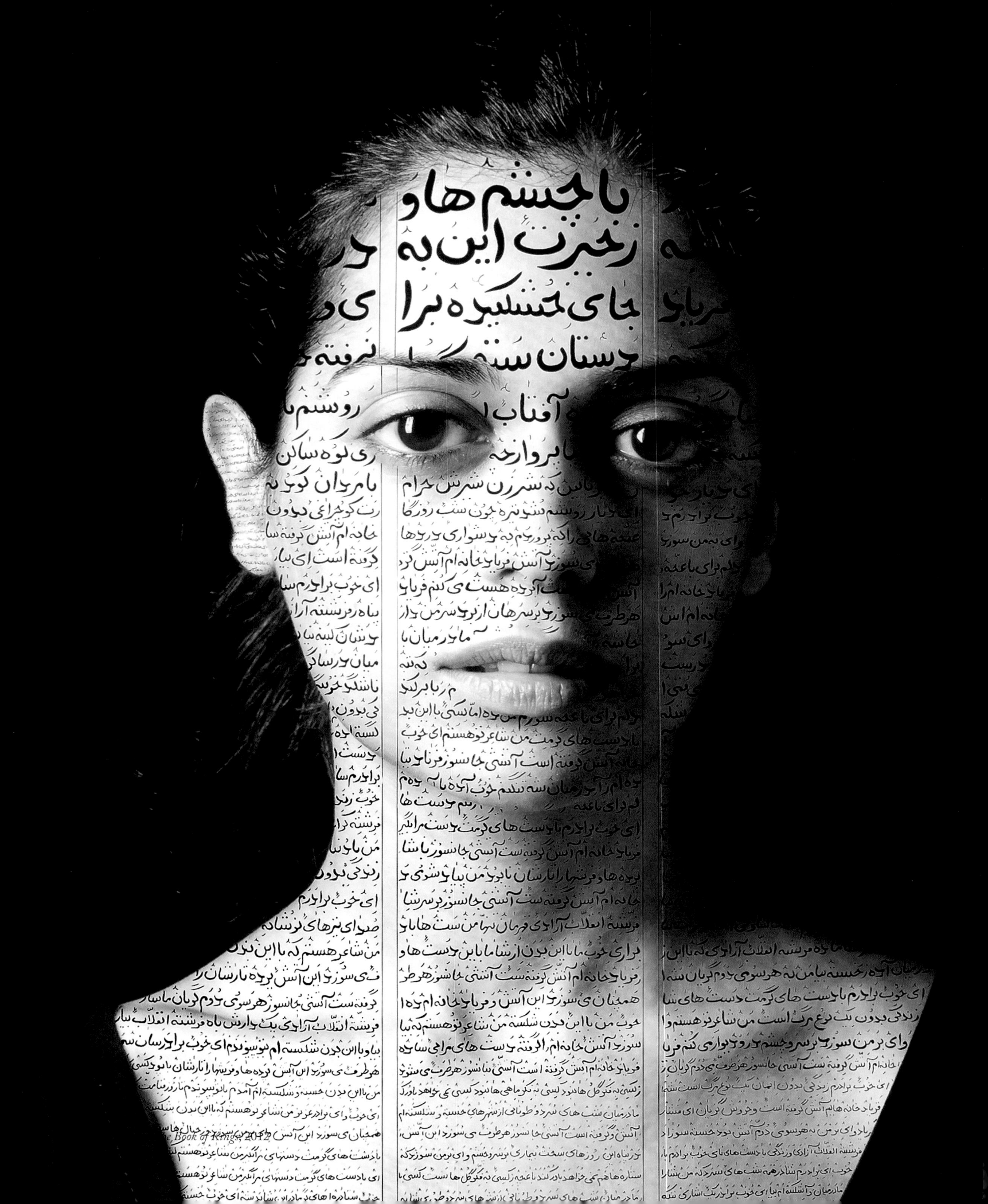

The Book of Kings, 2012

A CRY

Mehdi Akhavan-Sales

My house is on fire, soul burning,
ablaze in every direction.
Carpets and curtains threaded to dust.
Within the smoke of this raging fire
I sob, run to each corner
shout, scream, yelp
with the voice of a sad howl and bitter laughter.

My house is on fire,
a merciless fire,
burns without respite,
all images drawn with my blood on
every door and wall
in this damned and endless night.

Burn and
burn every blossom I grew with
much hardship
in these open urns.

And here come my enemies
on their rooftops with
their guileful victorious smirks
as I watch the burning flames
in the protection of the night.
I run every direction,
sobbing from this injustice.
I shout, scream, cry!

And the fire keeps on raging,
burning all memories, books and manuscripts,
all landscapes and views.
Putting out the fire with my blistering hands,
I pass out with its roar.
As the fire rages from yet another
direction circled in smoke.
Who will ever know as my being turns
into the non-being by the sunrise?

While these kind neighbors of mine are
happily sleeping in their bed
by dawn all that will be left
of me is a feast full of dust.
Alas, would any of these kind neighbors
rise in help?
As this cruel fire
burns my foundation
I shout, scream, cry!

Roja (detail), from *The Book of Kings*, 2012

FARHAD'S SEA OF TEARS LONGING FOR SHIRIN'S LOVE
from Nizami's *Khosrow and Shirin*

At times, intimate with the deer
Now again, leading the pace of Onagers.
At times, collecting tears of stag
Now again, combing lions' tails.
Days, in commune with the gazelles
Nights, sharing secrets with stag.
Not unlike, ship's propeller winding day and night
Oblivious to pain, pangs of hunger and thirst.
Adrift, like a ghost on an open road
Roam and wander incessantly for months on end.
Blind to obstacles on his path
Colliding and crashing, wounded and in pain.
Would not flinch at the arrow aiming his eye
For, he is gone and lost in sorrow.
Tumbling into the deep hole on his way
For, inattention hinders him off his ways.
Withdrawn, has lost interest in the world
Menace awaiting him at every corner.
With heart wistful and yearning
Nights abound with grief and sorrow.
What difference to be in a Hut or a Castle?
Whence, his howl pierces the rocks.
Love's fury, serves joy in his heart
Whence, separation's grief faults the mirth.
Seeking his star of fortune in his sight
Whence, washing his face with tears of blood.
Losing sleep when it's most needed
For, one shall not shut the door in friends' company.
Alien, to his own garment
For the lover's habit was at hand.
Repulsed by his own self-image, grotesque
Lest, he transfigures in lover's form.
Restless in his own skin day and night
Lest he steps out of his own self.
Wishing to abandon his own body
Lest, unified in one
Unaware, his bird (lover) no longer in cage
Gone out with the king, the house empty.

Translation by Shoja Azari

Gizbasti (detail), from *The Home of My Eyes*, 2015

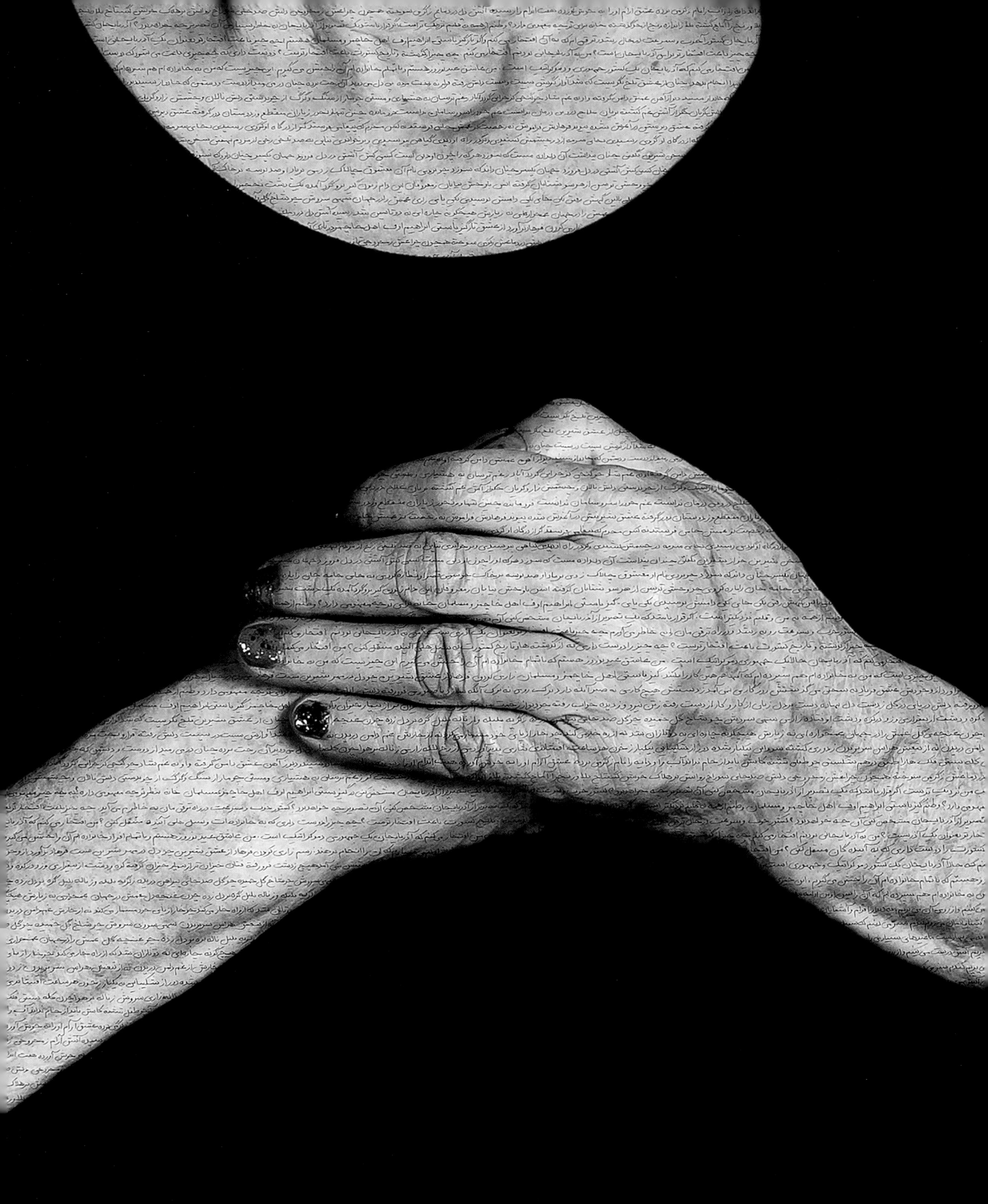

THE BOOK OF KINGS

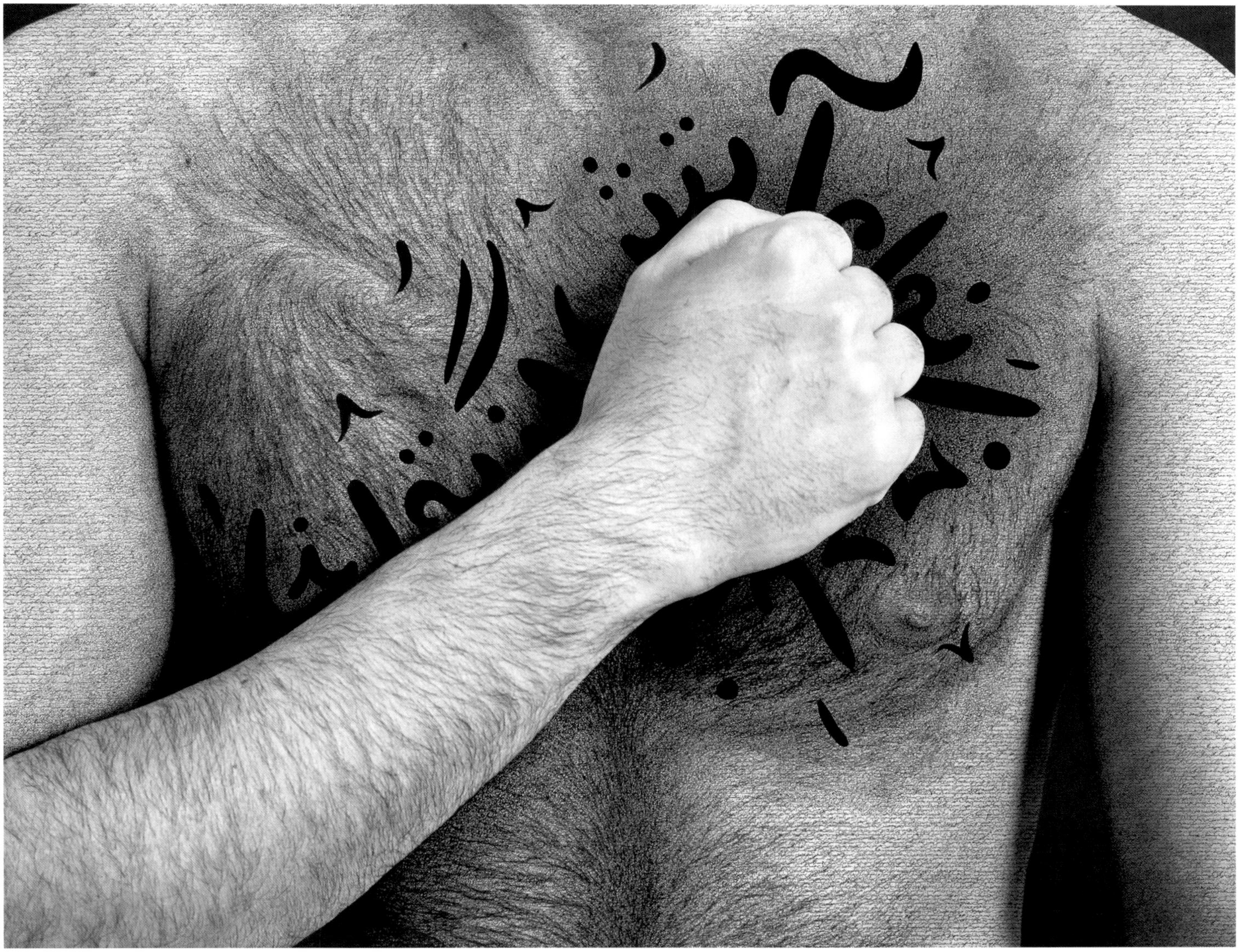

MY HOUSE IS ON FIRE, 2012

Ink on LE silver gelatin print, 47½ x 60¼ x 2 inches (120.7 x 153 x 5.1 cm). Photograph taken by Larry Barns

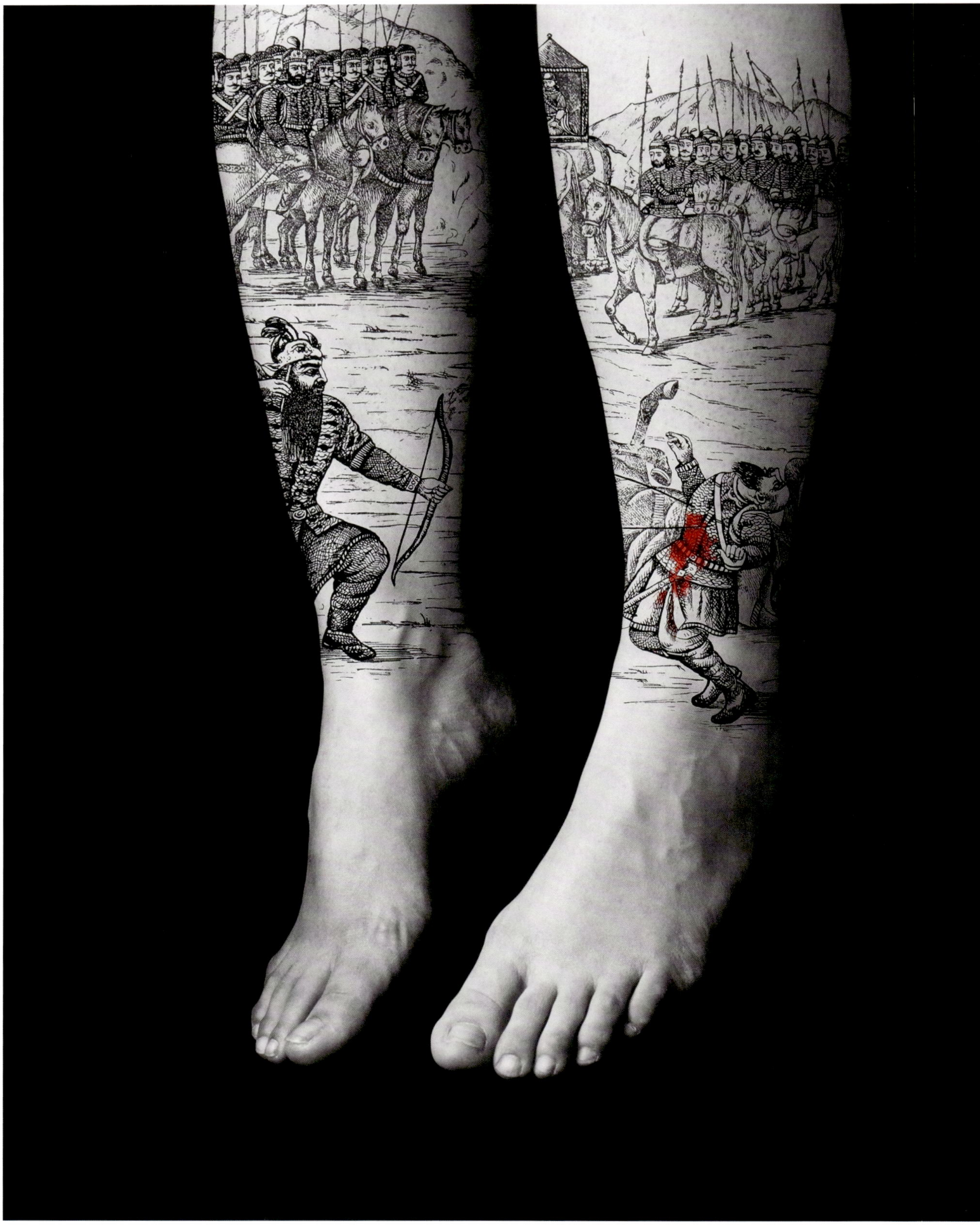

DIVINE REBELLION, 2012

Acrylic on LE silver gelatin print, 62¼ x 49¼ x 2 inches (158.1 x 125.1 x 5.1 cm). Photograph taken by Larry Barns

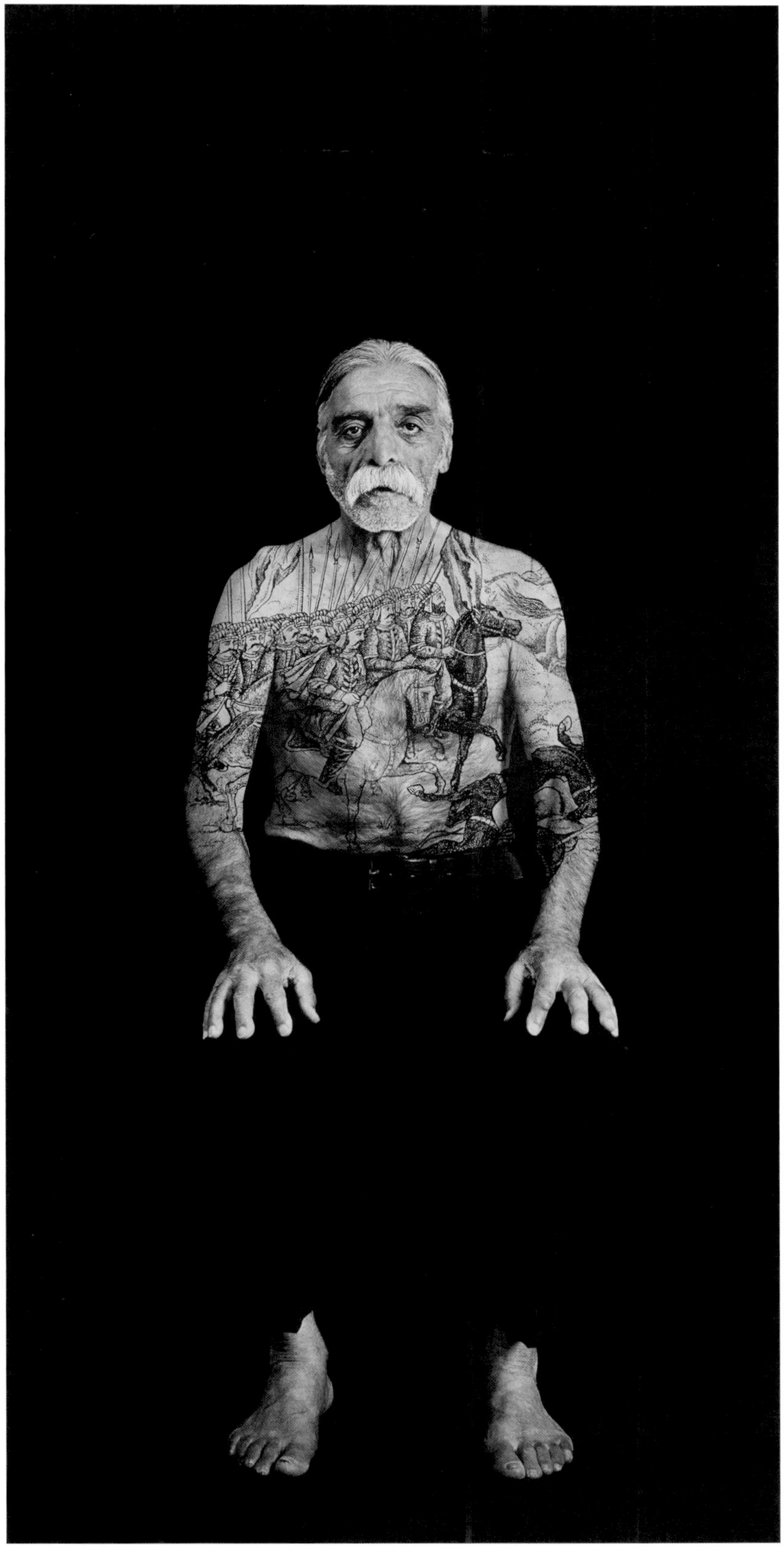

BAHRAM, 2012

Ink on LE silver gelatin print, 99¼ x 49⅜ x 2¼ inches (252.1 x 125.4 x 5.7 cm).
Photograph taken by Larry Barns. Courtesy of Shulamit Nazarian

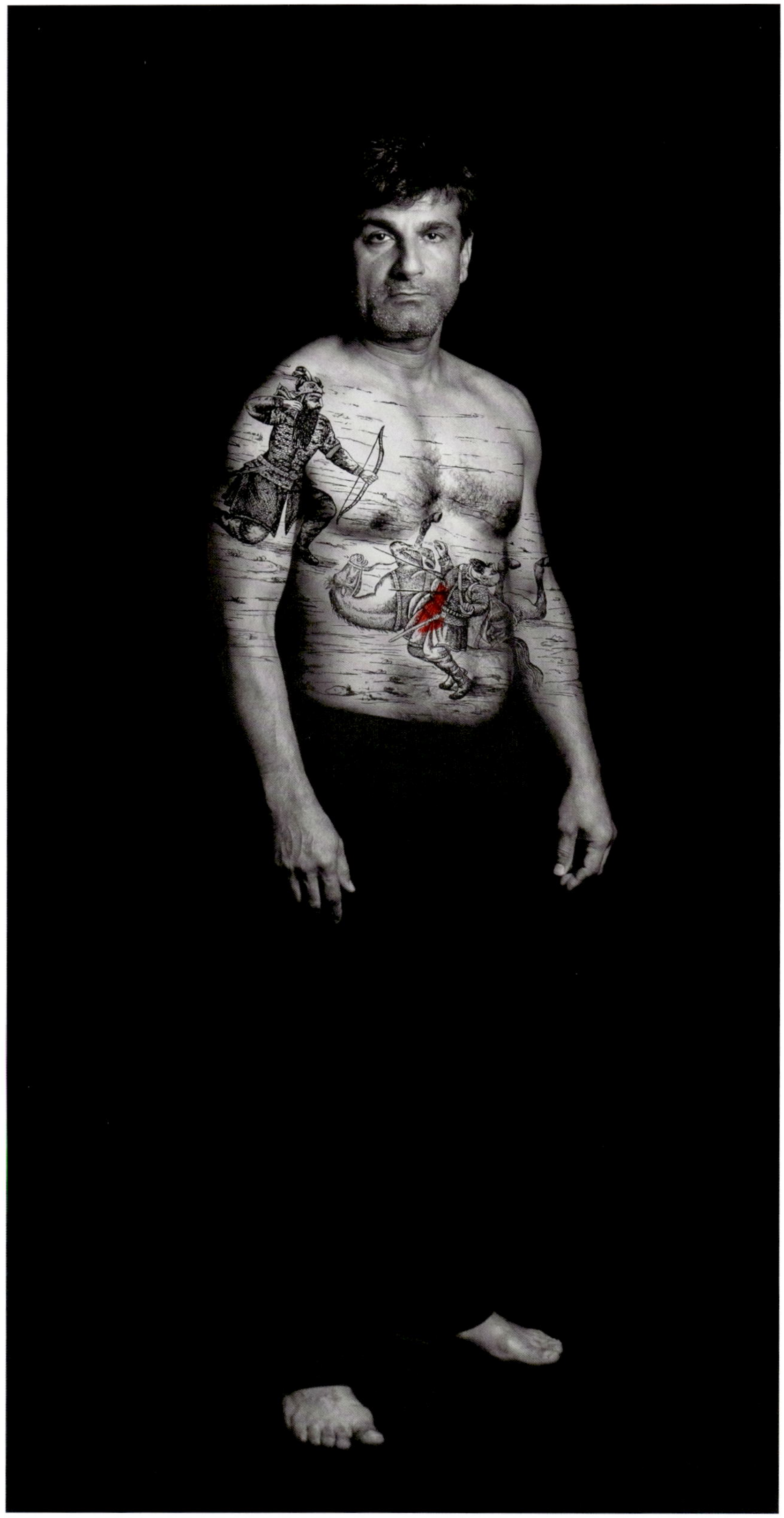

AMIR, 2012

Acrylic on LE silver gelatin print, 99¼ x 49¾ x 2¼ inches (252.1 x 125.1 x 5.7 cm).
Photograph taken by Larry Barns

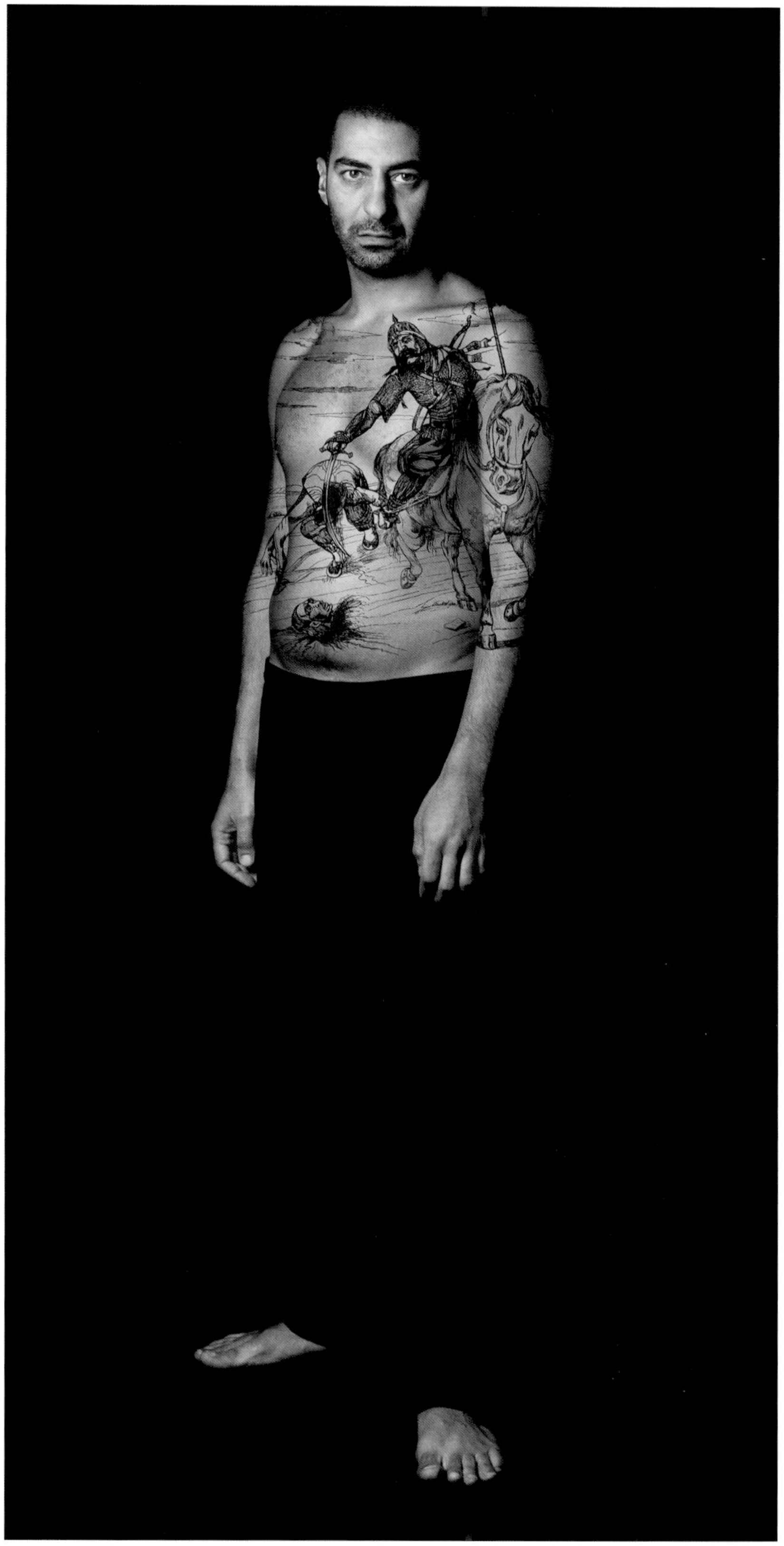

SHERIEF, 2012

Acrylic on LE silver gelatin print, 99¼ x 49¾ x 2¼ inches (252.1 x 125.1 x 5.7 cm). Photograph taken by Larry Barns

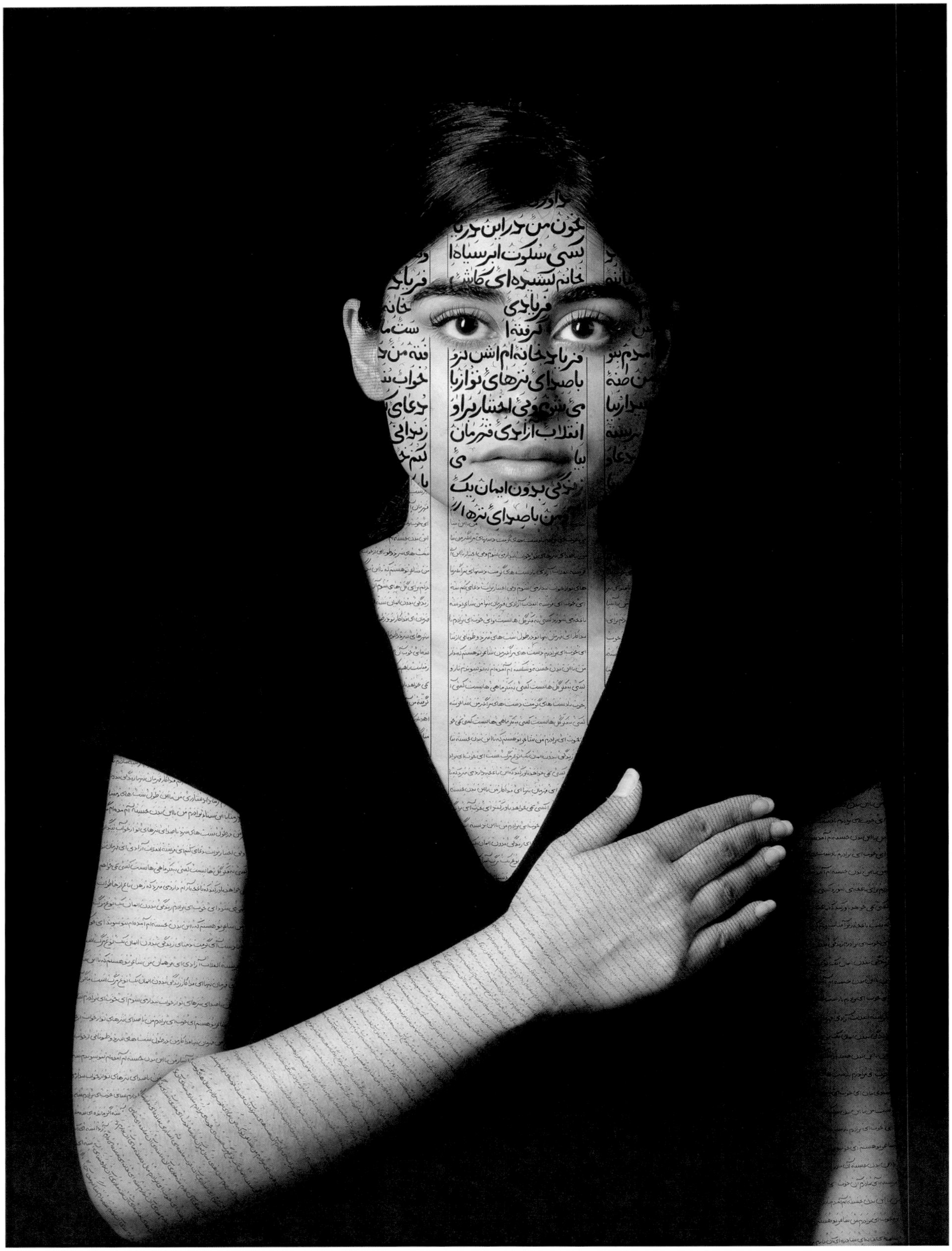

NIDA, 2012

Ink on LE silver gelatin print, 60¼ x 45¼ x 2 inches (153 x 114.9 x 5.1 cm). Photograph taken by Larry Barns. Private collection, New York, Courtesy of Sean Kelly Gallery

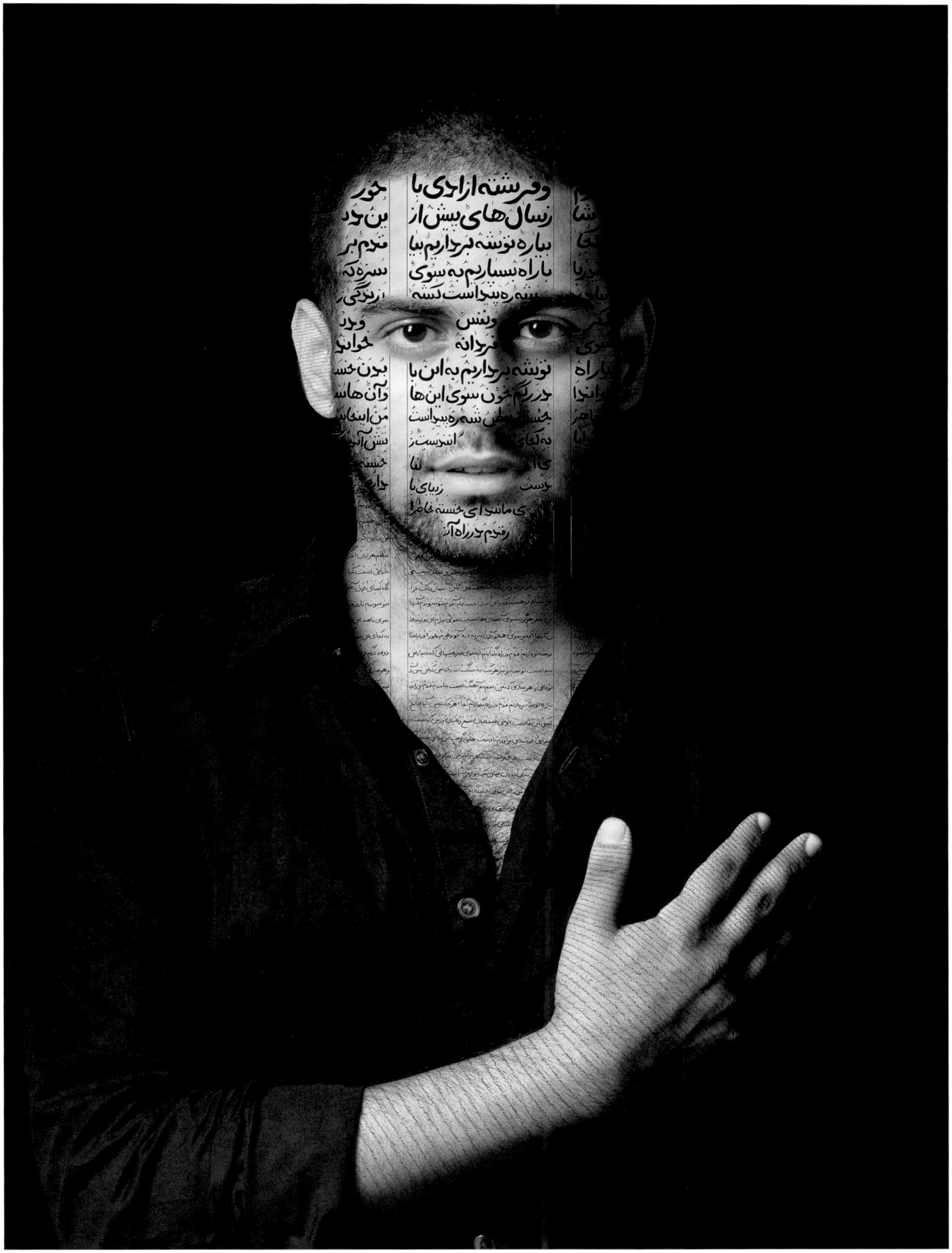

IBRAHIM, 2012

Ink on LE silver gelatin print, 60¼ x 45¼ x 2 inches (153 x 114.9 x 5.1 cm).
Photograph taken by Larry Barns

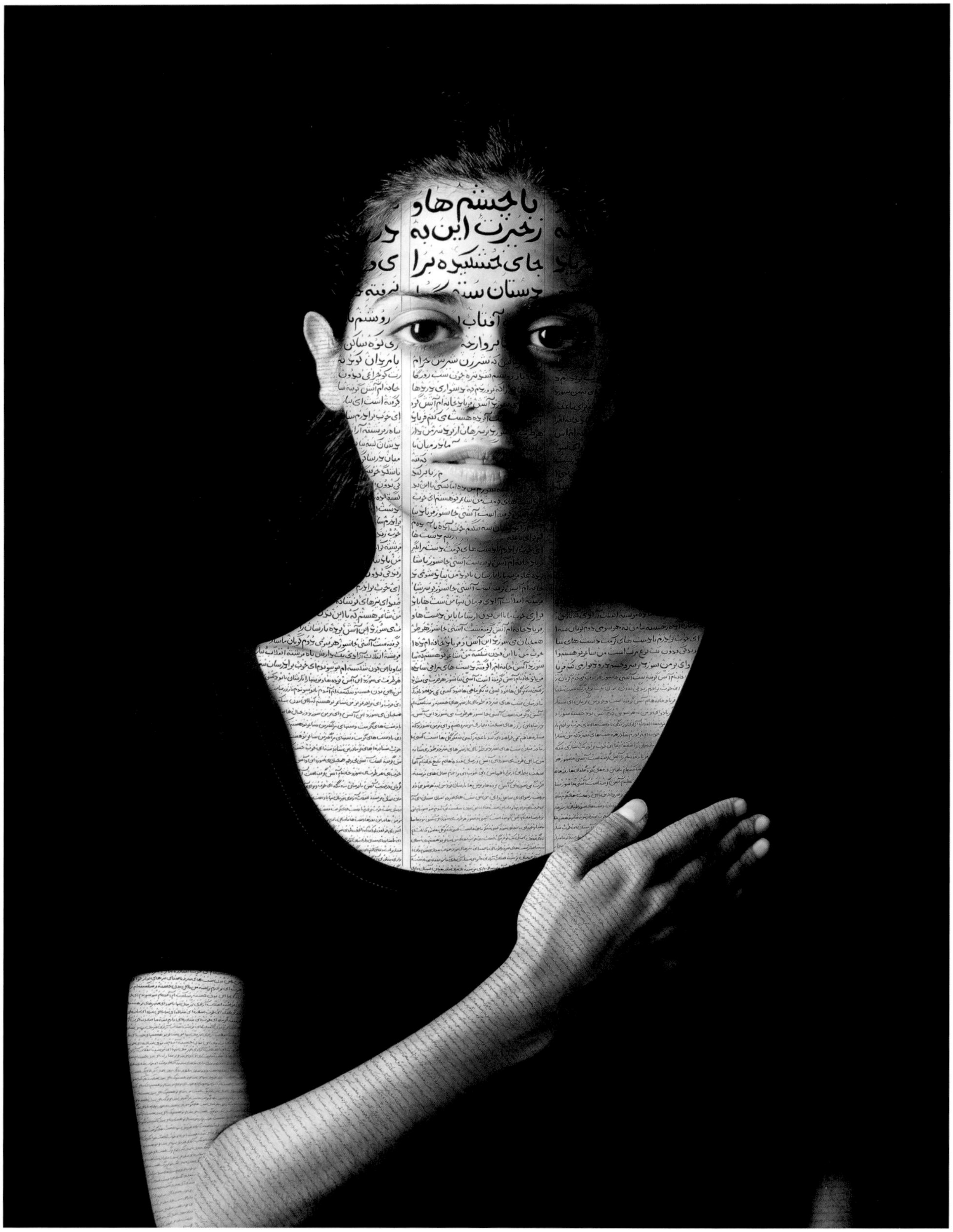

ROJA, 2012

Ink on LE silver gelatin print, 60¼ x 45¼ x 2 inches (153 x 114.9 x 5.1 cm). Photograph taken by Larry Barns. Courtesy of the collection of Art Berliner and Marian Lever

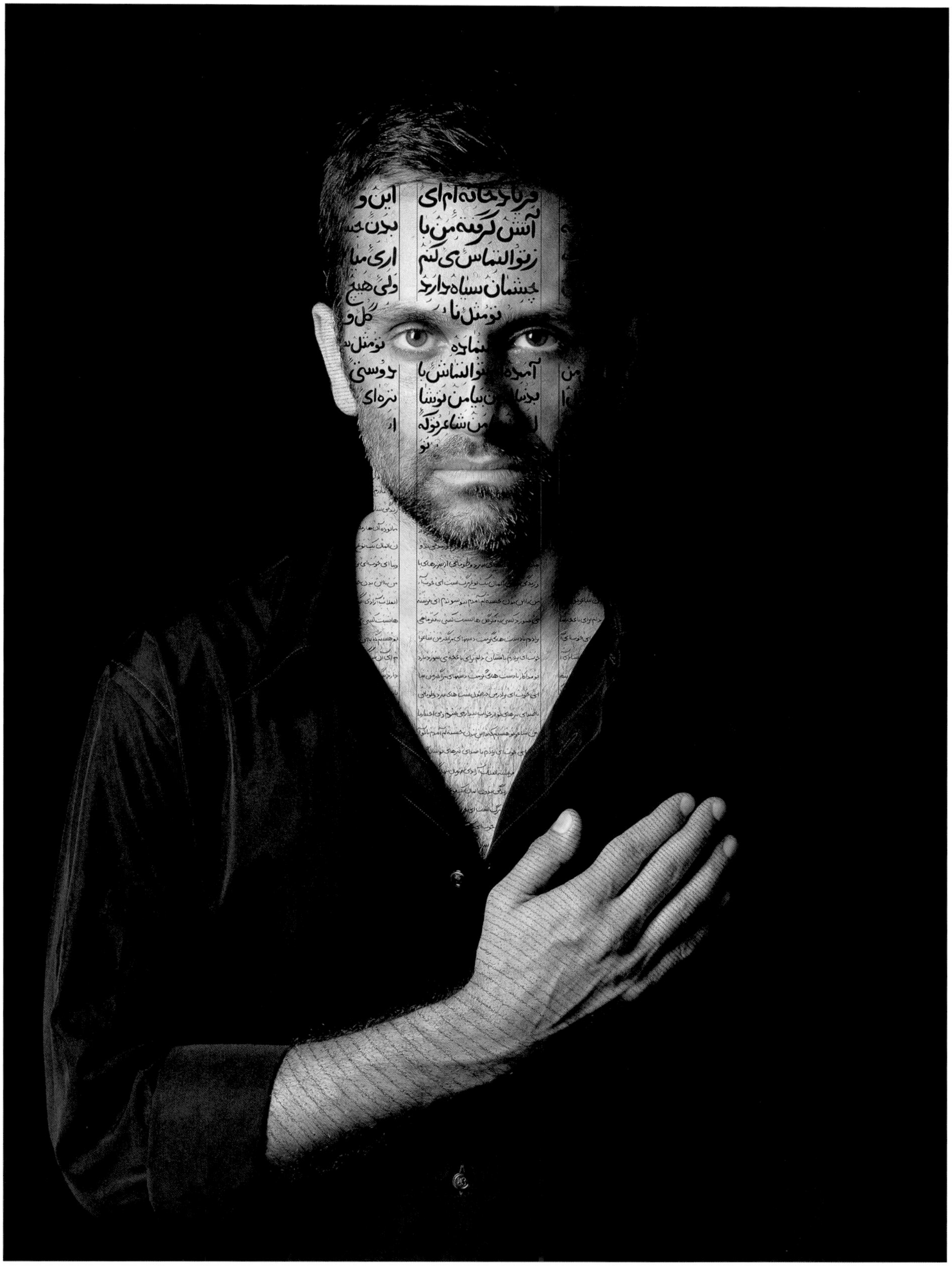

KOUROSS, 2012

Ink on LE silver gelatin print, 60¼ x 45¼ x 2 inches (153 x 114.9 x 5.1 cm). Photograph taken by Larry Barns

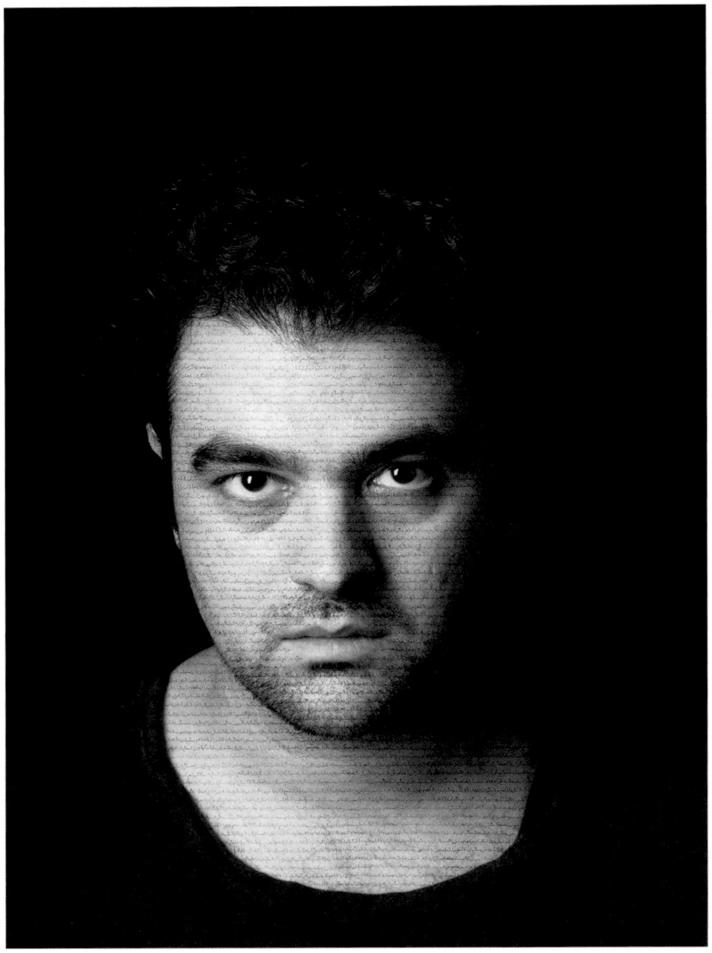

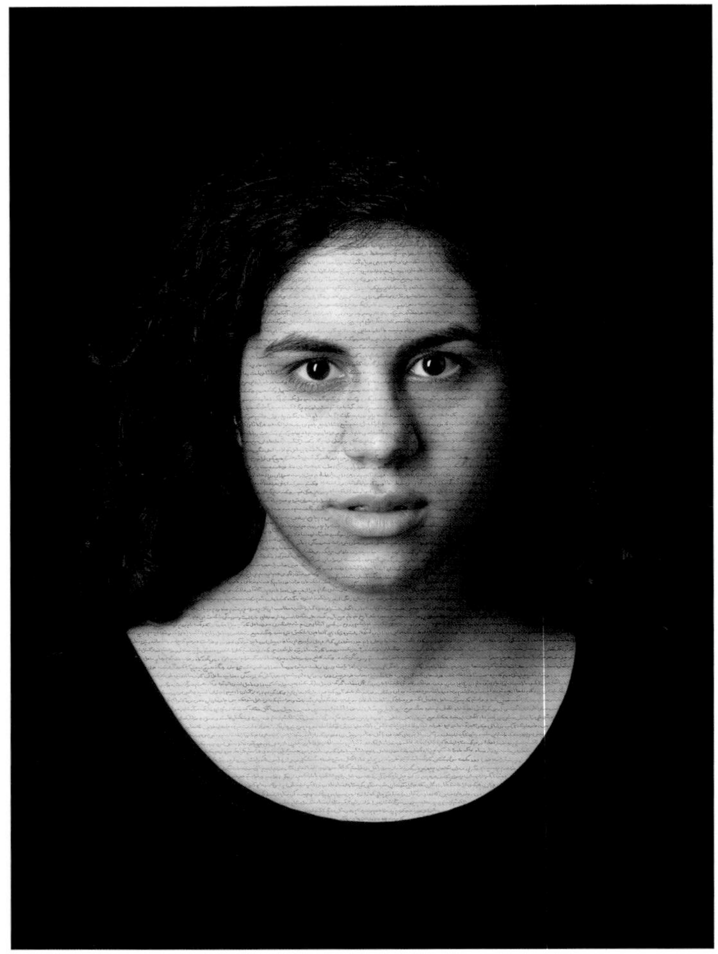

ROOZBEH, 2012

Ink on LE silver gelatin print, 40¼ x 30¼ x 2 inches (102.2 x 76.8 x 5.1 cm). Photograph taken by Larry Barns

SAMAN, 2012

Ink on LE silver gelatin print, 40¼ x 30¼ x 2 inches (102.2 x 76.8 x 5.1 cm). Photograph taken by Larry Barns

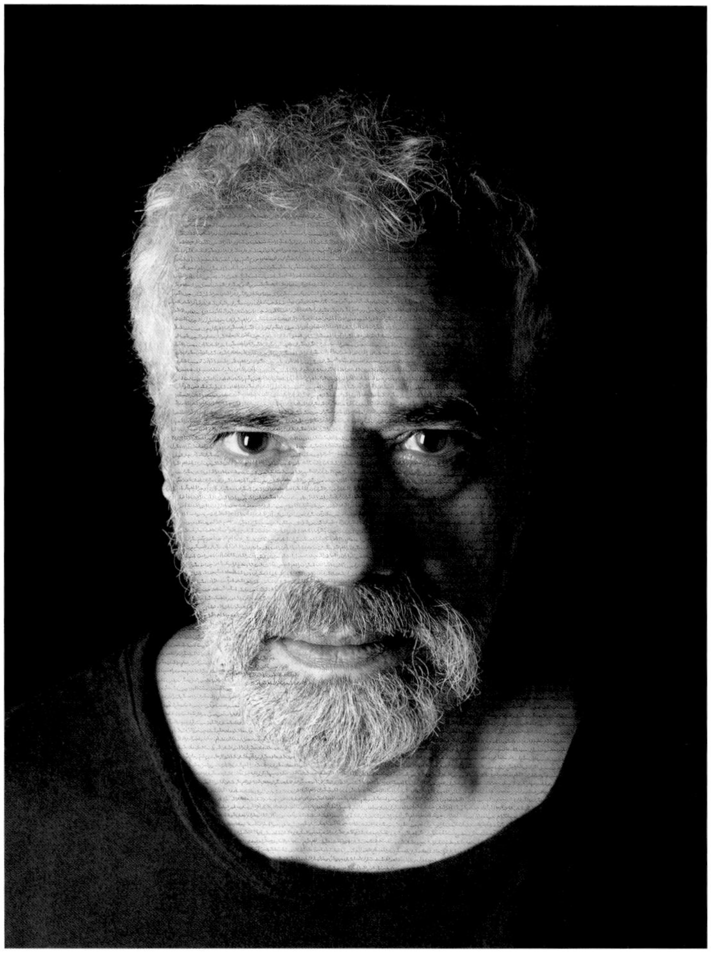

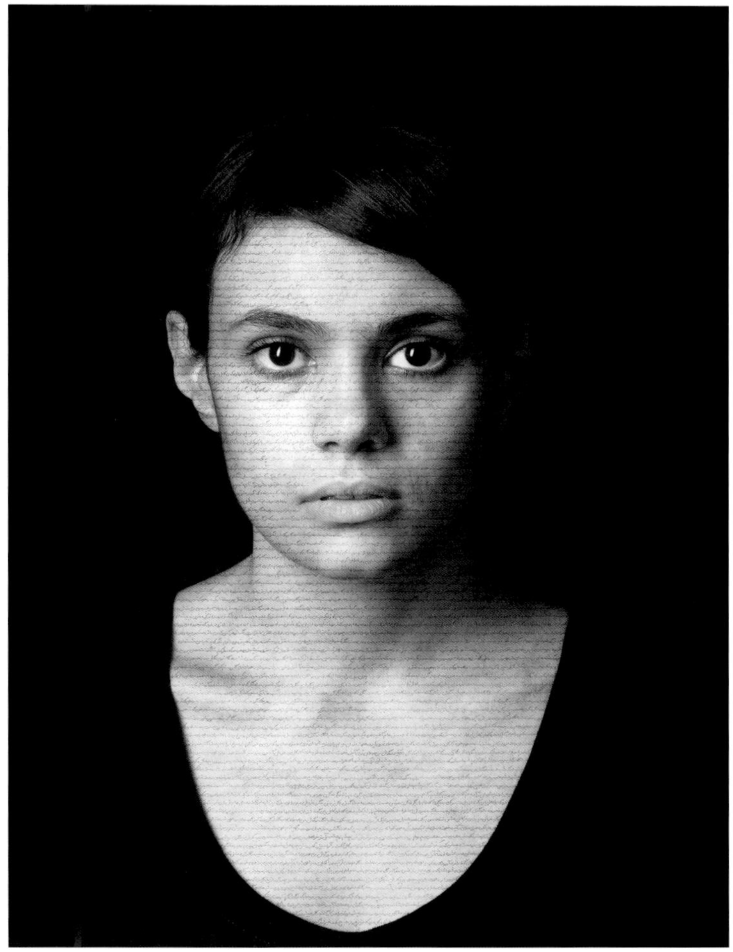

NICKZAD, 2012

Ink on LE silver gelatin print, 40¼ x 30¼ x 2 inches (102.2 x 76.8 x 5.1 cm). Photograph taken by Larry Barns

SARA JAFARI, 2012

Ink on LE silver gelatin print, 40¼ x 30¼ x 2 inches (102.2 x 76.8 x 5.1 cm). Photograph taken by Larry Barns

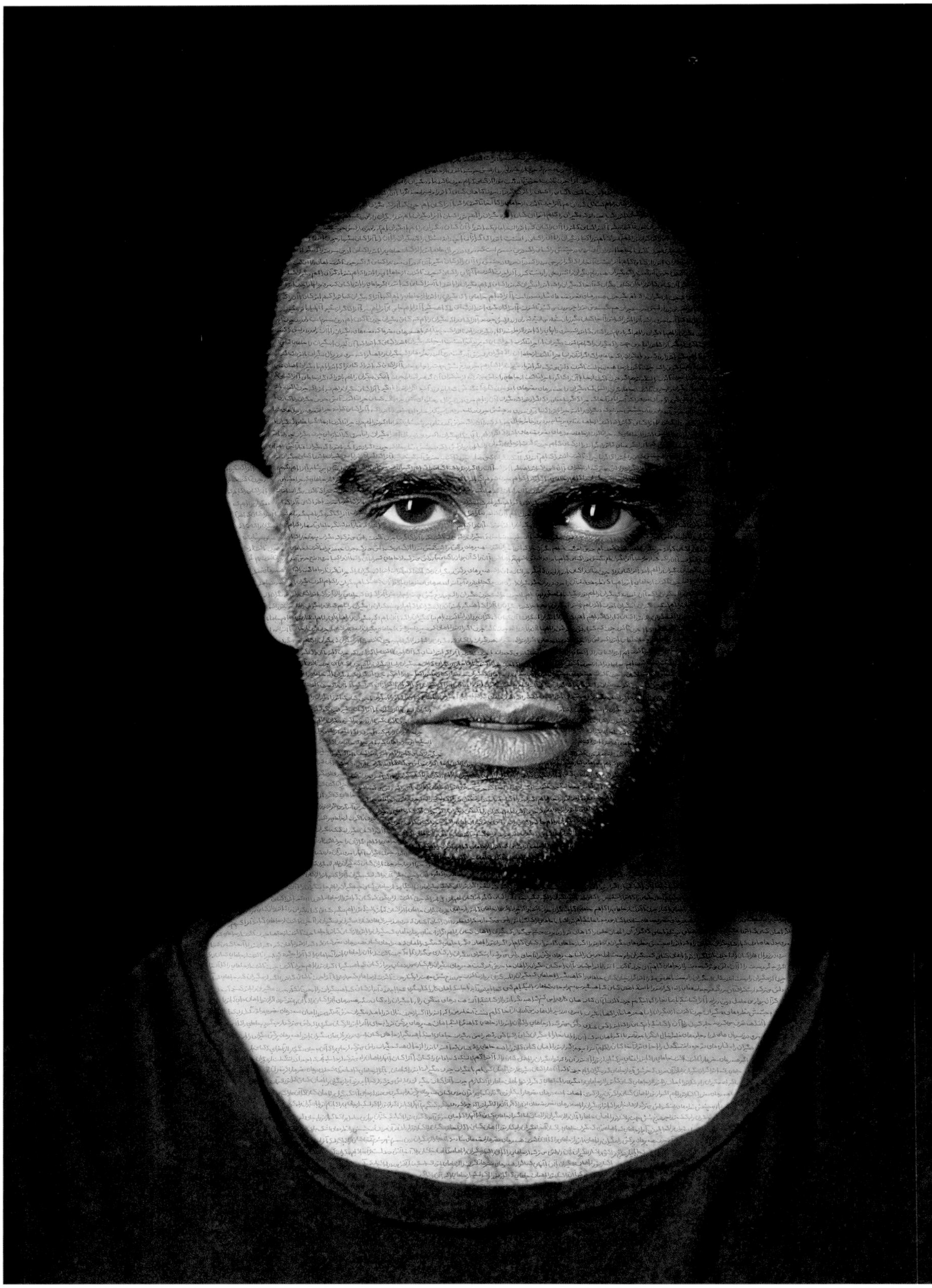

DAVOOD, 2012

Ink on LE silver gelatin print, 40¼ x 30¼ x 2 inches (102.2 x 76.8 x 5.1 cm).
Photograph taken by Larry Barns

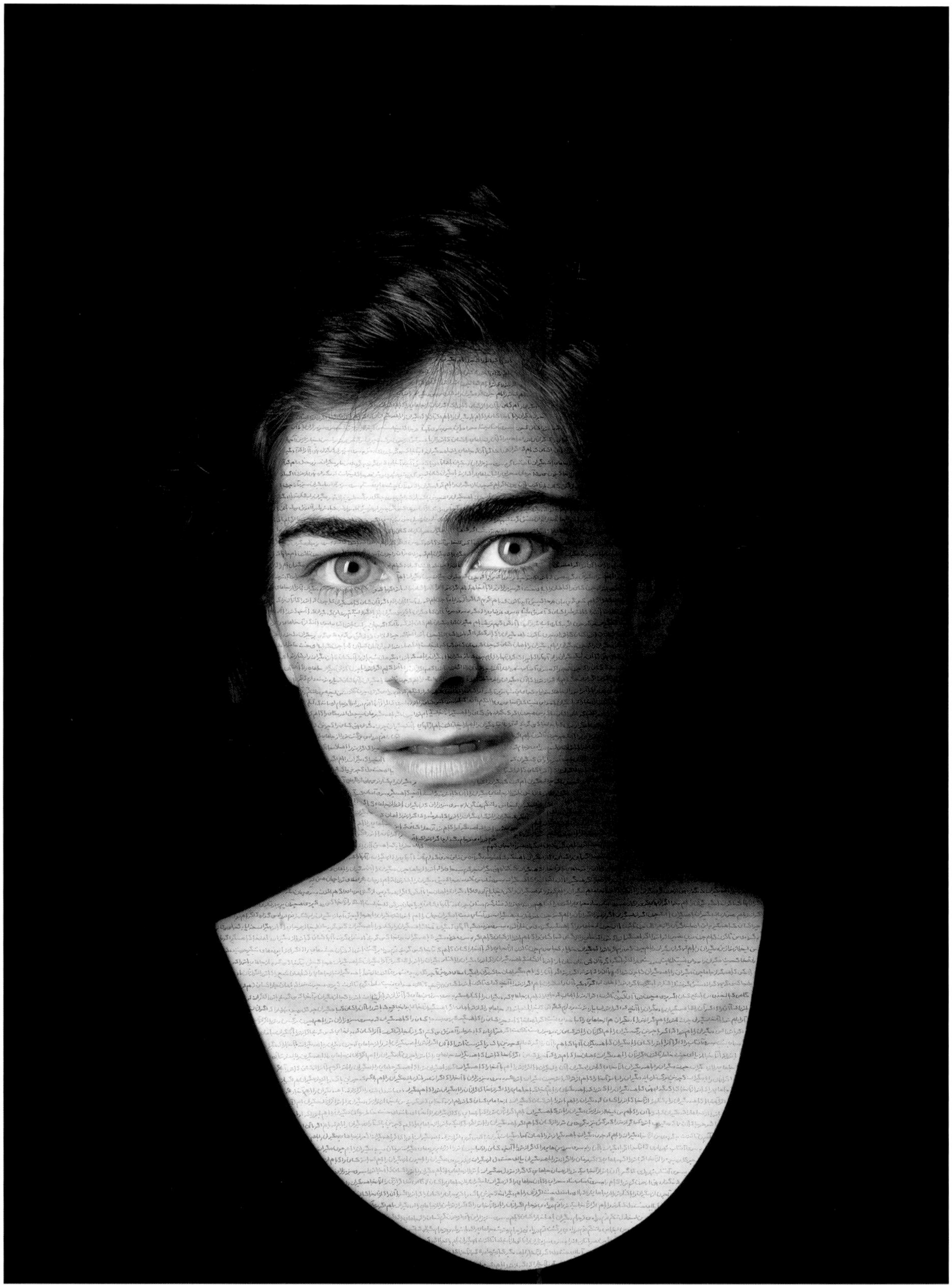

SARA ZANDIEH, 2012

Ink on LE silver gelatin print, 40¼ x 30¼ x 2 inches (102.2 x 76.8 x 5.1 cm).
Photograph taken by Larry Barns

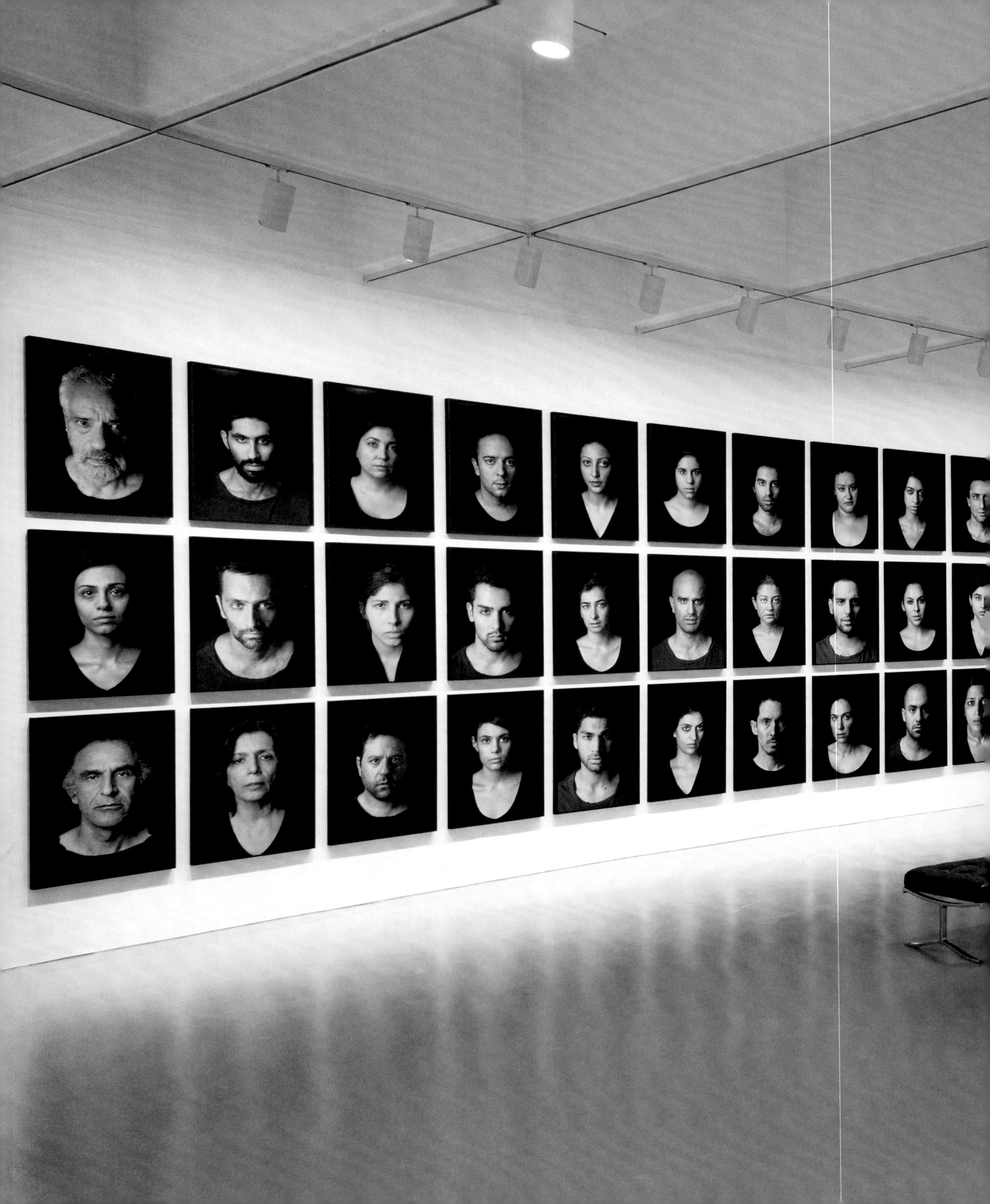

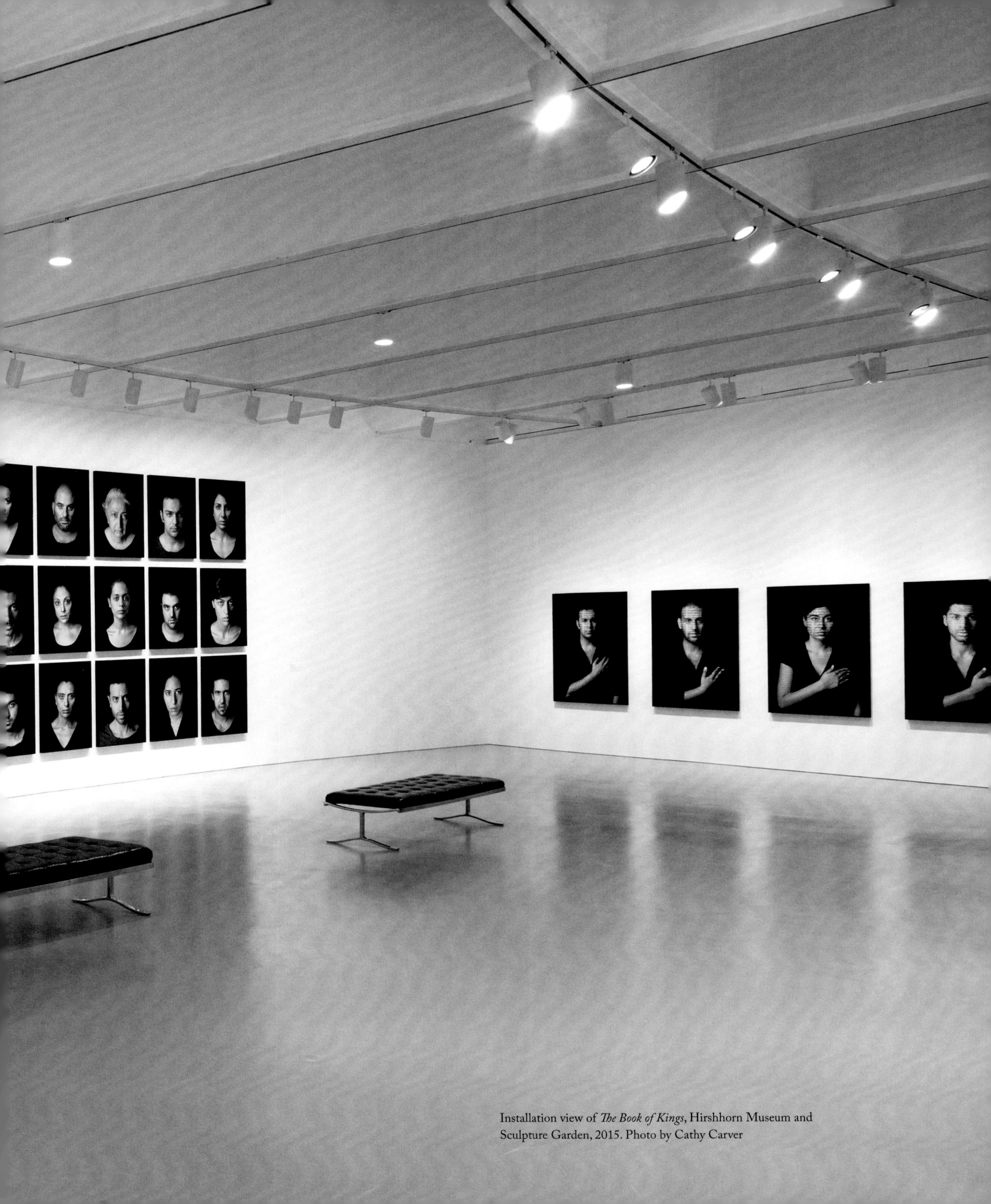

Installation view of *The Book of Kings*, Hirshhorn Museum and Sculpture Garden, 2015. Photo by Cathy Carver

OUR HOUSE IS ON FIRE

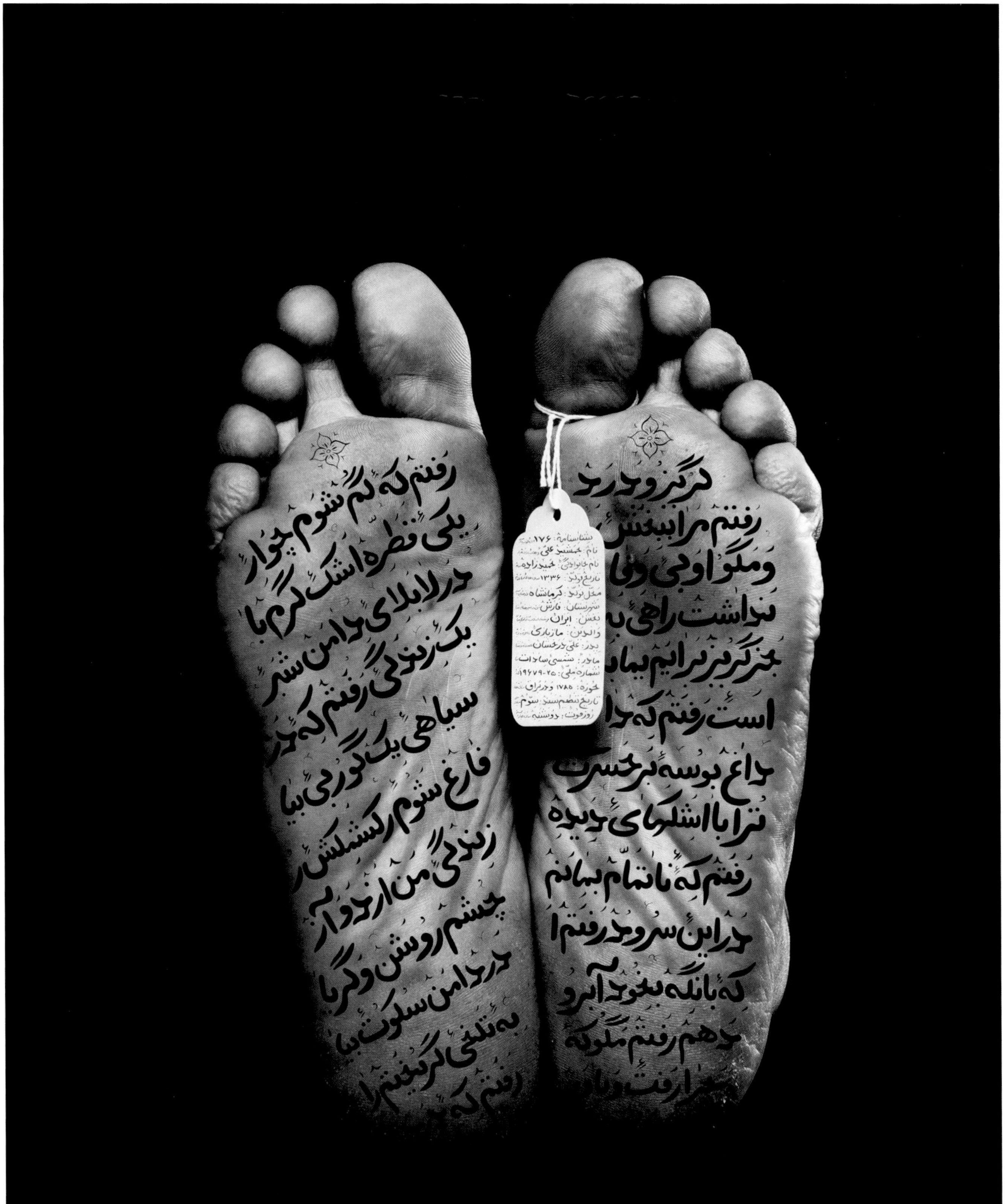

RAHIM, 2013

Ink on LE silver gelatin print, 61¼ x 49½ x 2 inches (155.6 x 124.8 x 5.1 cm).
Photograph taken by David Jiménez

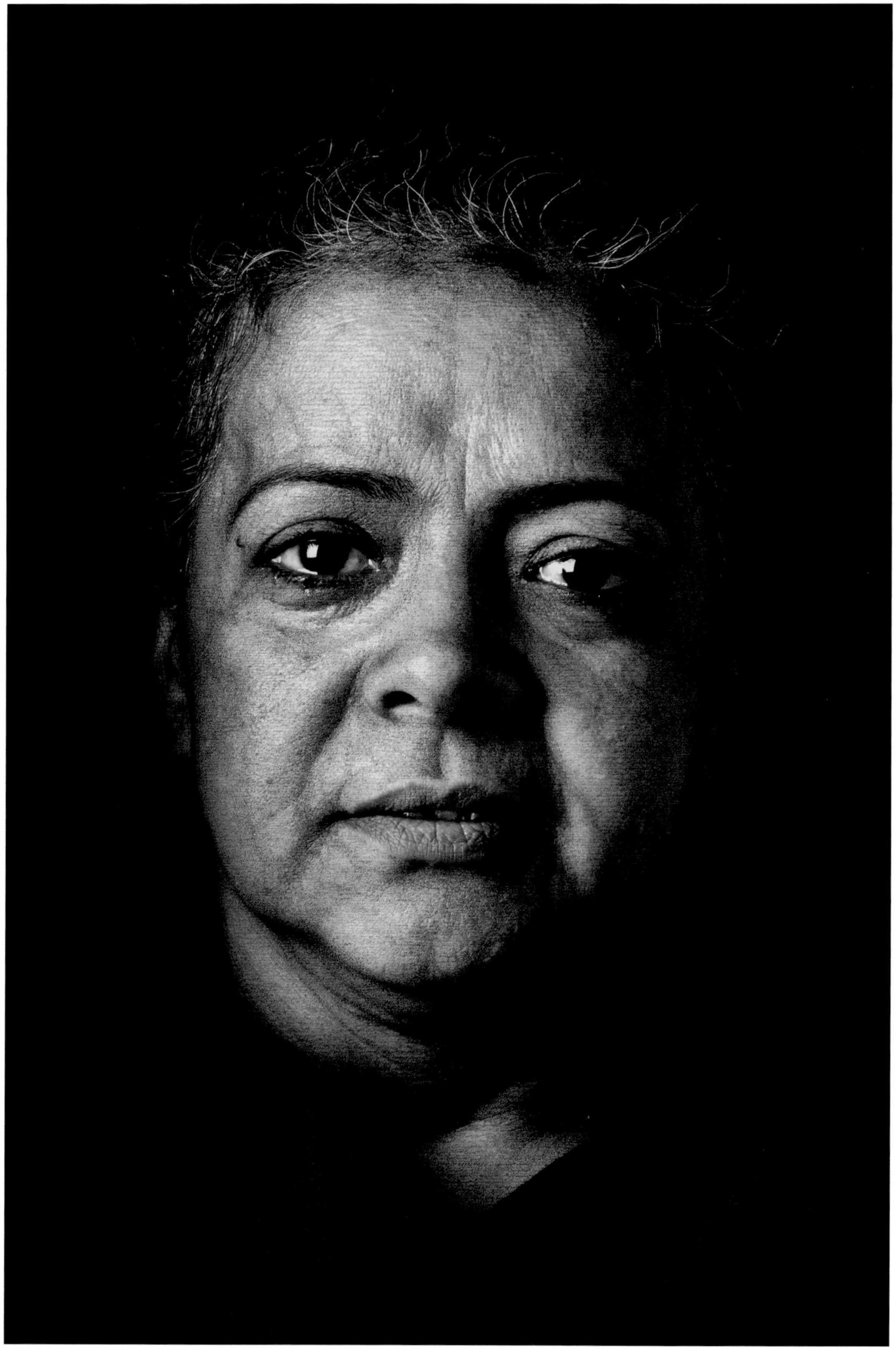

WAFAA, 2013

Digital C-print and ink, 63¼ x 41⅛ x 2 inches (160.7 x 104.5 x 5.1 cm).
Photograph taken by Larry Barns

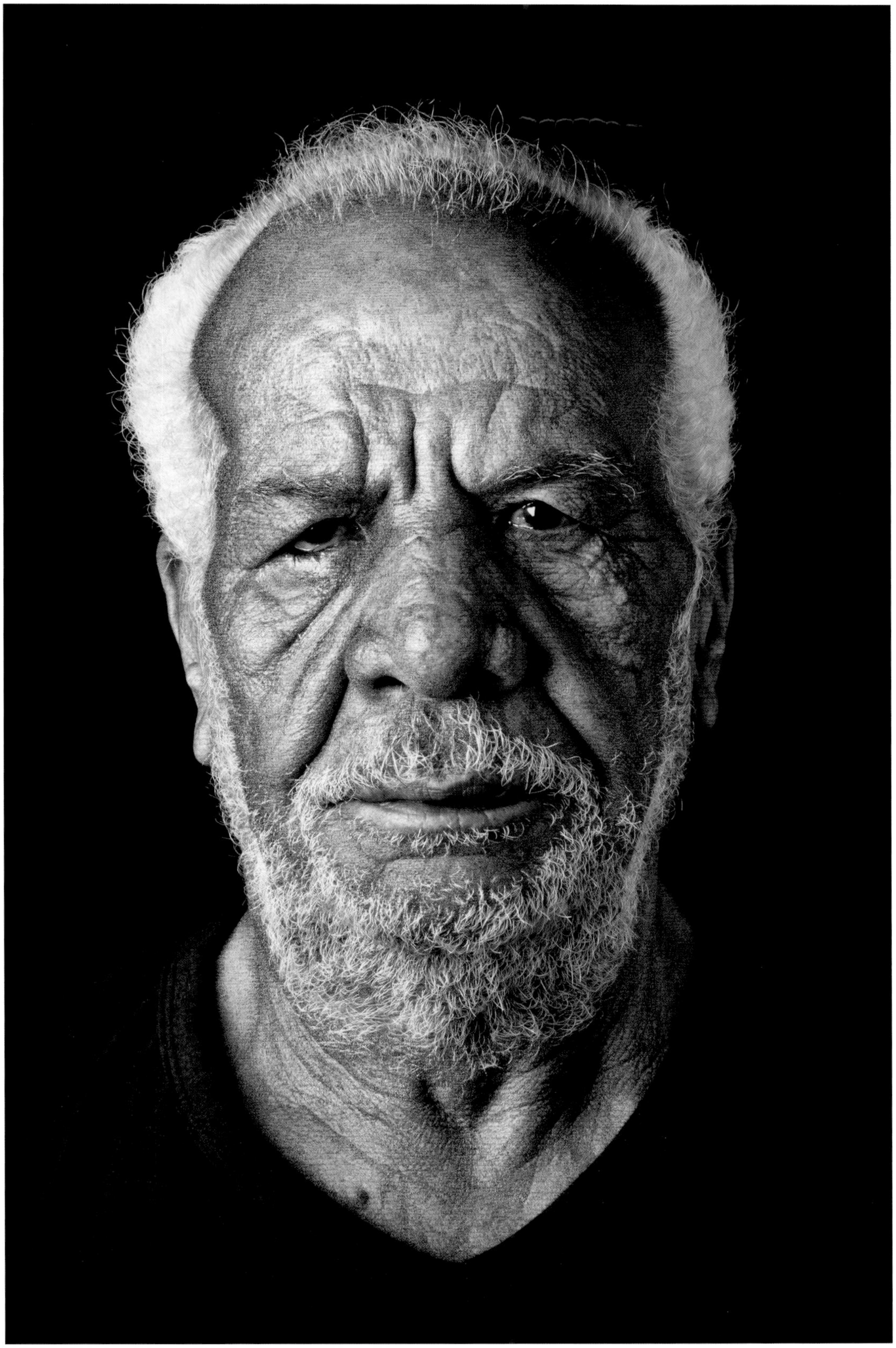

MAHMOUD, 2013

Digital C-print and ink, 63¼ x 41⅛ x 2 inches (160.7 x 104.5 x 5.1 cm).
Photograph taken by Larry Barns

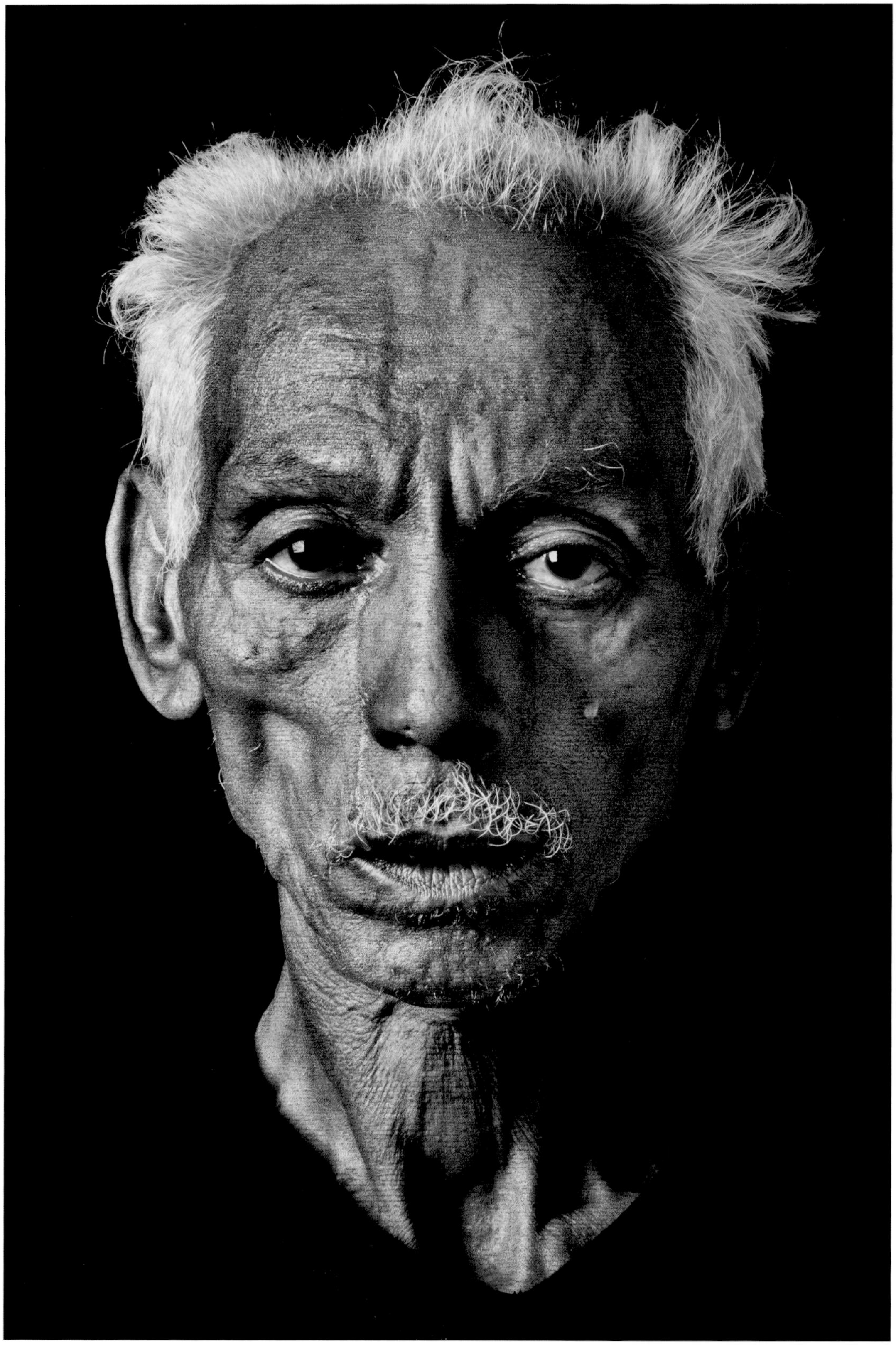

JAMAL, 2013

Digital C-print and ink, 63¼ x 41⅛ x 2 inches (160.7 x 104.5 x 5.1 cm).
Photograph taken by Larry Barns

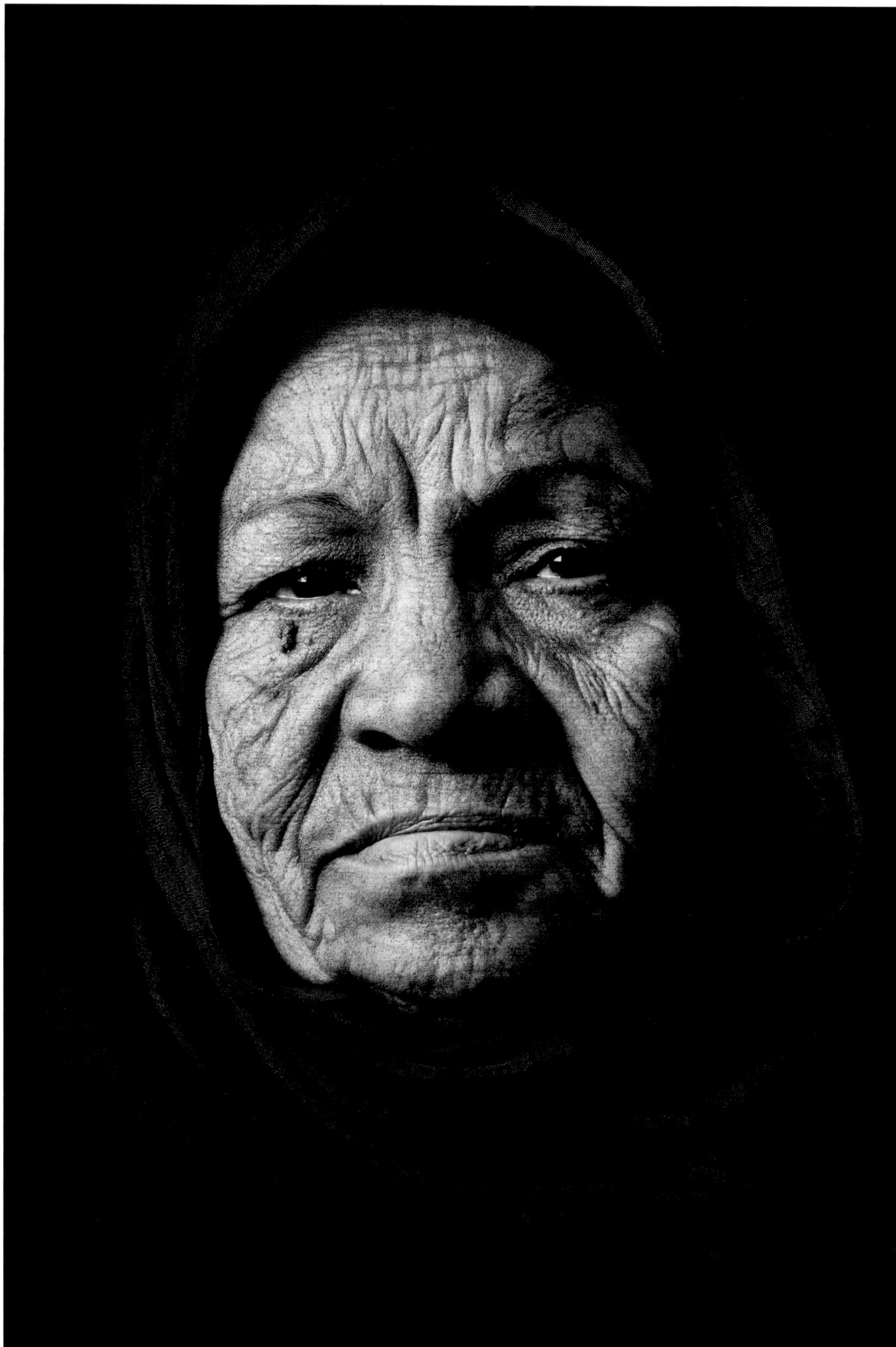

MONA, 2013

Digital C-print and ink, 63¼ x 41⅛ x 2 inches (160.7 x 104.5 x 5.1 cm).
Photograph taken by Larry Barns

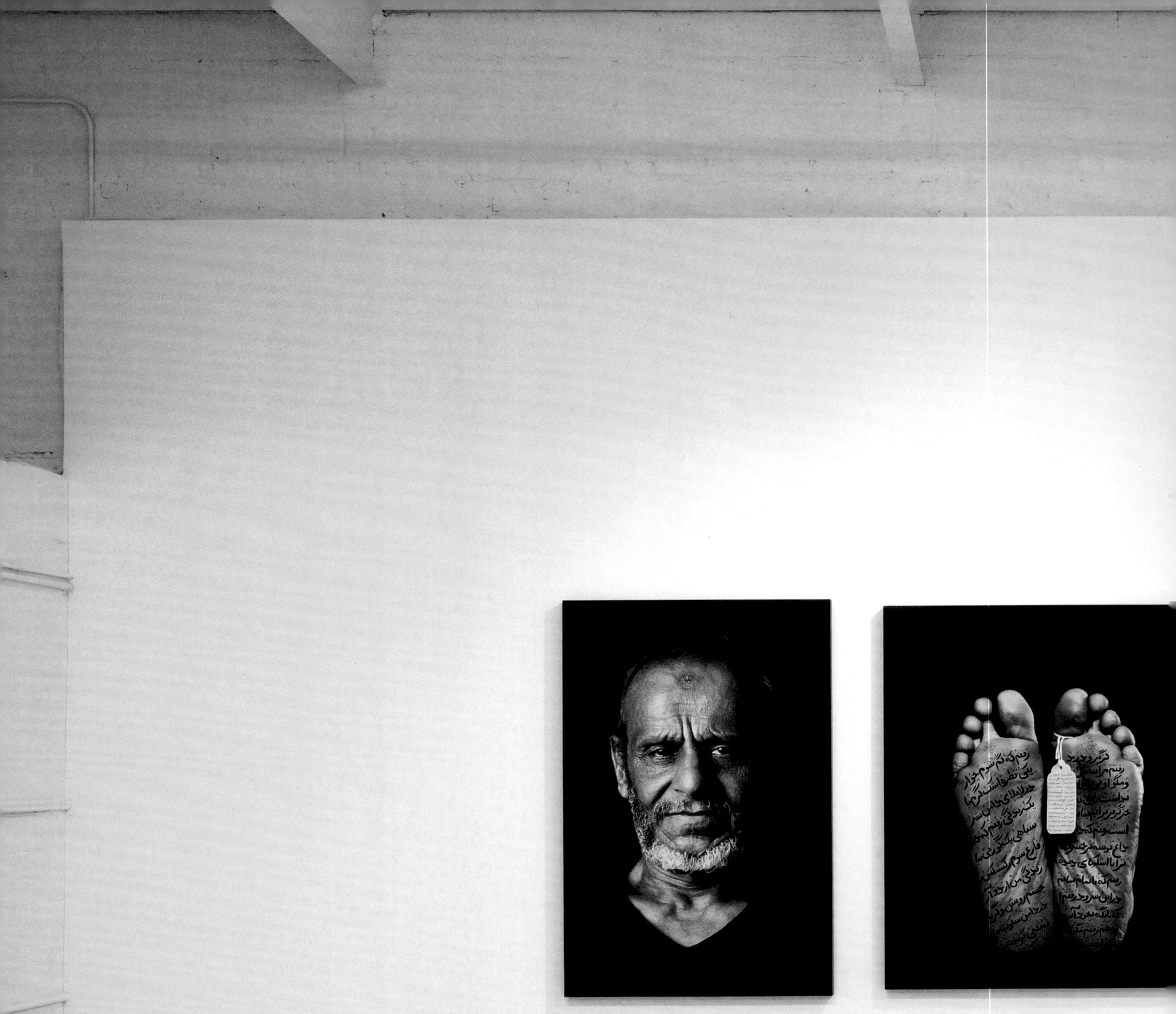

Installation view, *Shirin Neshat: Our House Is on Fire*, Robert Rauschenberg Foundation Project Space, New York, January 31–March 1, 2014. Photo by Glenn Steigelman

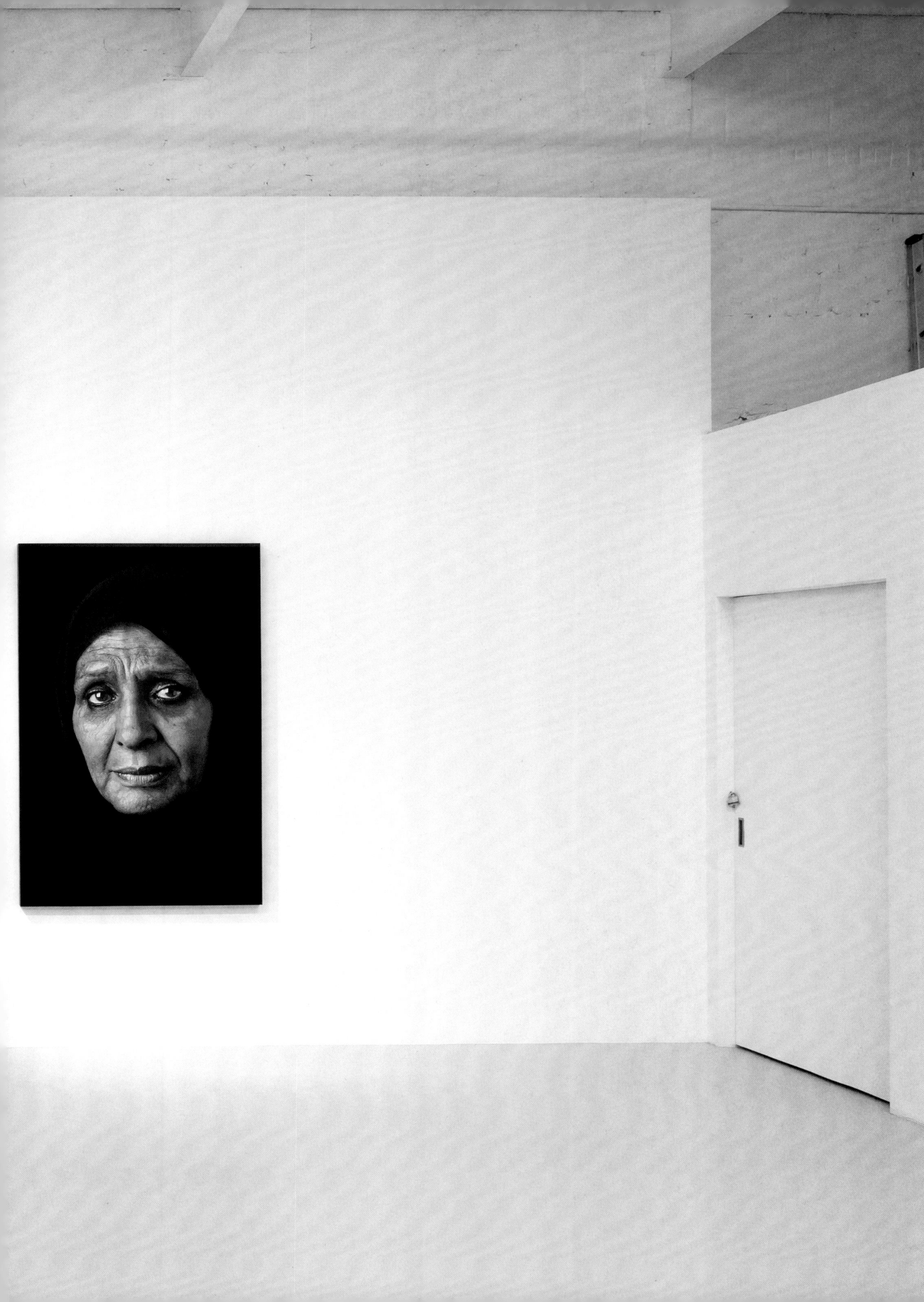

THE HOME OF MY EYES

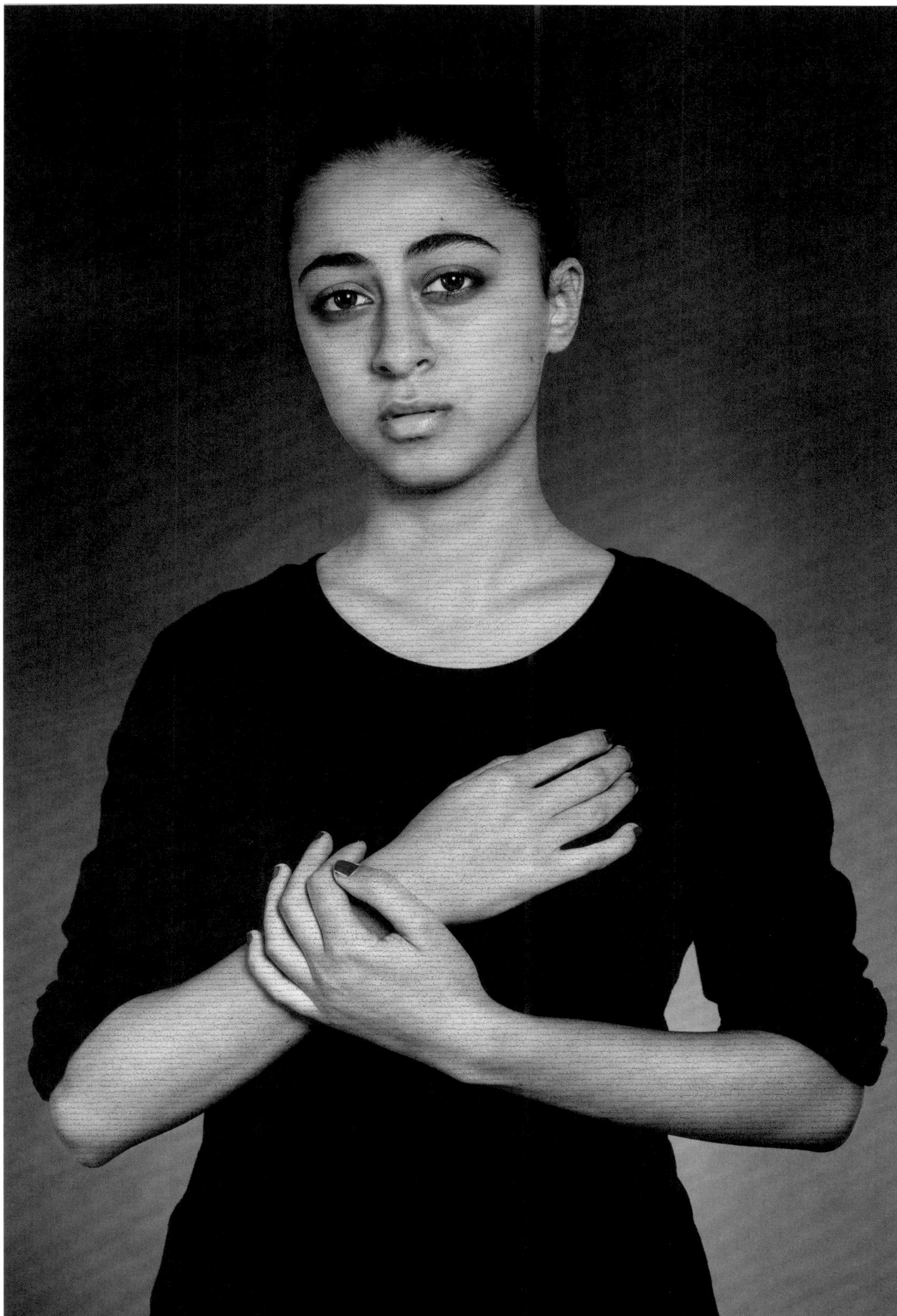

MALAKSIMA, 2015

Ink on LE silver gelatin print, 60 x 40 x 2 inches (152.4 x 101.6 x 5.1 cm).
Photograph taken by David Jiménez

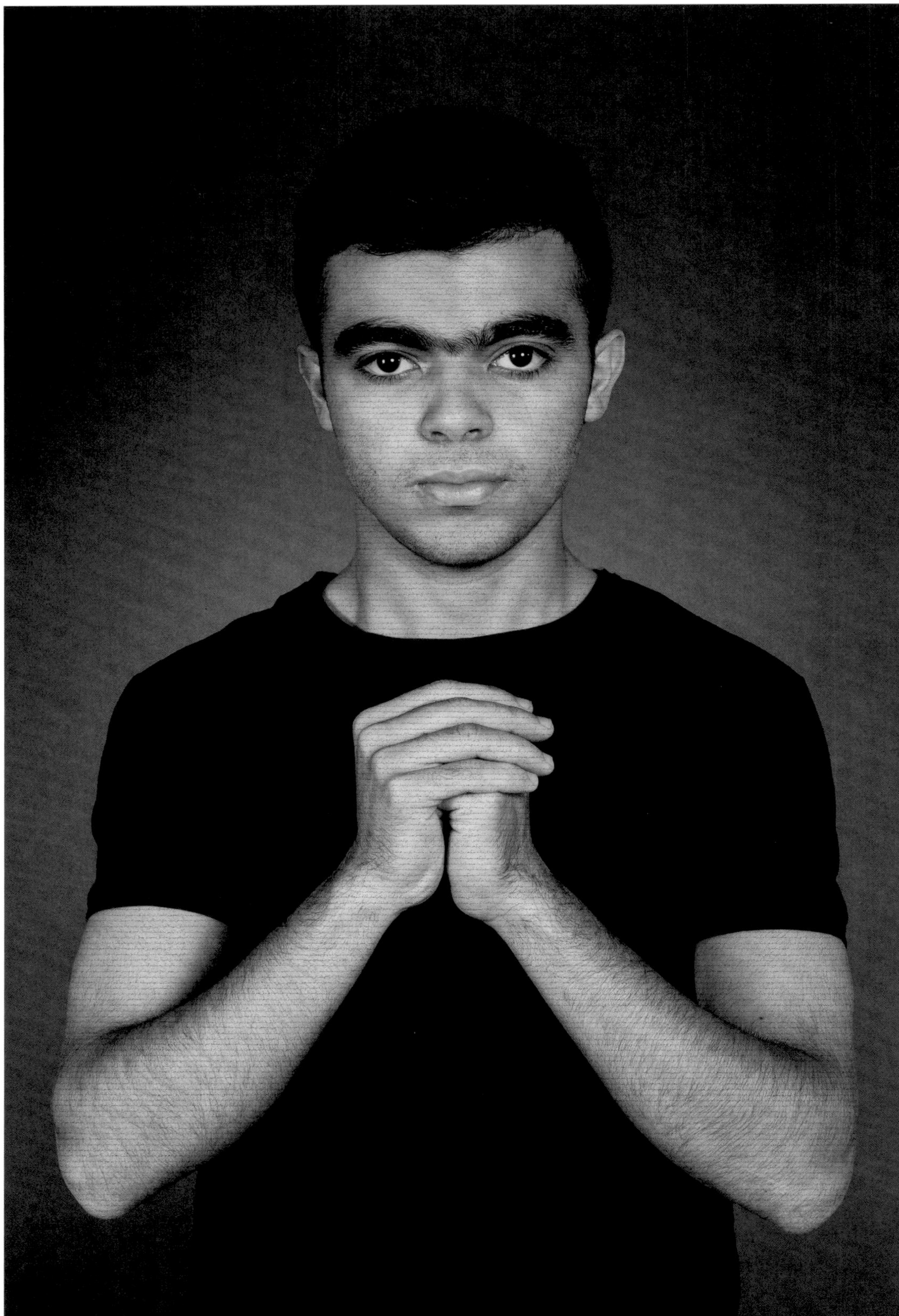

ADIL, 2015

Ink on LE silver gelatin print, 60 x 40 x 2 inches (152.4 x 101.6 x 5.1 cm).
Photograph taken by David Jiménez

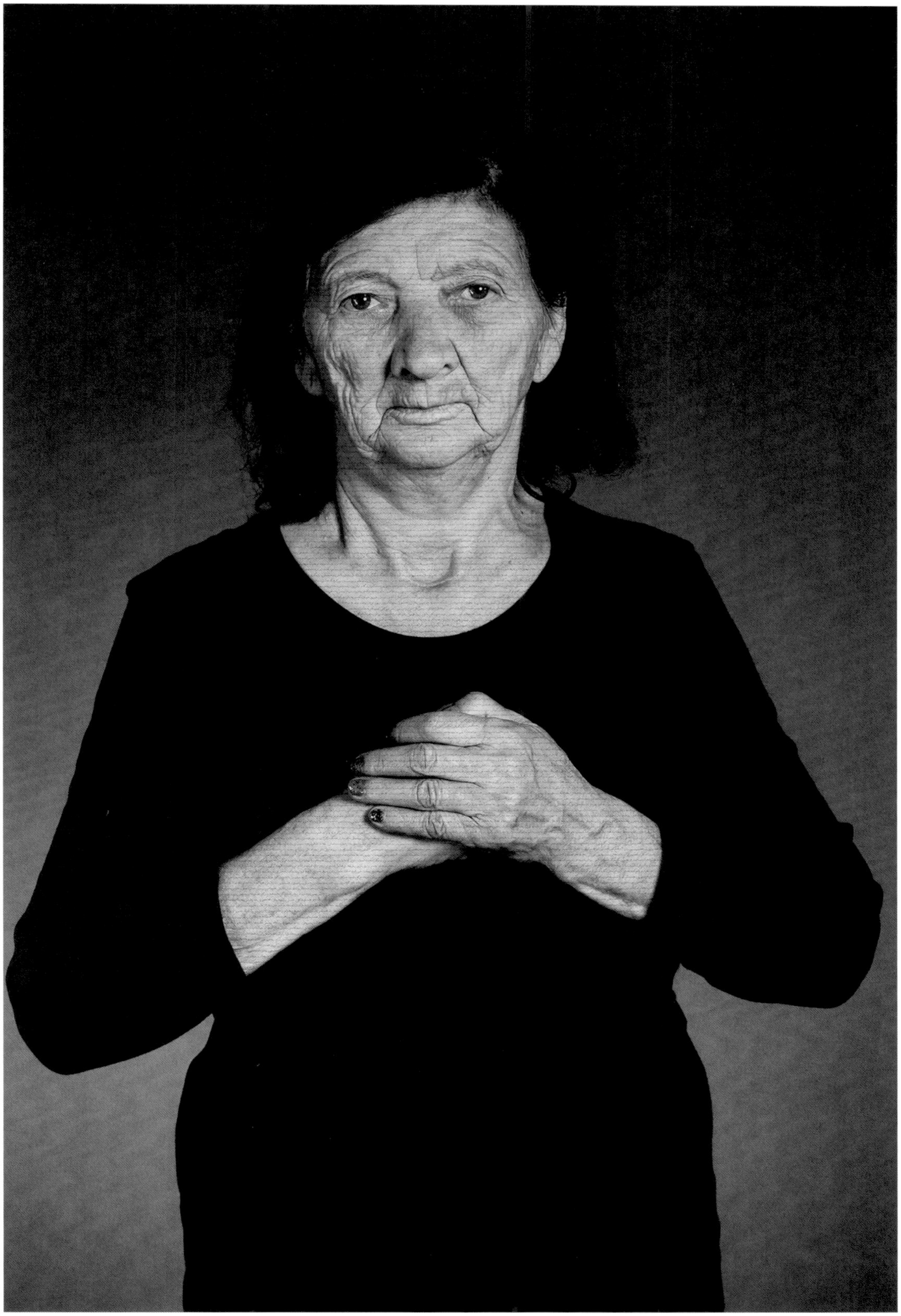

GIZBASTI, 2015

Ink on LE silver gelatin print, 60 x 40 x 2 inches (152.4 x 101.6 x 5.1 cm).
Photograph taken by David Jiménez

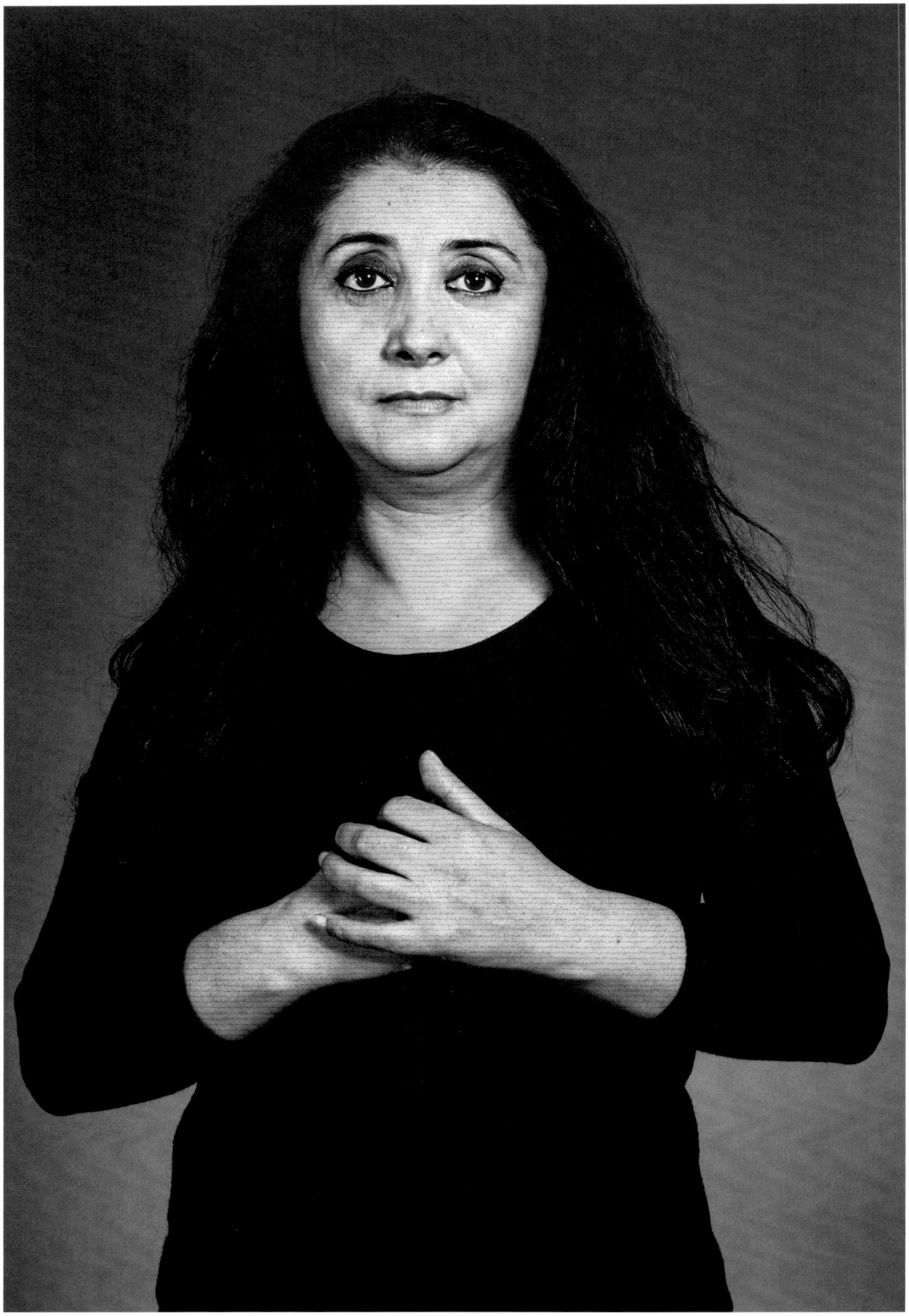

ILGARA, 2015

Ink on LE silver gelatin print, 60 x 40 x 2 inches (152.4 x 101.6 x 5.1 cm).
Photograph taken by David Jiménez

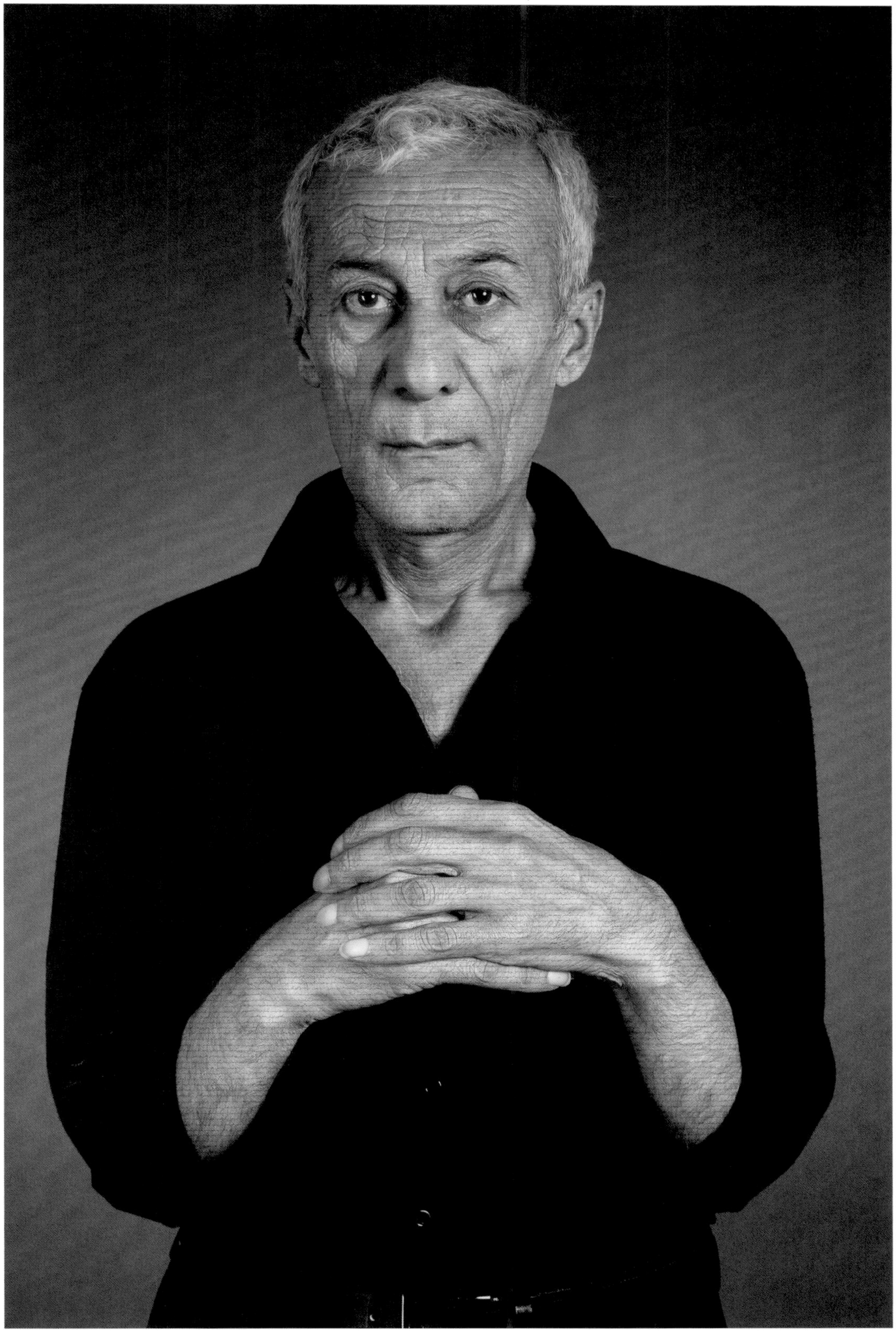

NAZIM, 2015

Ink on LE silver gelatin print, 60 x 40 x 2 inches (152.4 x 101.6 x 5.1 cm).
Photograph taken by David Jiménez

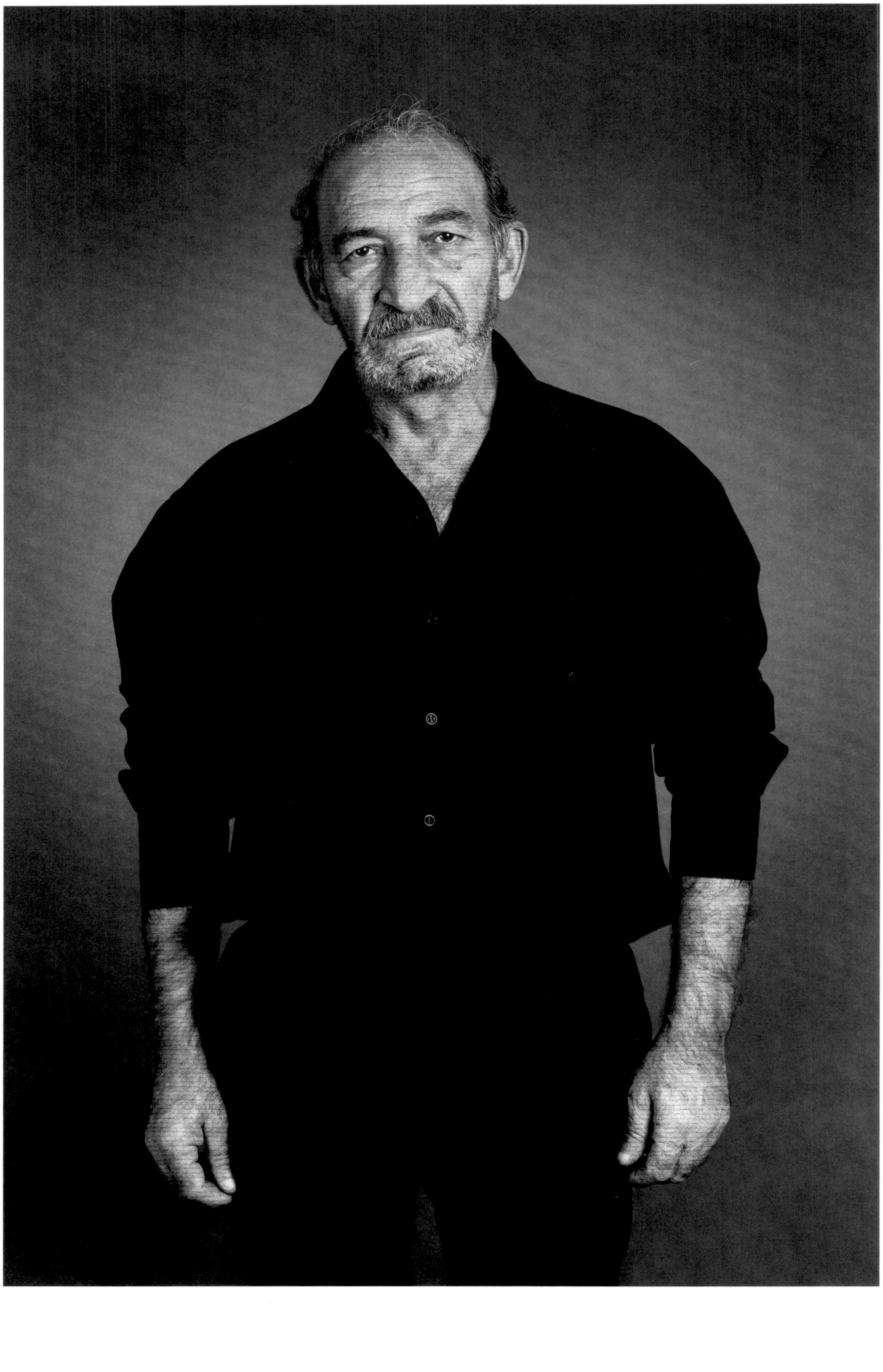

VAGIF, 2015

Ink on LE silver gelatin print, 72 x 48 x 2¼ inches (182.9 x 121.9 x 5.7 cm).
Photograph taken by David Jiménez

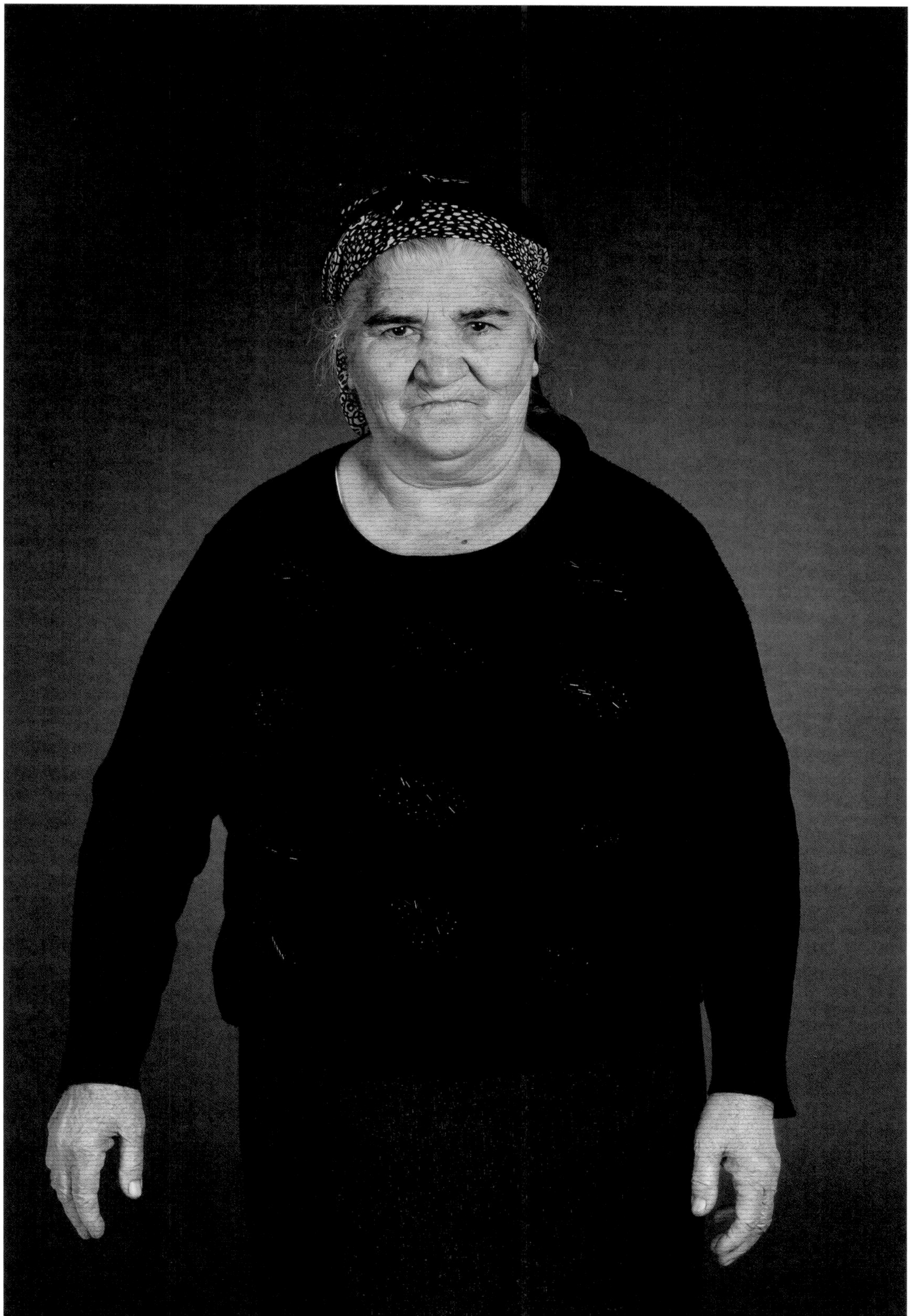

DURDANA, 2015

Ink on LE silver gelatin print, 72 x 48 x 2¼ inches (182.9 x 121.9 x 5.7 cm).
Photograph taken by David Jiménez

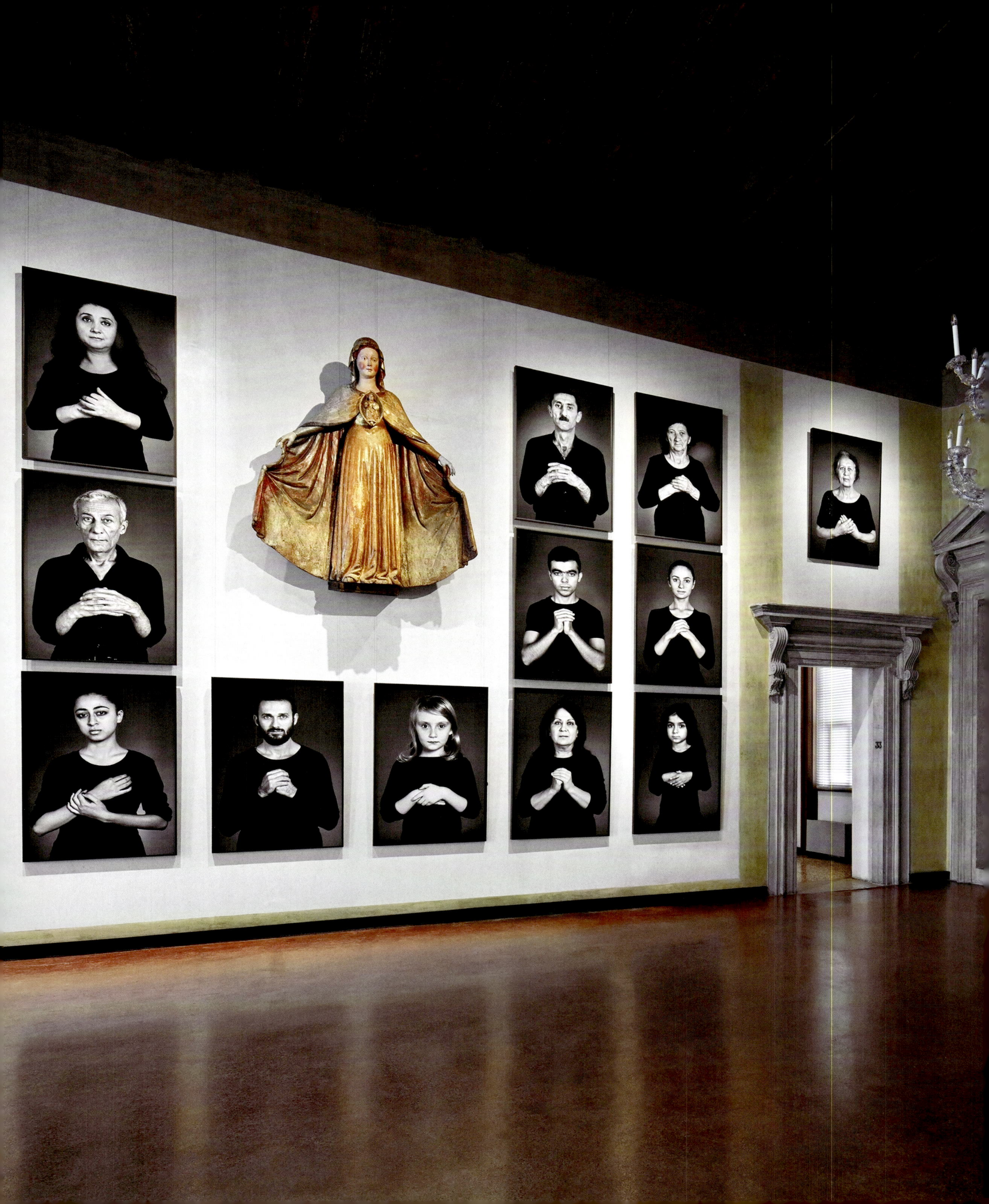

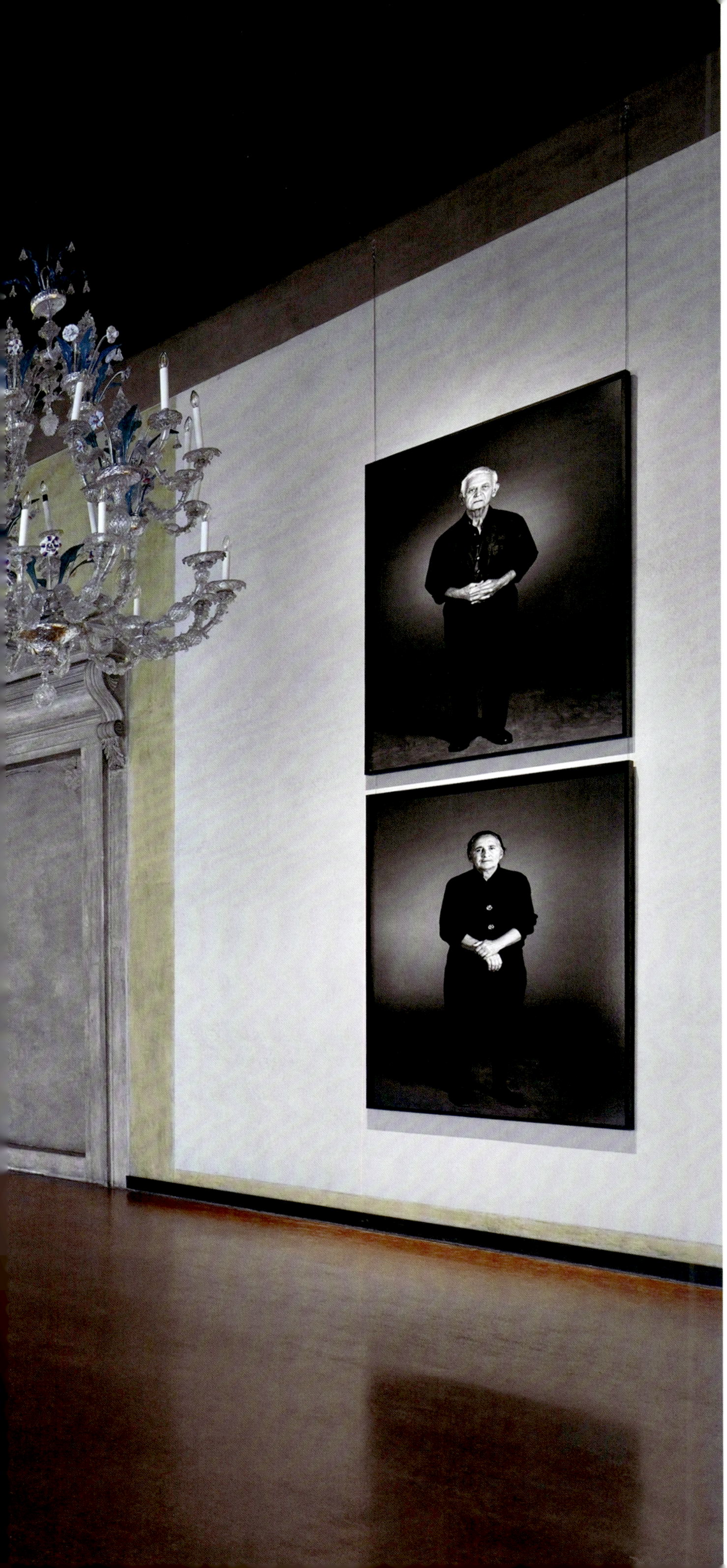

Installation view of *The Home of My Eyes*, Museo Correr, Venice, 2017. Photo by Philipp Ottendörfer

SHIRIN NESHAT: THE RAINBOW CATCHER
FARZANEH MILANI

The scene is etched forever on my life. Her voice still dances in my ears. My mother would choose a poetry book. Kiss it. Close her eyes to say a short prayer for the poet. Flip it open to a random page with her cigarette-stained index finger, and read a poem to her five children sitting in a circle around her. At times, our helpers around the house would join in. This was a moment of magic and wonder. In a hierarchical country where walls, veils, and codes of segregation abounded, poetry—like a shared ritual, like a national scripture—brought us all together. It created an egalitarian space, where women and men, young and old, literate and illiterate became equal partners-in-listening. It bridged divides across class, gender, ethnicity, and vastly varying levels of religiosity and literacy.

Imagining and, ultimately, creating such a safe and borderless space of communion and communication is the distinctive magic of Shirin Neshat's artistic universe. "In my art, I could create a universe where I felt at home," she explains.[1] "Perhaps that's why I became an artist. My imagination became my sanctuary . . . a place where I could build a fictional bridge between myself and my country."[2] Surely, the definition of home and homeland has evolved over the years for this diasporic artist. It has shifted from the national to the local, acknowledging the significance and primacy of experience, and concluding that "The idea of home is not the big things, it is not the bigger pictures of the architecture or the city, but it is the small things like the odor of your mother's cooking or the first day of spring and the way that you feel the smell of the blossoms, or the picnic with the family. It is not about the bigger things. It is the smallest little things . . ."[3]

From her early photographs to her feature films, Neshat has constructed—image by exquisite image—a space where connections and empathy are built across political and religious divides; where East and West prove to be imaginary constructs; the clash of civilizations leads to a dialogue among people; self-declared superiorities and pieties have no place; geography is not hierarchical; differences and similarities, common aspirations and shared challenges are acknowledged, and the power of the arts to liberate, connect, and heal is celebrated. "Politically conscious, humanitarian art is as necessary as the air we breathe today if we are to survive these trying times and not be condemned to repeat our endless cycle of terror and human tragedies," Neshat wrote recently in *The New York Times*.[4]

Iran, where Neshat comes from, is a country where art matters; where people grow up kissing books; where women, men, and children go on pilgrimage not only to the shrines of their holy saints, but also to the mausoleums of their quasi-sacred poets; where the very first word revealed to their prophet, who could actually not read, is a short command, "Read" (Surah 96), and a whole chapter of their holy book is titled "The Pen" (Surah 68). Neshat is the progeny of Scheherazade, a woman who knew how to transform a claustrophobic space of rage and revenge into a curative place of reconciliation. She was trained in a literary tradition whose daring storyteller volunteered to marry, against the advice of many, a king driven to vindictive fury and murder. At a time of national crisis, Scheherazade did not look away or remain uninvolved. She refused to be silently complicitous, justify the unjustifiable, and leave a tyrant to his perilous behavior. Knowing, but not fearing, consequences, she took a hazardous risk and engaged in political activism of the highest order. For one thousand and one patient nights, she cured a

1

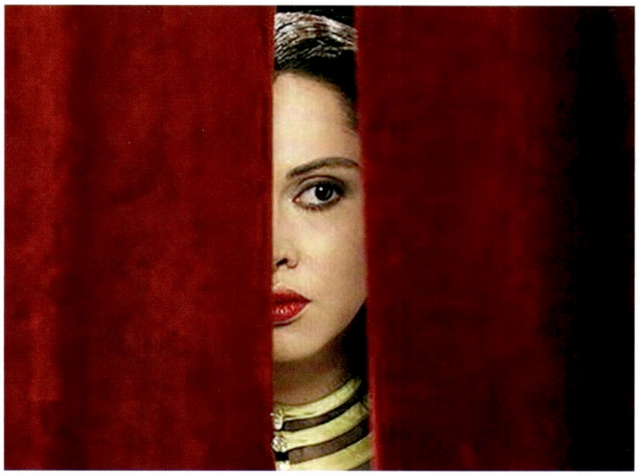

2

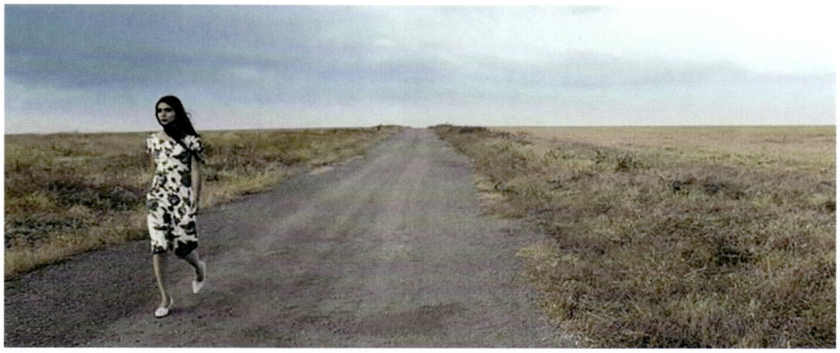

king turned serial killer with her stories. Under the looming threat of death, she relied on words rather than swords and triumphantly led the intransigent ruler to a place where absolutes did not rule, where good and evil, fragility and strength, pain and pleasure, victims and victimizers of both genders lived side by side. With infinite wisdom, she began every storytelling/therapy session with a short phrase, "There was one and there wasn't one." Who could listen to such an inspiring opener for two years and 271 consecutive nights and not be transformed by it?

Like her illustrious ancestor, Neshat declines to reduce life to binary opposites, to an either/or proposition. Hers is indeed a twilight zone where divergent views are synthesized, borders are crossed without a passport, walls demolished, stable categories trespassed, and bridges built. It is a liminal space where us and them, here and there, local and global are juxtaposed seamlessly, and from their stark contrast and confluence a new landscape is produced and marvels created—like the rainbow, formed when heaven and earth meet to celebrate the harmonious coexistence of falling rain with sunlight.

Deeply appreciative of the sacrosanct varieties and commonalities that define people and cultures, convinced that art always knows more than the artist just as dreams always know more than the dreamer, Neshat welcomes ambiguities and uncertainties, dives into unknown territories, summons the courage to be open to the unpredicted and the unpredictable. She travels nimbly between different media and venues, shifting from still photography and video installation to cinema and performing arts, moving from galleries and museums to movie theaters. As an intergeneric, commuter artist, she links converging narratives of highbrow and popular art. Unafraid to experiment, she blends Persian poetry, a key component of Iranian aesthetic sensibility, calligraphy, an exquisite whirling dance of words and letters on the page, and decorative motifs from Islamic, Persian, and Western painting, photography, performing arts, and cinematography.

To the perennial question asked of diasporic artists, "Where are you from?," Neshat's response is short: "I am a nomadic artist." And, indeed, she is nomadic not only in terms of geographical ruptures and national and international moves, but also in her wandering artistic journeys. "My nature is not to be fixated in one medium or style," she told Belinda Luscombe of *Time*.[5] Hers is the epitome of an artistic trajectory with an on-the-road mentality, one that refuses to stagnate in a familiar space. No wonder the image of an open road with no beginning and no end is a recurring motif in her work (fig. 2). It appears and reappears in several of her twenty-three video installations and in both her feature films. Just as a search for home and homeland characterizes Neshat's work, so does a sense of movement and

Fig. 1 Still from *Looking for Oum Kulthum*, 2017

Fig. 2 Still from *Faezeh*, 2008

mobility distinguish her art. It is a refreshing journeying between countries, languages, religions, and cultures.

And so it is that, on the magic carpet of Neshat's traveling art, we, her viewers, become fellow travelers of a wondrous voyage. Like Odysseus, who learned when he returned to Ithaca that both he and his Ithaca were no longer the same, we change with every journey and are reminded yet again that people—like countries—are full of paradoxes and ambiguities, that other cultures and languages, other faiths and rituals and artistic traditions are no less complex, no less worthy subjects of inquiry than any other. Together, we sail from one sea to another, from one universe of definitions and artistic conventions to another. We find ourselves mesmerized by the gateless ocean and follow our gaze to travel far and wide without being stopped by any obstacle (*Illusions and Mirrors*, 2013, p. 184; *Sarah*, 2016). We chase the wind and, in exquisite gardens, listen to the eloquent poetry of nature in its infinite glory. We dance with the dancing clouds, and find ourselves caressed by the roaming breeze. We hear the music of silence summon us to a place of unhurried reflection, spiritual transcendence, and joyous communion. It is as if death dies here, in these gardens, and time stops its tyrannical flow. It is as if the earth becomes, in the words of Elizabeth Barrett Browning, "crammed with heaven."

We also go to the heart of darkness, to the depths of cruelty and depravity. We witness political tyranny and religious fanaticism, cultural and political imperialism, and find ourselves appalled and shrinking. We see the ravages of prejudice, gender inequity, corruption and complacency, segregation and sexual abuse, physical violence and greed. We see dead female bodies floating Ophelia-like on weeping waters (*Mahdokht*, 2004; *Farokh Legna*, 2009). We see women torn by the pull and tug of conflicting impulses (*Soliloquy,* 1999–2000, p. 88); driven to madness (*Possessed*, 2001, p. 104); raped (*Faezeh*, 2008); suffering from anorexia (*Zarin*, 2006); sequestered in or forbidden to leave the family compound (*Pulse*, 2001; *Munis*, 2008); denied a public voice (*Turbulent*, 1998, p. 54); driven to suicide (*Munis)*. We see a young woman so desirous to become a mother and yet so frightened of her sexuality that she longs to become fertile like a woman-tree (*Mahdokht*). We watch the ravages of censorship and the atrocities reserved for those who speak truth to power (*The Last Word*, 2003; *Overruled*, 2012). We listen to warnings against love and pleasures of the flesh (*Fervor,* 2000). We witness memories turn into nightmares and the death of illusions and dreams, no less brutal than physical death (*Roja*, 2016, p. 194; *Sarah*, 2016; *Illusions and Mirrors*). We see men as prisoners in prisons of their own making, captive of restrictive definitions of masculinity (*Rapture*, 1999, p. 64), incapable of loving or being loved (*Farokh Legna*). We see violent wars and meet innocent-looking child-soldiers in killing fields (*Isaar*, 2003).

Remarkably, however, we always witness a creative mixture of human cruelty and courage; despair and hope; vulnerability and strength; harsh suffering and intense fellowship. We see violence and beauty, the sacred and the sacrilegious linked intricately (*Women of Allah*, 1993–97, p. 38; *Anchorage*, 1996). We find death as transience (*Soliloquy)* but also as birth and transit (*Passage*, 2001, p. 94). On the one hand, we see women enclosed within walls, their voices mutilated, their gaze controlled, their desire denied, their wanderlust kept under lock and key. On the other hand, we meet women who refuse to be confined by man-made rules, who do not descend into silence or inertia. We see them roam the streets, run, drive, fly, sail, sing, dance, cross the desert, explore forests and oceans, dream with their eyes wide open. We see them use their chadors as fluttering flags in the breeze (*Munis*), as sails to explore redemptive pathways and new frontiers in the ocean (*Rapture*), as wings to fly with (*Women without Men*, 2009). We see villains and victims, resistance and acquiescence next to each other in *The Book of Kings* (2012, p. 138). In the thirty-eight still photographs of *Women of Allah*, we see bodies that are veiled but whose faces, hands, and feet are turned defiantly into canvas, text, design, and subversive poetry—a staged spectacle, a living theater.

Although Neshat focuses her vigilant eyes on extremes, she never allows her art to become extremist. To the contrary, she "successfully combines different traditions and multiple languages into works of great emotional intensity . . . The artworks that result from this effort to confront and harmonize are never hybrids, but rather truly novel syntheses, where each element remains autonomous and is respected in terms of its specific original cultural and historical context."[6] Like the concurrent presence of light and darkness at the break of dawn and at twilight, what Iranians call "Wolf-and-Sheep," like the opening line of Charles Dickens' *A Tale of Two Cities*—"It was the best of times, it was the worst of times"[7]—her work in general and her last feature film in particular capture the paradoxical nature of life and its portrayal.

Poetic in its visual vocabulary, philosophical in its outlook, meticulous in its respect for facts, and skillfully complicated in its allegorical viewpoint, *Looking for Oum Kulthum* (2017, figs. 1, 3, 4), like Neshat's body of work, revolves around the intricate issue of who gets to represent whom. It also ponders the implications and meanings of segregation in its nuanced extremes, and subverts old stereotypes and familiar clichés about Muslim or Middle Eastern women. It examines the issue of sacrifice across a wide spectrum—from martyrdom for country, to singular devotion to career, to personal dedication to art—and probes how it intersects with the master narrative of motherhood that demands singleness of commitment and self-sacrifice from women. Characteristically, it also depends on its viewers' willingness to handle ambiguities, to welcome uncertainties, and to go on cross-cultural expeditions.

Looking for Oum Kulthum maps several voyages. It is the epic journey of a village girl, cross-dressed as a boy so she can sing in public, to become the most celebrated singer in the Arab world. Oum Kulthum's life had indeed a fairy-tale flavor to it—

3

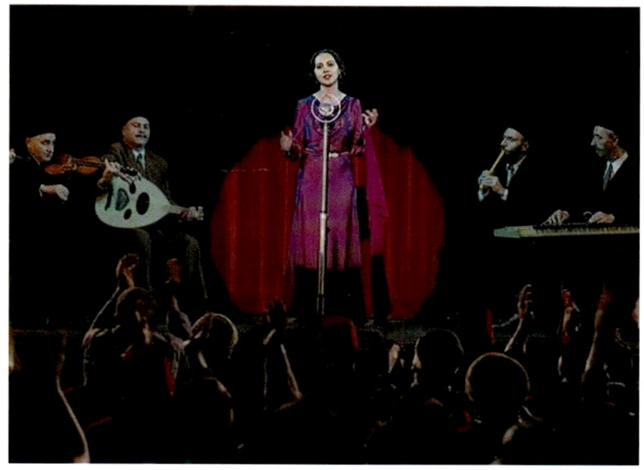

an independent and self-reliant Arab Cinderella who goes from rags to riches without tiny slippers or the help of a Prince Charming. Larger than life, she unveiled her body, uncaged her voice, and sang the song of a nation's soul. "It would not be an exaggeration to say that Um Kulthum embodied the cultural importance for the Arab world of Frank Sinatra, Elvis Presley, and The Beatles combined," writes David Shasha.[8] "Imagine a singer with the virtuosity of Joan Sutherland or Ella Fitzgerald, the public persona of Eleanor Roosevelt, and the audience of Elvis, and you have Umm Kulthum," maintains another.[9]

The film is also the difficult journey of a young Iranian filmmaker who is, in fact, looking for herself more than Oum Kulthum. Mitra wants to resolve her inner conflicts by studying the life of a woman whose circumstances and temperament differed from hers. Oum Kulthum was in control and fastidious; had no patience for self-revelation or public admission of any flaws—big or small. Mitra is voluble, emotional, and ready to confide. If one was glamorous and colorful, the other wears mostly black, as if to squeeze herself in as little space as possible. Greatness seems to be thrust upon one, while the other has to struggle for it and then feel guilty about being too ambitious and heartless. Mitra is consumed with contradictory aspirations, an intriguing and unresolved blend of certainties and doubts. On the one hand, she has internalized social norms and sanctions and wants to

Fig. 3 Still from *Looking for Oum Kulthum*, 2017

4

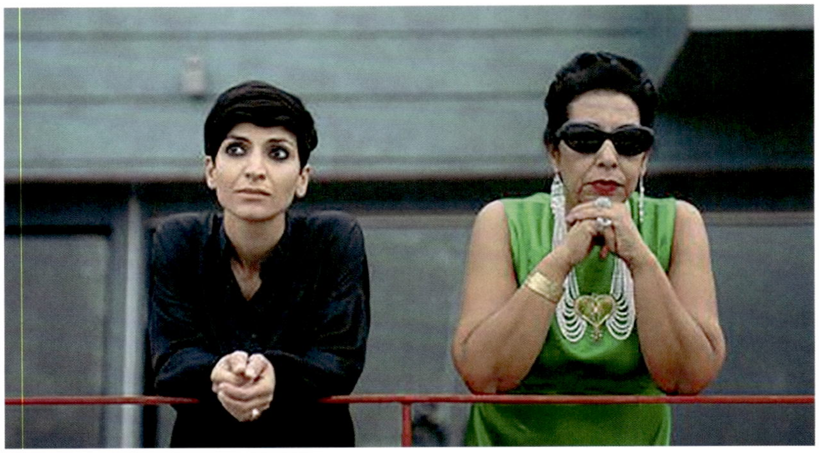

be a traditional mother. On the other hand, she is fully devoted to filmmaking. She can neither deny herself the privilege of listening to her mind and heart, nor free herself from what she has been taught in regard to ideal motherhood in a society that considers fatherhood an incontrovertible right and motherhood a privilege to be earned by self-sacrifice. She thus vacillates between two sets of values and aspirations. Unable to relinquish either, or to integrate the two, she is at war with herself. Frustrated, she finds herself compelled to change the facts of Oum Kulthum's life. She makes her lose her most valuable and cherished asset—her voice—in the most important concert of her life. Mitra eventually reorganizes her priorities, but she does not succeed in finishing her film.

Looking for Oum Kulthum is, perhaps most significantly, the sobering journey of Shirin Neshat, who wants to make a biopic but confronts many challenges and obstacles. To begin with, Oum Kulthum's life had a performative nature to it. From early childhood, when she appeared as a boy on stage, she had learned how to script her image, how to choreograph her public persona, how to look at herself through the eyes of her audience. She rarely, if ever, showed signs of vulnerability in public, and when the facade showed any cracks, she cloistered herself in the basement of her lush mansion, reemerging only when the mask was intact. Furthermore, Oum Kulthum is not only a music hall legend, but also a sacred national icon who personifies every Egyptian's, perhaps every Arab's, search for a voice. She articulates their longings, expresses their hopes and fears, and becomes known as Egypt's fourth Pyramid. How, then, can a biographer humanize such an icon, literally a national architectural treasure? How can she reconcile flawlessness and infallibility with the inherent imperfections of a lived life? How is she to portray the thousand and one paradoxes of a life metamorphosed into legend in a visual language that is proper and befitting? How can an Iranian woman who does not speak Arabic resurrect the world of an Egyptian woman who barely allowed the documentation of her private life? How can she prevent her autobiography from seeping into the biography she wants to produce? How, moreover, can she trespass the limits and limitations of biopics—especially in a region where traditionally the genre of life narratives is a literary and filmic misfit?

Rather than shying away from these paradoxes and obstacles, Neshat approaches them with candor, courage, creativity, and humility. Refusing to Hollywoodize her film, too conscientious to fabricate details of a life jealously held private, she proclaims her film to be self-reflexive—a film within a film. Acknowledging her challenges, she searches for a narrative strategy commensurate with the complicated subject at hand. She fragments both chronology and point of view, offers polycentric perspectives,

Fig. 4 Still from *Looking for Oum Kulthum*, 2017

and deploys innovative strategies and structures suited to the portrayal of the various ways in which Oum Kulthum broke all stereotypes (and Western viewers' expectations). With exacting, unblinking eyes, she navigates the extremes of worship and sanctification that have marked the telling of Oum Kulthum's life, and depicts her from the point of view of an Iranian film director and through the eyes of her Arab audience. We see Oum Kulthum sometimes as an adulated singer, other times as a woman deprived of her childhood, now as a challenger of cultural norms, a daring interloper in male territory, an appropriator of masculine prerogatives, including the stage and the microphone, and then, again, as a traditional woman, albeit one who knows how to navigate different political systems and outlast politicians.

Although Neshat shares certain similarities with Mitra, her outlook on life is different from her black-or-white, all-or-nothing philosophy. "What gives me a lot of pride from working on her story," Neshat says, "is that a lot of iconic women have had tragic endings and one of the reasons people make films about them is that they are dramatically interesting. People love the idea of the downfall of an iconic figure, like Princess Diana, Edith Piaf or Maria Callas, and especially with women. What's beautiful about Oum Kulthum is she never had that dip, she never did have a downfall, she sang until she died. She was most popular at the end. Four million people came to her funeral, she remained what she wanted to remain, whether you liked it or not. There is a lot of criticism about who she was, how she collaborated with the people in power but as an icon she is one who is not a tragic figure and this we must remember. Because as women we also need examples, we can have wonderful endings."[10]

Celebrating Oum Kulthum's iconic status as a diva while recognizing her flaws as a human being, Shirin Neshat finishes the film Mitra did not—could not—complete. Beyond all the twists and turns of Egyptian history and the vagaries of Oum Kulthum's life, she emphasizes her spellbinding voice and the magic and wonder she created in concert halls. She focuses her camera on the audience and shows how they were touched on the most elemental, emotional level, transported to paroxysms of joy, led to a non-hierarchical place, where young and old, women and men, rich and poor, veiled and unveiled, modern and traditional became equal partners-in-listening.

What a gift this safe and secure space of communion and communication! What a delight this voyage over the rainbow!

Farzaneh Milani is the Raymond J. Nelson Professor in the Department of Middle Eastern and South Asian Languages and Cultures and the Department of Women, Gender, and Sexuality Studies at the University of Virginia, Charlottesville.

NOTES

1 Alina Cohen, "How Shirin Neshat Got Her Start as an Artist," *Artsy*, March 1, 2019, at https://www.artsy.net/article/artsy-editorial-shirin-neshat-path-art-school-outcast-contemporary-art-icon.

2 Yasmine El Rashidi, "Egypt: Face to Face," *The New York Review of Books*, March 18, 2014, at https://www.nybooks.com/daily/2014/03/18/neshat-egypt-face-to-face/.

3 "An Encounter with Artist Shirin Neshat," DW Documentary, at https://www.youtube.com/watch?v=WoFouzeYy0o.

4 Shirin Neshat, "When Does Political Art Cross the Line?," *The New York Times*, December 5, 2018, at https://www.nytimes.com/2018/12/05/opinion/shirin-neshat-political-art.html.

5 Belinda Luscombe, "Visions of an Orthodox Beauty," *Time*, October 15, 2001, pp. 90–91.

6 Ida Gianelli, "Foreword," in *Shirin Neshat* (Milan: Charta, 2002), p. 9.

7 Charles Dickens, *A Tale of Two Cities* (New York: Penguin, 2003), p. 5.

8 David Shasha, "The Voice of Um Kulthum: A Place to Start the Dialogue," *The Huffington Post*, June 2, 2010.

9 Virginia Danielson, "Umm Kulthum Ibrahim," *Harvard Magazine*, July 1, 1997, at https://harvardmagazine.com/1997/07/umm-kulthum-ibrahim.

10 E. Nina Rothe, "The Price Women Pay: Talking with Shirin Neshat about 'Looking for Oum Kulthum' in Venice," *The Huffington Post*, September 13, 2017.

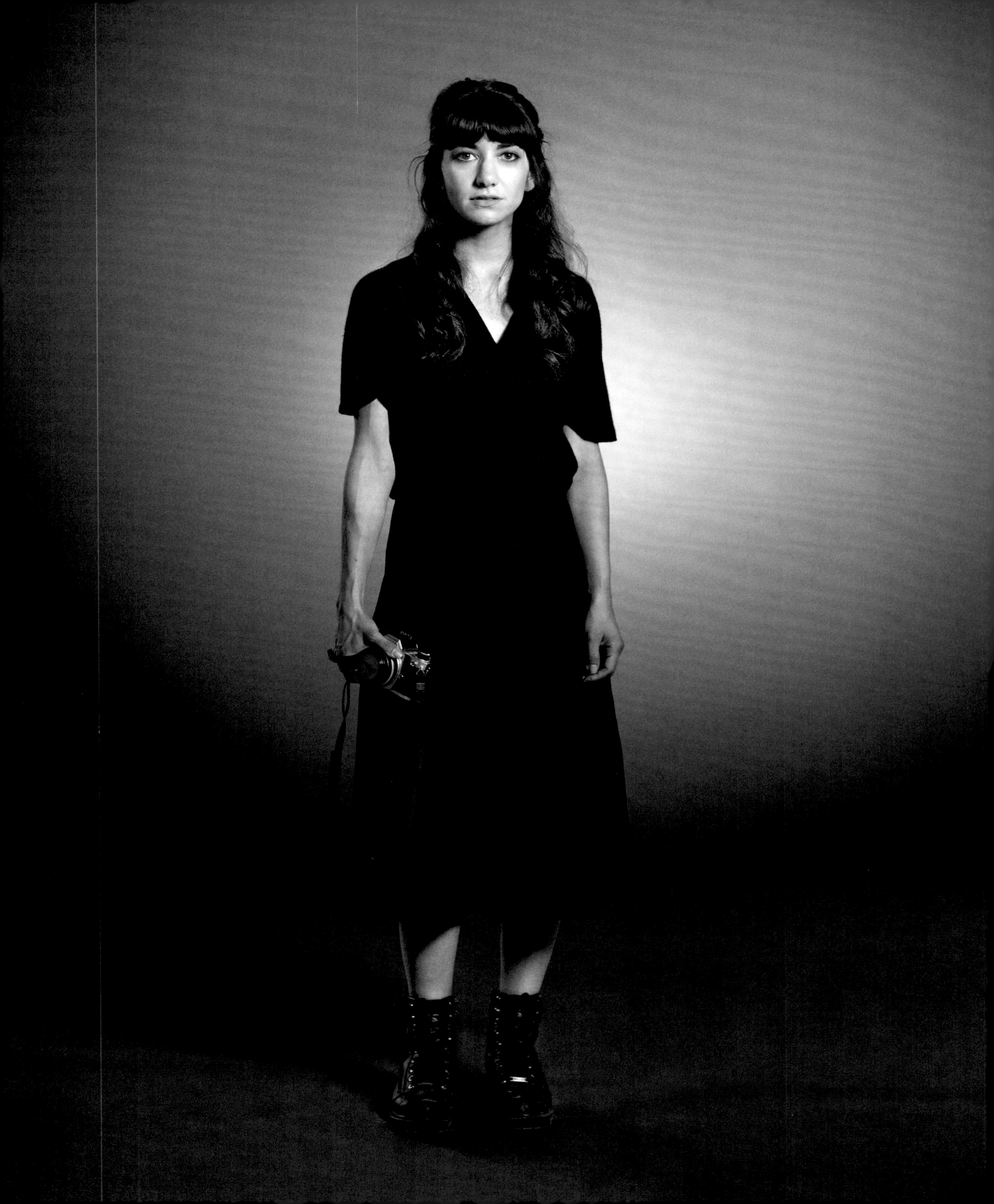

ILLUSIONS AND MIRRORS, ROJA, LAND OF DREAMS

In the winter of 2013, Neshat shot the video *Illusions and Mirrors*, commissioned by the fashion house Dior, on Long Island and in Yonkers, New York. The video follows the journey of a woman, played by Natalie Portman, who pursues a mysterious man across a beach and through a mansion. The result of the woman's journey is a confrontation with herself, as well as her mother, in the corridors and rooms of the house. The video is book-ended by images of the ocean, at the beginning seen in a blur, and at the end shown clearly. *Illusions and Mirrors* echoes mystical journeys found in other Neshat works, such as *The Logic of the Birds* (2001), suggesting that the point of view of the woman has changed through this dreamlike voyage into herself. "This film pays tribute to the black-and-white silent films made by Surrealist filmmakers such as Man Ray, Jean Cocteau, Luis Buñuel and, later, the wonderful experimental filmmaker Maya Deren," Neshat said of the work. "It is a big departure for me, as it moves away from all my past socio-political subjects regarding Iran and Islam and enters a very timeless and universal story."[1]

Illusions and Mirrors is the first video in what has become known as the *Dreamers* trilogy, which also includes *Roja* and *Sarah* (both 2016). As the title suggests, all three concern dreams. The videos, filmed entirely in U.S. locations, shift the focus of Neshat's work from meditations on political events and universal rituals of love and loss to the impact of exile on her perceptions of life in the United States. These videos, along with the artist's latest work, *Land of Dreams* (2019), return to some of her earliest American and European filmic influences, bringing them directly to bear on contemporary America.

In *Roja*, the title character (played by actress Roja Heydarpour, often taken for Neshat's doppelgänger) attends a performance of a song by The Seekers called "The Carnival Is Over," sung by a shirtless, presumably American, man at The Egg Center for the Performing Arts in Albany, New York (a location used fifteen years earlier in *Soliloquy*). The lyrics, about leaving a loved one, affect Roja deeply, and she is seen tearing up in the audience.

Previous spread
Simin (detail), from *Land of Dreams*, 2019. Photograph taken by Lina Bertucci

The man disapproves of her display of emotion and attempts to shame her: "I think you should come up onto the stage. You need to be seen. What's the matter, are you shy? I don't understand what you are doing out there hiding . . . I think you should come up here and tell your pretty lies to everyone who can see you, because in this story, you are going to be revealed."

Roja, a visualization of an actual dream of Neshat's, is evocative of how physical borders of exile become internalized and part of a person's psychology. After being harassed by the man, Roja leaves the building and treks through a desert, which rhymes geographically with parts of Iran although shot in a quarry in Pennsylvania. She confronts her mother, who turns monstrous as Roja takes flight from her. Roja is labeled a stranger, unjustly marked as a menacing figure, yet she cannot return home, for it has changed so much that it rejects her.

Land of Dreams consists of a series of photographic portraits and two videos shot in New Mexico in May and June 2019. The series tracks the movements of an Iranian photographer as she documents the dreams of rural Americans on a journey across the United States. She takes their photographs, records the dreams of her sitters, then delivers the dreams to an Iranian colony to be logged. According to Neshat, *Land of Dreams* represents her direct engagement with the United States under the presidency of Donald Trump, as hostile rhetoric about immigrants increases daily. The project confronts the long-standing tension between the U.S. and Iran, using political satire to evoke and examine some of the political and social absurdities shared by the two countries.

The videos are the most direct intersection to date of the immersive installation strategies found in photography series such as *The Book of Kings* and Neshat's multichannel approach to video. Debuting in this exhibition, *Land of Dreams* will be deployed throughout three rooms connected by a corridor. The first two rooms alternate between American homes and the Iranian colony, exploring the many dimensions between dreams and reality, between ordinary daily life and prejudices and fears that are lived internally. The final room of the exhibition features a large assemblage of the woman's images, installed floor to ceiling—an almost obsessive recording of the contemporary moment.

A feature-length version of *Land of Dreams*, in collaboration with Buñuel screenwriter Jean-Claude Carrière, is in development.

NOTE

1 Shirin Neshat quoted in "Illusions and Mirrors with Natalie Portman," *Wall Street International*, October 22, 2014, at https://wsimag.com/art/11787-illusions-and-mirrors-with-natalie-portman.

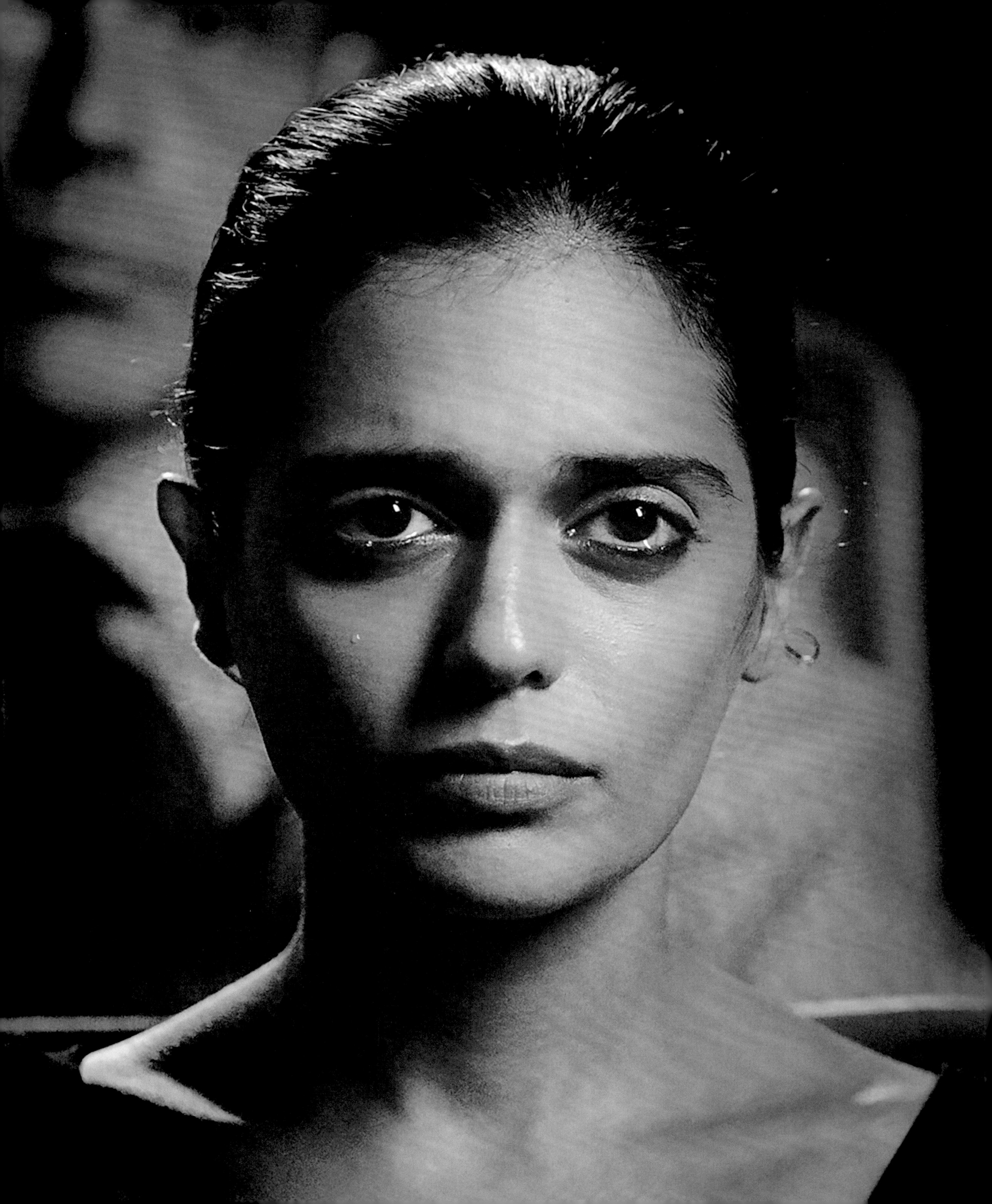

From the script of ROJA

I think you should come up onto the stage. You need to be seen.
What's the matter, huh, are you shy?
I don't understand what you are doing out there hiding.
Why don't you come onto the stage?
I think you should come on up here and tell your pretty lies to everyone where they can see you,
because in this story, now, you are going to be revealed,
you are going to be exposed as the deceitful, cunning, manipulative wretch that you are.

Get up here right now!

Still from *Roja*, 2016

ILLUSIONS AND MIRRORS

2013
SINGLE-CHANNEL VIDEO INSTALLATION
HD VIDEO
DURATION: 13 MINUTES, 22 SECONDS
FILMED IN NEW YORK

DIRECTOR: SHIRIN NESHAT
ACTRESS: NATALIE PORTMAN
DIRECTOR OF PHOTOGRAPHY: DARIUS KHONDJI
EDITORS: GEORGE CRAGG AND NARIMAN HAMED
MUSIC AND SOUND DESIGN: JOHNNY AZARI
EXECUTIVE PRODUCER: ANNIQUE DECAESTECKER
LINE PRODUCER: PAUL LAURENS
PRODUCTION MANAGER: DANI ROTSTEIN

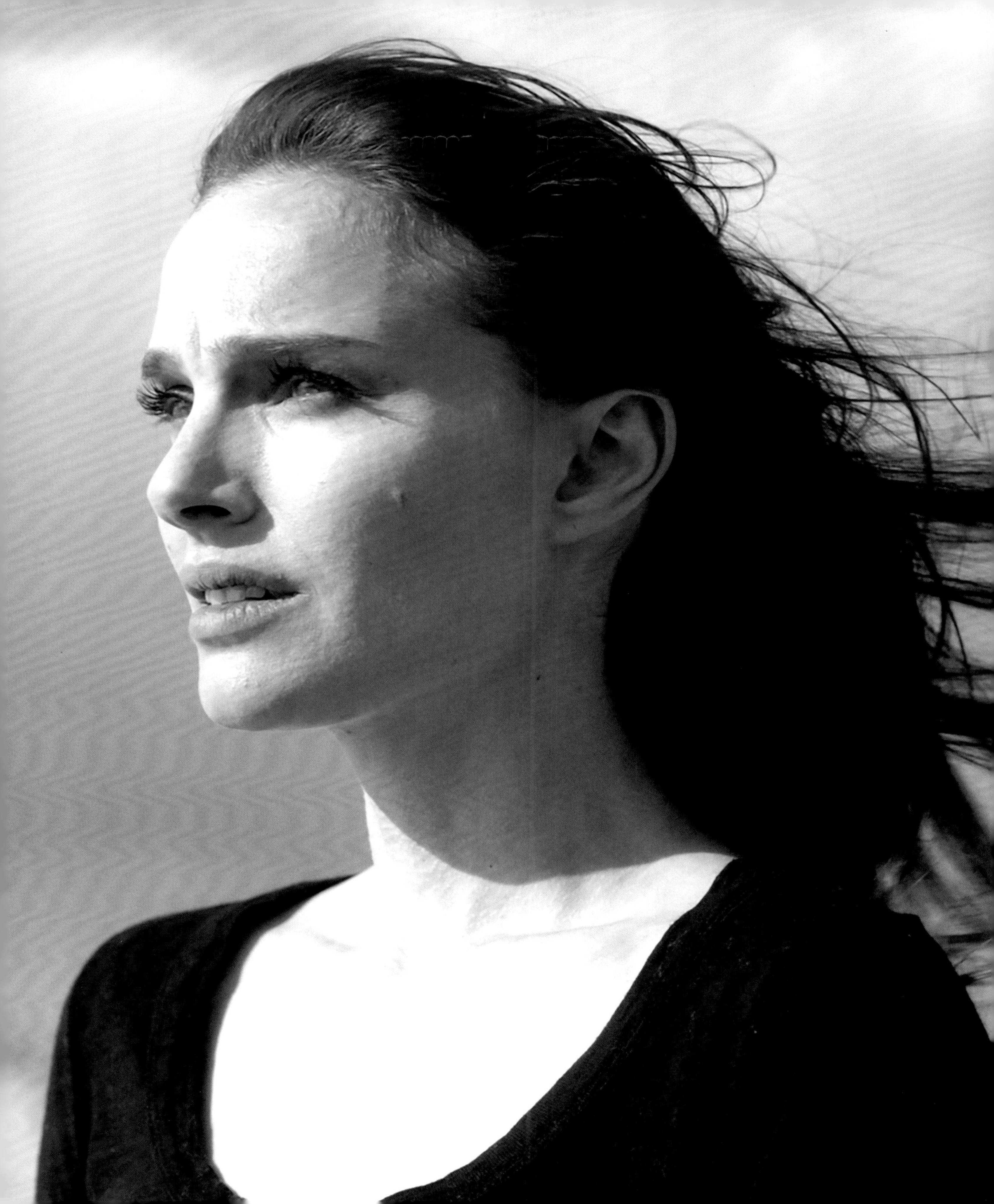

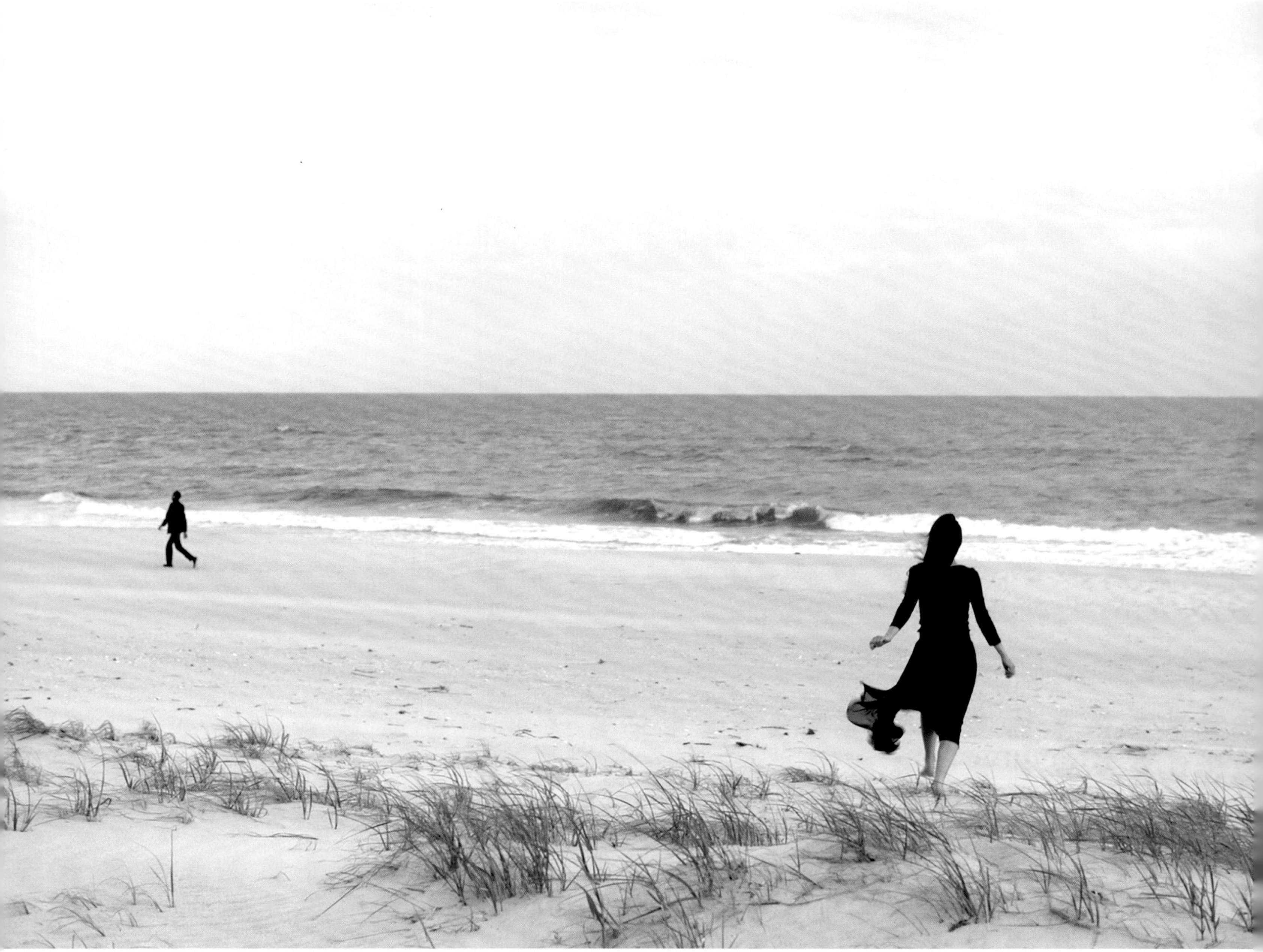

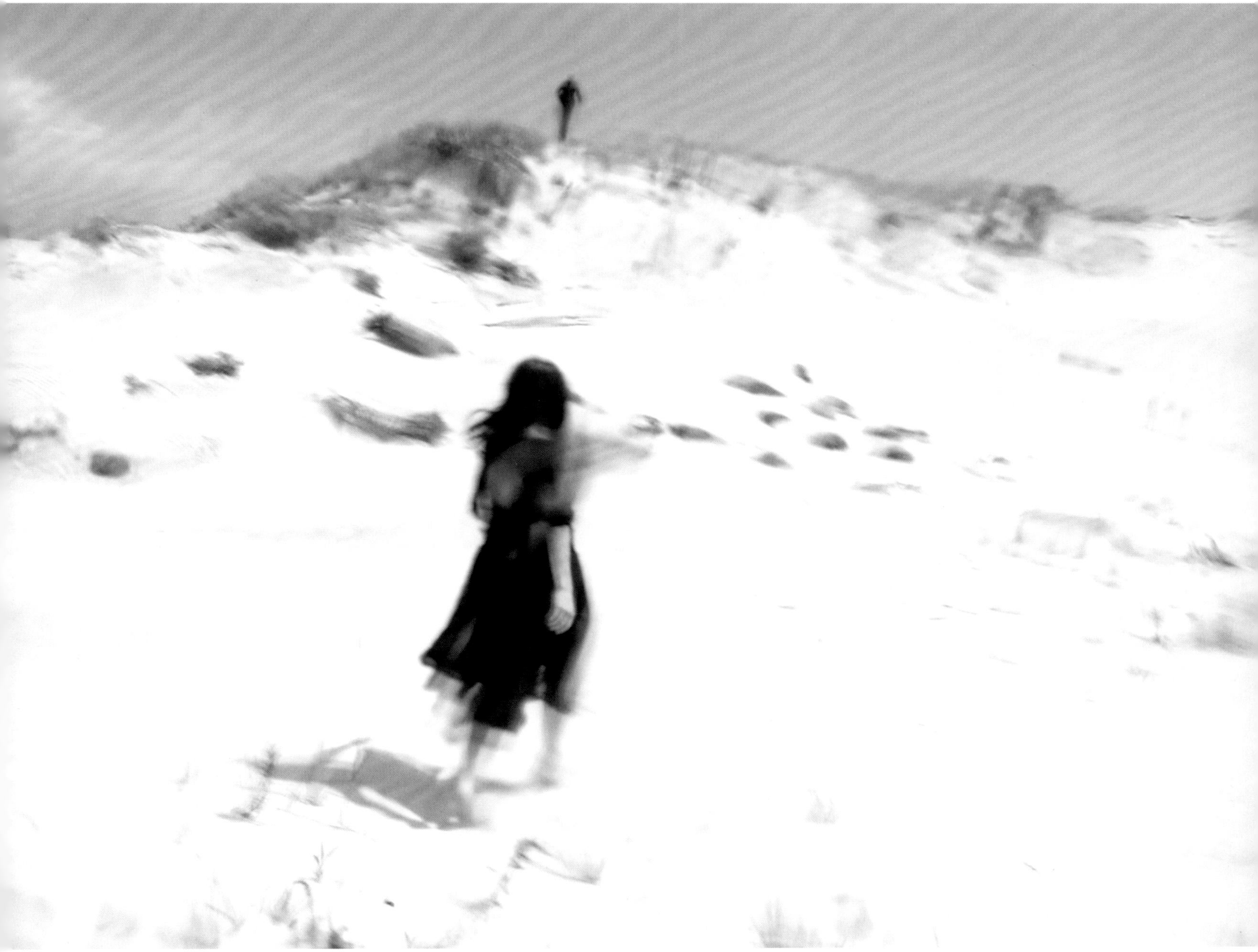

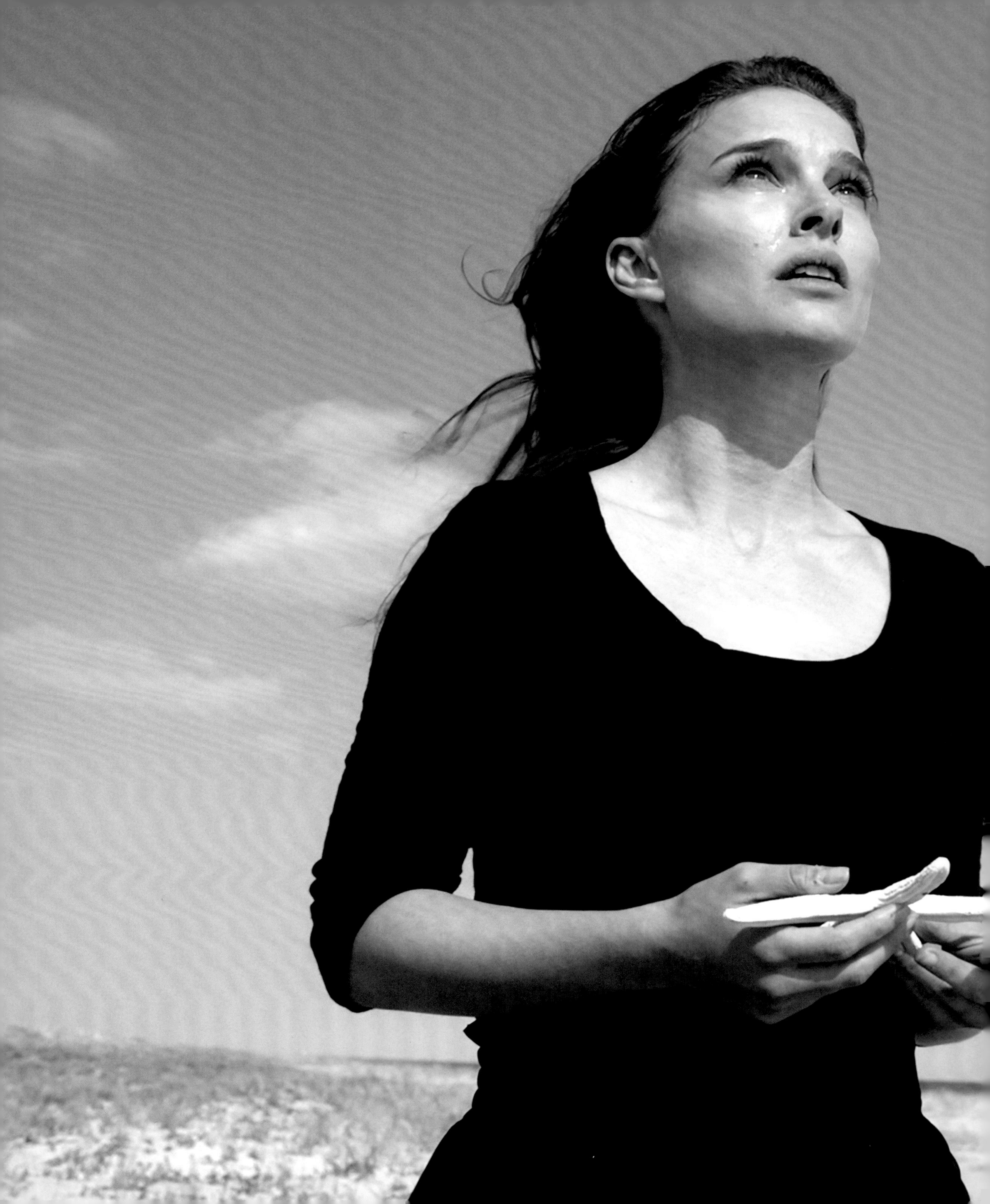

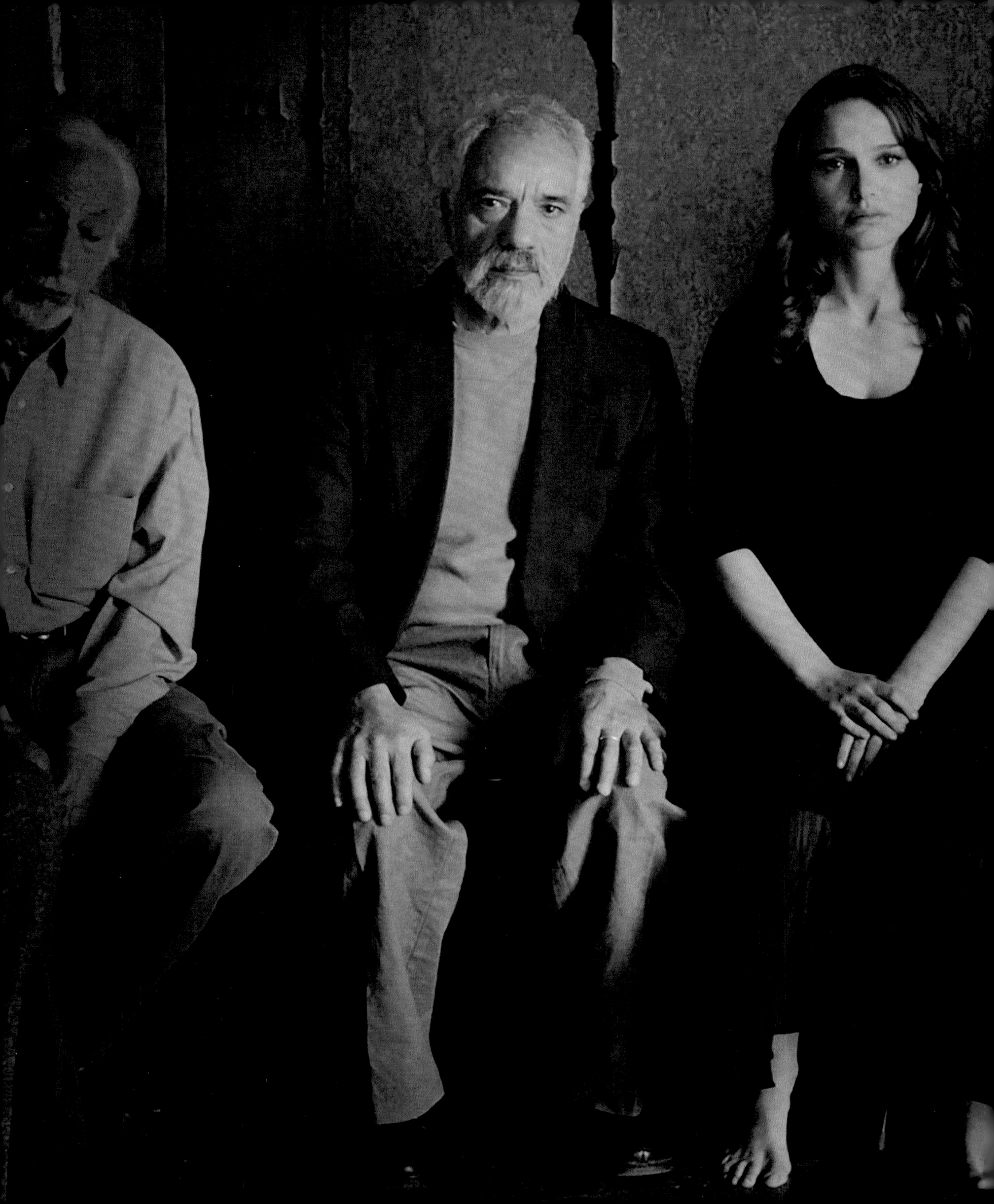

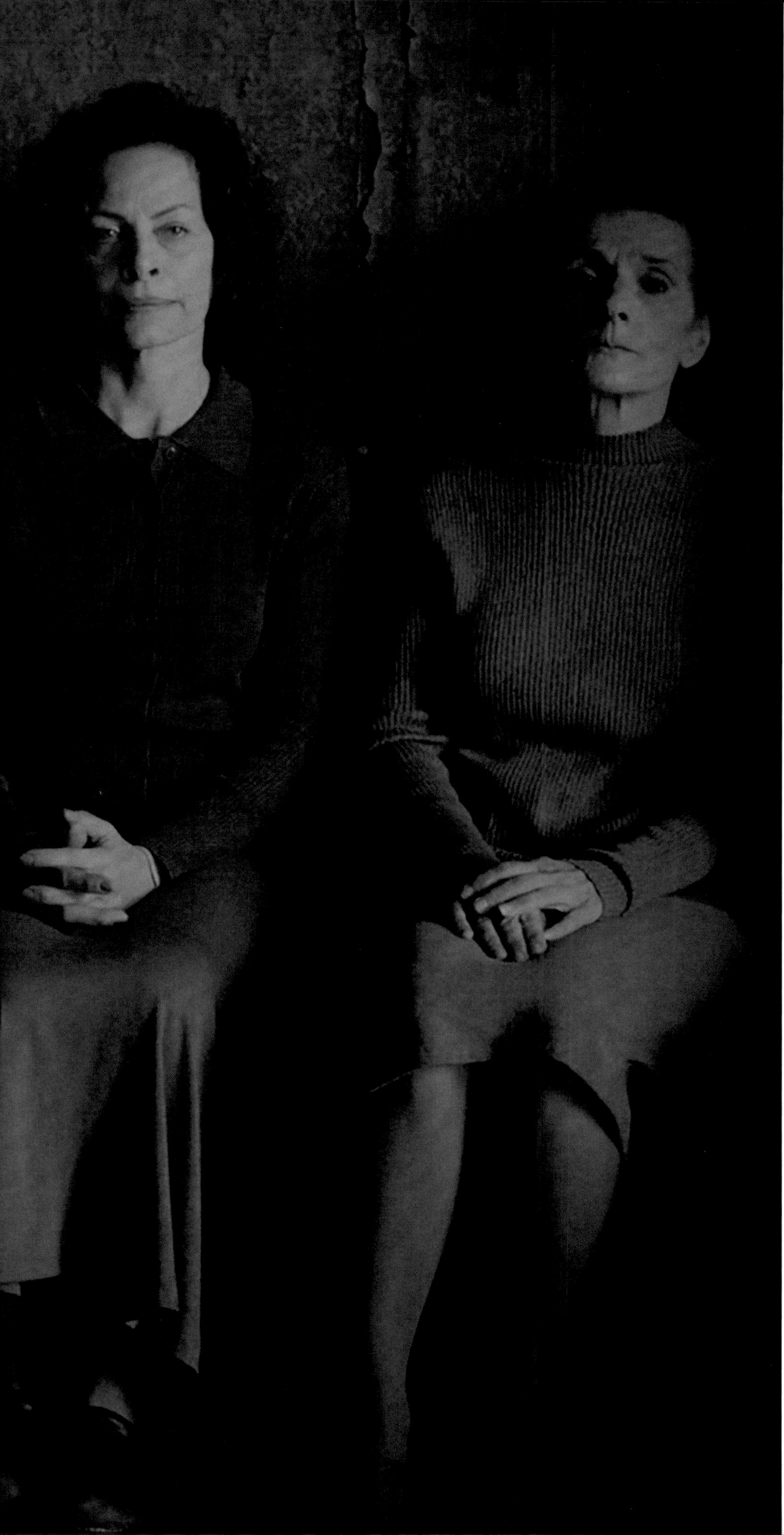

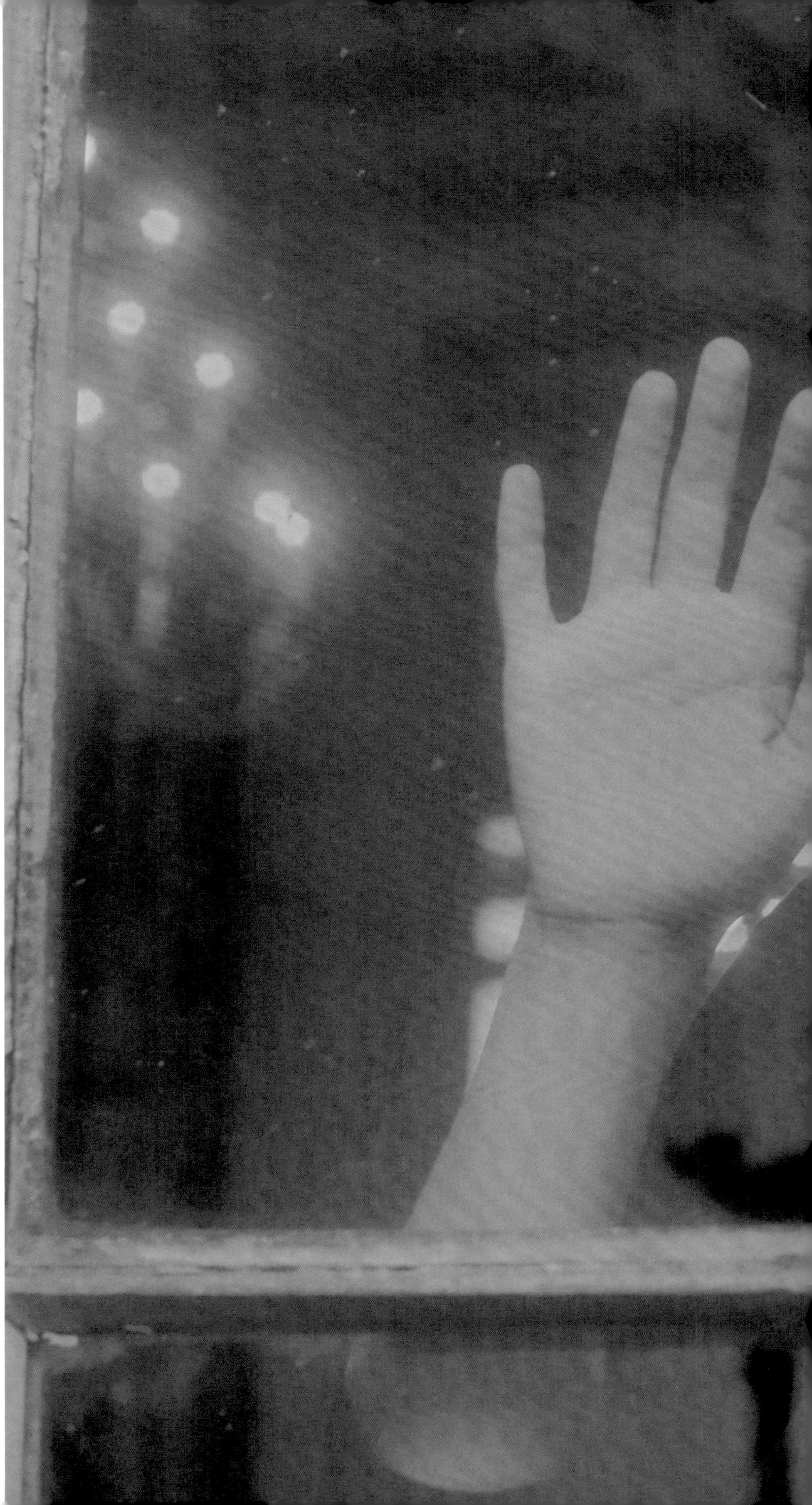

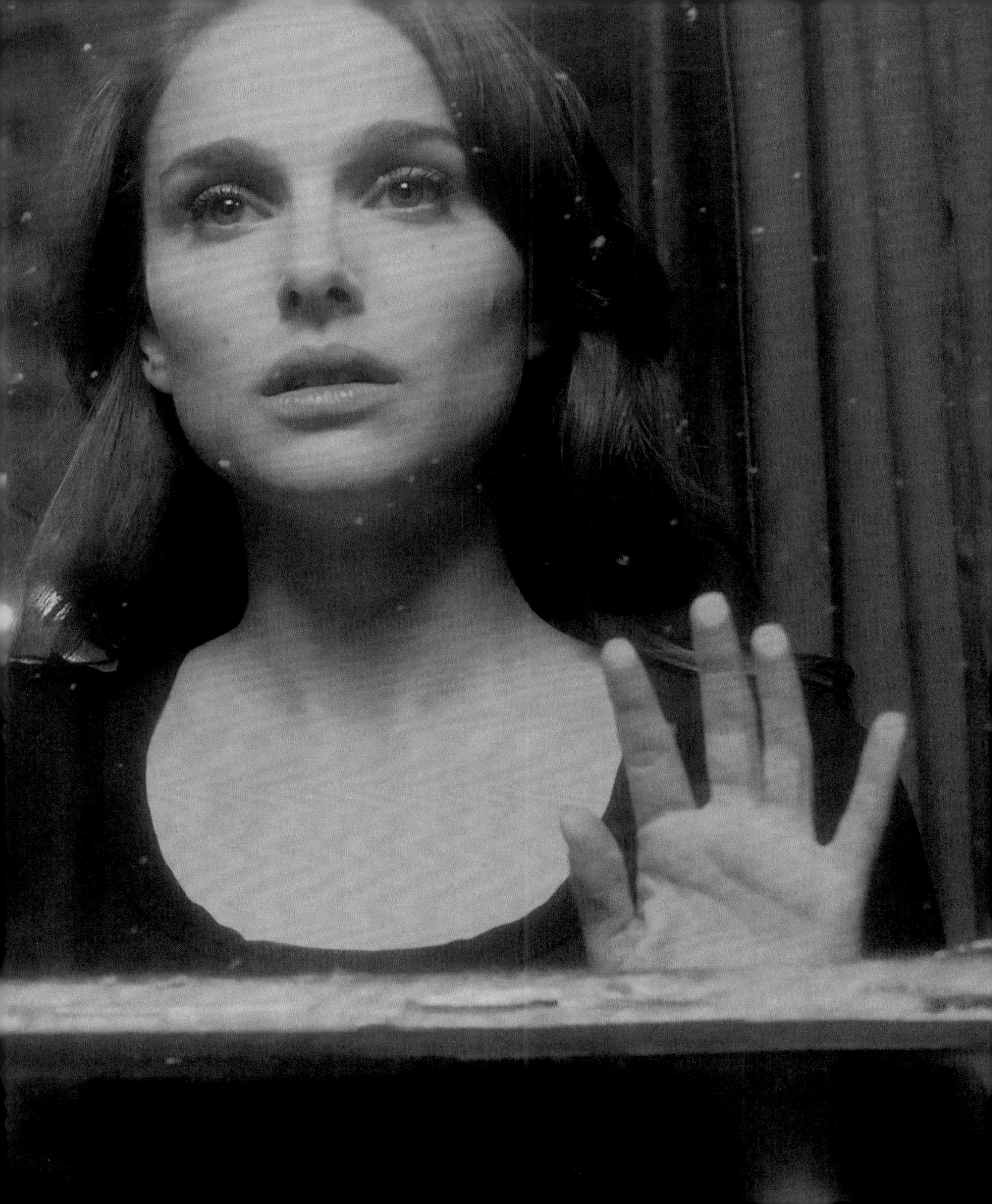

ROJA

2016
SINGLE-CHANNEL VIDEO INSTALLATION
HD VIDEO MONOCHROME
DURATION: 15 MINUTES, 20 SECONDS
FILMED IN NEW YORK AND PENNSYLVANIA

DIRECTOR: SHIRIN NESHAT
WITH ROJA HEYDARPOUR, TARANEH FARJAD, AND BILL STOKES
VOICE DUBBING: CHRISTOPHER SEARS
SONG PERFORMED BY: ANOHNI
PRODUCED AND EDITED BY: SHOJA AZARI
DIRECTOR OF PHOTOGRAPHY: GHASEM EBRAHIMIAN
MUSIC AND SOUND DESIGN: JOHNNY AZARI
PRODUCTION DESIGN AND COSTUME DESIGN: SHAHRAM KARIMI
HAIR AND MAKEUP ARTIST: MINA GHORAISHI
EXECUTIVE PRODUCERS: SHIRIN NESHAT AND GLADSTONE GALLERY
LINE PRODUCER: PAMELA MORIARTY
PRODUCTION MANAGER: KRISTAL MOSLEY

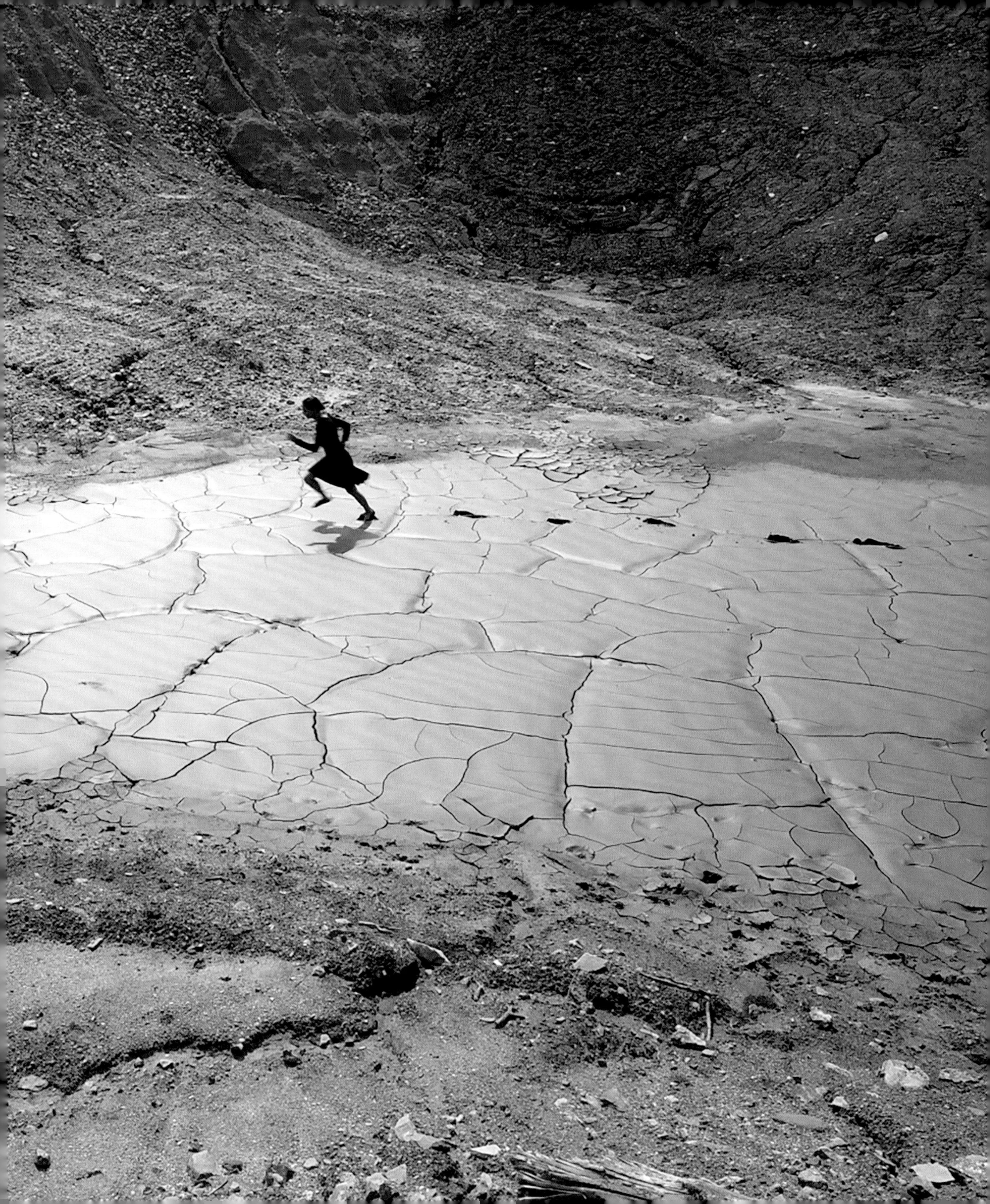

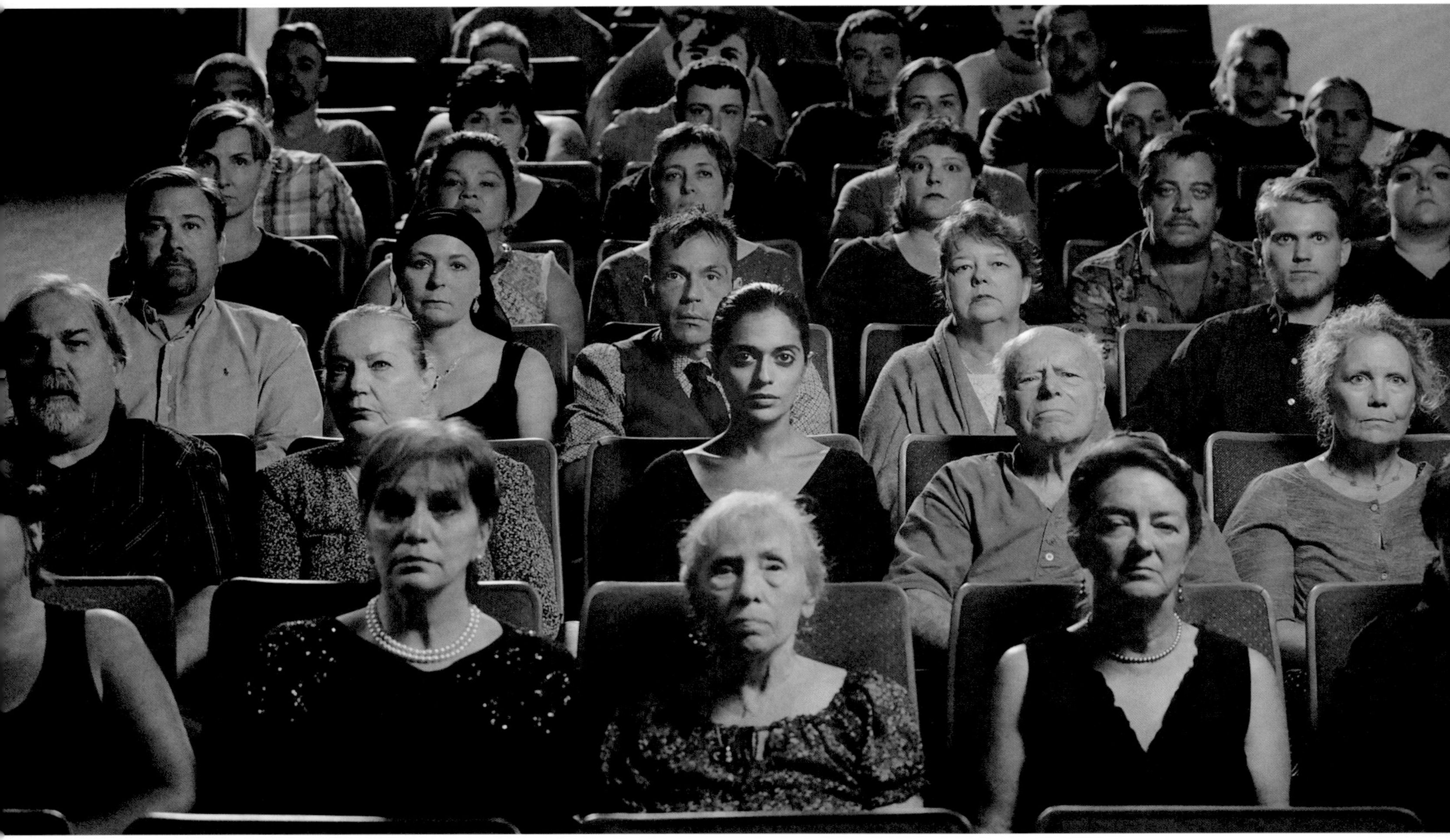

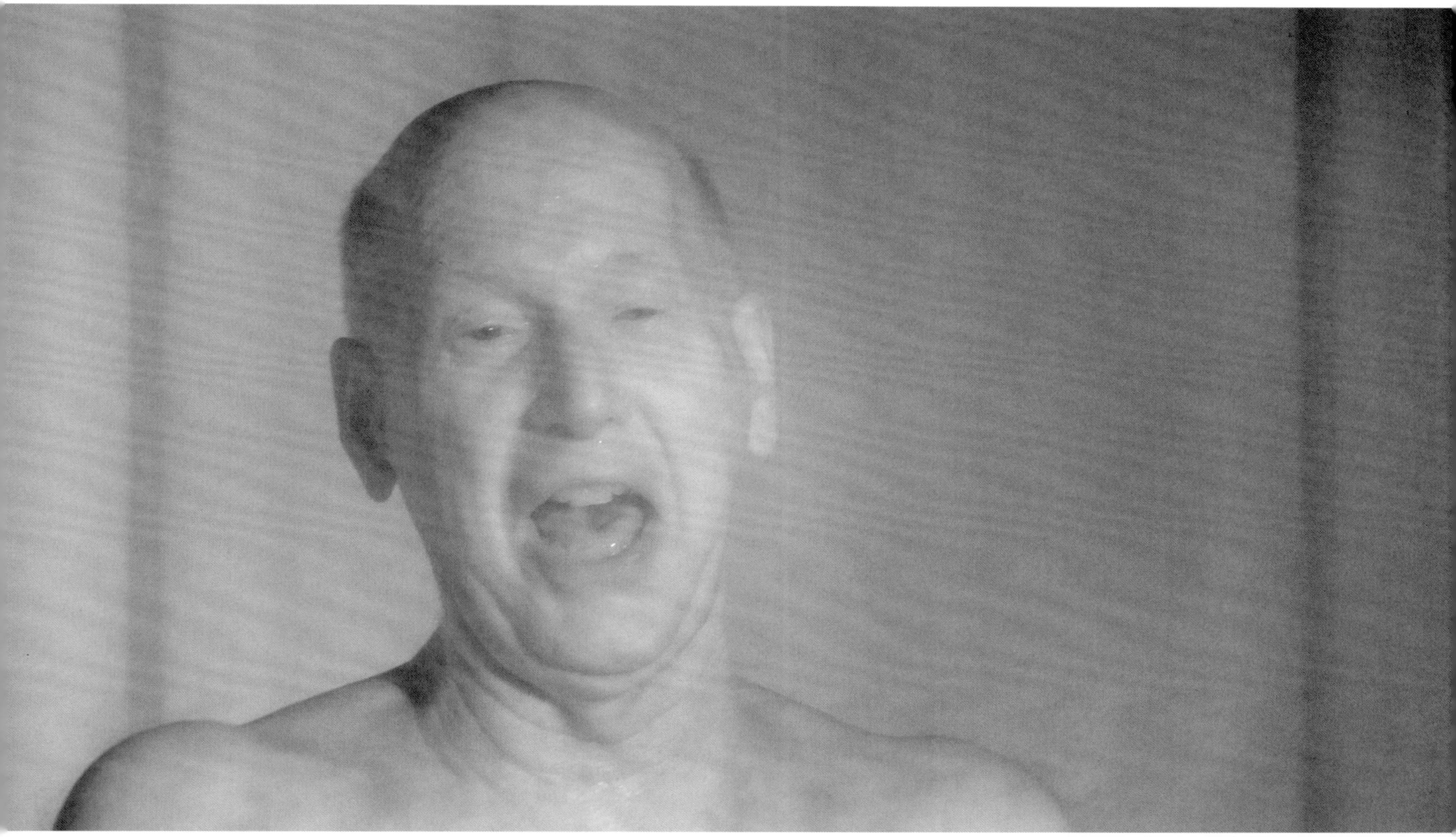

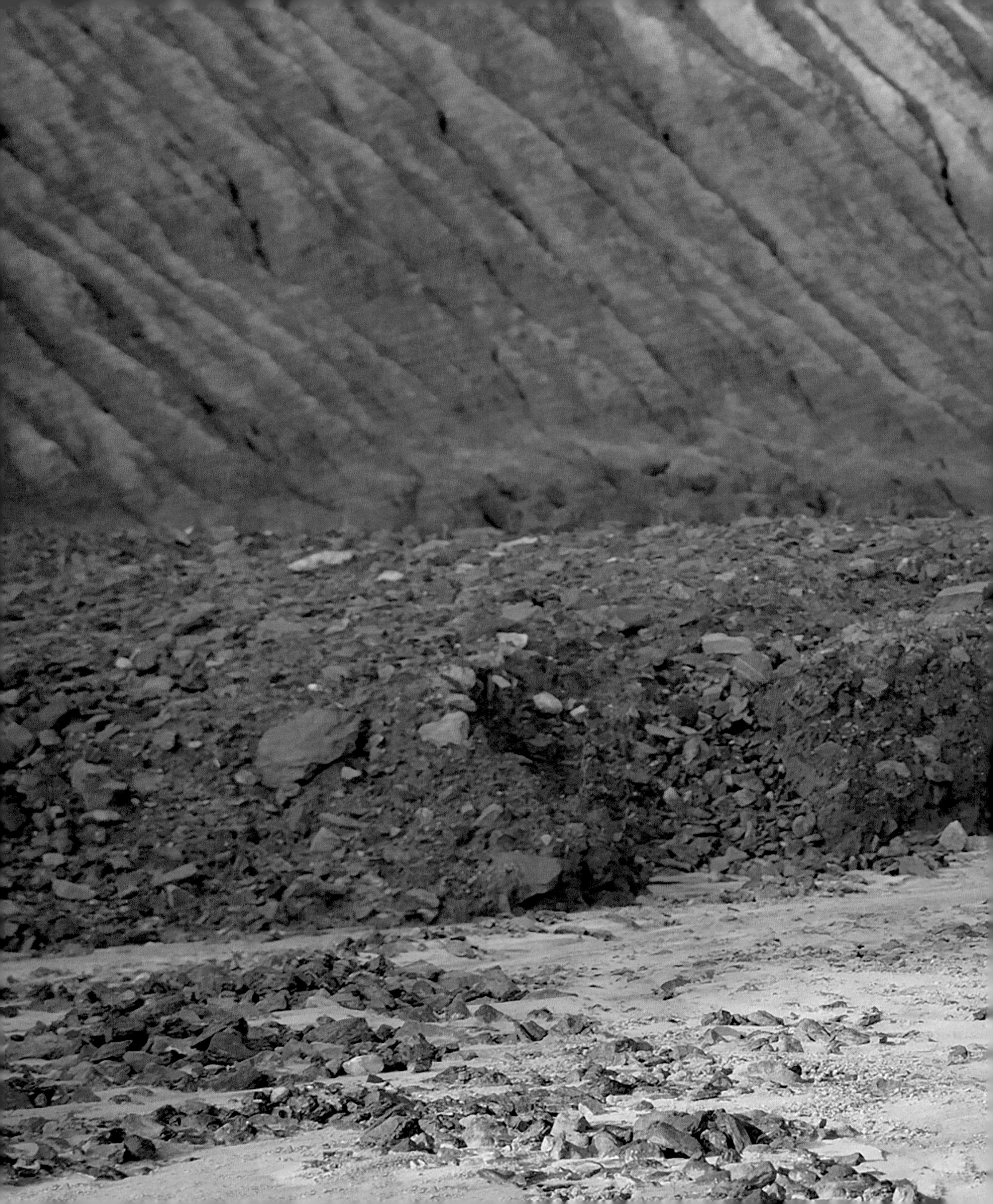

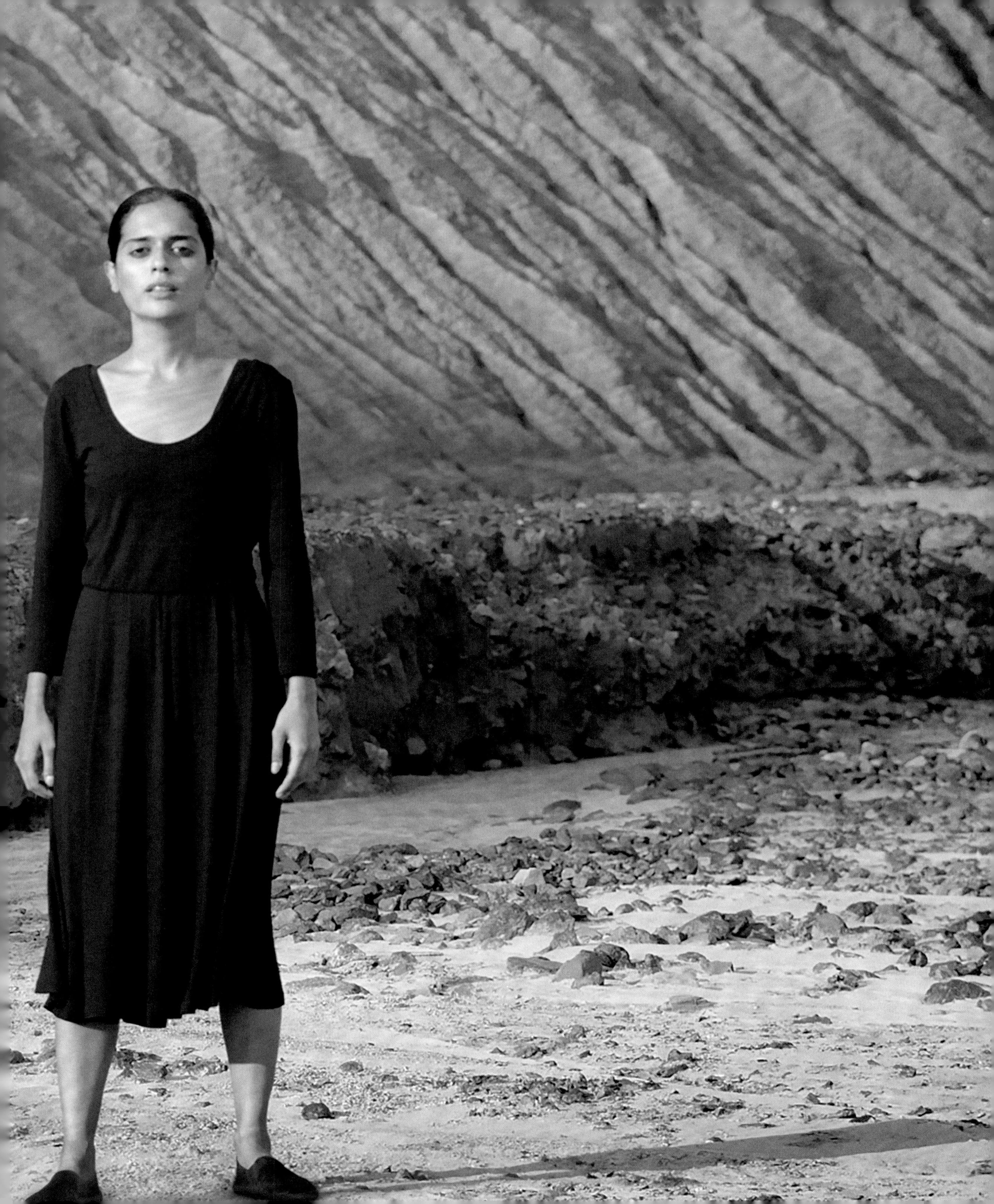

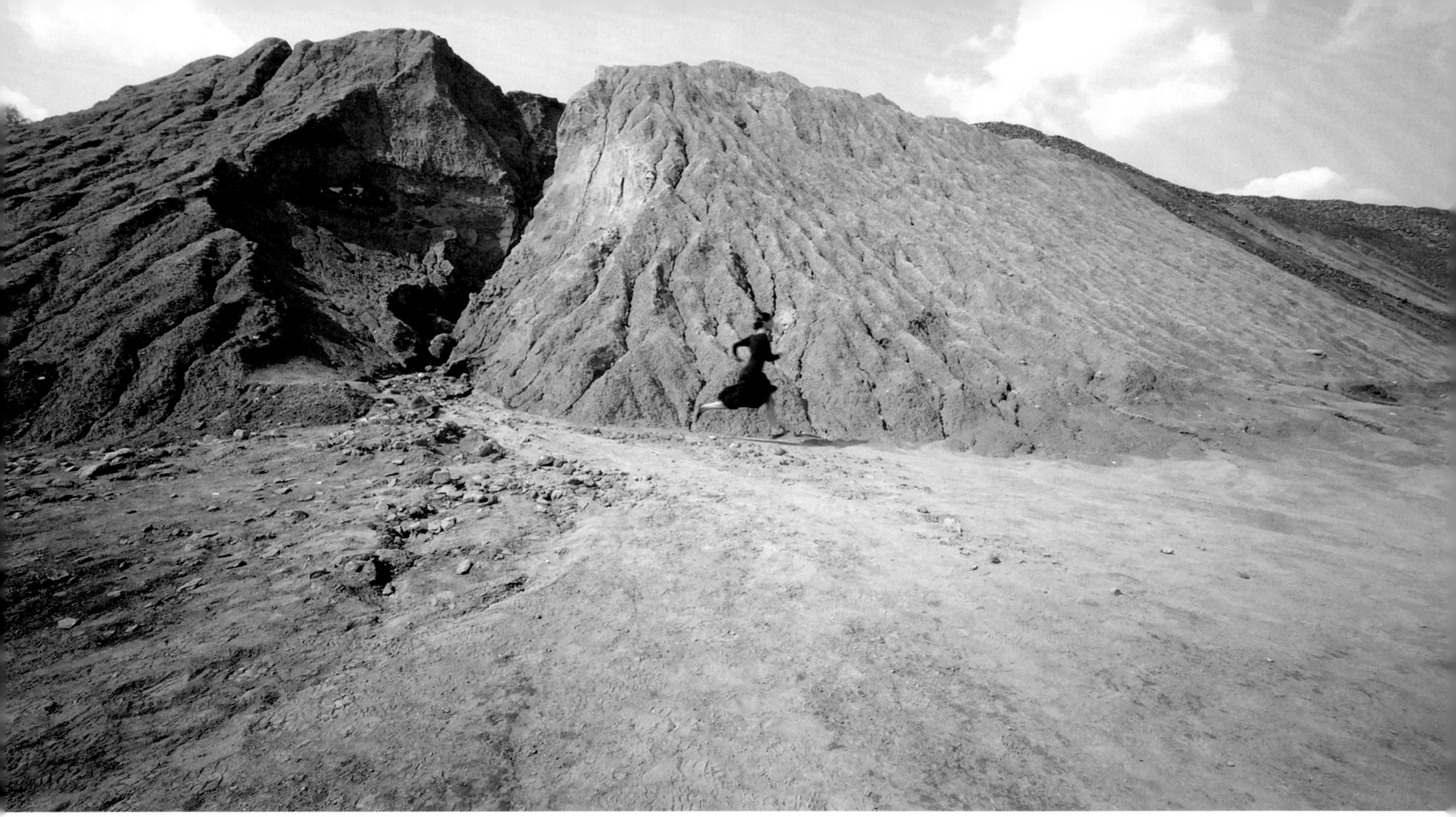

ROJA

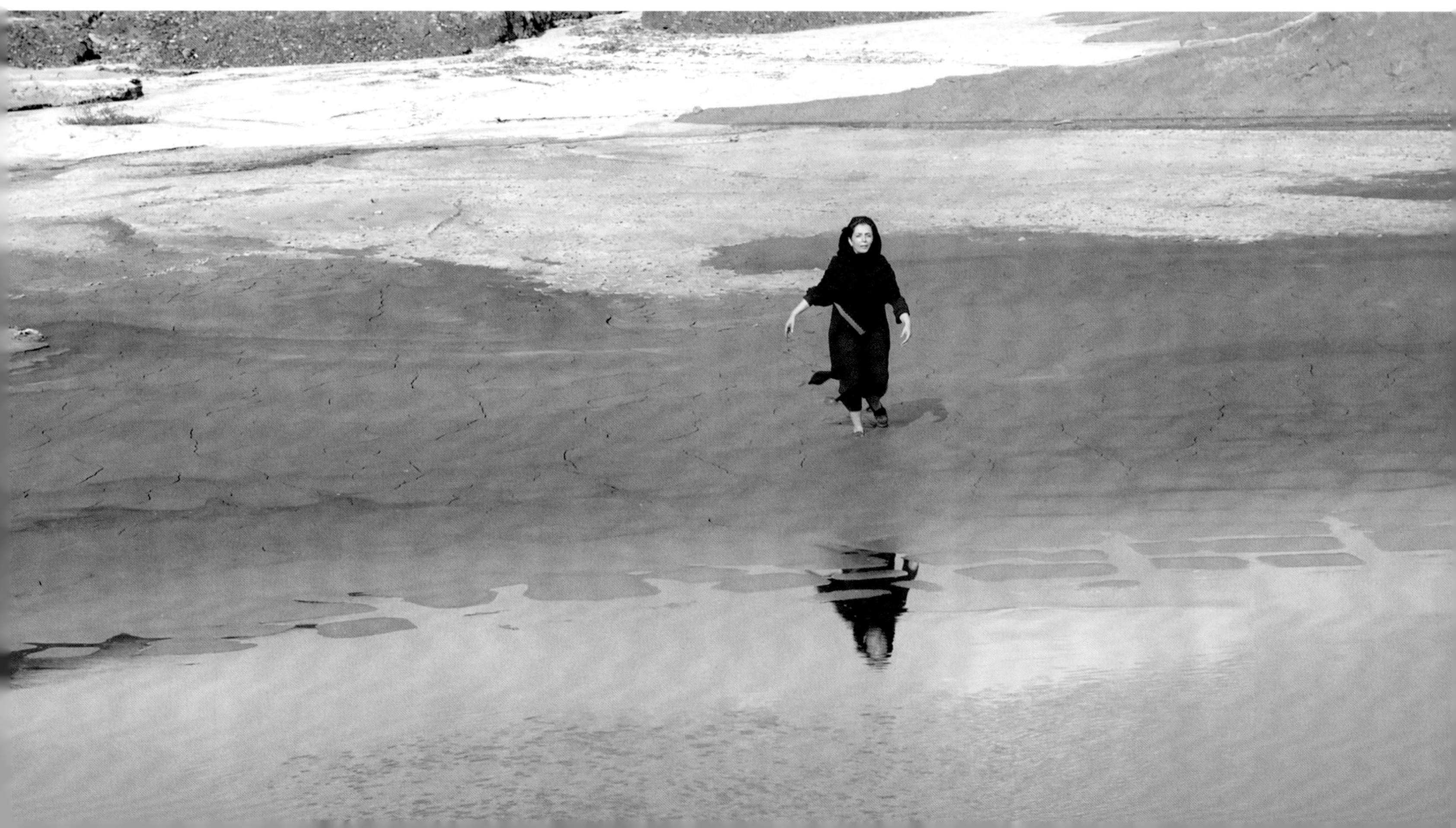

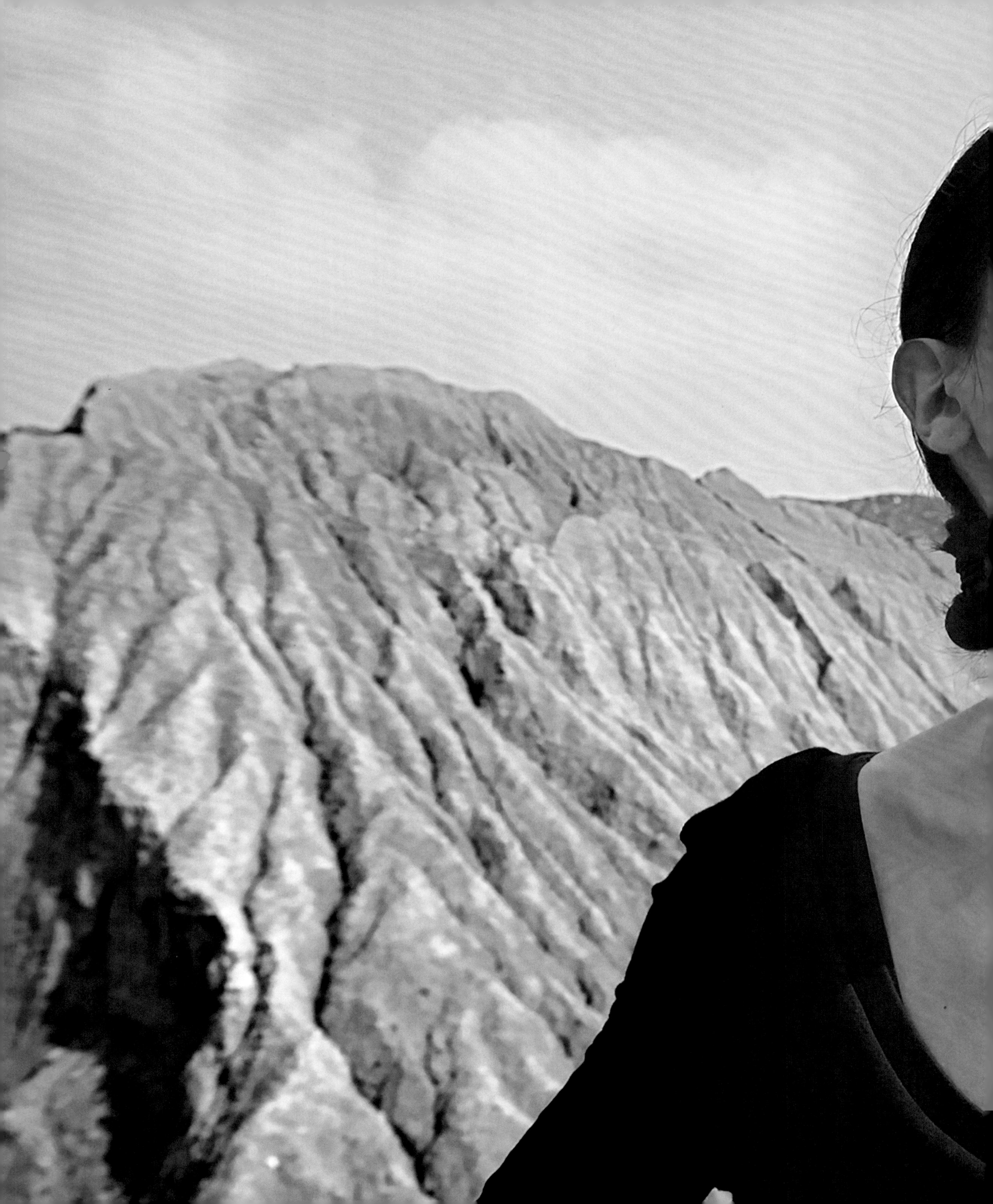

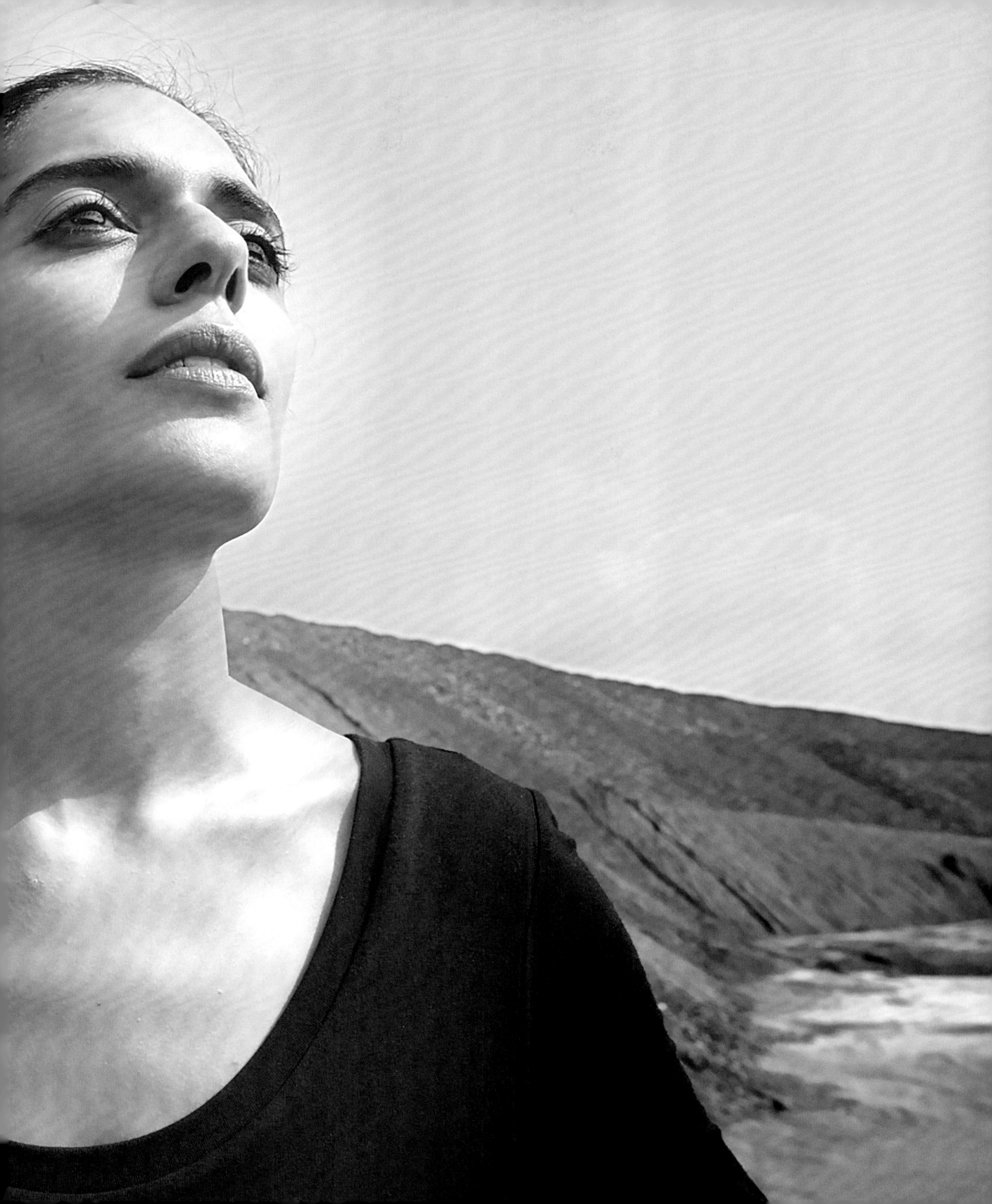

LAND OF DREAMS

AMERICA: LAND OF DREAMS, 2019
SINGLE-CHANNEL VIDEO INSTALLATION
HD VIDEO MONOCHROME
FILMED IN ALBUQUERQUE, FARMINGTON, LAS VEGAS, SANTA FE, NEW MEXICO
DIRECTOR: SHIRIN NESHAT
WITH SHEILA VAND
ADDITIONAL CAST: SHANNON K. DUNN, CRAIG FONES, PIP LUSTGARTEN, JOHN RADSPINNER, DAWN FERGUSON
CONCEPT BY: SHIRIN NESHAT
WRITTEN BY: SHOJA AZARI
EDITOR: SHOJA AZARI
DIRECTOR OF PHOTOGRAPHY: GHASEM EBRAHIMIAN
MUSIC AND SOUND DESIGN: JOHNNY AZARI
PRODUCTION DESIGN: RICK GILBERT
COSTUME DESIGN: KIM TRUJILLO
HAIR AND MAKEUP ARTIST: MINA GHORAISHI
PRODUCED BY: SHOJA AZARI AND SOL TRYON
EXECUTIVE PRODUCERS: GLADSTONE GALLERY AND GOODMAN GALLERY

THE COLONY, 2019
SINGLE-CHANNEL VIDEO INSTALLATION
HD VIDEO MONOCHROME
FILMED IN ALBUQUERQUE AND SHIPROCK, NEW MEXICO
DIRECTOR: SHIRIN NESHAT
WITH SHEILA VAND AND MOHAMED GHAFFARI
CONCEPT BY: SHIRIN NESHAT
WRITTEN BY: SHOJA AZARI
EDITOR: SHOJA AZARI
DIRECTOR OF PHOTOGRAPHY: GHASEM EBRAHIMIAN
MUSIC AND SOUND DESIGN: JOHNNY AZARI
PRODUCTION DESIGN: RICK GILBERT
COSTUME DESIGN: KIM TRUJILLO
HAIR AND MAKEUP ARTIST: MINA GHORAISHI
PRODUCED BY: SHOJA AZARI AND SOL TRYON
EXECUTIVE PRODUCERS: GLADSTONE GALLERY AND GOODMAN GALLERY

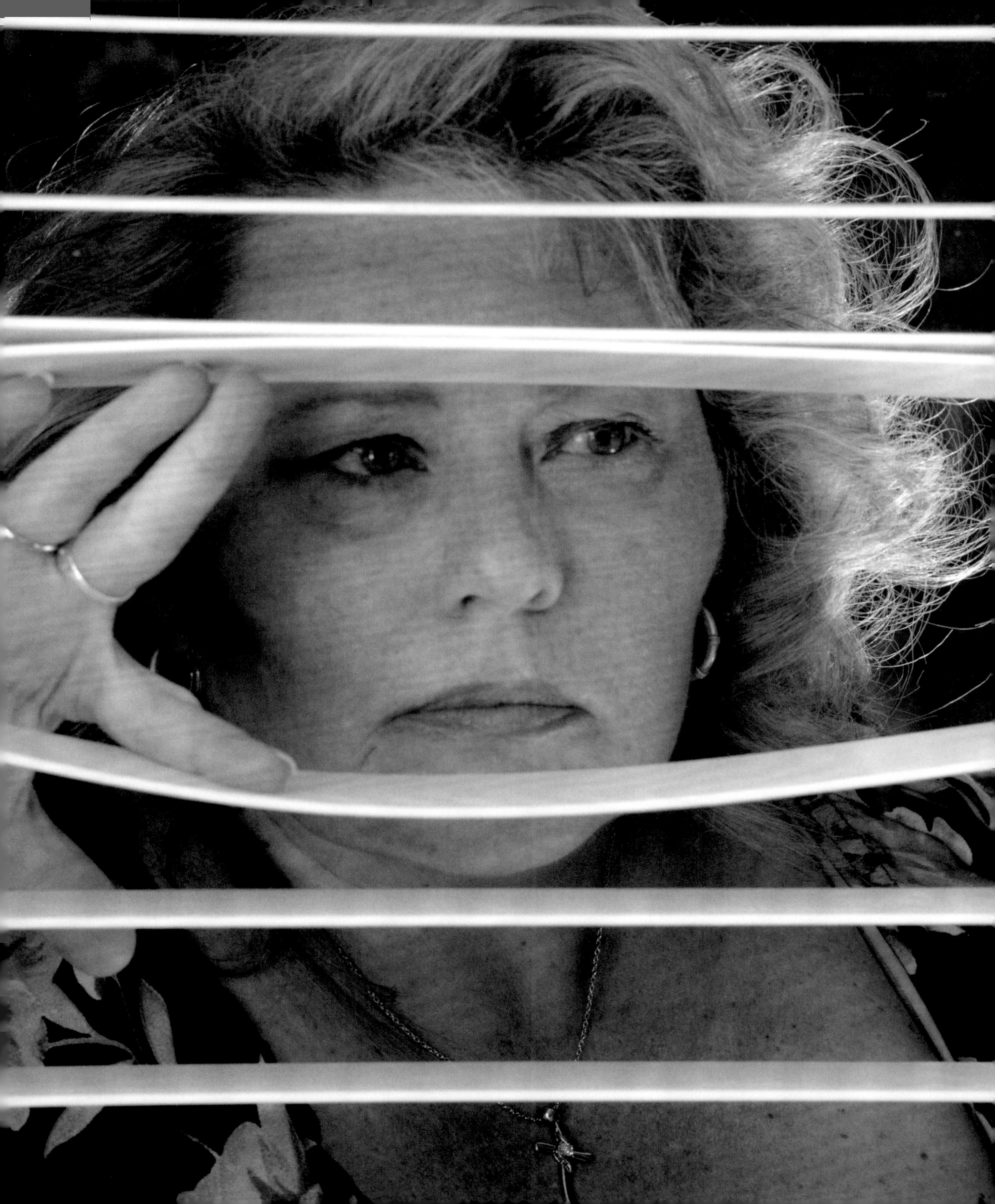

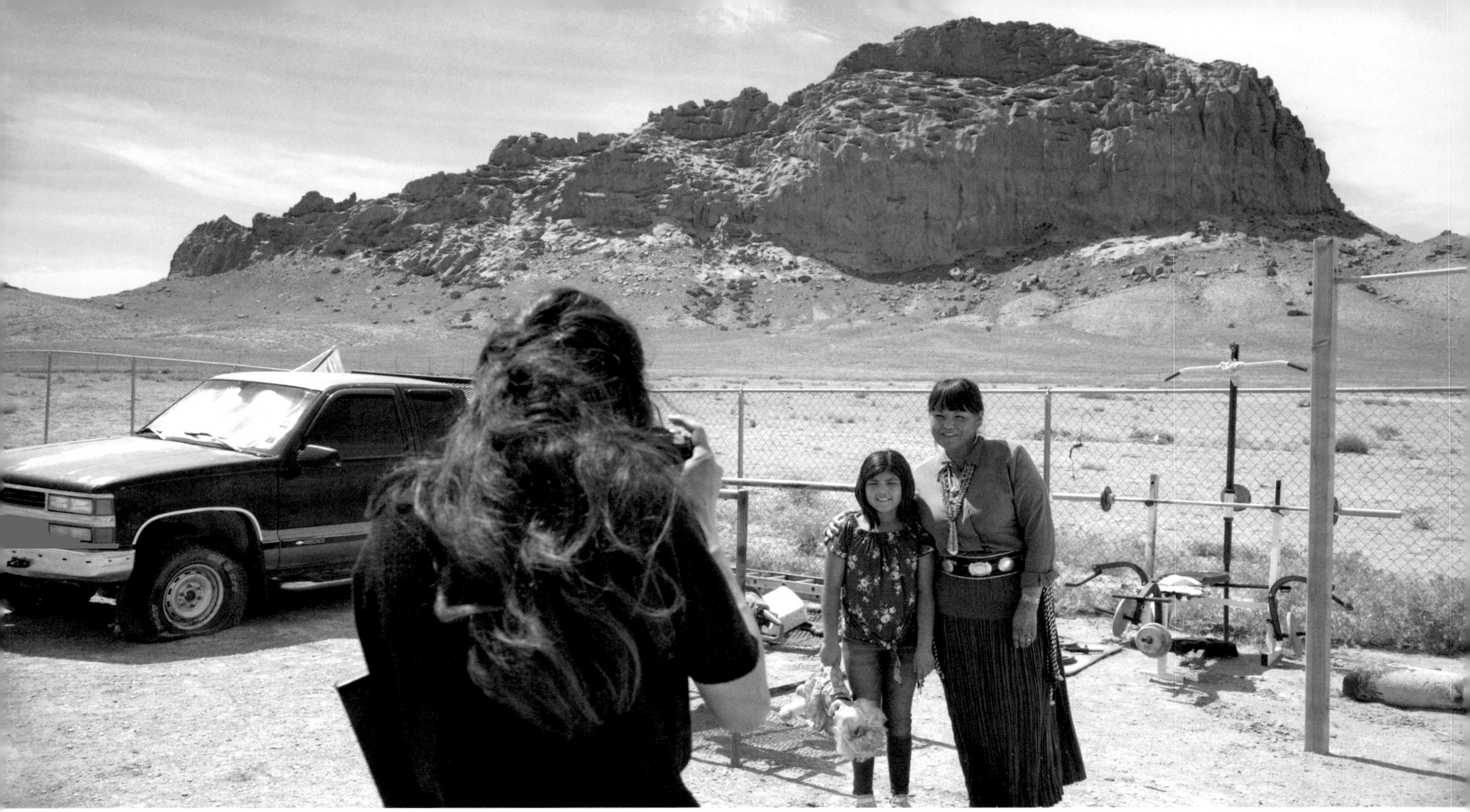

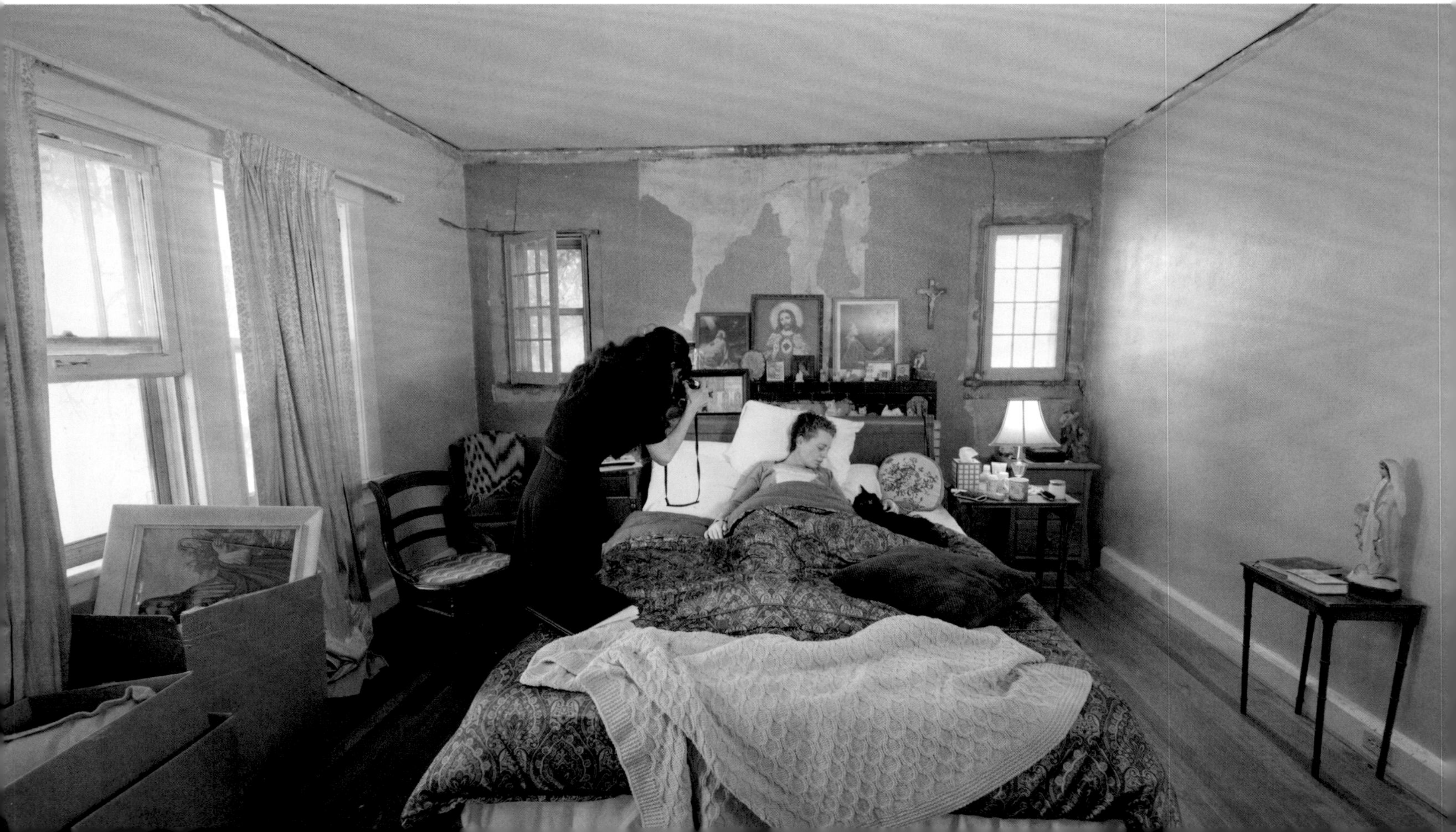

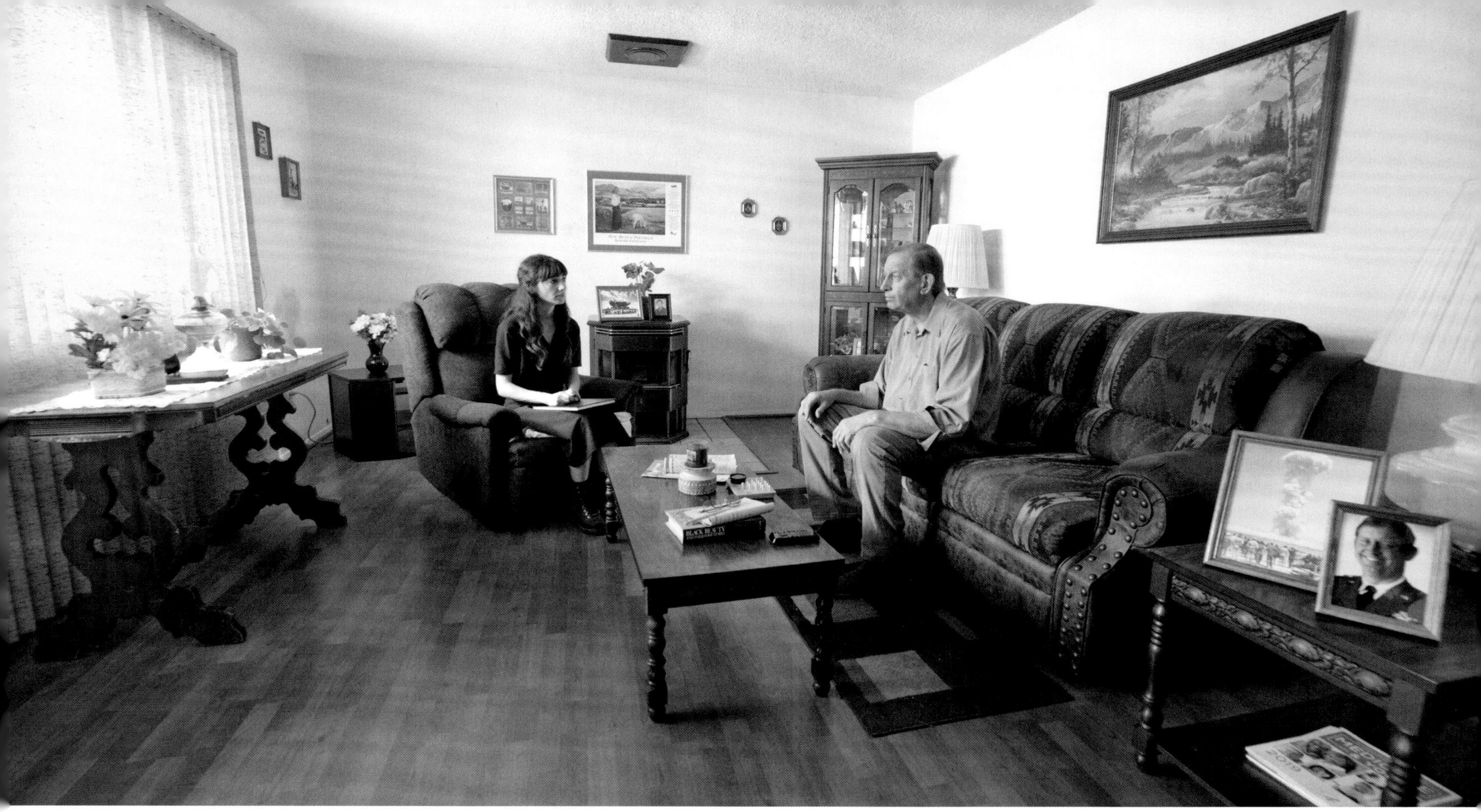
BLACK BEAUTY

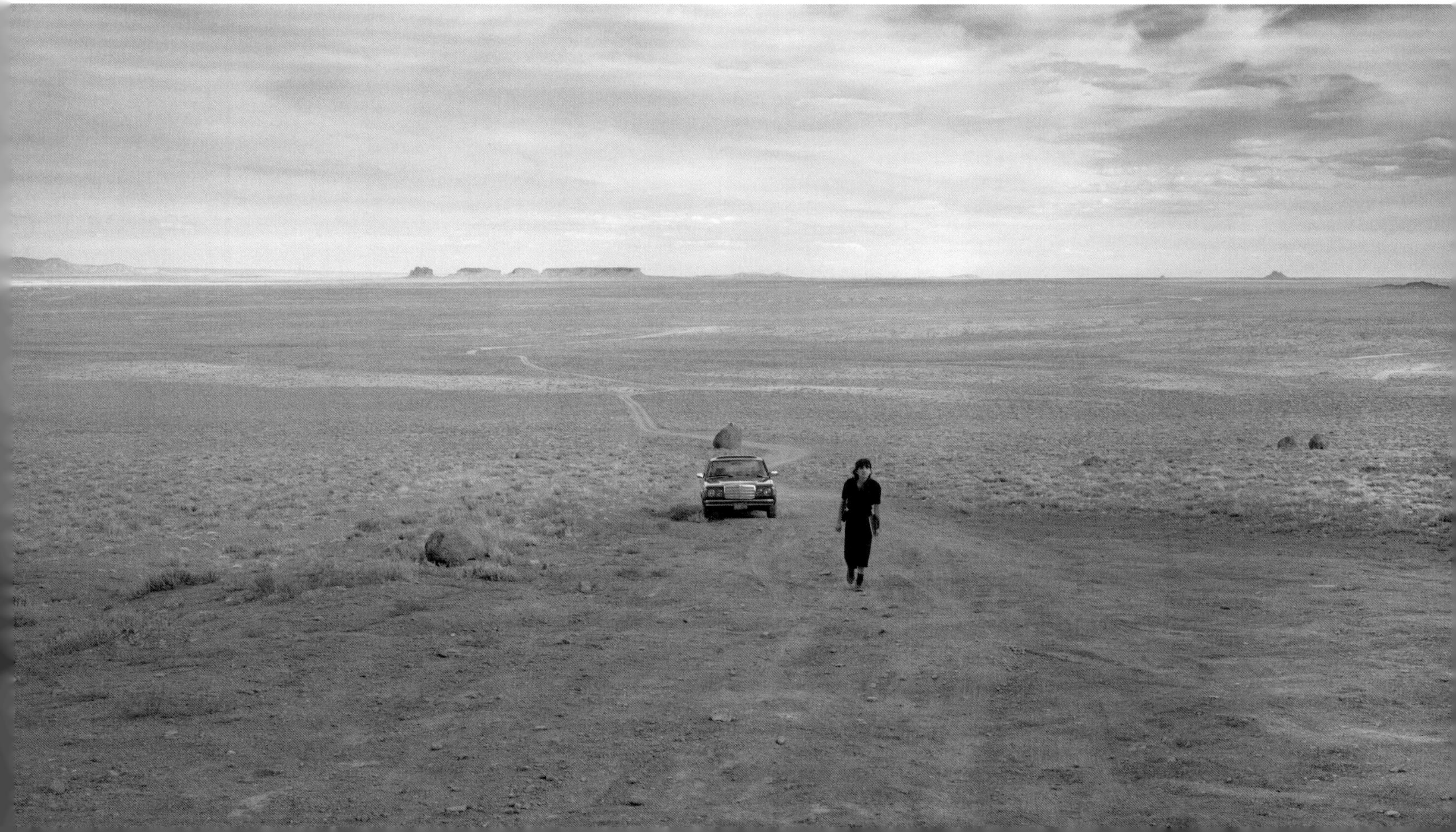

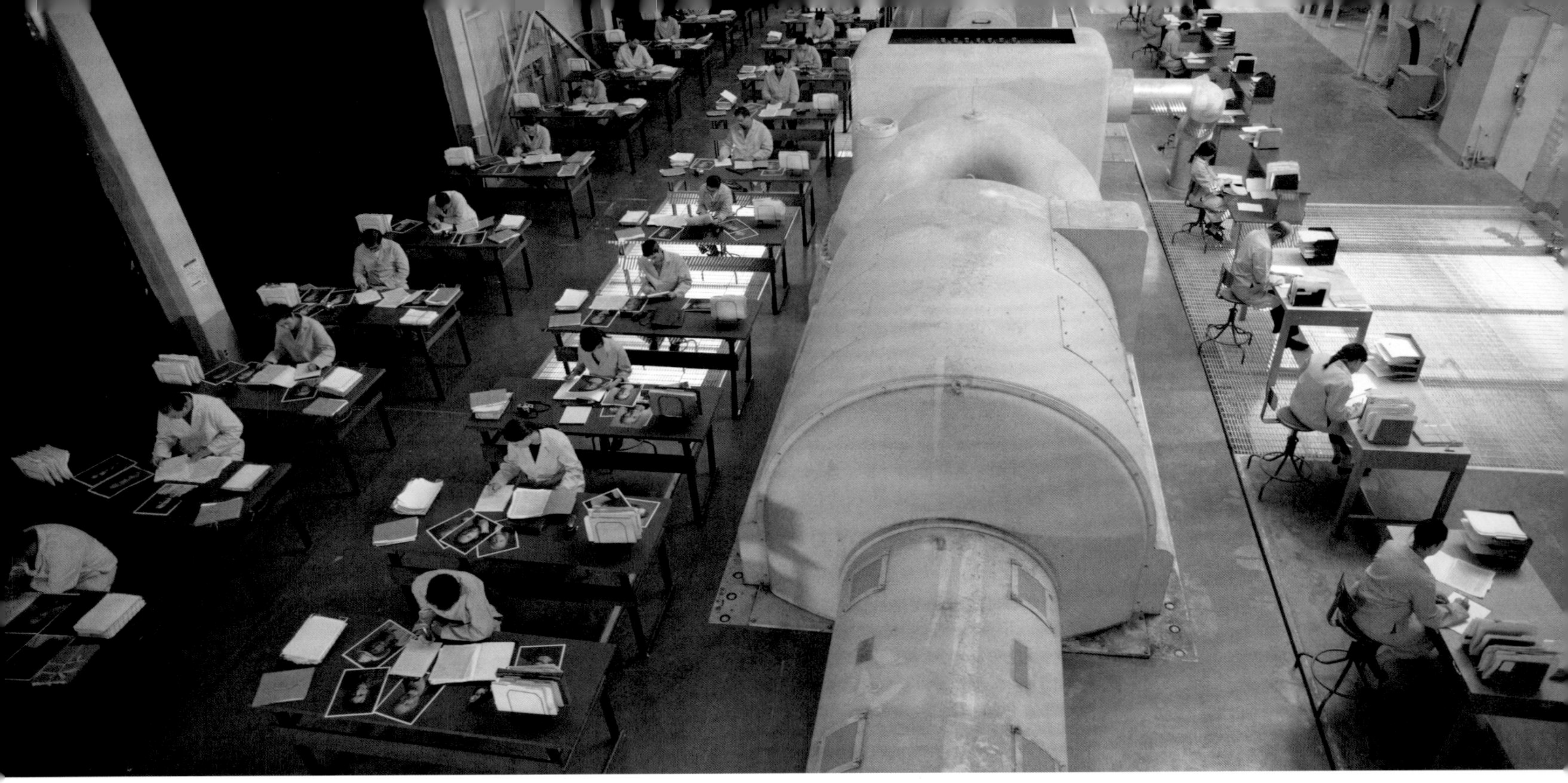

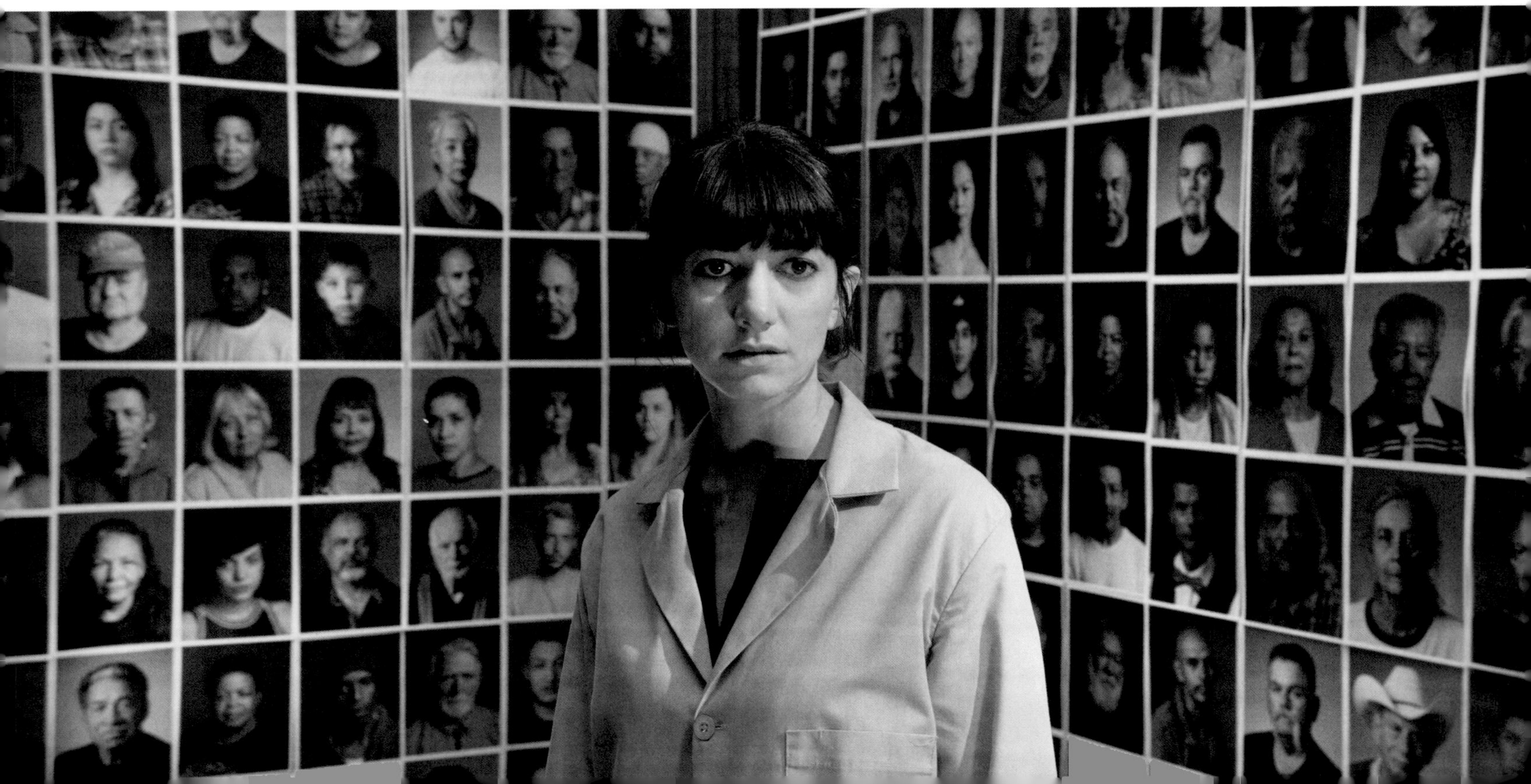

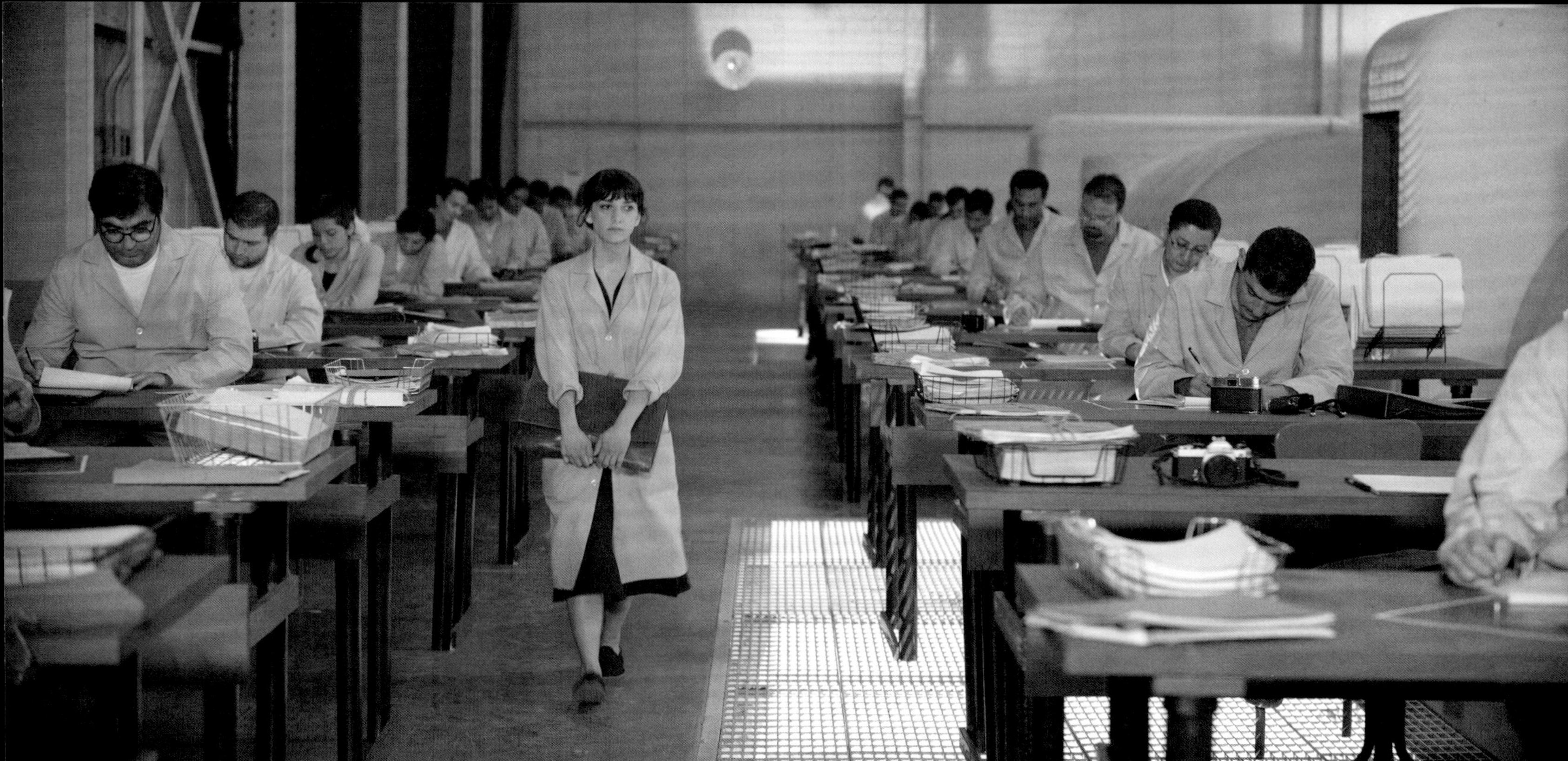

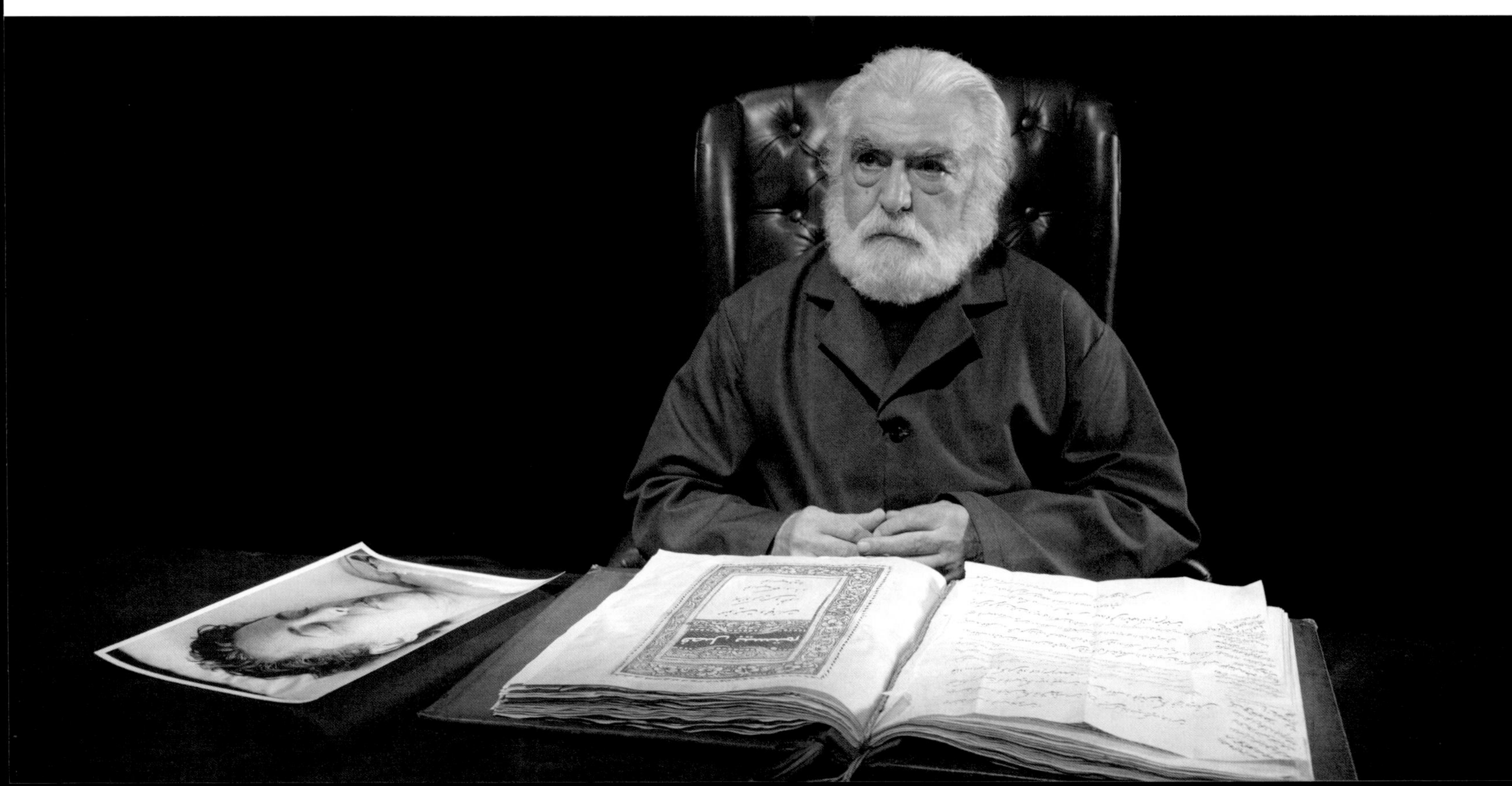

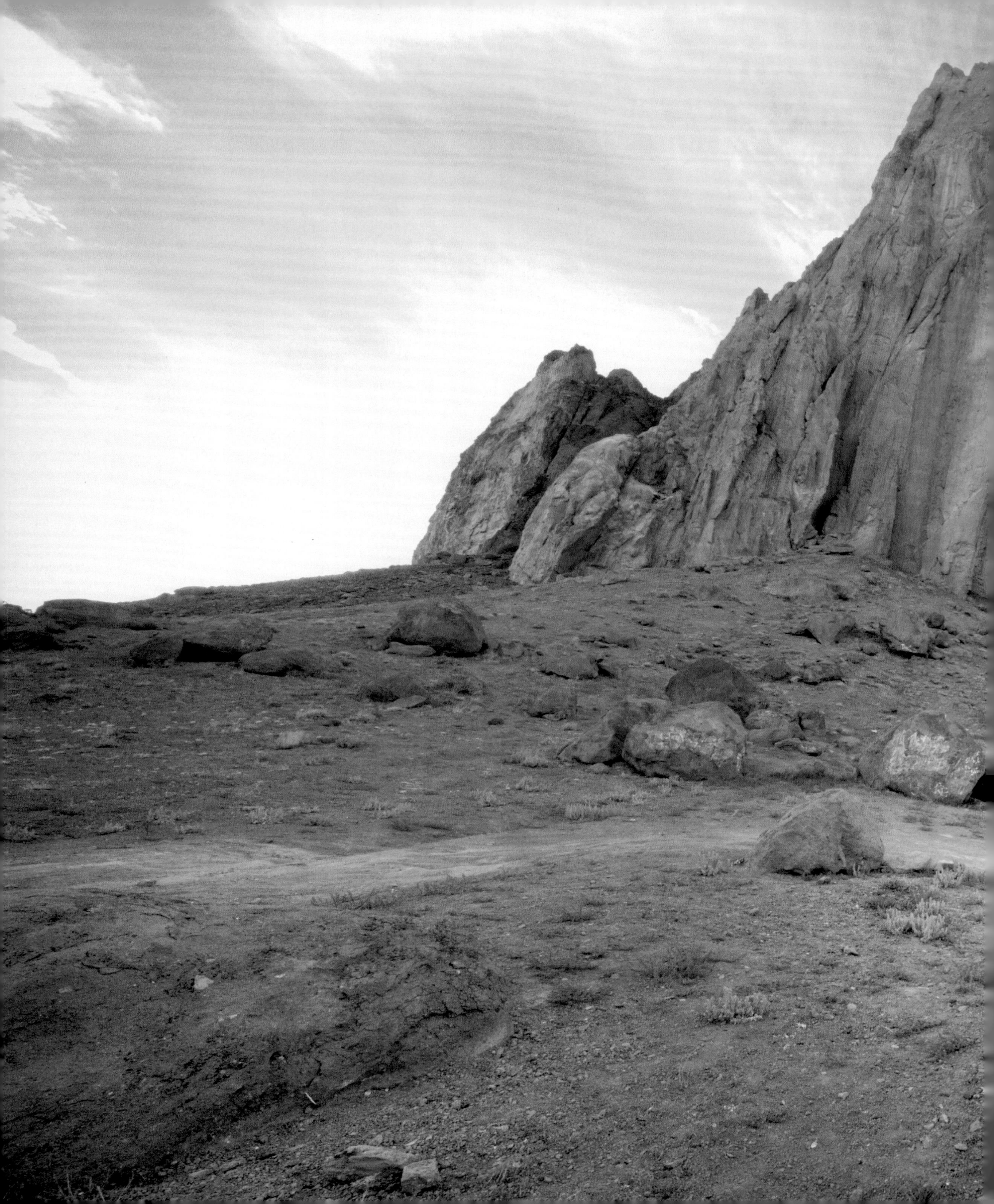

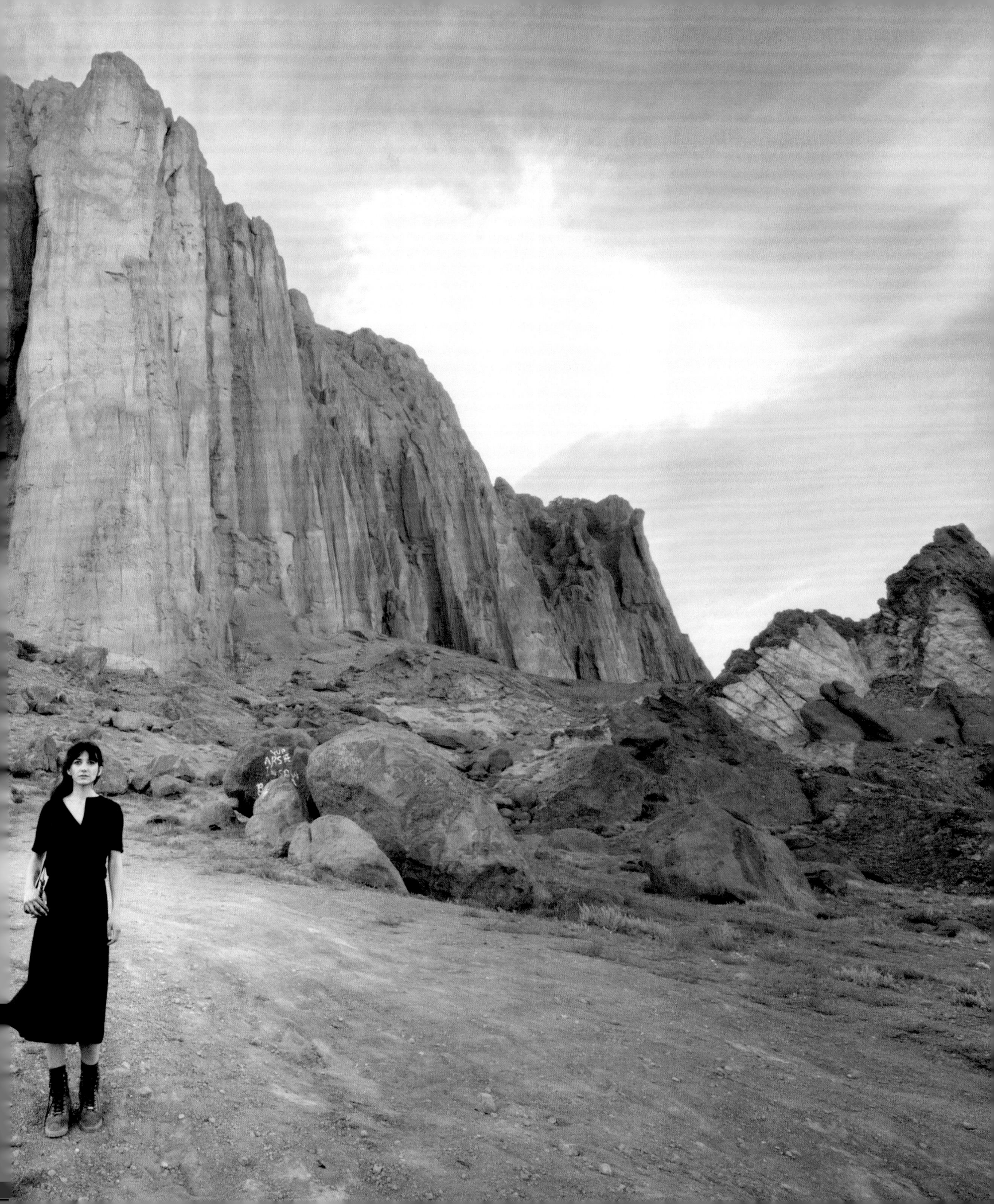

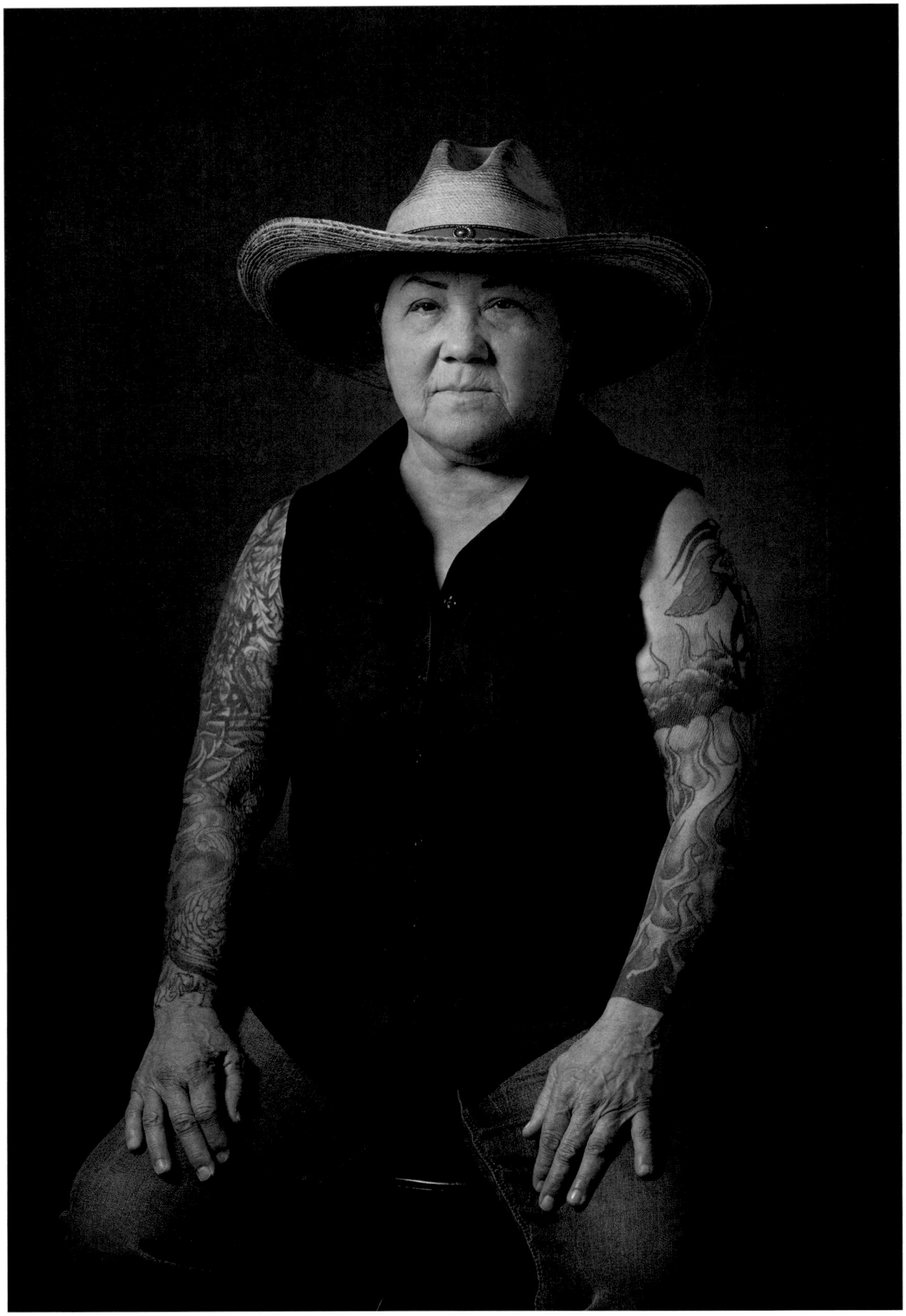

CONSUELO QUINTANA, 2019

Digital C-print and ink, dimensions variable.
Photograph taken by Lina Bertucci

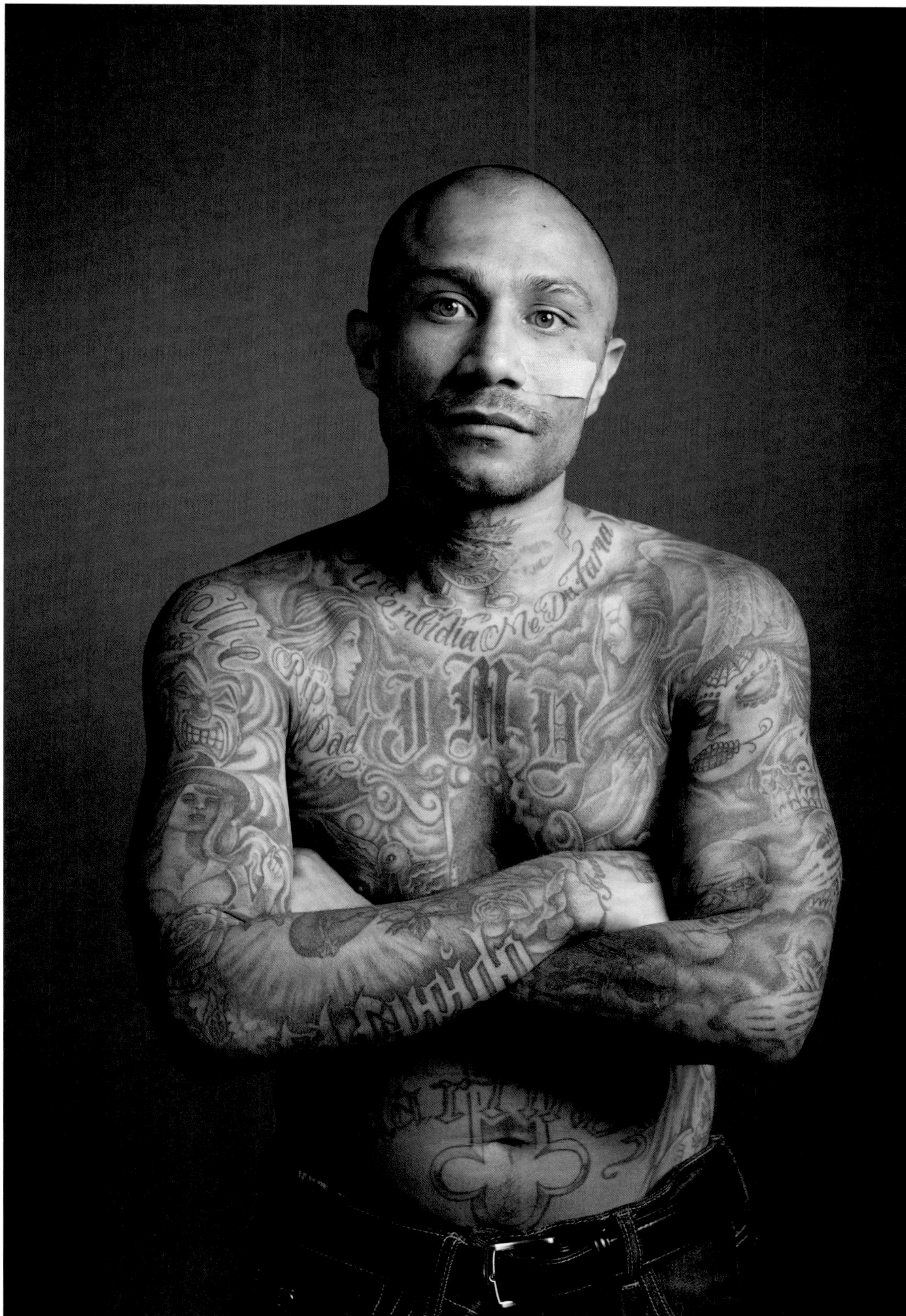

MANUEL MARTINEZ, 2019

Digital C-print and ink, dimensions variable.
Photograph taken by Lina Bertucci

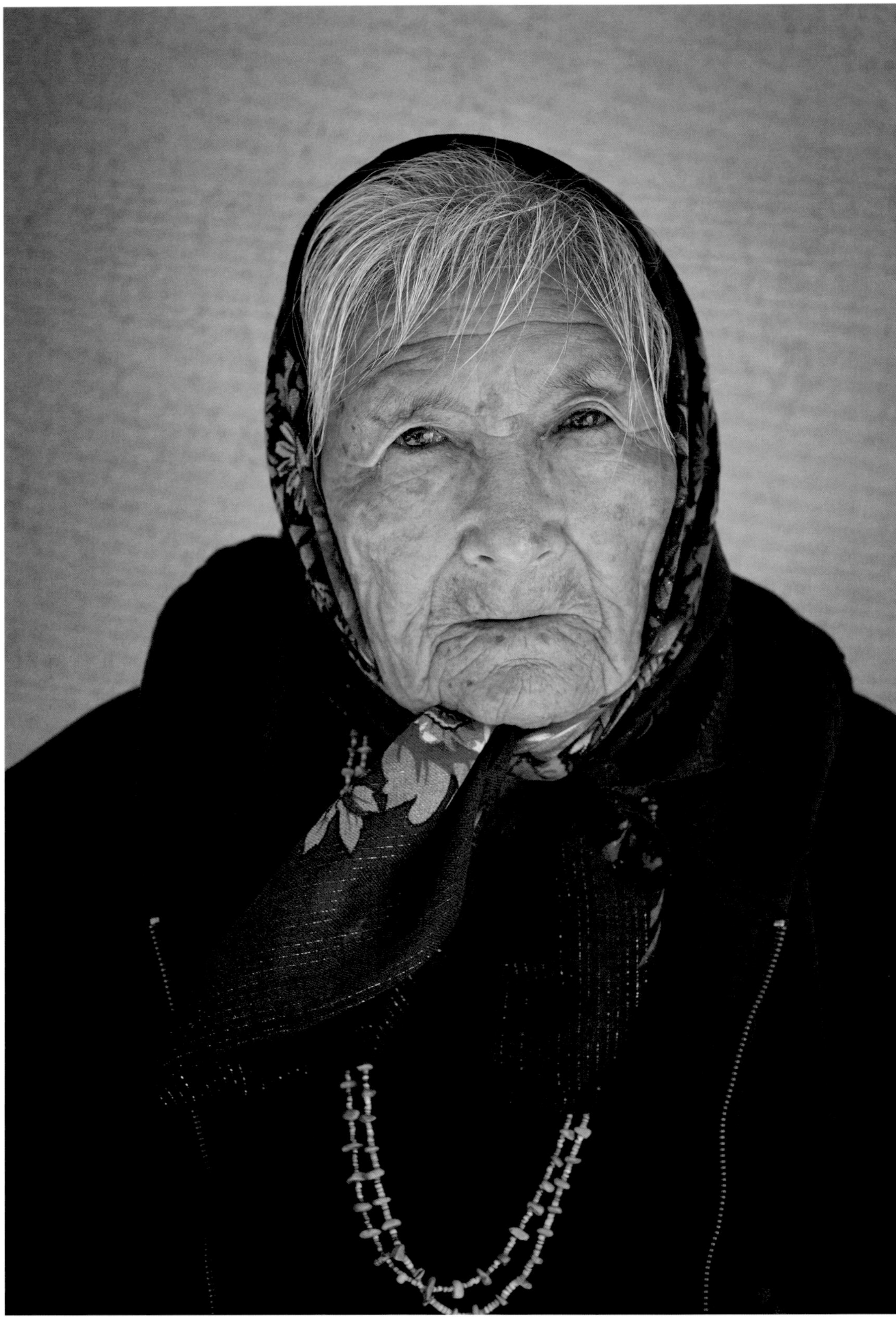

MRS. KING, 2019

Digital C-print and ink, dimensions variable.
Photograph taken by Lina Bertucci

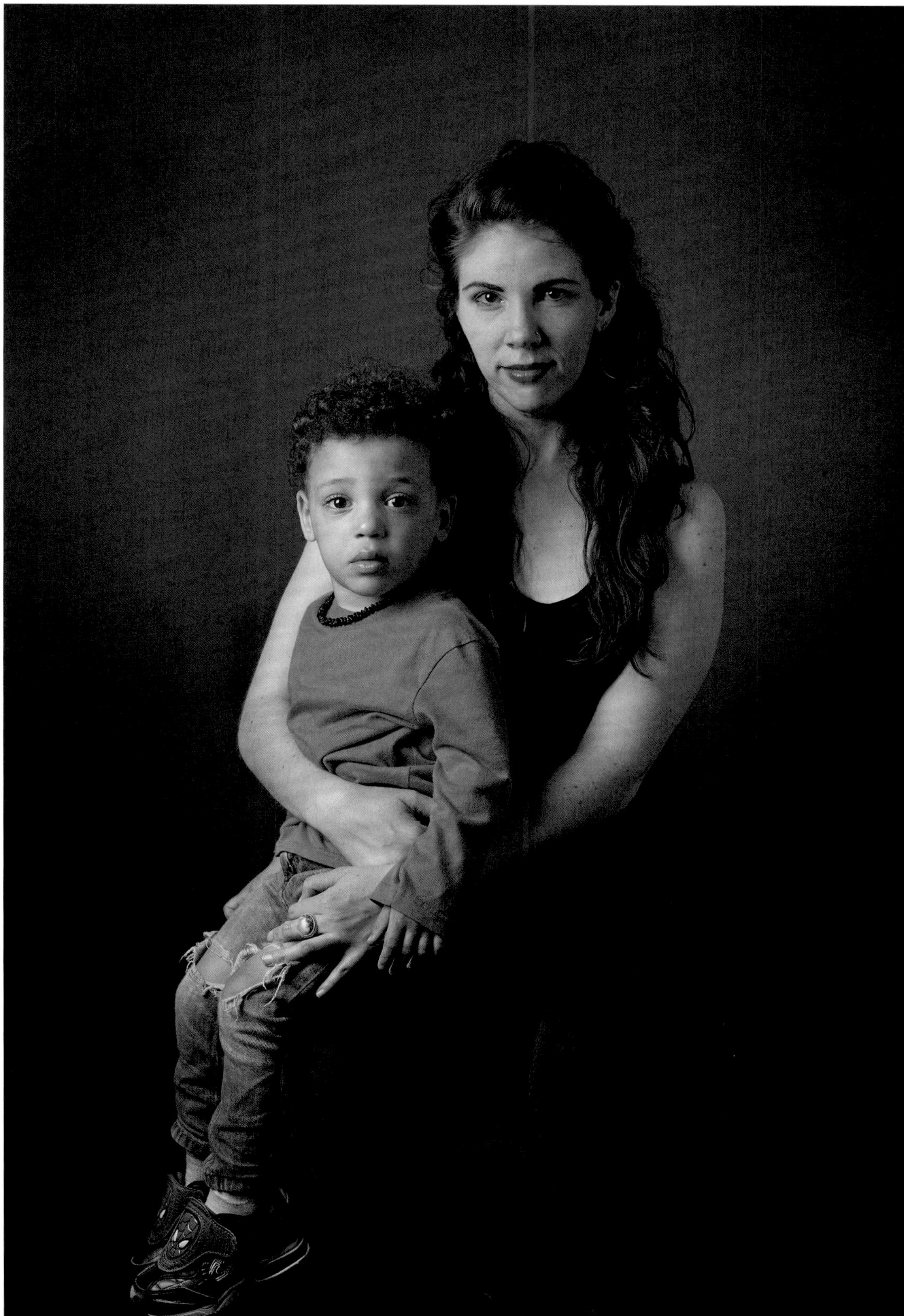

MAGALI AND PHOENIX RUTSCHMAN, 2019

Digital C-print and ink, dimensions variable.
Photograph taken by Lina Bertucci

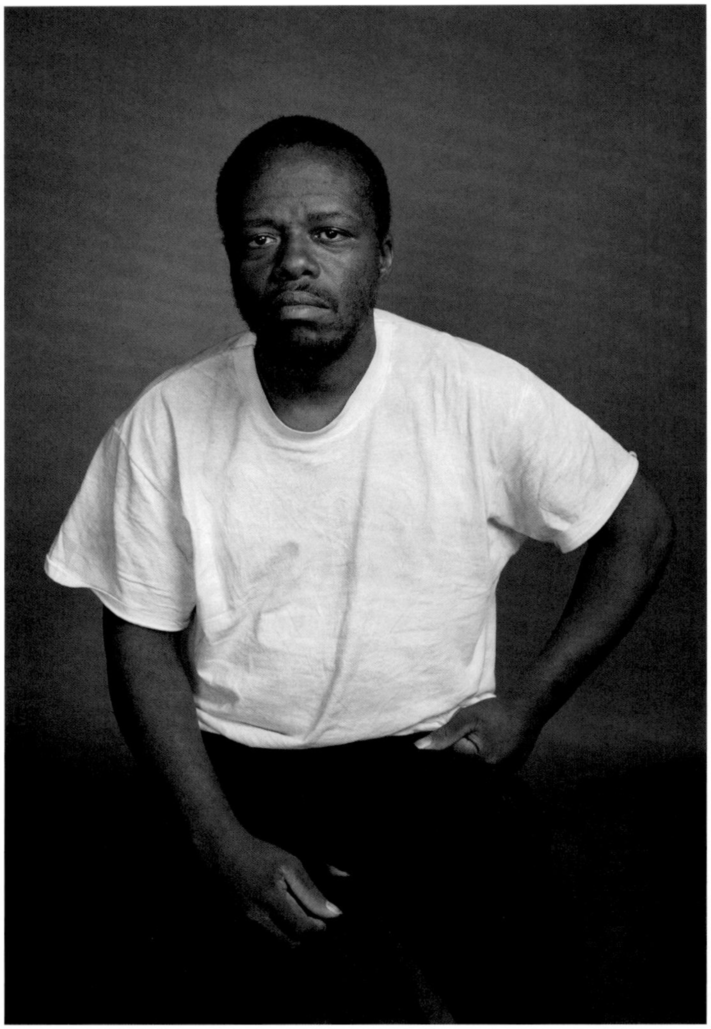

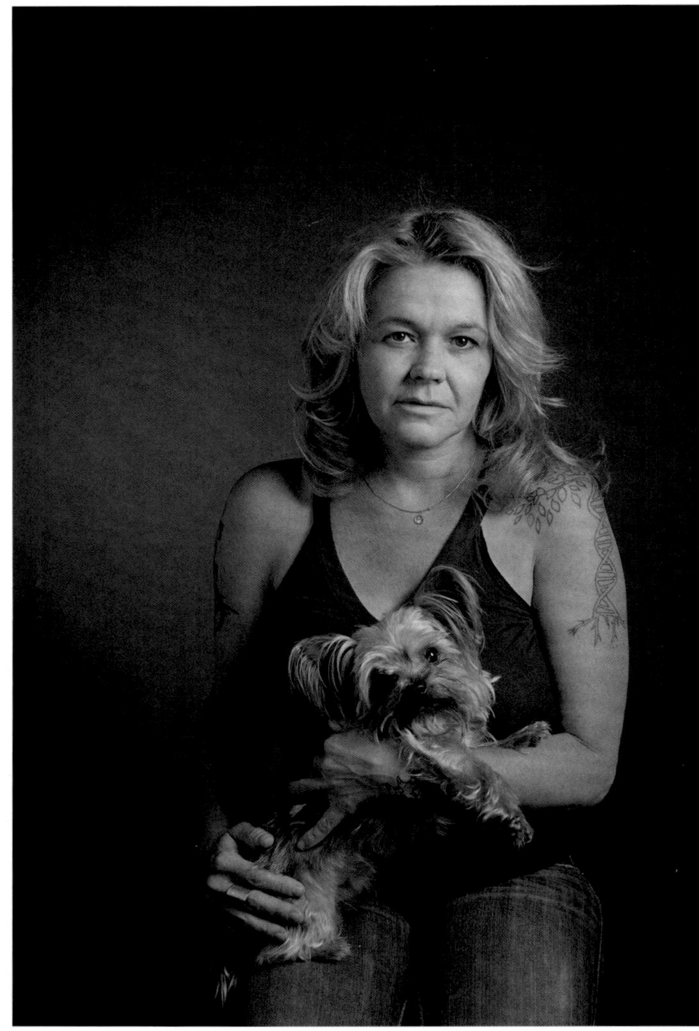

DAVID MILLER, 2019

Digital C-print and ink, dimensions variable.
Photograph taken by Lina Bertucci

JENASIS GREER, 2019

Digital C-print and ink, dimensions variable.
Photograph taken by Lina Bertucci

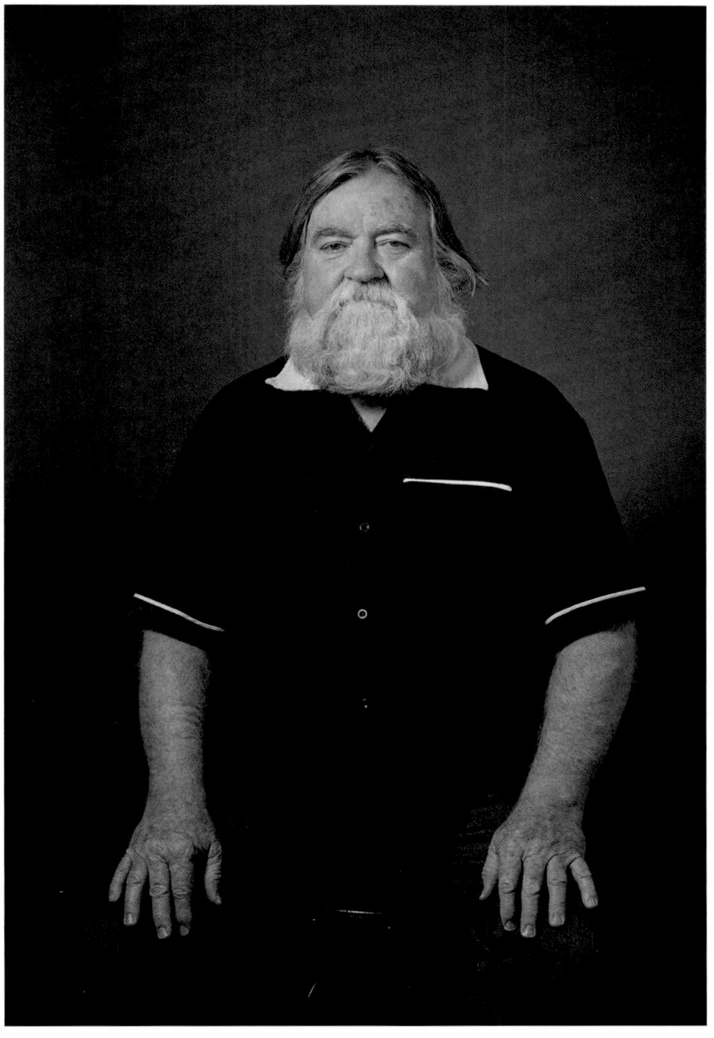

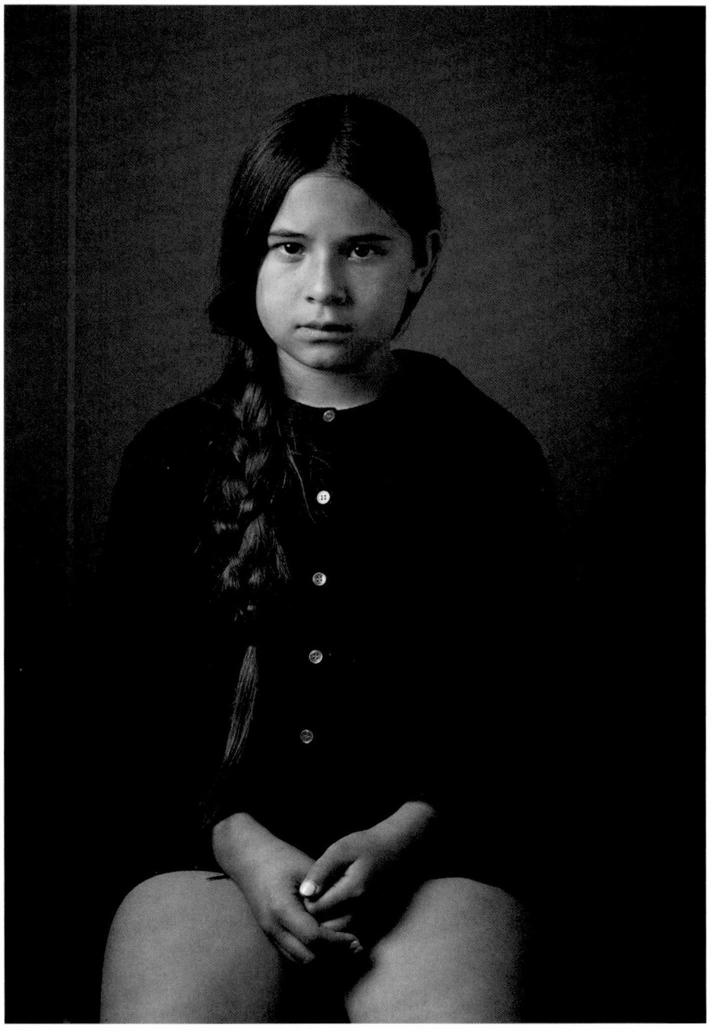

GREG FITCH, 2019

Digital C-print and ink, dimensions variable.
Photograph taken by Lina Bertucci

KATALINA ESPINOZA, 2019

Digital C-print and ink, dimensions variable.
Photograph taken by Lina Bertucci

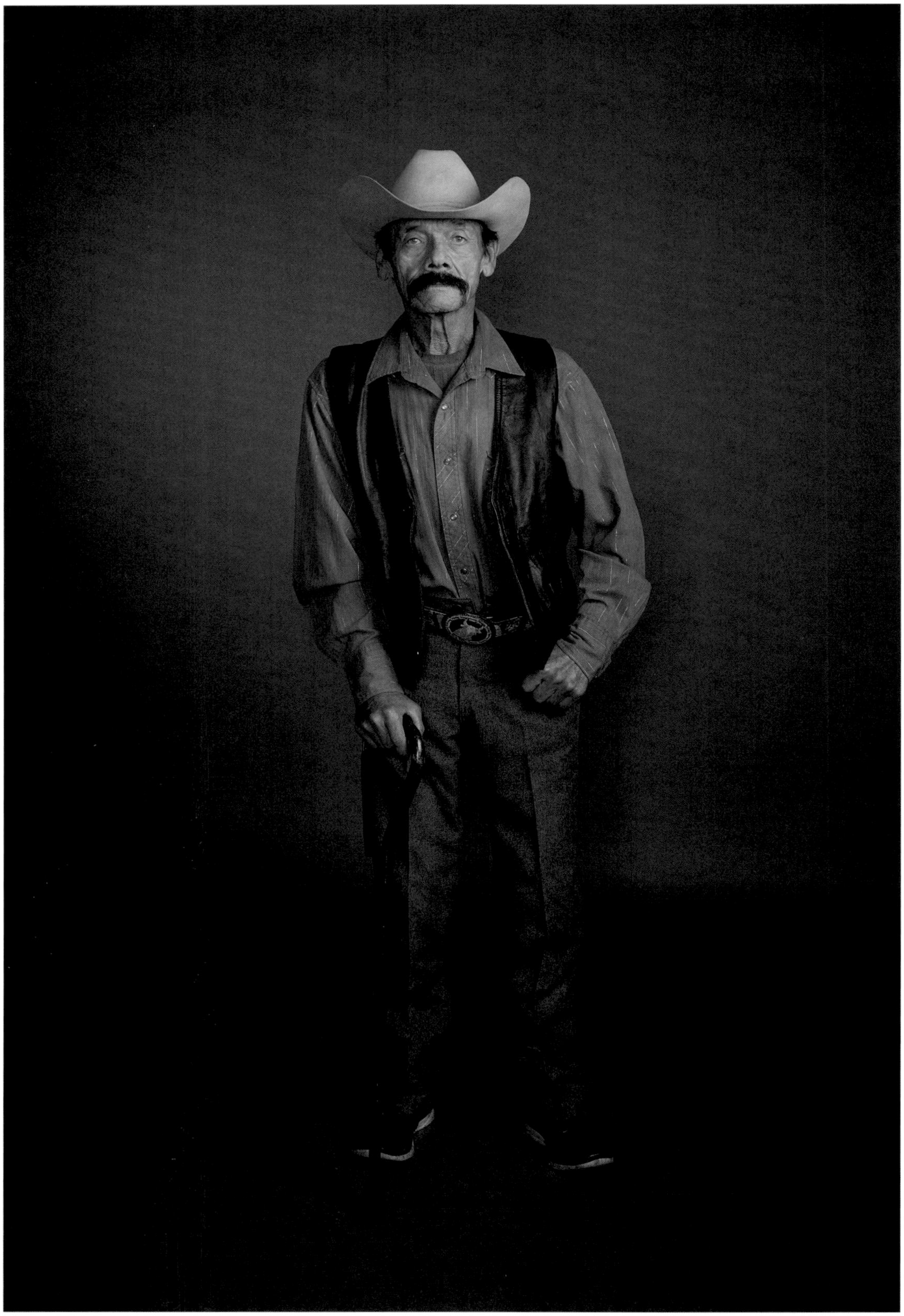

ENRIQUE ZEPEDA, 2019

Digital C-print and ink, dimensions variable.
Photograph taken by Lina Bertucci

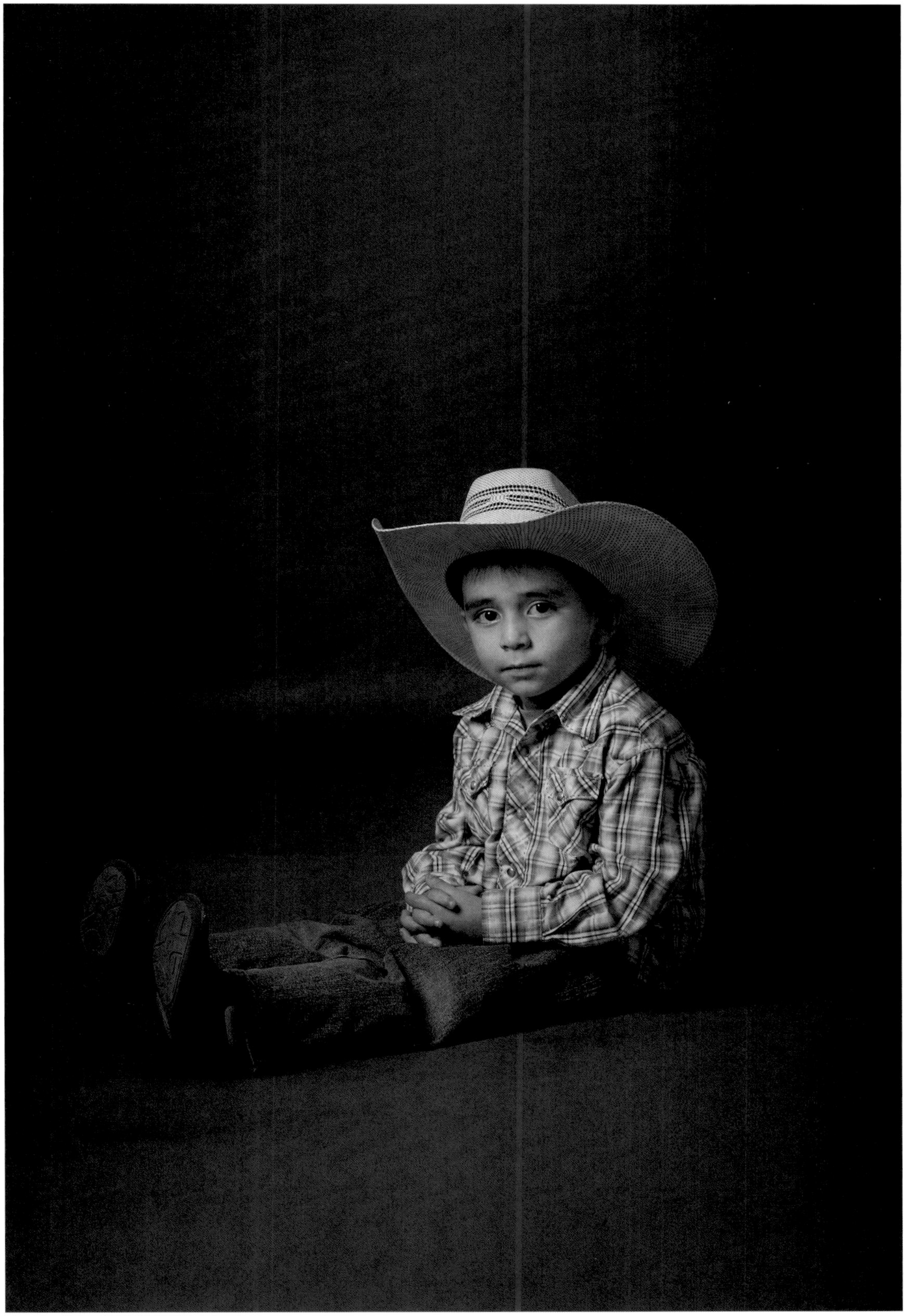

ISAAC SILVA, 2019

Digital C-print and ink, dimensions variable.
Photograph taken by Lina Bertucci

FROM SKIN TO SOUL: THE CINEMATIC JOURNEY OF SHIRIN NESHAT GODFREY CHESHIRE

Shirin Neshat is one of the world's great filmmakers.

That judgment comes from a film critic who is well aware it is not common parlance among critics and cinephiles, in the U.S. or elsewhere, for a number of reasons that manifestly have to do with the nature of Neshat's film work and how it has been displayed and discussed over the last two decades.

Regarding its nature: the main body of her cinema consists of roughly two dozen short films made between 1996 and 2016. Though filmmakers from Georges Méliès to Man Ray to Maya Deren gained substantial reputations for work done in the short form, it is generally a much more difficult feat than that faced by film artists who make feature films. Growing out of her celebrated work as a photographer, moreover, Neshat's films have generally been displayed in art galleries, which means in turn that they have been written about via the academic language and perspectives of art critics rather than film critics.

Though born and raised in Iran, Neshat began her artistic career in New York in the 1990s, a particularly vital era for gallery-based innovation, eclecticism, public performance, and the mixing of media. Thus it is understandable that her work has been seen in relation to that of artists such as Bruce Nauman, Nam June Paik, Bill Viola, Cindy Sherman, and Gary Hill. Yet to imagine her film work of this period removed from the gallery context is to invite another set of associations, cinematic ones that might include names such as Tarkovsky, Kieslowski, Bergman, and Antonioni, artists whose films Neshat discovered while beginning her own work as a maker of moving pictures.

From another perspective, appreciating Neshat's cinema also means perceiving its connection to two Iranian artists for whom she has long expressed profound affinities: poet-filmmaker Forugh Farrokhzad and filmmaker-poet Abbas Kiarostami (figs. 1, 2). The work of all three artists poses questions not only about relationships between the verbal and the visual, but also between traditional and modernistic forms, both within Iranian culture and between Iran and the world.

To best understand the greatness and importance of Neshat's work in the short-film form necessarily entails seeing it *as a whole*, to grasp the special aims and achievements of each film in relation to the others, and to follow their formal and thematic developments as they unfold across the body of work. But to imagine a chronological display of her short films—a Shirin Neshat film festival, so to speak—immediately poses questions about *how* they should be displayed.

Many of the films consist of two, three, or four simultaneous frames and are meant to be shown on separate screens with the viewer positioned between them, as can easily be done in a gallery. These same films, though, can be displayed in ways that give them a more conventional cinematic aspect, with the frames positioned alongside each other. But should they? Given that both ways of viewing the films are now possible, perhaps it would be best to suggest that it's not necessary to see either as the "correct" or best way; both can be illuminating. Indeed, just as the "gallery" way of seeing the films sets up a kind of visual/intellectual dialogue between or among the images, a similar dialogue can take place between the gallery way and the "cinema" way, with the latter having certain advantages in underscoring these short works as *films* as opposed to "video installations," a term Neshat herself still uses for them

1

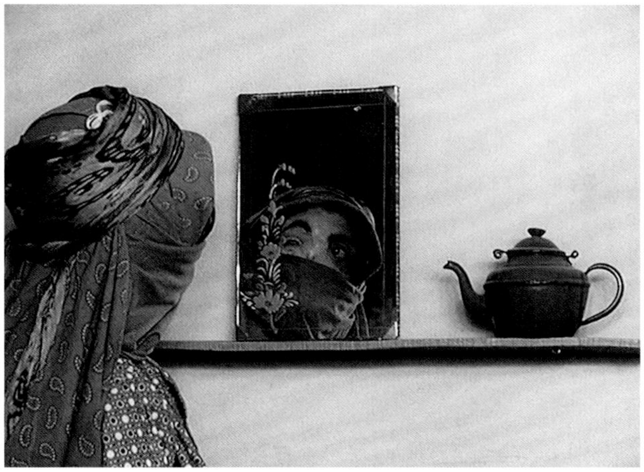

2

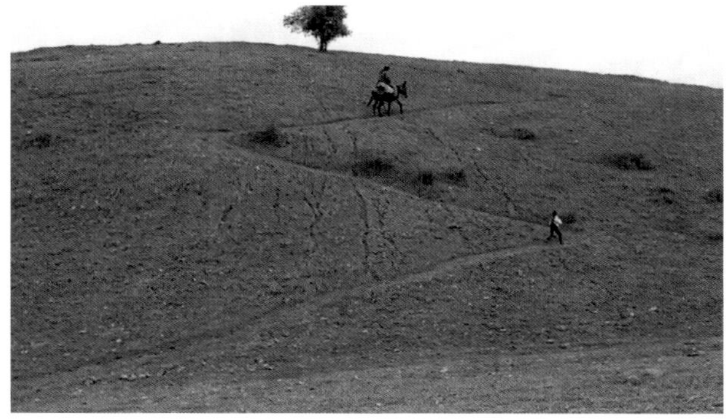

despite the fact that most were shot (very beautifully) on 16mm or 35mm film.

Since her early films and photography came from an implicitly feminist perspective and include "exotic" images of Islamic art, architecture, and traditionally clad woman, they fit within certain fashionable academic discourses (especially regarding gender and power), qualities that also brought charges of "Orientalizing" their subjects. Yet, while not denying a certain validity to these discourses or the objections just noted, the act of moving beyond them, like the effort to see beyond the films' gallery origins, can help us discern two key aspects of their achievements as cinema: the formal and the personal.

Every Neshat film displays a distinctive strategy in how it visually frames bodies, buildings, and landscapes, and in combining these with sounds and music, sometimes allying both to a defined narrative, sometimes not. To see the films in sequence is to be struck by how cogently, deliberately, and imaginatively these strategies evolve over time. Each film involves *new* formal challenges and advances; none ever simply repeats those of a previous film.

Likewise, especially since Neshat herself appears in some of the films, it's perhaps inevitable to assume the existence of an autobiographical dimension in the work. Yet that dimension is not, as in many autobiographical artworks, limited to progressions reflected in physical appearances and the outward facts of a life. Rather, it is recorded in the films' unfolding formal *vision* as well, and depicts the kind of spiritual journey familiar to readers of Iranian mystical literature: from outer to inner, from circumference to center, from skin to soul.

The following brief overview of nineteen titles from Neshat's short-film work, mainly but not strictly chronological, reflects groupings of works that are either used by Neshat herself (e.g., the *Dreamers* trilogy) or that seem appropriate to the work's organic development.

TWO PRELUDES (1996–97)

Neshat has said that, having left Iran at age seventeen, she was shocked to return in 1991 and see the changes wrought by revolution and the emergence of the Islamic Republic, especially in the images of militant, armed, chador-clad, martyrdom-seeking women. When she begins making images, in the photographic series *Women of Allah*, these female figures dominate, as a way for the artist to evoke/contemplate archaic powers in herself and her native culture.

When her images begin to move, in *Anchorage* (single-screen color video, 1996), Neshat is in center-frame, dressed in black, surrounded by black, only her bare feet, face, and hands showing. Three "acts" unfold in alternating frontal long shots and close-ups: she prays, she pulls out a pistol and fires

Fig. 1 Still from *The House Is Black*, 1962, directed by Forugh Farrokhzad. Courtesy of Ebrahim Golestan

Fig. 2 Still from *Where Is the Friend's House?*, 1987, directed by Abbas Kiarostami. Photo courtesy of mk2 films

(at the camera, at us), she sings a lullaby. Beyond its challenging identification of the artist with an Islamic culture that is both her and not-her, the film almost seems a whimsical evocation of the early days of cinema, from the studio-bound figure studies of Edison to the seriocomic, head-on violence of Edwin Porter's *The Great Train Robbery*.

As if continuing the early-cinema analogies, *The Shadow under the Web* (four-screen color video, 1997) delivers us to the era of the Lumière brothers, when the camera goes outdoors to observe moving human figures in diverse locales. Here, seen mostly in long shot, a chador-clad woman (Neshat) runs through locations that include a mosque's courtyard, a bazaar, and a residential area; the only sounds are her footsteps and heavy breathing. Storyless, the film is the first to use a foreign location (Istanbul), Middle Eastern/Islamic architecture, and the figure of a fleeing woman—a motif that will recur.

THE TRILOGY (1998–2000)

Here Neshat's cinema begins in earnest, with three highly original, brilliantly realized two-screen black-and-white films that mark her first work with three important collaborators: creative partner Shoja Azari, cinematographer Ghasem Ebrahimian, and performer/composer Sussan Deyhim. Each a stylized dramatic situation hinging on the gendering of Islamic social spaces, with all the psychological and power imbalances that reality implies, the boldly imagined films rest on a panoply of binaries: male/female, individual/group, dark/light, left/right, action/stasis, doing/watching, etc.

As *Turbulent* (16mm B&W, 1998; p. 54) opens, on the left screen a man in a white shirt (Azari) faces the camera in medium shot as an auditorium of men sits behind him, while on the right, a woman (Deyhim) in black stands alone in an empty space. The man sings (lip syncs) a confident, powerful song that wins enthusiastic applause from the crowd. Then the woman unleashes her own, solitary song, a keening lament that seems to come from the depths of her being. The crowning touch: the man in white seems to hear the woman—psychically?—and his abashed expression registers that her song is both an angry protest and a cry for freedom.

Rapture (16mm B&W, 1999; p. 64) takes place in and around a hulking coastal fortress (it was shot in Morocco), all of the action seen in distanced, elegantly composed long shots. On the left screen, white-shirted men conduct what look like military exercises, while on the right, chador-clad women watch them, immobile, from beyond the fort. Then the women begin to move, purposefully, and the men stop and watch from their ramparts. Ultimately, the women reach a beach and put to sea in small black boats: an action obviously intended to be read as either suicidal or a lunge for freedom, or both. With its precise geometric crowd choreography mixing lines and circles, the film recalls the compositional grandeur of Sergei Eisenstein and the early films of Fritz Lang.

Fervor (16mm B&W, 2000) transpires, like *Anchorage*, in three acts. In the first act, the distanced, geometrical compositions of *Rapture* recur as the camera watches a man and a woman pass each other on intersecting country roads. In the second act, the two enter a building where white-clad men and black-clad women sit on opposite sides and watch a male performer who, explicating a religious painting behind him, exhorts them to abjure Satan and temptations of the flesh. The man and woman exchange looks that are decidedly at odds with this message, and leave early. In the last act, they pass on the street, their mutual interest still evident. In *Fervor*, the impositions of religion are clearer than before, the characters are individuals rather than bodies or types, and the stark division between woman and man is suddenly if provisionally bridged—opening a world of possibilities.

TWO BLACK-AND-WHITE FILMS (2001)

The single-screen *Possessed* (35mm B&W, 2001; p. 104) was the first of two back-to-back collaborations with Iranian American star Shohreh Aghdashloo, the first times Neshat worked with a prominent movie actor. Both films depict women in states of mental isolation. In *Possessed*, the woman Aghdashloo plays moves though a town, her flowing hair uncovered. She appears to be on the brink of madness. She enters a square and at first is ignored, until she screams, which causes people in the square to start fighting with each other, as if her madness were contagious. If most of Neshat's female characters can be considered partial self-portraits, the ones in this and the following film suggest her passion for solitary rebellion can leave her cut off from the larger world.

In the single-screen *Pulse* (35mm B&W, 2001), the only Neshat film comprised of a single shot, the camera gazes across a darkened room. As it slowly tracks forward, details of the room's furnishings begin to be discernible, until it reaches the far wall and the back of a woman (Aghdashloo) who leans into an old radio listening raptly to a song (Sussan Deyhim singing a Rumi lyric). The radio and song seem to be her only links to the world outside the room. The film ends after the camera tracks back to the room's other side.

FOUR COLOR FILMS (1999–2002)

Like *The Shadow under the Web*, the two-screen *Soliloquy* (16mm color, 1999) presents Neshat as a black-clad woman on a visual odyssey, though this is the first film to make the West/East divide (in her life and work) explicit and to equate it with Christian/Muslim. Both screens initially show her gazing out of windows at different landscapes. Eventually she moves: on the right screen, she passes through the streets and architectures of an Islamic city (Turkey again), finally reaching and entering a mosque; on the left screen, she drives into a bustling Western city (New York, including World Trade Center interiors) before entering a modernistic church (filmed in Albany) and observing white-clad celebrants in a ceremony. Both screens end with her exiting the mosque/church and disappearing into the landscapes.

While *Soliloquy* has autobiographical implications in paralleling Neshat's own situation with the cultures she observes, *Passage* (35mm color, 2001; p. 94) has a more immediate personal spur. Invited by Philip Glass to make a film for him to score, she created one inspired by the recent death of her father, her first in 35mm and the first single-screen work since *Anchorage*. *Passage* opens with a line of men carrying a shroud-wrapped body along a seashore and over a rocky terrain; it then intercuts this movement with shots of a circle of chador-clad women chanting as they dig a grave. While the circle-and-line compositions recall *Rapture* (also shot in Morocco), and Glass' rhythmic score complements Ebrahimian's elegant camera movements, *Passage* moves beyond the binary patterns of previous films with the addition of a third element: the figure of a little girl who, in the film's last minute, generates a wall of fire that surrounds both the men and the women. This is the first time Neshat's presumed alter ego is a child.

Given the views of the World Trade Center in *Soliloquy* and the theme of death in *Passage*, it's eerily appropriate that Neshat's next color film was, she has said, inspired by the events of 9/11 and offers an allegorical vision of refuge. Significantly, the two-screen *Tooba* (35mm color, 2002; p. 114) is her first film with no overt reference to the Islamic world (it's also her first collaboration with cinematographer Darius Khondji). Filmed in Mexico, it opens with the camera slowly pulling back (right screen) from the wizened face of a placid native woman, apparently sleeping, who is revealed to be embedded in a tree atop a hill (a setting that recalls Kiarostami's Koker trilogy), while a group of men (left screen) aggressively traverse a rocky landscape and are seen chanting in a circle at night. The men arrive at the hilltop and find the tree surrounded by a low wall, which they easily surmount. But rather than attack the tree, they simply stop, surrounding it almost protectively. While the film introduces a suggestion of Latin American magical realism to Neshat's work, it also evokes the ancient Persian idea of paradise as a walled garden: a place of refuge and natural solace.

The Last Word (35mm color, 2003) must be counted doubly significant as Neshat's first film with dialogue and perhaps her most directly autobiographical and political film. Reflecting an interrogation she says she underwent the last time she left Iran, the work has a surreal, Kafkaesque air. After a brief prologue written and spoken in Farsi (untranslated), a young woman with uncovered dark hair walks through a dimly lit hallway along which she sees various strange people, then enters a large room and takes a seat at a long table facing a white-haired man, her inquisitor, behind whom several young men scurry around carrying books. The inquisitor cajoles, accuses, berates, and threatens the frightened young woman, behind whom appear a little girl with a yoyo and a matronly woman who brushes her hair. The young woman refuses to speak until, climactically, she exultantly declaims a passionate, defiant Forugh Farrokhzad poem that leaves the men in stunned silence, after which she calmly walks out. The bold assertion here of art's ultimate authority over political power could not be clearer.

WOMEN WITHOUT MEN SHORT FILMS (2004–9)

In 2002, Neshat began working on an adaptation of *Women without Men*, Shahrnush Parsipur's celebrated novel set during the 1953 coup against the government of Mohammad Mossadegh. The feature (co-credited to Azari), which received wide acclaim on its release in 2009, incorporated four of five short films Neshat based on Parsipur's fiction; following the book, each bears the name of one of the main female characters. Seen apart from the feature, these films remain among her most distinctive and accomplished in the short form. Her only ventures into period filmmaking, with Casablanca filling in for Tehran, they benefit considerably from the skills of cinematographer Martin Gschlacht, composer Ryuichi Sakamoto, and production designers Shahram Karimi and Katharina Woppermann.

The one short that wasn't used in the feature, and thus can be considered a prelude to the others, the three-screen *Mahdokht* (Super 35mm color, 2004), offers a dreamlike, magical-realist vision of rural groves of trees, yellow-clad children playing, and an image that recurs in Neshat's work: a woman floating in water. (The other films in the series are all single-screen.) Opening in a bordello, *Zarin* (Super 35mm color, 2006) follows an emaciated prostitute as she ventures through the city to a bathhouse, where she scrubs her body with a desperate intensity. (This is the first Neshat film to depict sex and nudity.) In *Faezeh* (Super 35mm color, 2008), the title character, a conservative young woman, enters an enclosed estate where she has visions of her own rape and the white-clad bride of her friend Munis' brother. Depicting the urban riots spurred by the anti-Mossadegh coup, *Munis* (Super 35mm, color, 2008) sees its politically minded heroine witness the death of a young communist, then float down from a rooftop to converse with his soul. In *Farokh Legha* (Super 35mm, color, 2009), the title character is a society woman hosting a tony party on her country estate until it is invaded by soldiers led by an imperious army captain. Besides registering the political tumult of 1953, this film offers one of the richest evocations of an era of Iranian history rarely captured by cinema.

DREAMERS (2013–16)

From the early achievement of her first brilliant trilogy, Neshat's short-film work to date comes full circle with another masterful de facto trilogy in black-and-white (the first film shot by Khondji, the other two by Ebrahimian). While the earlier films mostly looked outward, to issues of appearance, identity, and sociology, these turn inward, to the realms of psychology and dream: completing the journey from skin to soul. Rather than engaging binary and seemingly implacable opposites, the newer films traverse shifting dreamscapes that suggest the anxieties and challenges faced by anyone caught between cultures; they also depict father and mother figures alternately threatening and welcoming. Cinematically, the *Dreamers* trilogy evokes influences from poetic and Surrealist auteurs including Jean Cocteau, Luis Buñuel, and Maya Deren; the use of distorting glass in front of the lens, seen in all three films, descends from Man Ray.

Made in collaboration with Natalie Portman, and establishing the dream logic that governs all three narratives, *Illusions & Mirrors* (ARRI Alexa, B&W, 2013; p. 184) follows the actress from a beach along a path to a large house, which she enters and explores, seeing various individuals and groups of people before coming upon a matronly woman comforting a young woman, who lunges at the protagonist and screams; the film ends with her back on the beach, seemingly at peace. *Roja* (2K ARRI AlexaXT Video B&W, 2016; p. 194) opens with the title character, a young woman, in a theater watching a burly older man, who performs an emotional song titled "The Carnival Is Over," then urges her to come on stage. Instead, she exits the building and finds herself facing a strange landscape that includes a lake and a woman who walks toward her, at first appearing merely curious but suddenly turning hostile when she gets close; Roja reacts by elevating into the sky. *Sarah* (2K ARRI AlexaXT Video B&W, 2016), inspired by Akira Kurosawa's *Dreams*, opens with its young title character floating underwater in a stream, looking up at the sky; next, in a forest surrounded by smoke that seems left from a recent fire, she sees a seated woman, then a road that is traversed by a company of marching, chanting soldiers, and later, a group of chador-clad women who seem engaged in a religious processional. Then Sarah sees a placid lake over which the sun hovers; she walks into it, looking as becalmed as the women in the last frames of the two previous films.

LOOKING FOR OUM KULTHUM (2017)

In *Women without Men*, Neshat crossed the divide between short and feature filmmaking in an ingenious and bracingly organic way; it was as if the imaginary walls dividing the short films made from Parsipur's fiction simply melted away, revealing the unified cinematic whole they always implied or suggested. In her second feature, *Looking for Oum Kulthum* (made in collaboration with Azari), Neshat provocatively moves in the opposite direction, unveiling a whole that calls attention to the imaginary dividing lines it contains, lines that in some ways recall the binary divisions of her early films. So: we have a celebrated Iranian visual artist setting out to contemplate and dramatize the work of a legendary Egyptian singer. Beyond the obvious contraries of Persian and Arabic, iconic and musical, past and present, artistic subject and object, and with Morocco playing Egypt, Neshat provides a mirror image of herself in Mitra (Neda Rahmanian), an Iranian-born filmmaker attempting to make a biopic about Oum Kulthum and confronted by all the challenges such an enterprise would entail for any filmmaker but also the additional ones that come from being a woman: everything from the disdain of crew members to her agonizing separation from her son. Invoking the Iranian tradition of films about filmmakers and filmmaking, *Looking for Oum Kulthum* may not be entirely successful on its own terms, but it is a brave and forward-looking film, one that again shows Neshat with her eyes on the artistic horizon, looking for barriers to sunder and worlds to bridge.

Godfrey Cheshire is a film critic, journalist, and filmmaker based in New York City.

CHRONOLOGY
ED SCHAD

1957

March 26: Neshat is born in Qazvin, Iran, the fourth of five children, to Ali, a medical doctor and intellectual, and Mahin, a homemaker.

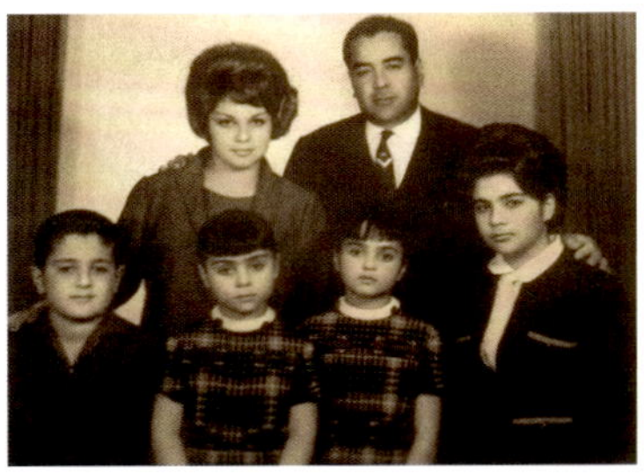

1960s AND EARLY 1970s

Neshat attends elementary school in Qazvin, then is sent to Tehran to a Catholic high school. Due to medical issues, she returns to Qazvin to continue high school. She is an avid moviegoer as a child, though going to the cinema is problematic for adults. In conservative circles, cinema is taboo.

1963

Women are granted the right to vote in Iran under Mohammed Reza Pahlavi.

1967

February 13: Poet Forugh Farrokhzad dies in a car accident.

1975

Neshat is sent to the United States at the age of seventeen to finish her education. She lives with her sister Mahdokht in the Westwood area of Los Angeles, and later resides with a Jewish French family on Manning Avenue. She speaks no English on arrival.

February 3: Internationally renowned Egyptian singer Oum Kulthum dies in Egypt of a kidney condition. Four million people attend her funeral.

1976–77

Neshat attends University High School in Los Angeles. Though her family is not political, she often finds herself, uncomfortably, as the youngest person at political gatherings where the talk is about overthrowing the shah. She meets Mansoor Ehsan, who later exerts a large influence on her *Women of Allah* series of photographs.

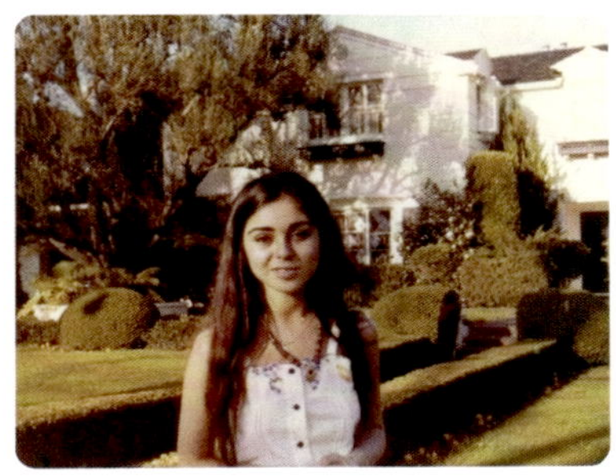

1978

January: The Islamic Revolution in Iran begins. Mohammed Reza Pahlavi escapes the country. Ayatollah Ruhollah Khomeini orders an election in the new Islamic Republic, and Abolhassan Banisadr is elected the first president in 1980.

1979

Neshat moves to Berkeley to attend college, living on the outskirts of San Rafael. She studies printmaking with Sylvia Lark, and sculpture and mixed media with Harold Paris. To support herself, she works part-time in a florist shop. She attends an Indian dance and music school and becomes a student of Kathak dance.

On a trip to Peru with university friends, her Iranian passport is stolen. With no proof of her relationship to Iran or her student visa, she is adrift in Lima, unable to return to the States or to legally remain in Peru. UC Berkeley provides proof that she is a student, and the U.S. Embassy allows her to return to California.

November 4: The Iran hostage crisis begins.

1980

The Iran-Iraq War begins, lasting until 1988. News of the war will greatly inform Neshat's *Women of Allah* series. She receives the vast majority of war news through U.S. outlets.

The wearing of the hijab is made mandatory in government and public offices in Iran, and in 1983 it becomes mandatory for all women.

April 7: The U.S. severs diplomatic relations with Iran. There is no postal service between Iran and the U.S. Any communication between Neshat and her family in Iran is by telephone, which is not easy to facilitate, or by hand-carried letters.

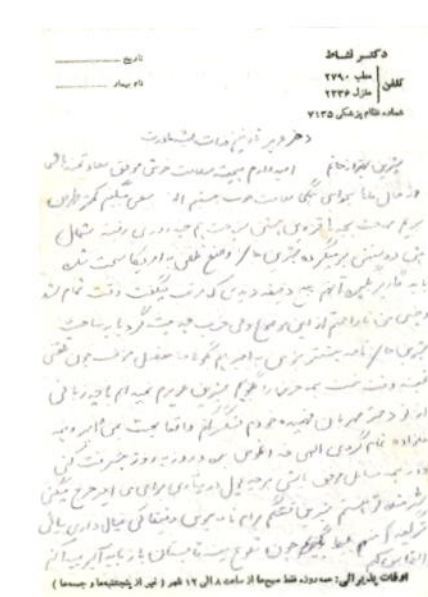

1981

Neshat encounters anti-Iran protests at Berkeley.

January 20: Iran releases fifty-two American hostages on the day of Ronald Reagan's inauguration as president of the United States.

1983

Neshat receives an MFA from UC Berkeley. She moves to New York, leaving nearly all her belongings in an apartment in Marin County, including dozens of paintings, prints, and collages she had made while studying at the university. Living in the East Village, she works at a hair salon and later at a Midtown textile office, where she designs fabrics. Soon after quitting her job, she meets future husband Kyong Park, founder of Storefront for Art and Architecture, and runs Storefront as co-director for the next ten years.

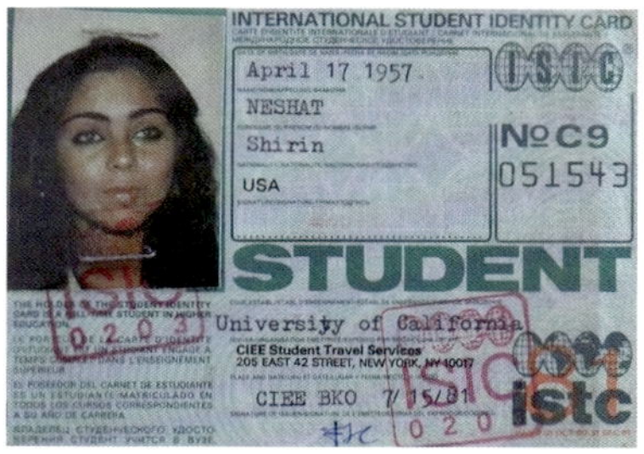

1985

As war with Iraq dominates all life in Iran, Neshat shepherds the visa and passport process of her brother Amir, the youngest member of her family, through multiple countries in Europe. She is finally able to meet him in St. Martin to accompany him into the U.S.

1986

July: Neshat becomes a citizen of the United States.

As co-director of Storefront, she works with Mel Chin and architects like Zaha Hadid, Peter Cook, and Jean Nouvel. The work of many other artists encountered there—Kiki Smith, Alfredo Jaar, Antonio Muntadas, Dan Graham, Nam June Paik, Mary Miss—will have a direct influence on her own creative production.

1987

May: The Iran-Contra hearings begin in the U.S. Congress.

1988

August 20: The Iraq-Iran War ends.

November 16: Neshat marries Kyong Park.

1990

August 26: Mehdi Akhavan-Sales, pioneer of free verse in Iranian poetry, dies in Tehran. He is buried in Tus, near the grave of Abolqasem Ferdowsi, author of the national epic poem of Iran and Persia, *The Book of Kings*.

November 11: Neshat's son Cyrus is born. He is named after the Persian king Cyrus the Great.

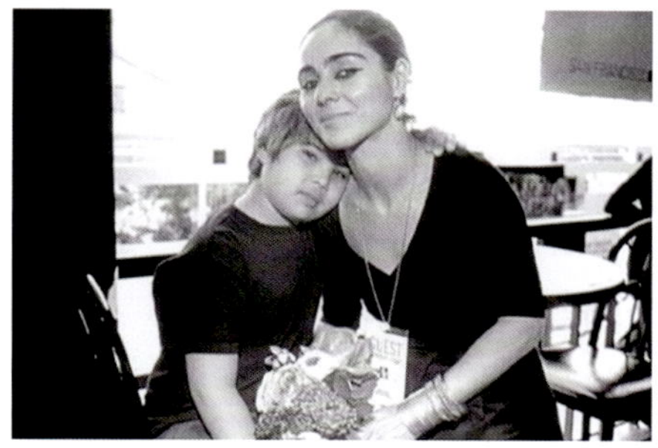

1991

May: Neshat makes her first trip to Iran since leaving the country twelve years before, bringing along her son Cyrus. She takes a bus tour to Kashan.

Summer/Fall: She receives an artist residency at Henry Street Settlement on the Lower East Side of Manhattan. She begins drawing human body parts like hands, feet, and eyes, writing on them with Farsi text. Though never exhibited, these works lead to her later photography work.

1992

Neshat works closely with Vito Acconci and Steven Holl to manage the new facade construction of Storefront for Art and Architecture.

Farzaneh Milani publishes *Veils and Words*, one of the first studies in English to introduce contemporary female literary voices in Iran to global audiences.

Shahrnush Parsipur's *Women without Men* is published.

June: Neshat makes a second trip to Iran.

Fall: She begins work on the first wave of the *Women of Allah* photos, working with Brazilian photographer Plauto, whom she met at Storefront.

1993

April: Neshat has her first solo exhibition, *Unveiling,* at Franklin Furnace in New York.

1994

Early 1994: Neshat works with photographer Cynthia Preston on the second wave of *Women of Allah*, which takes up the idea of martyrdom. Neshat met Preston in upstate New York and borrowed the guns in the photos from her neighbors, who were hunters.

February 18–June 12: She participates in *Beyond the Borders: Art by Recent Immigrants* at the Bronx Museum. The show garners important early press exposure for Neshat.

Late 1994: Neshat meets and works with photographer Larry Barns on more photos for *Women of Allah*. Barns had lived in Iran during a stint in the Peace Corps and speaks Farsi.

1995

June: Neshat's work is included in curator Fumio Nanjo's group exhibition *Transculture* at the Venice Biennale. Due to this exhibition, she has her first commercial gallery exhibition at Annina Nosei.

August: Neshat makes her third and final trip to Iran.

September 30–October 28: *Women of Allah* is on view at Annina Nosei Gallery in New York. Cindy Sherman is the first person to buy Neshat's work.

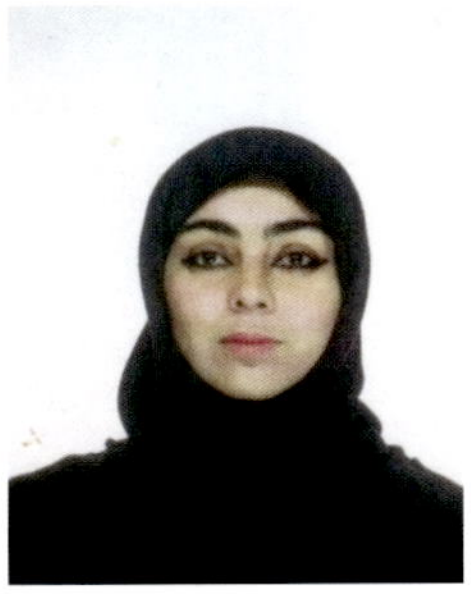

1996

Indicative of the quick renown of the *Women of Allah* series, Neshat shows the work at Haines Gallery, San Francisco; Galleria Lucio Amelio, Naples; Marco Noire Contemporary Art, Turin; and Centre d'Art Contemporain, Fribourg, all in the course of one year. She participates in the Austrian Triennial on Photography, Graz, in June, and the Biennale of Sydney in July. As she begins to contemplate a move into film and video, she undertakes intense study of film, especially Iranian cinema.

June 20: Commissioned by Creative Time, she makes her first film, *Anchorage,* which is designed for and shown only once at the base of the Brooklyn Bridge in the Anchorage.

1997

October 5–November 9: Neshat participates in *On Life, Beauty, Translations and Other Difficulties* at the 5th International Istanbul Biennial, curated by Rosa Martínez.

October: She participates in the Johannesburg Biennale. Okwui Enwezor is artistic director.

November: Neshat meets Shoja Azari, her future partner, and through Azari, Ghasem Ebrahimian, while working on her video *Turbulent*. She also becomes reacquainted with Sussan Deyhim, whom she met during her time in the Bay Area.

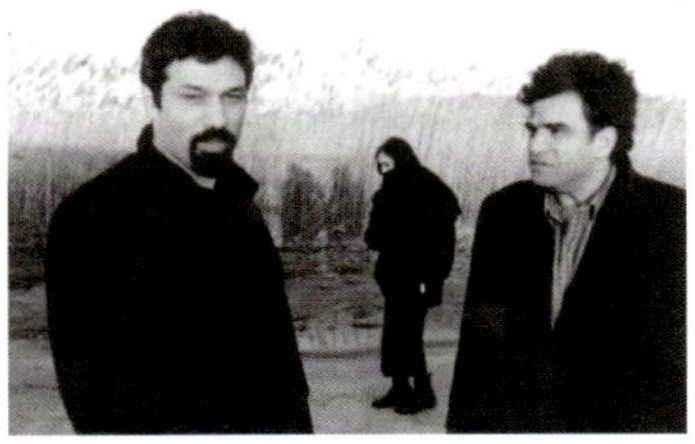

1998

Neshat separates from her husband Kyong Park.

January: She shoots the video *Turbulent* in a high school auditorium on the Lower East Side of Manhattan in two days: one to film the male singer (Azari), and a second to film the female singer (Deyhim).

Spring/Summer: Neshat, Azari, and Ebrahimian travel to Essaouira, Morocco, to scout for the video *Rapture*. The choice of Essaouira is partially inspired by its use as a location in Orson Welles' *Othello*. The video is shot in the fall.

1999

In relatively close succession in Iran, Neshat's seventeen-year-old nephew Iman dies of cancer, followed by her father Ali. Neshat is in the U.S. at the time, but is able to see her sister Mayram soon after, during the filming of *Soliloquy*.

Articles are published against Neshat's work in daily newspapers in Iran.

The Whitney Museum of American Art purchases *Rapture*. Neshat cites this as her most significant early sale.

Summer and Fall: *Soliloquy* is shot in various locations around the World Trade Center, Saint Ann's Church in New York City, the Empire State Plaza in Albany, New York, and Mardin, Turkey. Neshat and her crew are shadowed by the Turkish government during shooting. Some of the film crew are jailed and their passports confiscated. Neshat bails her crew members out of jail.

May 2–August 1: *Focus: Shirin Neshat, Rapture* is held at The Art Institute of Chicago and features an installation of the video *Rapture*. In the wake of this exhibition, Neshat is invited to join Barbara Gladstone Gallery in New York.

June 13–November 17: She participates in the Venice Biennale, winning the First International Prize for *Turbulent*.

November: *Soliloquy* debuts at the Carnegie International.

Fall/Winter: Neshat shoots *Fervor* in Marrakech, Morocco, over two weeks.

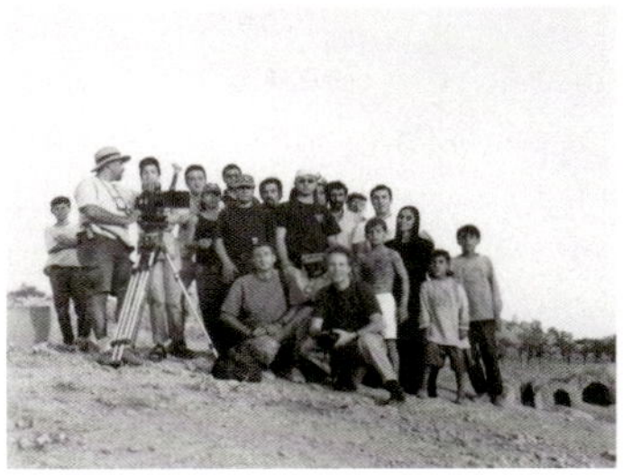

2000

Neshat wins the Grand Prix at the Kwangju Biennale and the Visual Art Award from the Edinburgh International Film Festival.

March 23–June 4: *Rapture* is shown in the Whitney Biennial.

May 26–July 30: She participates in the Biennale of Sydney.

2001

Neshat is given a photocopied manuscript of Parsipur's *Women without Men* by Hamid Dabashi. Editions of the text are difficult to find in Farsi because the book has been banned in Iran.

Neshat's work is included in the Chicago International Film Festival and the San Francisco International Film Festival. She has a solo exhibition at the National Museum of Contemporary Art in Athens.

Spring: She collaborates with Philip Glass to create *Passage*, filmed in the Moroccan coastal town of Essaouira. On the same trip, she shoots *Possessed* and *Pulse*.

September 11: The Twin Towers in New York City are destroyed by terrorists. Neshat's son is enrolled in school across the street from the Towers, and as the tragedy unfolds, she and Azari run on foot to get him out of school and bring him home. Along the way, they witness people jumping from windows and eventually see both buildings collapse.

October 5: *The Logic of the Birds* premieres at the Kitchen in New York. Commissioned by Performa and written and filmed by Neshat, Azari, and Ehrahimian, it is based on Attar's *The Conference of the Birds* and features Deyhim's voice and composition. The performance is altered in the wake of 9/11 and responds, in part, to the events.

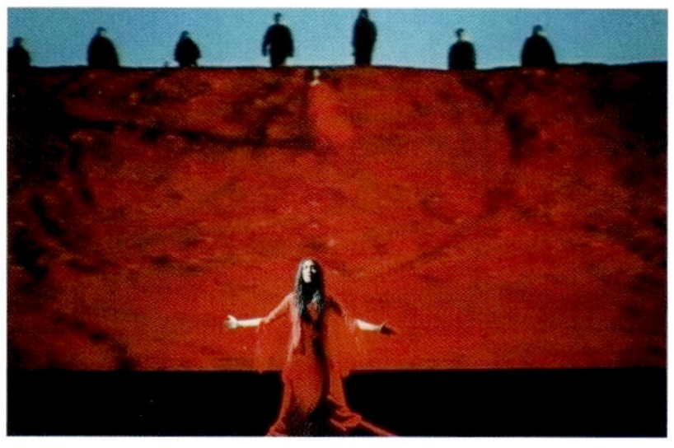

2002

Neshat wins the Infinity Award from the International Center of Photography in New York and has a solo exhibition at the Walker Art Center in Minneapolis.

June: She participates in *Moving Pictures* at the Guggenheim Museum.

Summer: The film *Tooba* is shot in the villages of Tiracoz and Cuilapan de Guerrero in Oaxaca, Mexico, featuring an isolated tree. The visuals for the film are partially inspired by Abbas Kiarostami. *Tooba* is shown as a two-channel video installation at documenta 11 in Kassel.

August: Neshat participates in the Locarno International Film Festival.

2003

Neshat is honored at the First Annual Risk Takers in the Arts Celebration awarded by the Sundance Institute in New York. She wins the ZeroOne Award from the Universität der Künste Berlin.

May: She participates in the Tribeca Film Festival.

September: She participates in the ICP Triennial of Photography and Video at the International Center of Photography in New York.

Winter: Screenwriters Laboratory of the Sundance Institute helps Neshat to develop and begin production on the feature film *Women without Men*, an adaptation of Shahrnush Parsipur's novel of the same name. The screenplay is a collaboration between Neshat and the author, and the cinematography is by Darius Khondji, who also shot *Tooba*. She flies back and forth between New York and Berlin to work with script consultant Franz Rodenkirchen and her European producers, eventually becoming a resident in Berlin for a time. The first installment of the film, *Mahdokht*, is shot in Marrakech, but is eliminated from the final film.

2005

Neshat's visit to Luang Prabang, Laos, inspires the *Games of Desire* video and a photographic series in a temple by the Mekong River, which explores the tradition of the *lam*, a Laotian custom of reciting courtship songs.

Zarin, a second video related to the *Women without Men* project, is shot.

January: A solo exhibition is held at the Hamburger Bahnhof, Museum für Gegenwart in Berlin.

July: Neshat wins the Hiroshima Freedom Prize from the Hiroshima City Museum of Art.

2006

April: Neshat has a solo exhibition at the Stedelijk Museum, Amsterdam.

October: She wins the Dorothy and Lillian Gish Prize in New York, given annually to an individual who has "made an outstanding contribution to the beauty of the world and to mankind's enjoyment and understanding of life."

2007

The remainder of shooting for *Women without Men* is undertaken in Casalanca, Marrakech, and Rabat.

February: Neshat participates *in Lights Camera Action* at the Whitney Museum in New York.

June: She joins the board of the Andy Warhol Foundation and serves an eight-year term.

2008

Neshat works intensely on post-production of *Women without Men*.

October 25: Tahereh Saffarzadeh, the controversial Iranian poet and translator of the Qur'an, known equally for her feminism and her celebration of the authority of Islam, dies. Her poetry features prominently in Neshat's *Women of Allah* series.

2009

June 19: Protests against the 2009 Iranian presidential election results spur the founding of Iran's Green Movement. The color green is associated with presidential candidate Mir-Hossein Mousavi.

July 1: Neshat helps mobilize a three-day hunger strike in front of the UN Building in New York to bring international attention to human rights violations committed by the Iranian government and to petition for the release of jailed student protesters in Iran.

September 14: She wins the Silver Lion for Best Director at the 66th Venice Film Festival for *Women without Men*. Neshat and her collaborators wear green in support of Iran's Green Movement.

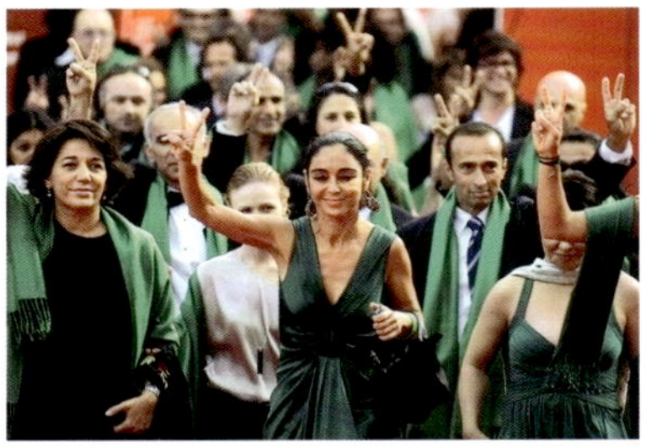

2010

The Huffington Post declares Neshat "Artist of the Decade."

January: By invitation of Yvonne Force Villareal and Doreen Remen of the Art Production Fund, two *Women of Allah* photos are featured on top of New York taxis for a month.

December: Neshat delivers her TEDWomen lecture "Art in Exile" at the Paley Center for Media in Washington, D.C.

2011

Neshat is named one of the most influential women in the world by the London *Financial Times*.

January: She and Azari travel to Egypt for research on the life of Egyptian singer Oum Kulthum.

November 11–12: *Overruled*, a performance commissioned by Performa, based on Neshat's earlier film *The Last Word*, is performed at Cedar Lake in New York City. The performance features actor Mohammed Ghaffari, composer Mohsen Namjoo, and singer Shadi Yousefian.

Winter: Neshat shoots photos for *The Book of Kings* series.

2012

September 12–November 17: *The Book of Kings* debuts at Galerie Jérôme de Noirmont in Paris.

2013

April 7–July 7: Her first major U.S. retrospective, *Shirin Neshat*, is held at the Detroit Institute of Arts.

April 13–September 8: *The Book of Kings* is shown at the Faurschou Foundation in Beijing.

June 6–September 1: *Written on the Body*, a survey of Neshat's work, is held at Espacio Fundación Telefónica in Madrid.

Fall: Neshat shoots photos for *Our House Is on Fire*, commissioned by the Robert Rauschenberg Foundation, at Townhouse, a nonprofit art space in Cairo near Tahrir Square. Over the course of two weeks, she meets and interviews Egyptian citizens about their experiences during the Arab Spring.

Winter: Commissioned by Dior, Neshat shoots *Illusions and Mirrors* on Long Island and at a mansion in Yonkers, New York.

2014

Neshat wins the Crystal Award from the World Economic Forum for her contributions to the world through art.

She is commissioned by Toledo Contemporanea to produce a series of portraits (nine total) inspired by the work of El Greco on the occasion of the 400th anniversary of the artist's death.

January 31: *Our House Is on Fire* debuts at the Robert Rauschenberg Foundation.

June 18: Shakespeare's *The Tempest*, a collaboration between Krzysztof Pastor, Neshat, and Azari, premieres at the Dutch National Opera & Ballet in Amsterdam. The performance uses video by Neshat and music by Henry Purcell, Thomas Tallis, Robert Johnson, Matthew Locke, and Michel van der Aa, as well as traditional Iranian music.

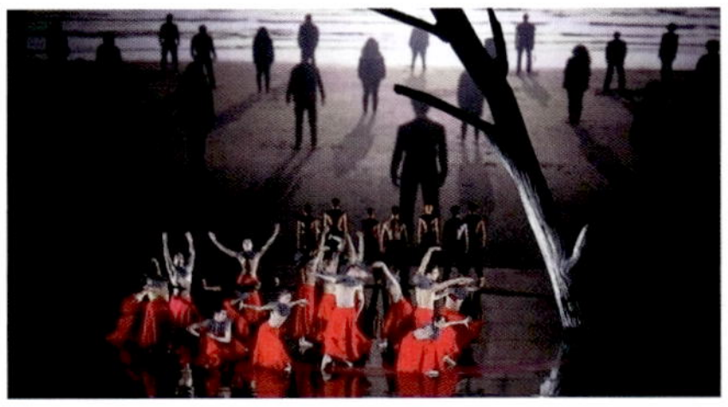

September 25–26: *Passage Through the World*, a collaboration between Neshat, Azari, and Mohsen Namjoo, debuts at Teatro Margherita in Bari, Italy. After visiting the city of Bari, emblematically projected for centuries as an ideal bridge between European and Asian cultures, the three artists enlist a group

of women of the old city who are the last witnesses of the rites of lamentation in funeral ceremonies, and the band Faraualla, dedicated to the valorization of the traditional music and popular culture of Puglia. The performance is partially based on Pier Paolo Pasolini's 1960 documentary *Stendali*.

November 9, 2014–February 15, 2015: *Afterwards*, a survey of Neshat's work, opens at Mathaf: Arab Museum of Modern Art in Doha.

2015

March 24–August 31: *The Home of My Eyes* shows at the Yarat Contemporary Art Centre in Baku, Azerbaijan. The series of portraits were commissioned by Yarat in collaboration with the curator Dina Nasser-Khadivi.

May 18–September 20: *Facing History*, a large survey of Neshat's work, is held at the Hirshhorn Museum and Sculpture Garden in Washington, D.C.

2016

Neshat shoots the video *Roja* in a coal mine in Pennsylvania and in upstate New York. The video *Sarah* is shot around Neshat and Azari's home in the Adirondack Mountains.

July 4: Abbas Kiarostami, a major influence on Neshat and generations of Iranian filmmakers, dies in Paris.

September–December: The feature film *Looking for Oum Kulthum* is shot in Morocco.

August: Neshat has her first solo exhibition in Africa, at the Goodman Gallery in Johannesburg.

2017

Neshat receives the Praemium Imperiale Award in Tokyo along with Mikhail Baryshnikov, El Anatsui, Rafael Moneo, and Youssou N'Dour.

May 13–November 26: *The Home of My Eyes* is exhibited at Museo Correr in Venice. The show is curated by Thomas Kellein.

July 1–October 29: *Shirin Neshat* shows at Kunsthalle Tübingen.

August 6: *Aida*, directed by Neshat at the invitation of Markus Hinterhäuser and the Salzburg Festival, premieres at Großes Festspielhaus. The production is conducted by Riccardo Muti and features Anna Netrebko as Aida.

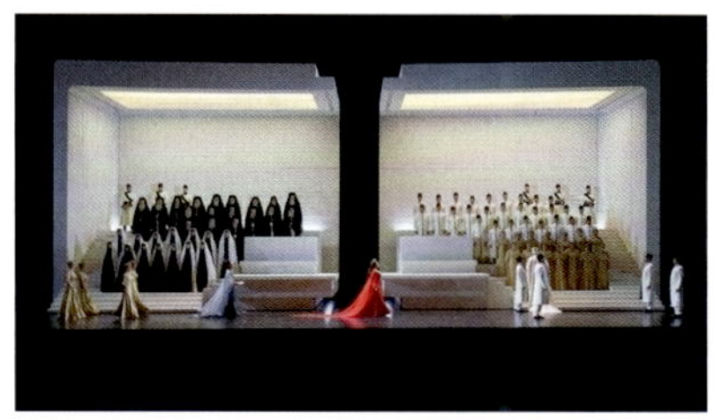

September 2: After six years in production, *Looking for Oum Kulthum* premieres at the Toronto International Film Festival.

Winter: Neshat moves her studio from Soho in Manhattan to Bushwick in Brooklyn.

2018

January 18–April 22: A survey exhibition of Neshat's work, *Frauen in Gesellschaft*, is held at the Neue Galerie Graz, Austria.

March 20–September 7: *Looking for Oum Kulthum* is shown at the Faurschou Foundation in Copenhagen.

March 23–May 20: The *Dreamers* trilogy shows at Kunstraum Dornbirn, Austria.

October 3: The National Portrait Gallery in London unveils Neshat's commissioned portrait of female education activist Malala Yousafzai.

Late November–early December: Neshat joins Azari and Ehrahimian on a road trip across the United States to scout locations for *Land of Dreams*. They settle on locations in New Mexico.

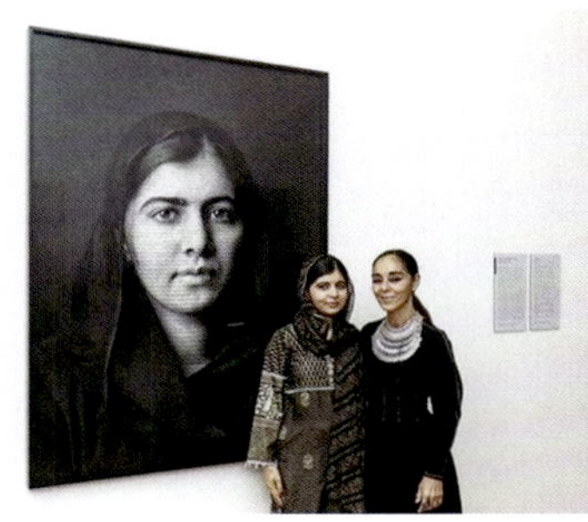

2019

May: Neshat shoots portraits for *Land of Dreams* in New Mexico.

Mid-June: She shoots video for *Land of Dreams* at Shiprock Pinnacle in Navajo Nation, New Mexico.

EXHIBITION CHECKLIST

Unless otherwise noted, all art is copyright Shirin Neshat and courtesy of Gladstone Gallery, New York and Brussels.

All artwork measurements listed below are framed dimensions.

WOMEN OF ALLAH

I Am Its Secret, 1993 (p. 39)
From *Women of Allah* series
Ink on RC print
54⅞ x 39⅛ x 1⅞ inches (139.4 x 99.4 x 4.8 cm)
Photograph taken by Plauto

Offered Eyes, 1993 (p. 45)
From *Women of Allah* series
Ink on RC print
52⅜ x 36¼ x 1⅞ inches (133 x 92.1 x 4.8 cm)
Photograph taken by Plauto

Unveiling, 1993 (pp. 15, 34, 46)
From *Women of Allah* series
Gelatin silver print and ink
59¾ x 39¾ inches (151.8 x 101 cm)
Photograph taken by Plauto
Purchase, with funds from the Photography Committee. Inv. N.: 2000.267.
Whitney Museum of American Art, New York, NY, U.S.A.

Allegiance with Wakefulness, 1994 (p. 49)
From *Women of Allah* series
Ink on LE silver gelatin print
52 x 42⅜ x 1⅞ inches (132.1 x 107.6 x 4.8 cm)
Photograph taken by Cynthia Preston

Faceless, 1994 (p. 48)
From *Women of Allah* series
Ink on RC print
56½ x 37 x 2 inches (143.5 x 94 x 5.1 cm)
Photograph taken by Cynthia Preston

Grace Under Duty, 1994 (p. 16)
From *Women of Allah* series
Ink on LE silver gelatin print
50¼ x 41¼ x 1⅞ inches (127.6 x 104.8 x 4.8 cm)
Photograph taken by Robert Wesler

Guardians of Revolution, 1994 (p. 43)
From *Women of Allah* series
Ink on LE silver gelatin print
47½ x 43¾ x 1⅞ inches (120.7 x 111.1 x 4.8 cm)
Photograph taken by Cynthia Preston

My Beloved, 1995 (p. 42)
From *Women of Allah* series
Ink on LE silver gelatin print
65⅜ x 47⅜ x 2 inches (166.1 x 120.3 x 5.1 cm)
Photograph taken by Cynthia Preston
Courtesy of Goodman Gallery, Johannesburg, Capetown, and London

Rebellious Silence, 1994 (pp. 37, 40)
From *Women of Allah* series
Ink on LE silver gelatin print
51⅞ x 36½ x 1⅞ inches (131.8 x 92.7 x 4.8 cm)
Photograph taken by Cynthia Preston

Untitled, 1994/2015
From *Women of Allah* series
Ink on LE silver gelatin print
65⅜ x 47⅜ x 2 inches (166.1 x 102.3 x 5.1 cm)
Photograph taken by Cynthia Preston

All Demons Flee, 1995 (p. 51)
From *Women of Allah* series
LE silver gelatin print
45½ x 65½ x 1⅞ inches (115.6 x 166.4 x 4.8 cm)
Photograph taken by Bahman Jalali

Bonding, 1995 (p. 12)
From *Women of Allah* series
Ink on RC print
34⅜ x 56⅞ x 1¾ inches (87.3 x 144.5 x 4.4 cm)
Photograph taken by Kyong Park

Untitled, 1995 (p. 50)
From *Women of Allah* series
LE silver gelatin print
65½ x 45½ x 2 inches (166.4 x 115.6 x 5.1 cm)
Photograph taken by Bahman Jalali

Untitled, 1995 (p. 52)
From *Women of Allah* series
LE silver gelatin print
65½ x 45½ x 2 inches (166.4 x 115.6 x 5.1 cm)
Photograph taken by Bahman Jalali

Untitled, 1995 (p. 53)
From *Women of Allah* series
LE silver gelatin print
65½ x 45½ x 2 inches (166.4 x 115.6 x 5.1 cm)
Photograph taken by Bahman Jalali

Identified, 1995 (p. 41)
From *Women of Allah* series
Ink on RC print
58¾ x 43¼ x 1⅞ inches (149.2 x 109.9 x 4.8 cm)
Photograph taken by Cynthia Preston

Speechless, 1996 (p. 47)
From *Women of Allah* series
Ink on RC print
52 x 39¼ x 1⅞ inches (132.1 x 99.7 x 4.8 cm)
Photograph taken by Larry Barns

Untitled, 1996 (p. 17)
From *Women of Allah* series
Ink on RC print
53 x 39¼ x 1⅞ inches (134.6 x 99.7 x 4.8 cm)
Photograph taken by Larry Barns

Untitled, 1996 (p. 44)
From *Women of Allah* series
Ink on RC print
58½ x 43 x 1⅞ inches (148.6 x 109.2 x 4.8 cm)
Photograph taken by Kyong Park

Whispers, 1997 (p. 31)
From *Women of Allah* series
Ink on LE gelatin silver print
50⅜ x 82⅝ x 1⅞ inches (128 x 209.9 x 4.8 cm)
Photograph taken by Larry Barns

TURBULENT

Turbulent, 1998 (p. 54)
Two-channel video installation
16mm black-and-white film transferred to video
Duration: 10 minutes
Filmed in New York City
Director: Shirin Neshat
Director of Photography: Ghasem Ebrahimian
Female Performer, Vocalist, Composer: Sussan Deyhim
Male Performer: Shoja Azari
Vocalist for Male Performer: Shahram Nazeri
Poetry by: Jalal al-Din Rumi
Production Manager: Bahman Soltani
Producer: Marco Noire Contemporary Art

RAPTURE

Rapture, 1999 (p. 64)
Two-channel video installation
16mm black-and-white film transferred to video
Duration: 13 minutes
Filmed in Morocco
Director: Shirin Neshat
In Collaboration with: Shoja Azari
Director of Photography: Ghasem Ebrahimian
Music and Sound Design: Sussan Deyhim
Production Managers: Hamid Fardjad and Bahman Soltani
Costume Designer: Noureddine Amir
Producer: Galerie Jérôme de Noirmont
Courtesy of Noirmontartproduction, Paris

SOLILOQUY

Soliloquy Series, 1999 (p. 91)
LE silver gelatin print
43¾ x 79¼ x 2¼ inches (111.1 x 201.3 x 5.7 cm)
Photograph taken by Larry Barns
Courtesy of Goodman Gallery, Johannesburg, Capetown, and London

Soliloquy Series, 1999 (p. 90)
LE silver gelatin print
50⅝ x 66 x 2 inches (128.6 x 167.6 x 5.1 cm)
Photograph taken by Larry Barns

Soliloquy Series, 2000 (p. 89)
Chromogenic print
63½ x 47½ x 2 inches (161.3 x 120.7 x 5.1 cm)
Photograph taken by Larry Barns

Soliloquy Series, 2000 (p. 93)
Chromogenic print
60¼ x 48¼ inches (153 x 122.6 cm)
Photograph taken by Larry Barns
The Broad Art Foundation, Los Angeles

Soliloquy Series, 2000 (p. 92)
Chromogenic print
48¼ x 60¼ inches (122.6 x 153 cm)
Photograph taken by Larry Barns
The Broad Art Foundation, Los Angeles

PASSAGE

Passage, 2001 (p. 94)
Single-channel video installation
35mm color film transferred to video
Duration: 11 minutes, 30 seconds
Filmed in Morocco
Director: Shirin Neshat
In Collaboration with: Shoja Azari
Music Composition: Philip Glass
Director of Photography: Ghasem Ebrahimian
Production Designer: Shahram Karimi
Costume Designer: Noureddine Amir
Line Producer: Hamid Fardjad
Producer: Barbara Gladstone

POSSESSED

Possessed, 2001 (p. 104)
Single-channel video installation
16mm and 35mm black-and-white film transferred to video
Duration: 9 minutes, 30 seconds
Filmed in Morocco
Director: Shirin Neshat
In Collaboration with: Shoja Azari
Director of Photography: Ghasem Ebrahimian
Music: Sussan Deyhim
Actress: Shohreh Aghdashloo
Line Producer: Hamid Fardjad
Art Director: Shahram Karimi
Costume Designer: Noureddine Amir
Producer: Barbara Gladstone

TOOBA

Tooba, 2002 (p. 114)
Two-channel video installation
35mm color film transferred to video
Duration: 12 minutes, 43 seconds
Filmed in Mexico
Director: Shirin Neshat
In Collaboration with: Shoja Azari
Cast: María de Los Ángeles
Director of Photography: Darius Khondji
Music and Sound Design: Sussan Deyhim
Production Designer: Shahram Karimi
Editor: Sam Neave
Production Manager/Assistant Director: Sol Tryon
Line Producer: Alice Christov-Moore
Producer: Barbara Gladstone

THE BOOK OF KINGS

My House Is on Fire, 2012 (p. 139)
From *The Book of Kings* series
Ink on LE silver gelatin print
47½ x 60¼ x 2 inches (120.7 x 153 x 5.1 cm)
Photograph taken by Larry Barns

Divine Rebellion, 2012 (p. 140)
From The Book of Kings series
Acrylic on LE silver gelatin print
62¼ x 49¼ x 2 inches (158.1 x 125.1 x 5.1 cm)
Photograph taken by Larry Barns

Amir, 2012 (p. 142)
From *The Book of Kings* series
Acrylic on LE silver gelatin print
99¼ x 49¼ x 2¼ inches (252.1 x 125.1 x 5.7 cm)
Photograph taken by Larry Barns

Bahram, 2012 (p. 141)
From *The Book of Kings* series
Ink on LE silver gelatin print
99¼ x 49⅜ x 2¼ inches (252.1 x 125.4 x 5.7 cm)
Photograph taken by Larry Barns
Courtesy of Shulamit Nazarian

Sherief, 2012 (p. 143)
From *The Book of Kings* series
Acrylic on LE silver gelatin print
99¼ x 49¼ x 2¼ inches (252.1 x 125.1 x 5.7 cm)
Photograph taken by Larry Barns

Roja, 2012 (pp. 134, 146)
From *The Book of Kings* series
Ink on LE silver gelatin print
60¼ x 45¼ x 2 inches (153 x 114.9 x 5.1 cm)
Photograph taken by Larry Barns
Courtesy of Art Berliner and Marian Lever

Rahul, 2012
From *The Book of Kings* series
Ink on LE silver gelatin print
60¼ x 45¼ x 2 inches (153 x 114.9 x 5.1 cm)
Photograph taken by Larry Barns

Nida, 2012 (p. 144)
From *The Book of Kings* series
Ink on LE silver gelatin print
60¼ x 45¼ x 2 inches (153 x 114.9 x 5.1 cm)
Photograph taken by Larry Barns
Private collection, New York, Courtesy of Sean Kelly Gallery

Kouross, 2012 (p. 147)
From *The Book of Kings* series
Ink on LE silver gelatin print
60¼ x 45¼ x 2 inches (153 x 114.9 x 5.1 cm)
Photograph taken by Larry Barns

Ibrahim, 2012 (p. 145)
From *The Book of Kings* series
Ink on LE silver gelatin print
60¼ x 45¼ x 2 inches (153 x 114.9 x 5.1 cm)
Photograph taken by Larry Barns

Ali, 2012
From *The Book of Kings* series
Ink on LE silver gelatin print
40¼ x 30¼ x 2 inches (102.2 x 76.8 x 5.1 cm)
Photograph taken by Larry Barns

Ali Sharma, 2012
From *The Book of Kings* series
Ink on LE silver gelatin print
40¼ x 30¼ x 2 inches (102.2 x 76.8 x 5.1 cm)
Photograph taken by Larry Barns

Anwar, 2012
From *The Book of Kings* series
Ink on LE silver gelatin print
40¼ x 30¼ x 2 inches (102.2 x 76.8 x 5.1 cm)
Photograph taken by Larry Barns

Davood, 2012 (p. 150)
From *The Book of Kings* series
Ink on LE silver gelatin print
40¼ x 30¼ x 2 inches (102.2 x 76.8 x 5.1 cm)
Photograph taken by Larry Barns

Farokh, 2012
From *The Book of Kings* series
Ink on LE silver gelatin print
40¼ x 30¼ x 2 inches (102.2 x 76.8 x 5.1 cm)
Photograph taken by Larry Barns

Morad, 2012
From *The Book of Kings* series
Ink on LE silver gelatin print
40¼ x 30¼ x 2 inches (102.2 x 76.8 x 5.1 cm)
Photograph taken by Larry Barns

Lili, 2012
From *The Book of Kings* series
Ink on LE silver gelatin print
40¼ x 30¼ x 2 inches (102.2 x 76.8 x 5.1 cm)
Photograph taken by Larry Barns

Leah, 2012
From *The Book of Kings* series
Ink on LE silver gelatin print
40¼ x 30¼ x 2 inches (102.2 x 76.8 x 5.1 cm)
Photograph taken by Larry Barns

Mariam, 2012
From *The Book of Kings* series
Ink on LE silver gelatin print
40¼ x 30¼ x 2 inches (102.2 x 76.8 x 5.1 cm)
Photograph taken by Larry Barns

Nazy, 2012
From *The Book of Kings* series
Ink on LE silver gelatin print
40¼ x 30¼ x 2 inches (102.2 x 76.8 x 5.1 cm)
Photograph taken by Larry Barns

Ghada, 2012
From *The Book of Kings* series
Ink on LE silver gelatin print
40¼ x 30¼ x 2 inches (102.2 x 76.8 x 5.1 cm)
Photograph taken by Larry Barns

Roozbeh, 2012 (p. 148)
From *The Book of Kings* series
Ink on LE silver gelatin print
40¼ x 30¼ x 2 inches (102.2 x 76.8 x 5.1 cm)
Photograph taken by Larry Barns

Sara Jafari, 2012 (p. 149)
From *The Book of Kings* series
Ink on LE silver gelatin print
40¼ x 30¼ x 2 inches (102.2 x 76.8 x 5.1 cm)
Photograph taken by Larry Barns

Omer, 2012
From *The Book of Kings* series
Ink on LE silver gelatin print
40¼ x 30¼ x 2 inches (102.2 x 76.8 x 5.1 cm)
Photograph taken by Larry Barns

Sara Nafici, 2012
From *The Book of Kings* series
Ink on LE silver gelatin print
40¼ x 30¼ x 2 inches (102.2 x 76.8 x 5.1 cm)
Photograph taken by Larry Barns

Navid, 2012
From *The Book of Kings* series
Ink on LE silver gelatin print
40¼ x 30¼ x 2 inches (102.2 x 76.8 x 5.1 cm)
Photograph taken by Larry Barns

Najla, 2012
From *The Book of Kings* series
Ink on LE silver gelatin print
40¼ x 30¼ x 2 inches (102.2 x 76.8 x 5.1 cm)
Photograph taken by Larry Barns

Saman, 2012 (p. 148)
From *The Book of Kings* series
Ink on LE silver gelatin print
40¼ x 30¼ x 2 inches (102.2 x 76.8 x 5.1 cm)
Photograph taken by Larry Barns

Golshid, 2012
From *The Book of Kings* series
Ink on LE silver gelatin print
40¼ x 30¼ x 2 inches (102.2 x 76.8 x 5.1 cm)
Photograph taken by Larry Barns

Negin, 2012
From *The Book of Kings* series
Ink on LE silver gelatin print
40¼ x 30¼ x 2 inches (102.2 x 76.8 x 5.1 cm)
Photograph taken by Larry Barns

Zakaria, 2012
From *The Book of Kings* series
Ink on LE silver gelatin print
40¼ x 30¼ x 2 inches (102.2 x 76.8 x 5.1 cm)
Photograph taken by Larry Barns

Sara Zandieh, 2012 (p. 151)
From *The Book of Kings* series
Ink on LE silver gelatin print
40¼ x 30¼ x 2 inches (102.2 x 76.8 x 5.1 cm)
Photograph taken by Larry Barns

Shirin, 2012
From *The Book of Kings* series
Ink on LE silver gelatin print
40¼ x 30¼ x 2 inches (102.2 x 76.8 x 5.1 cm)
Photograph taken by Larry Barns

Ahmed, 2012
From *The Book of Kings* series
Ink on LE silver gelatin print
40¼ x 30¼ x 2 inches (102.2 x 76.8 x 5.1 cm)
Photograph taken by Larry Barns

Rahul, 2012
From *The Book of Kings* series
Ink on LE silver gelatin print
40¼ x 30¼ x 2 inches (102.2 x 76.8 x 5.1 cm)
Photograph taken by Larry Barns

Kouross, 2012
From *The Book of Kings* series
Ink on LE silver gelatin print
40¼ x 30¼ x 2 inches (102.2 x 76.8 x 5.1 cm)
Photograph taken by Larry Barns

Mosaeb, 2012
From *The Book of Kings* series
Ink on LE silver gelatin print
40¼ x 30¼ x 2 inches (102.2 x 76.8 x 5.1 cm)
Photograph taken by Larry Barns

Roja, 2012
From *The Book of Kings* series
Ink on LE silver gelatin print
40¼ x 30¼ x 2 inches (102.2 x 76.8 x 5.1 cm)
Photograph taken by Larry Barns
Collection of BNY Mellon

Ramin, 2012
From *The Book of Kings* series
Ink on LE silver gelatin print
40¼ x 30¼ x 2 inches (102.2 x 76.8 x 5.1 cm)
Photograph taken by Larry Barns

Nickzad, 2012 (p. 149)
From *The Book of Kings* series
Ink on LE silver gelatin print
40¼ x 30¼ x 2 inches (102.2 x 76.8 x 5.1 cm)
Photograph taken by Larry Barns

Taraneh, 2012
From *The Book of Kings* series
Ink on LE silver gelatin print
40¼ x 30¼ x 2 inches (102.2 x 76.8 x 5.1 cm)
Photograph taken by Larry Barns

Sara Khaki, 2012
From *The Book of Kings* series
Ink on LE silver gelatin print
40¼ x 30¼ x 2 inches (102.2 x 76.8 x 5.1 cm)
Photograph taken by Larry Barns

Fahimeh, 2012
From *The Book of Kings* series
Ink on LE silver gelatin print
40¼ x 30¼ x 2 inches (102.2 x 76.8 x 5.1 cm)
Photograph taken by Larry Barns

ILLUSIONS AND MIRRORS

Illusions and Mirrors, 2013 (p. 184)
Single-channel video installation
HD video
Duration: 13 minutes, 22 seconds
Filmed in New York
Director: Shirin Neshat
Actress: Natalie Portman
Director of Photography: Darius Khondji
Editors: George Cragg and Nariman Hamed
Music and Sound Design: Johnny Azari
Executive Producer: Annique DeCaestecker
Line Producer: Paul Laurens
Production Manager: Dani Rotstein

OUR HOUSE IS ON FIRE

Ahmed, 2013
From *Our House Is on Fire* series
Digital C-print and ink
63¼ x 41⅛ x 2 inches (160.7 x 104.5 x 5.1 cm)
Photograph taken by Larry Barns

Ghada, 2013
From *Our House Is on Fire* series
Digital C-print and ink
63¼ x 41⅛ x 2 inches (160.7 x 104.5 x 5.1 cm)
Photograph taken by Larry Barns

Karim, 2013
From *Our House Is on Fire* series
Digital C-print and ink
63¼ x 41⅛ x 2 inches (160.7 x 104.5 x 5.1 cm)
Photograph taken by Larry Barns

Wafaa, 2013 (p. 156)
From *Our House Is on Fire* series
Digital C-print and ink
63¼ x 41⅛ x 2 inches (160.7 x 104.5 x 5.1 cm)
Photograph taken by Larry Barns

Jamal, 2013 (p. 158)
From *Our House Is on Fire* series
Digital C-print and ink
63¼ x 41⅛ x 2 inches (160.7 x 104.5 x 5.1 cm)
Photograph taken by Larry Barns

Sayed, 2013
From *Our House Is on Fire* series
Digital C-print and ink
63¼ x 41⅛ x 2 inches (160.7 x 104.5 x 5.1 cm)
Photograph taken by Larry Barns

Nady, 2013
From *Our House Is on Fire* series
Digital C-print and ink
63¼ x 41⅛ x 2 inches (160.7 x 104.5 x 5.1 cm)
Photograph taken by Larry Barns

Mona, 2013 (p. 159)
From *Our House Is on Fire* series
Digital C-print and ink
63¼ x 41⅛ x 2 inches (160.7 x 104.5 x 5.1 cm)
Photograph taken by Larry Barns

Souad, 2013
From *Our House Is on Fire* series
Digital C-print and ink
63¼ x 41⅛ x 2 inches (160.7 x 104.5 x 5.1 cm)
Photograph taken by Larry Barns

Mahmoud, 2013 (p. 157)
From *Our House Is on Fire* series
Digital C-print and ink
63¼ x 41⅛ x 2 inches (160.7 x 104.5 x 5.1 cm)
Photograph taken by Larry Barns

Saleh, 2013
From *Our House Is on Fire* series
Digital C-print and ink
63¼ x 41⅛ x 2 inches (160.7 x 104.5 x 5.1 cm)
Photograph taken by Larry Barns

Mohammed, 2013
From *Our House Is on Fire* series
Digital C-print and ink
63¼ x 41⅛ x 2 inches (160.7 x 104.5 x 5.1 cm)
Photograph taken by Larry Barns

Rahim, 2013 (p. 155)
From *Our House Is on Fire* series
Digital C-print and ink
61¼ x 49⅛ x 2 inches (155.6 x 124.8 x 5.1 cm)
Photograph taken by Larry Barns

Kamal, 2013
From *Our House Is on Fire* series
Digital C-print and ink
61¼ x 49⅛ x 2 inches (155.6 x 124.8 x 5.1 cm)
Photograph taken by Larry Barns

THE HOME OF MY EYES

Agayar, 2015
From *The Home of My Eyes* series
Ink on LE silver gelatin print
60 x 40 x 2 inches (152.4 x 101.6 x 5.1 cm)
Photograph taken by David Jiménez

Amil, 2015
From *The Home of My Eyes* series
Ink on LE silver gelatin print
60 x 40 x 2 inches (152.4 x 101.6 x 5.1 cm)
Photograph taken by David Jiménez

Rahim, 2015
From *The Home of My Eyes* series
Ink on LE silver gelatin print
60 x 40 x 2 inches (152.4 x 101.6 x 5.1 cm)
Photograph taken by David Jiménez

Akram, 2015
From *The Home of My Eyes* series
Ink on LE silver gelatin print
60 x 40 x 2 inches (152.4 x 101.6 x 5.1 cm)
Photograph taken by David Jiménez

Eldar, 2015
From *The Home of My Eyes* series
Ink on LE silver gelatin print
60 x 40 x 2 inches (152.4 x 101.6 x 5.1 cm)
Photograph taken by David Jiménez

Esmiralda, 2015
From *The Home of My Eyes* series
Ink on LE silver gelatin print
72 x 48 x 2¼ inches (182.9 x 121.9 x 5.7 cm)
Photograph taken by David Jiménez

Farid, 2015
From *The Home of My Eyes* series
Ink on LE silver gelatin print
60 x 40 x 2 inches (152.4 x 101.6 x 5.1 cm)
Photograph taken by David Jiménez

Farida, 2015
From *The Home of My Eyes* series
Ink on LE silver gelatin print
60 x 40 x 2 inches (152.4 x 101.6 x 5.1 cm)
Photograph taken by David Jiménez

Gafar, 2015
From *The Home of My Eyes* series
Ink on LE silver gelatin print
60 x 40 x 2 inches (152.4 x 101.6 x 5.1 cm)
Photograph taken by David Jiménez

Nikas, 2015
From *The Home of My Eyes* series
Ink on LE silver gelatin print
60 x 40 x 2 inches (152.4 x 101.6 x 5.1 cm)
Photograph taken by David Jiménez

Rabil, 2015
From *The Home of My Eyes* series
Ink on LE silver gelatin print
60 x 40 x 2 inches (152.4 x 101.6 x 5.1 cm)
Photograph taken by David Jiménez

Husniya, 2015
From *The Home of My Eyes* series
Ink on LE silver gelatin print
60 x 40 x 2 inches (152.4 x 101.6 x 5.1 cm)
Photograph taken by David Jiménez

Tamasha, 2015
From *The Home of My Eyes* series
Ink on LE silver gelatin print
60 x 40 x 2 inches (152.4 x 101.6 x 5.1 cm)
Photograph taken by David Jiménez

Humay, 2015
From *The Home of My Eyes* series
Ink on LE silver gelatin print
60 x 40 x 2 inches (152.4 x 101.6 x 5.1 cm)
Photograph taken by David Jiménez

Sabina M., 2015
From *The Home of My Eyes* series
Ink on LE silver gelatin print
60 x 40 x 2 inches (152.4 x 101.6 x 5.1 cm)
Photograph taken by David Jiménez

Samima, 2015
From *The Home of My Eyes* series
Ink on LE silver gelatin print
60 x 40 x 2 inches (152.4 x 101.6 x 5.1 cm)
Photograph taken by David Jiménez

Novruz, 2015
From *The Home of My Eyes* series
Ink on LE silver gelatin print
60 x 40 x 2 inches (152.4 x 101.6 x 5.1 cm)
Photograph taken by David Jiménez

Zuleykha, 2015
From *The Home of My Eyes* series
Ink on LE silver gelatin print
60 x 40 x 2 inches (152.4 x 101.6 x 5.1 cm)
Photograph taken by David Jiménez

Vagif, 2015 (p. 168)
From *The Home of My Eyes* series
Ink on LE silver gelatin print
72 x 48 x 2¼ inches (182.9 x 121.9 x 5.7 cm)
Photograph taken by David Jiménez

Durdana, 2015 (p. 169)
From *The Home of My Eyes* series
Ink on LE silver gelatin print
72 x 48 x 2¼ inches (182.9 x 121.9 x 5.7 cm)
Photograph taken by David Jiménez

Aydin G., 2015
From *The Home of My Eyes* series
Ink on LE silver gelatin print
72 x 48 x 2¼ inches (182.9 x 121.9 x 5.7 cm)
Photograph taken by David Jiménez

Tahir, 2015
From *The Home of My Eyes* series
Ink on LE silver gelatin print
81 x 54 x 2¼ inches (205.7 x 137.2 x 5.7 cm)
Photograph taken by David Jiménez

Aida, 2015
From *The Home of My Eyes* series
Ink on LE silver gelatin print
81 x 54 x 2¼ inches (205.7 x 137.2 x 5.7 cm)
Photograph taken by David Jiménez

Gabil, 2015
From *The Home of My Eyes* series
Ink on LE silver gelatin print
60 x 40 x 2 inches (152.4 x 101.6 x 5.1 cm)
Photograph taken by David Jiménez

Adil, 2015 (p. 164)
From *The Home of My Eyes* series
Ink on LE silver gelatin print
60 x 40 x 2 inches (152.4 x 101.6 x 5.1 cm)
Photograph taken by David Jiménez

Ilgara, 2015 (p. 166)
From *The Home of My Eyes* series
Ink on LE silver gelatin print
60 x 40 x 2 inches (152.4 x 101.6 x 5.1 cm)
Photograph taken by David Jiménez

Javid, 2015
From *The Home of My Eyes* series
Ink on LE silver gelatin print
60 x 40 x 2 inches (152.4 x 101.6 x 5.1 cm)
Photograph taken by David Jiménez

Anna, 2015
From *The Home of My Eyes* series
Ink on LE silver gelatin print
60 x 40 x 2 inches (152.4 x 101.6 x 5.1 cm)
Photograph taken by David Jiménez

Gizbasti, 2015 (pp. 137, 165)
From *The Home of My Eyes* series
Ink on LE silver gelatin print
60 x 40 x 2 inches (152.4 x 101.6 x 5.1 cm)
Photograph taken by David Jiménez

Sabina H., 2015
From *The Home of My Eyes* series
Ink on LE silver gelatin print
60 x 40 x 2 inches (152.4 x 101.6 x 5.1 cm)
Photograph taken by David Jiménez

Nazim, 2015 (p. 167)
From *The Home of My Eyes* series
Ink on LE silver gelatin print
60 x 40 x 2 inches (152.4 x 101.6 x 5.1 cm)
Photograph taken by David Jiménez

Malaksima, 2015 (p. 163)
From *The Home of My Eyes* series
Ink on LE silver gelatin print
60 x 40 x 2 inches (152.4 x 101.6 x 5.1 cm)
Photograph taken by David Jiménez

Hasan, 2015
From *The Home of My Eyes* series
Ink on LE silver gelatin print
60 x 40 x 2 inches (152.4 x 101.6 x 5.1 cm)
Photograph taken by David Jiménez

Kanan, 2015
From *The Home of My Eyes* series
Ink on LE silver gelatin print
60 x 40 x 2 inches (152.4 x 101.6 x 5.1 cm)
Photograph taken by David Jiménez

Vugar, 2015
From *The Home of My Eyes* series
Ink on LE silver gelatin print
60 x 40 x 2 inches (152.4 x 101.6 x 5.1 cm)
Photograph taken by David Jiménez

Khadija, 2015
From *The Home of My Eyes* series
Ink on LE silver gelatin print
60 x 40 x 2 inches (152.4 x 101.6 x 5.1 cm)
Photograph taken by David Jiménez

ROJA

Roja, 2016 (p. 194)
Single-channel video installation
HD video monochrome
Duration: 15 minutes, 20 seconds
Filmed in New York and Pennsylvania
Director: Shirin Neshat
With Roja Heydarpour, Taraneh Farjad, and Bill Stokes
Voice Dubbing: Christopher Sears
Song Performed by: Anohni
Produced and Edited by: Shoja Azari
Director of Photography: Ghasem Ebrahimian
Music and Sound Design: Johnny Azari
Production Design and Costume Design: Shahram Karimi
Hair and Makeup Artist: Mina Ghoraishi
Executive Producers: Shirin Neshat and Gladstone Gallery
Line Producer: Pamela Moriarty
Production Manager: Kristal Mosley

Untitled, from *Roja* series, 2016 (cover)
LE silver gelatin print
51½ x 76½ x 2¼ inches (130.8 x 194.3 x 5.7 cm)
Photograph taken by Larry Barns

LAND OF DREAMS

All *Land of Dreams* works are courtesy of Gladstone Gallery, New York and Brussels, and Goodman Gallery, Johannesburg, Capetown, and London

America: Land of Dreams, 2019
Single-channel video installation
HD video monochrome
Filmed in: Albuquerque, Farmington, Las Vegas, Santa Fe, New Mexico

Director: Shirin Neshat
With Sheila Vand
Additional cast: Shannon K. Dunn, Craig Fones, Pip Lustgarten, John Radspinner, Dawn Ferguson
Concept by: Shirin Neshat
Written by: Shoja Azari
Editor: Shoja Azari
Director of Photography: Ghasem Ebrahimian
Music and Sound Design: Johnny Azari
Production Design: Rick Gilbert
Costume Design: Kim Trujillo
Hair and Makeup Artist: Mina Ghoraishi
Produced by: Shoja Azari and Sol Tryon
Executive Producers: Gladstone Gallery and Goodman Gallery

The Colony, 2019
Single-channel video installation
HD video monochrome
Filmed in: Albuquerque and Shiprock, New Mexico
Director: Shirin Neshat
With Sheila Vand and Mohamed Ghaffari
Concept by: Shirin Neshat
Written by: Shoja Azari
Editor: Shoja Azari
Director of Photography: Ghasem Ebrahimian
Music and Sound Design: Johnny Azari
Production Design: Rick Gilbert
Costume Design: Kim Trujillo
Hair and Makeup Artist: Mina Ghoraishi
Produced by: Shoja Azari and Sol Tryon
Executive Producers: Gladstone Gallery and Goodman Gallery

Land of Dreams (photographic series), 2019
Digital C-print and ink
Dimensions variable
Installation of variable dimensions
Photographs taken by Lina Bertucci

Alfonso Garduno, 2019
Allegra Edwards, 2019
Alysha Tobin, 2019
Amanda Martinez, 2019
Andre Luna, 2019
Andrew Szeman, 2019
Ann Rupprecht, 2019
Anna Garcia, 2019
Anthony Tobin, 2019
Aria Hernandez, 2019
Ava Poafpybitty, 2019
Barbara Newton, 2019
Brandt Davis, 2019
Bruce Lorenzo Coleman, 2019
Carlie Encinias, 2019
Carlois Miller, 2019
Carly Drobnick, 2019
Clay Drobnick, 2019
Collin Rogers, 2019
Connor Cowboy, 2019
Consuelo Quintana, 2019 (p. 212)
David Armstrong, 2019
David Martinez, 2019
David Miller, 2019 (p. 216)
Denise Calloway, 2019
Dominique Evans, 2019
Dwayne Stewart, 2019
Edward Nicolas, 2019
Eloisa Pena, 2019
Enrique Zepeda, 2019 (p. 218)
Florence Villanueva, 2019
Fred Daily, 2019
Gary Dixon, 2019
Glen Talley, 2019
Gloria and Molly Rivera, 2019
Greg Fitch, 2019 (p. 217)
Herbie Nelson, 2019
Ignacio Lucerno, 2019
Isaac Silva, 2019 (p. 219)
James Brockwny, 2019
James Chaney, 2019
James Reynolds, 2019
James Sanchez, 2019
Jenasis Greer, 2019 (p. 216)
Jerry Villas, 2019
Joe Medino, 2019
Joe Melendez, 2019
Judy Long, 2019
Julie Ann Duran, 2019
Katalina Espinoza, 2019 (p. 217)
Katherine Marquez, 2019
Kaycheri Rappaport, 2019
Kenneth Morse, 2019
Kevin Bogort, 2019
Kiana Poafpybitty, 2019
Kim Knifechief, 2019
Lance Madrid, 2019
Larry King, 2019
Leo Mickey Grace, 2019
Leroy Rael, 2019
Louis Atencio, 2019
Louis Medina, 2019
Madison Cowboy, 2019
Madison Maldonado, 2019
Magali and Phoenix Rutschman, 2019 (p. 215)
Manuel Martinez, 2019 (p. 213)
Marcos Espinoza, 2019
Margaret Labounty, 2019
Maria Alma Rivera, 2019
Marie Overstreet, 2019
Marina Medina, 2019
Marquez Espinoza, 2019
Martha Johnsen, 2019
Martha Perez, 2019
Mary Larance, 2019
Melissa Greene, 2019
Michael Golden, 2019
Michael Martinez, 2019
Michael Morse, 2019
Michelle Cowboy, 2019
Millicent Wilson, 2019
Mrs. King, 2019 (p. 214)
Natani Hinton, 2019
Nathan Vooge, 2019
Nick Slindler, 2019
Pacifico Baca, 2019
Patrick Clay Goetsch, 2019
Patti Stewart Goetsch, 2019
Paul Cowboy, 2019
Paul Espinoza, 2019
Paulita Cowboy, 2019
Pearl Cowboy, 2019
Phil Chavez, 2019
Phillip Alderete, 2019
Preciliano Romero, 2019
Prescilla Antonio, 2019
Prescilla Quintana, 2019
Priscilla Wolf, 2019
Raven Brewer-Beltz, 2019
Riley Caldwell, 2019
Robert Flores, 2019
Robert Gallecos, 2019
Robert Garcia, 2019
Robert Lenick, 2019
Robert Saucedo, 2019
Rodger Larance, 2019
Ron Querry, 2019
Rose Atencio, 2019
Russell Thompson, 2019
Sandra Skatzes, 2019
Sarah Montano, 2019
Savannah Torres, 2019
Schonzono Pino, 2019
Sean Williams, 2019
Sharon Davis, 2019
Simin, 2019 (p. 178)
Stephanie Poafpybitty, 2019
Sylvia Hays, 2019
Tammy Drobnick, 2019
Tokala Poafpybitty, 2019
Tracy Parks, 2019
Vanessa Wheatly, 2019
Vicky Hemmes, 2019
Victoria Jones, 2019
Yvette Johnson, 2019
Yvette Larson, 2019
Zachariah Morse, 2019
Zelma King, 2019

ACKNOWLEDGMENTS

Shirin Neshat's photographs, videos, and films, rooted in her Iranian heritage, are lyrical, beautiful, and saturated with influences and references, some of which are familiar to audiences in the United States. They are also full of stories that one may not have heard and metaphors one may be shy to interpret about a country one may not understand. Her work is full of voices: of exiles, of poets, of people caught in the turbulence of political movements, and of inspiring collaborators. Thus, in presenting a large-scale exhibition of her work, with special attention to some of her most metaphorical and mysterious projects, we owe a great debt to many people who have helped our team at The Broad enter the fascinating and complex history that lies behind Neshat's art.

It is hard to overstate the openness, patience, and inspiration that the artist herself has extended to us in this project. Shirin Neshat and her studio bring remarkable energy to any task with which they are involved, and they have been constantly generous with the loan of artworks and their time in supervising and advising on every detail of the catalogue and exhibition. We thank Giulia Theodoli for being the point person on the project, as well as Rodin Hamidi, Michael Lantz, and Elham Asadi. From the bottom of our hearts, we thank Shirin, who has brought us closer to her wonderful culture through her dynamic work. She is a voice of courage and of empathy at a time when the walls between nations and people are often more affirmed than transcended.

At every stage of the exhibition, Barbara Gladstone and the many staff members of Gladstone Gallery have been wonderful to work with and open to our efforts in presenting such an ambitious presentation of Neshat's work. They are a key lender to the exhibition and the source of much of the photography of the artist's work and installations presented in this catalogue. We thank Caroline Luce, artist liaison, for her support, advice, and diligence in working through the many details of the exhibition and catalogue. We also thank Alexis Hager, Andy Rosenwald, Alex Wixon, and Sarah Willis.

Early in the process of planning the exhibition, conversations with Sanam Khamneipur, Bita Shafipour, and Philip Grant led us to books we needed to read, people we needed to meet, and stories that we needed to hear. These conversations continued with meetings and conversations with Abbas Milani, Nasrin Rahimieh, Farzaneh Milani, Shulamit Nazarian, Ali Razi, Alireza Ardekani, and Sholeh Wolpé, all of whom helped us immensely to start and extend our study. We thank Shoja Azari, Sussan Deyhim, Ghasem Ebrahimian, and Kyong Park for allowing us to interview them during our research.

At The Broad, adding to the many thanked in our Founding Director Joanne Heyler's Foreword, we are grateful to Katayoun Bahrami for translating and providing many insights about the poems and cultural references in Neshat's work. In addition to this tremendous effort, our conversations about Iran and exile, as well as her assistance in thinking through idiomatic constructions in Farsi and the details of Iranian culture, have been incredibly helpful. Thanks also to Lauren Cook, who provided important research for the chronology of Neshat's career.

With regard to the catalogue, we thank Katayoun, Jocelyn Lopez-Anleu, and Sarah Loyer, who reviewed the final text edits. We are grateful to Jeannine Guido and Christine Steiner for helping navigate the rights and reproduction process. We also thank Madeleine Casella and Diana Pulling at the Museum of Modern Art in New York for helping to organize the recording of the conversation between Shirin and Glenn Lowry.

We are incredibly grateful to Shiffman & Kohnke design studio for their beautiful and lyrical graphic design for this publication. Specifically, we thank Tracey Shiffman and James Ihira for their hard work and professionalism at every stage. We thank Philomena Mariani for editing and working with our many writers, and at Prestel, we thank Karen Farquhar and Amelia Rina for all their help in the printing, contract, and marketing process. Especially, we thank our co-publisher Mary DelMonico for her dedication, attention, and energy in developing this publication.

Finally, we want to again thank our Founders, Eli and Edythe Broad, as well as our Founding Director, Joanne Heyler, for their belief in this exhibition, their counsel, and their ongoing support and encouragement. Their collective vision has made this important exhibition possible.

ED SCHAD
Curator and Publications Manager, The Broad

The exhibition *Shirin Neshat: I Will Greet the Sun Again* was organized by The Broad, Los Angeles, and curated by Ed Schad.

Exhibition dates: October 19, 2019–February 16, 2020

Exhibition Lenders:
The Artist and Gladstone Gallery, New York, and Brussels
Goodman Galley, Johannesburg, Capetown, and London
The Whitney Museum of American Art
Shulamit Nazarian
BNY Mellon
Art Berliner and Marian Lever
Private collection, New York

Published in 2019 by The Broad and DelMonico Books

The Broad
221 South Grand Avenue
Los Angeles, CA 90012
www.thebroad.org

DelMonico Books, an imprint of Prestel, a member of Verlagsgruppe Random House GmbH

Prestel Verlag
Neumarkter Strasse 28
81673 Munich

Prestel Publishing Ltd.
14-17 Wells Street
London WC1T 3PD

Prestel Publishing
900 Broadway, Suite 603
New York, NY 10003

www.prestel.com

Editor in Chief: Ed Schad
Designer: Tracey Shiffman and James Ihira, Shiffman & Kohnke
Production Director: Karen Farquhar, DelMonico Books
Scanning and Separations: Echelon Color
Printed and bound in China

ISBN: 978-3-7913-5875-8

Library of Congress Control Number: 2019907995

PHOTOGRAPH CREDITS

Unless otherwise noted, all works by Shirin Neshat and installation photos of works by Shirin Neshat © Shirin Neshat and were provided for publication courtesy of Shirin Neshat and Gladstone Gallery.

p. 10: Courtesy of Darius Khondji
p. 14: © AB Svensk Filmindustri, Photo: Sven Nykvist
pp. 15 (left), 16 (left): Courtesy of Franklin Furnace Archive, Inc.
p. 18 (top): Reprinted by permission of Penguin Random House LLC
pp. 20 (right), 221 (left): Courtesy of Ebrahim Golestan
p. 22 (left): Photo by Stefan Hauer
p. 22 (right): Photo by David Regen
pp. 28, 171: Photo by Philipp Ottendörfer
p. 34: Digital image © Whitney Museum of American Art/ Licensed by Scala/Art Resource, NY
p. 125: Courtesy of Electronic Arts Intermix (EAI), New York
p. 127 (left): Courtesy of Bridgeman Images
p. 128: Andy Warhol © The Andy Warhol Foundation for the Visual Arts, Inc./Artist Rights Society (ARS), The Elvis Presley Foundation
p. 130: Photo by Jonathan Leijonhufvud, © Shirin Neshat & Faurschou Foundation
p. 152: Photo by Cathy Carver
p. 160: Photo by Glenn Steigelman
p. 221 (right): Courtesy of mk2 films
p. 230 (left): Damien Meyer: Getty Images
p. 231 (left): © Monika Ritterhaus